Java Certification

for Programmers and Developers

Java Certification
for Programmers
and Developers

Barry Boone

McGraw-Hill

New York ▪ San Francisco ▪ Washington, D.C. ▪ Auckland
Bogota ▪ Caracas ▪ Lisbon ▪ London ▪ Madrid
Mexico City ▪ Milan ▪ Montreal ▪ New Delhi
San Juan ▪ Singapore ▪ Sydney
Tokyo ▪ Toronto

McGraw-Hill

A Division of The **McGraw·Hill** Companies

The views expressed in this book are solely those of the author, and do not represent the views of any other party or parties.

3 4 5 6 7 8 9 0   DOC/DOC   9 0 2 1 0 9 8 7

P/N 0-07-006661-2
PART OF
ISBN 0-07-913657-5

The sponsoring editor for this book was Judy Brief. It was set in Sabon by Maya Riddick freelance designer. The Chapter opener art was photographed by and icons designed by Natalie Fortin freelance designer.

Printed and bound by R.R. Donnelley & Sons Company.

 This book is printed on recycled, acid-free paper containing a minimum of 50% recycled de-inked fiber.

Product or brand names used in this book may be trade names or trademarks. Where we believe that there may be proprietary claims to such trade names or trademarks, the name has been used with an initial capital or it has been capitalized in the style used by the name claimant. Regardless of the capitalization used, all such names have been used in an editorial manner without any intent to convey endorsement of or other affiliation with the name claimant. Neither the author nor the publisher intends to express any judgement as to the validity or legal status of any such proprietary claims.

Contents

Part II   Developer Certification Study Guide   421

Chapter 19:   *Creating Clean APIs*   423

Chapter 20:   *Advanced Graphical User Interfaces*   439

Acknowledgements

Many people helped make this book as good as it can be. First, thanks to my amazing wife Mary for listening to all that was going on with the book and helping me through the writing process. Thanks to Judy Brief, my outstanding editor at McGraw-Hill, for recognizing this book's potential and working so hard to realize that vision. Bill Adler, my excellent agent, also saw the strong need for this book and got it to the right people. Many thanks to Mike Bridwell and Annie Kolvin from Sun who so generously gave their time and insights into making this book accurate and who supplied me with much valuable information. And thanks especially to Siobhan Flanagan from Sun for her help in obtaining a Sun-written Foreword to this book and helping explain Sun's insights into Java certification.

Foreword

Less than two years ago, companies throughout the U.S. and the world began using the Java(TM) technology as their development language of choice. The reasons are obvious: the Java language enables developers to write programs faster and more securely. In the software market, cutting down time-to-market is crucial to success, and developers report development times that are 2-3 times faster than C and C++ and that includes time to get up and running on the Java language. The competitive edge the Java technology gives companies has led to its explosive growth.

The growth in the use of Java technology has created a tremendous need for knowledgeable people to design applications in the Java language, which has created a dilemma for companies seeking knowledgeable Java programmers. Companies can't rely on these programmers having "five years of Java expertise." Similarly, Java programmers claiming to know Java have no way to prove to prospective employers and clients that they have mastered the language.

Sun(TM) developed the Sun Java Certification program to identify individuals with a high standard of competence in the Java language. Java certification demonstrates to employers that a programmer is well prepared to do the job. Programmers can prove they know the Java language in-depth, which may ultimately translate into greater productivity and employment opportunities.

Sun certifies Java software professionals at two levels: as a programmer, which tests for a strong working knowledge of the Java language, and as a developer, which assesses the ability to implement real-world solutions. The Sun Certified Java Programmer exam tests for overall Java knowledge as well as programming concepts and applet development skills. The Sun Certified Java Developer assesses the ability to perform complex programming through an application assignment which is followed by an exam on the knowledge required to perform the assignment.

As this book explains, becoming a Sun Certified Java Programmer and Developer is not easy. You must not only be familiar with the Java language: You must have used it in the real world, developing applications that solve real problems to gain the level of expertise you need to pass the tests.

Only through time and experience can you gain a better knowledge of the Java language. This book will help augment your understanding of it. Sun strongly recommends taking Java Applications Programming and Java Programming Workshop prior to attempting the Sun Certified Java Developer assignment and exam.

Additional information on the Java Certification program is available on the World Wide Web at: www://sun.com/sunservice/suned.

Good Luck

Bill Richardson

Vice President and General Manager

SunService Division, Sun Microsystems, Inc.

Sun Educational Services

Sun, the Sun logo, Java, and Sun Microsystems are trademarks or registered trademarks of Sun Microsystems, Inc.

Introduction

What this Book is All About

To distinguish yourself from the growing crowd of Java programmers, you should become Sun certified. To prepare for the certifications exams, you should read this book.

What Does It Mean to Become Sun Certified in Java?

Sun offers certification in the Java language at two levels:

- as a *programmer*, which tests for basic understanding of the language and your ability to code given a set of specifications, and
- as a *developer*, which tests for advanced Java knowledge in putting together real-world applications using Java.

When you are Sun certified as a Java programmer and Java developer, your employers, peers, and friends know that you can walk the walk and talk the talk. It's not just you saying so; it's Sun, the inventor of the Java language.

As you know, the Java programming market is red-hot. Companies are paying huge sums to programmers who can demonstrate expertise in Java. Consulting and contracting firms specializing in personnel placement cannot get knowledgeable Java programmers fast enough.

As the Java market heats up even more, programmers will need a way to distinguish themselves as *Java experts* in an increasingly crowded field. Certification is your means of separating yourself from those less knowledgeable.

What are the Exams Like?

The Programmer exam contains around 70 questions. These consist mostly of analyzing programming snippets and identifying true and false statements about the way the language works, and supplying short class definitions and method calls.

For the programming snippets, you'll be asked a variety of questions. Do they produce the expected results? What do they write to the standard output? Do they even compile in the first place?

There are three types of questions:

1. Multiple choice, where you select as many valid answers as are listed.
2. Single choice, where there is only one right answer from a list.
3. Short answer, where you'll be asked to enter a single line of code—or sometimes just a single word, such as a specific class name or keyword.

The Programmer test focuses on all the basics of Java, including classes, objects, methods, exceptions, threads, user interfaces, applets, and some of Java's core classes, such as String and Math.

The Developer exam consists of two parts:

1. A programming assignment.
2. A set of five short-answer questions.

The programming assignment asks you to develop a front-end to a database residing on the Internet. The short-answer exam asks you questions about this coding assignment.

You take both exams on a computer at one of hundreds of locations around the country. The Programmer exam is graded by the computer right after you take it. The Developer exam is graded by a third party, independent assessor, so that there's no conflict with Sun.

Why Use Java Certification for Programmers and Developers to Prepare for the Exams?

The exams are not free, and they are not easy. I know of a number of Java *instructors* who failed the test on their first try, because they did not study!

It's best to have a clear idea of what you need to know before you plunk down your money and walk into the exam. After all, you don't want to fail, and you don't want to waste your time and money when you can pass the first time with a little preparation.

Java Certification for Programmers and Developers helps programmers with a basic understanding of Java take and pass the Java certification exams with flying colors.

Java Certification for Programmers and Developers is written as a study guide. This book explains the specific concepts and coding assignments found in the Certification exams. It carefully separates what is and is not on the test. This book also contains complete practice tests and programming assignments similar to the ones on the exams—all with detailed answers—so that when you walk into the test, you'll know you'll pass.

This book aims to make you a Java expert.

In addition to helping programmers pass these exams, this book can help Java programmers become experts in their field. I cover important Java features not on the test at the end of each chapter. That way, even when the test does not explicitly require you to know a particular topic, you'll still learn about the topic in detail. After all, as a certified programmer, you'll be expected to be a Java expert.

The CD that comes with this book contains all the source code presented in this book, the sample questions, and many other resources to help programmers study for these tests.

Where Else Can You Go to Prepare for the Test?

There are a number of Internet and Web-based resources that add information to what appears in this book.

I teach a Web-based class through a company called DigitalThink. DigitalThink uses *Java Certification for Programmers and Developers* as the text book for this Web-based course. Taking a course on-line allows you to interact with other students, learn about the experiences of those who have taken the exams, ask questions of tutors, and ask questions of me. You can find the Java certification course offered by DigitalThink by visiting http://www.digitalthink.com.

McGraw-Hill maintains a wonderful Web site for this book. It's at http://www.computing.mcgraw-hill.com/

Sun posts information regarding the certification exams at http://www.sun.com/sunservice/suned/java_certification.html. You can find the most up-to-date numbers to call to sign up for the exam and all the test locations throughout the U. S. and the world at this Web site.

Sun also offers instructor-led courses you can attend through Sun Educational Services. You can find these courses by following the Internet link in the previous paragraph.

And finally, my company, Blue Horse Software, Inc., offers products and services to help you learn Java. Drop by my Web page at http://www.learnjava.com to learn more.

What Should You Know Before You Start Studying?

I assume you already know something about programming in Java. This book does not teach Java programming from scratch; there are many great books available on that topic. Just peruse the bookshelves at your local bookstore, or visit one of the excellent Web-based bookstores, such as Amazon.com or cbooks.com, and search for "Java programming."

I expect that you know how to do things like write a simple "Hello, world" program and how to define a class with instance variables and instance methods. You don't need to be an expert to begin studying for the exams, but you should have done some Java programming before. If you're not sure you know enough to begin studying for the exams, try this simple exercise.

Exercise 0.1

> Write a stand-alone, character-mode program that greets a person by name. The person's name should be supplied as a command-line argument.

For example, you should be able to invoke your program from the command-line by typing:

```
java Hello Barry
```

and, in the standard output, the program should display:

```
Hello, Barry
```

(I know that some development environments, such as Metrowerks Code-Warrior, ask you to enter command-line parameters in a separate window. Follow the procedures for your particular development environment when working through the instructions in this book.)

You might not realize it at first glance, but if you can write this program, you know how to do many basic things in Java, including:

- Define a class.
- Write a `static` method.
- Work with an array.
- Invoke a method.
- Access a class variable.
- Work with Java's String class.
- Write a String to the standard output.

Even though this list appears fairly long, the program itself can be written in four or five lines of code. The answer to this exercise appears at the end of this introduction.

The majority of test questions for both exams are quite a bit more complicated and trickier than this exercise, but the point is that you should already know something about Java before you begin to study for the exam. If you feel comfortable writing this simple program, you're ready to use this book to start preparing to become a Sun Certified Java Programmer and a Sun Certified Java Developer—and win the accolades and respect that goes with these titles.

What is My Background?

If we're going to be spending some time together, you might as well know a bit about me.

I am a Sun Certified Java Programmer and Sun Certified Java Developer. I'll share my experiences in taking these tests in these pages.

I live in Seattle, but I travel all around the country teaching. I love teaching. The thrill of working with students when they "get it" and understand a concept is always an exciting moment. Books are a natural extension of my love of learning and teaching, and I hope this fun comes across while you're studying.

I am the author of two previous books on Java: *Java Essentials for C and C++ Programmers* and *Learn Java on the Macintosh*, with Dave Mark. I've had some great conversations with readers since these books were first published. I have taught classes in Java and object-oriented programming throughout the U.S. In doing so, I've discovered what confuses students learning Java and what they need to know to get through the tougher concepts.

I've consulted to and worked for Fortune 500 companies on object-oriented design and development for the past eleven years, writing many real-world applications that play a role in this book.

I am currently co-teaching a number of Web-based Java classes with Ken Arnold at DigitalThink (www.digitalthink.com). These classes provide me with continuing feedback as to what students are interested in and where they are focusing their efforts.

For the past four years I've been president of Blue Horse Software, Inc., which can be found at www.learnjava.com. I've done all my consulting and work with students through this company. My email address is barryb@bluehorse.com.

How is this Book Organized?

This book is structured like a self-study course. Each chapter contains sections describing:

- what's on the test
- objectives for that chapter
- the concepts for that chapter
- examples of how to use Java to implement these concepts
- exercises you can work through to ensure you have learned the objectives

- review questions
- the complete answers to the exercises and review questions to make sure you've learned what you need to learn

Java Certification for Programmers and Developers is divided into three sections.

- The first section helps make sure you can figure out how an existing program works and that you can program in Java given a set of specifications. These skills are at the heart of the Programmer exam.
- The second section ensures you can use Java to solve problems, design a solution, and write your own code. These abilities are the crux of the Developer exam.
- The third section contains sample tests and programming assignments you can use to prepare for the exams. These practice exams are modeled on the actual exams and are of the same degree of difficulty that you'll find in the real tests.

Java Certification for Programmers and Developers covers in depth those topics that are on the test. However, if I only covered the material on the test questions, this would not be a complete Java review. In addition to becoming an expert, sometimes you just want to know about the other stuff. So, at the end of each chapter, I'll list those Java topics that are *not* on the test and provide a quick overview of these topics. This will help round out your knowledge of Java and might even provide you with some insight into things that are on the test.

To help you reconcile the divergent paths of studying as quickly as possible and studying as thoroughly as possible, I've used a variety of callouts to make sure you can easily distinguish between what you *need* to know to pass the exam, what is good background information, and what you'll be *expected* to know by your peers as you enter the world as a certified programmer and developer.

This book is a review of Java for those who have already programmed in Java—at least a little. I'll list what you should know at the start of each chapter.

I'll list the objectives for each chapter at the beginning of the chapter, and I'll repeat each objective as I cover it in the sections within the chapter.

I'll make sure the key concepts in each chapter are easy to spot so that you can quickly review a chapter and be certain you've gotten the important information.

Each chapter contains lots of exercises you can use to test yourself and review what you've learned. You can also use the exercises as a starting point to pursue your own investigations into how Java works.

Tips, advice, shortcuts, and tricks have this icon.

I've given anything that can get you into trouble this icon.

I've also marked general background information, such as design issues and concepts, so that you can see more easily what are the things you need to study and what are background explanations to help you understand why a feature is designed the way it is.

What Do You Do Once You're Ready to Take the Test?

Once you've studied and feel comfortable that you know what you need to know, you can sign up for the test. To become a Sun Certified Java Programmer, you need to take and pass exam 310-020 for Java 1.0.2, or exam 310-022 for Java 1.1. This test is administered through Sylvan Prometric™. You can schedule an exam by calling Sun Educational Services or an Authorized Prometric Test Center. Part III of this book provides phone numbers to call to schedule your exam.

To become a Sun Certified Java Developer, you need to first be a Sun Certified Java Programmer. Then, you must successfully complete a programming assignment and pass exam 310-021. These exams are also administered through Sylvan Prometric.

No matter where you are, don't worry—there are test centers throughout the U.S. and around the world, so you'll find a place you can go to get certified.

Onward!

You're ready to prepare for the test. Good luck and have fun as you become a certified expert in the Java programming language.

Answers to the exercises

Exercise 0.1

Here's a version that fulfills the requirements of the exercise:

```
class hello {
    public static void main(String[] args) {
        System.out.println("Hello, " + args[0]);
    }
}
```

This version is fine, but we can improve it by checking whether the user has supplied a command-line argument so we don't get an ArrayIndex-OutOfBoundsException if a name was not supplied:

```
class hello {
    public static void main(String[] args) {
        if (args.length > 0) // safety feature
            System.out.println("Hello, " + args[0]);
        else
            System.out.println("Hello, someone");
    }
}
```

Whether you wrote the exact program I've written is not important. What is important is that you should feel familiar with defining a class, writing a main() method, accessing an element in an array, and writing to the standard output. If you can do these things, you probably know enough Java to tackle this book. If you know much more than this, that's fine, too. Either way, I'll help you focus on what the test will cover so that you'll pass on your very first try.

Study for Programmers

Object-Oriented Programming

Before tackling this chapter, you should already be familiar with object-oriented concepts including classes, objects, instance methods, class methods, instance variables, class variables, and inheritance. You should know how to define a class in Java, and you should be able to implement methods and define variables.

In this chapter, we'll look at Java's features that relate to object-oriented programming. In particular, we'll create class hierarchies and use keywords that limit access to classes and class members.

What's on the Test

There are a two types of object-oriented questions on the test:

1. those that test how well you know Java's object-oriented *keywords,* and
2. those that test for your understanding of object-oriented *design.*

What does this mean? First, you've got to know which keywords you use to restrict access to class members within the same package and between packages. Second, you've got to be able to arrange classes in hierarchies and understand the difference between 'is a' and 'has a' relationships.

Objectives for this Chapter

- Create object-oriented hierarchies using 'is a' and 'has a' relationships.
- Define classes, including member variables and member methods.
- Define and use packages, using the package and import keywords.
- Use the class modifiers public, abstract, and final appropriately.
- Distinguish legal and illegal orderings of top-level Java source file elements, including package declarations, import statements, public class declarations, and non-public class declarations.
- Declare variables and methods using the private, protected, public, static, final, native, or abstract modifiers.
- Identify when variables and methods can be accessed based on access control keywords.

Object-Oriented Relationships Using 'is a' and 'has a'

Create object-oriented hierarchies using 'is a' and 'has a' relationships.

Here's an example of the kind of thing you've got to understand for the test. (And putting aside the test for moment, you've got to understand this problem and its solution to be an effective Java programmer.) How would you define a class hierarchy with these classes?

1. An Employee class that maintains an employee number.

2. A Full-time employee class that
   a) maintains an employee number,
   b) maintains the number of hours worked that week, and
   c) calculates its own pay using its own `salary()` method.

3. A Retired employee class that
   a) maintains an employee number,
   b) maintains the number of years worked, and
   c) calculates pay using its own `salary()` method.

Then, using these classes and the resulting class hierarchy, create an object for a full-time employee named Ralph Cramden.

Think about for this for a moment, then read on...

Perhaps you're thinking of something like this for the class hierarchy:

Figure 1-1
A Hierarchy that
Works in Theory

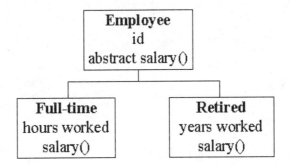

At first blush, this *seems* to work. We have Employee at the top level, defining an instance variable and an `abstract` method that both Full-time and Retired employees inherit. We would create a new instance of the Full-time employee class for Ralph.

Figure 1-1 certainly fits the classes into a class hierarchy. So what's the problem? Here's an example of where the design in Figure 1.1 falls apart.

Ralph Cramden is hired as a bus driver when he's 25. At that time, the program creates a new Full-time instance for him. Over the years the application accumulates references to this object throughout the system, because Ralph's on various lists for medical benefits, employee phone numbers, and so on. The application runs fine for years. But after 20 years he decides to retire to spend more time with his wife. Now we want to represent Ralph as an instance of the Retired class. Does this mean we create a new object for him, that we try to find all the references to the old object and replace it with the new object? And what happens if he takes time off in the middle of his career? What happens if he works in a temporary position in which his salary is calculated differently from other employees? Do we constantly create new objects to represent our employee named Ralph Cramden?

We only want to create one object for Ralph. Clearly, then, something's wrong with the design. What's wrong is that we did not fully grasp the difference between 'is a' and 'has a' for our particular domain.

The phrase 'is a' defines a direct relationship between a superclass and a subclass: a subclass is a type of a superclass. The phrase 'has a' describes a relationship between a part of an object and another object, usually of a different type: an object has a part that is another object.

Sure, a Full-time employee or a Retired employee 'is an' Employee. However, we would be much better off saying that the Employee class 'has a' part that 'is a' Status, and that an employee's Status is either Full-time or Retired. Now our hierarchy looks like this:

Figure 1-2
A Hierarchy that
Works in Practice

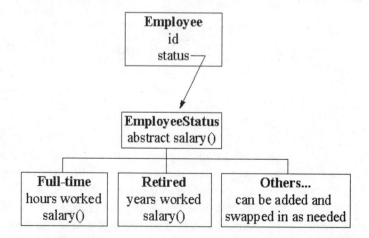

With this arrangement, we can keep the same Employee object forever and simply change its status when we need to. We can add to our status hierarchy as the needs of the application change. If Ralph took a leave of absence at the birth of his son, we can define a class to represent that new type of status and use a new instance of this class as Ralph's current status. If Ralph worked part-time for a while as he pursued a bowling career, an instance of a class called Part-time could be swapped in as his new status.

Our hierarchy works smoothly because we have used 'has a' and 'is a' correctly for our domain: an Employee 'has a' status; Part-time, Full-time, or Retired 'is a' Status.

This example shows why creating class hierarchies falls somewhere between engineering and craft. You use your skills to make trade-offs until you find something that works in practice. The primary skills you use are your ability to discern between 'is a' and 'has a' relationships for the domain you're working in, and your ability to imagine scenarios that test your design.

Tip

Our next step is to start implementing the classes and class hierarchies you design.

Exercise 1.1

Create classes for 2DShape, Circle, Square, and Point. Points have an (x, y) location. Circles have an (x, y) location, as well as a radius. Squares have an (x, y) location, as well as a length. Which are the superclasses, and which are the subclasses? Are any classes related by a 'has a' relationship?

Exercise 1.2

Define a class hierarchy to represent a shipment of coffee beans. The beans have some different characteristics and behavior in an inventory system depending on whether they are *untested*, or whether they have been tested and have been found to be *stale* or *fresh*. A shipment of beans is first entered into the inventory system before it is tested. What classes might you need? How are these classes related in 'is a' and 'has a' relationships? Which kind of class should you create an instance of when the shipment first arrives, before it is tested? What should you do after the shipment is tested?

Review: Classes, Variables, and Methods

Define classes, including member variables and member methods.

Objectives

I assume you can already create classes and define member variables and methods. Here's a quick review.

Classes

A class definition has some or all of these components:

```
[keywords] class MyClass [extends Superclass] [implements Inter-
face] {
   // class variables
   // static initializers
   // instance variables
   // constructors
   // class methods
   // instance methods
```

Member Variables

Here is an example of a class that inherits from class Object and defines three instance variables.

```
class Movie  {
   String name;
   int runningTime;
   boolean thumbsUp;
}
```

The first instance variable is an object reference to an instance of class String. The next two are primitive data types. These instance variables allow Movie objects to store their own unique values.

A static variable belongs to the class, not to the objects.

```
class Movie  {
   static int id;
   String name;
   int runningTime;
   boolean thumbsUp;
}
```

The id variable can be accessed from any class that can access Movie, starting from when Movie is first loaded into the Java Virtual Machine. Because it is declared as static, the id variable exists exactly once, no matter how many objects are created—even if no objects are created. In addition to static, we'll get into the other keywords for member variables (public, protected, private, and final) later in this chapter.

Member Methods

To define a method, simply declare the method within the class it belongs to, stating the method's keywords, return type, name, parameters, and any exceptions it might throw. In this chapter, we're concerned with the object-oriented design aspects of methods—where they fit into a class hierarchy and which classes can access them. How you define a return type, specify parameters, define any exceptions a method might throw, override and overload methods, and define native and synchronized methods is discussed in Chapter 8. In addition to native and synchronized, method definitions can be modified by the keywords public, protected, private, final, and abstract. These last five keywords all relate to object-oriented design, so we'll look at them later in this chapter. You can also define a static method to assign it to the class.

Here's an example of defining a method for our Movie class. (We'll use access control keywords in the next section.)

```
class Movie  {
    static int id;
    String name;
    int runningTime;
    boolean thumbsUp;
    boolean letsSeeIt() {
        return thumbsUp && (runningTime < 130);
    }
}
```

The letsSeeIt() method says that we'll see movies that have been given a thumbs-up by the reviewer and that have a running time of less than two hours and ten minutes.

Let's move on from this review and organize the classes we create into packages.

Packages

Define and use packages, using the package and import keywords.

To help you work more easily with a whole bunch of classes at once, Java allows you to group classes into packages. Packages help you associate classes with a particular function. For example, the Abstract Window Toolkit package (java.awt) is used for building user interfaces. As another example, the Input/Output package (java.io) is used for reading from and writing to streams. The classes in a package may or may not be related in a class hierarchy. They are, however, related in purpose.

Packages have three effects on your object-oriented design. Packages:

1. allow you to define stricter access control
2. make it easier to reuse common names
3. collect classes so that they can be shared more easily between applications

We'll look briefly at each of these three aspects; then we'll fill in the details.

Access Control

By default, all of your classes can reference other classes in the same package, and all methods can invoke other methods and access variables in the same package. (If you do not explicitly define a package, all of your classes are placed within the same, *default* package.)

The keywords public and protected do not affect access between classes and members *in the same package*. The keyword private, however, does restrict access to the class that defines the private member.

Table 1 shows what happens when a class *within the same package* as a public and default class tries to access members of the public and default classes. These members are defined with different access control keywords. (Figure 1-3 helps you visualize what I mean here.)

Figure 1-3
A Class Accessing
Members of Other
Classes Within the
Same Package

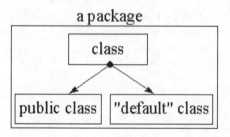

In the table, the entry "yes" indicates a class can access the member in the class type named for that column; the entry "no" indicates a class cannot access the member. (In the table, a "default" class is a class defined without any access control keywords; a "default" member is a member defined without any access control keywords.)

	public class	"default" class
public member	yes	yes
protected member	yes	yes
private member	no	no
"default" member	yes	yes

Classes in the same package can access each others' variables and methods, except for `private` members. Classes outside of the package can only see classes that are defined as `public` and can only access methods and variables defined using the `public` or `protected` keyword. What's more, only subclasses of classes with `protected` members can access those `protected` members outside a package.

Table 1-2 shows a method in a class *outside the same package* as a `public` and default class trying to access members with different access control keywords. Figure 1-4 shows this using images:

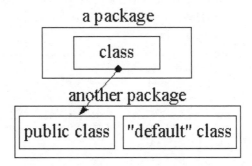

	public class	"default" class
Table 1-2 Access for a Class Outside a Package Defining a Public and "Default" Class		
public member	yes	no
protected member	yes if the accessing class is a subclass of this class; otherwise, no	no
private member	no	no
"default" member	no	no

Tip

Notice that access is much more restrictive than when the accessing class is in the same package as the public and "default" class. Packages allow you to fine-tune how and when others can make use of your classes.

Reuse Names

With a package, you can fully qualify a class name so that Java knows where to look for it. This allows you to use the same class name as one defined in another package. That is, fully qualifying a class name allows you to reuse common class names, since you can specify where Java should look to find where these classes are defined.

For example, perhaps you've decided to use the class names Point and Rectangle in your own package called `COM.Bluehorse.shapes`. However, you also want to use the `java.awt` classes called Point and Rectangle. One way to proceed is to import the AWT classes, using the `import` statement at the top of your file:

```
import java.awt.Point;
import java.awt.Rectangle;
```

Whenever you want to refer to Java's Point or Rectangle class, you can do so directly, as in:

```
new Point(10, 10);
```

You can reference your own classes by fully qualifying them. For example, you could create a new instance of your own Point class like this:

```
new COM.Bluehorse.shapes.Point(10, 10);
```

Sharing Classes Between Applications

Tip

When placing a collection of classes into its own package, you should strip out the application-dependent aspects of these classes. In a good design, a package will contain application-independent classes that you can reuse in any number of applications.

Since classes within the same package are placed in their own directory, you can easily refer to the entire collection of classes and use them in another application, without worrying about whether you are importing extra baggage that belongs to application-specific classes. For example, you can import all the classes in a package named shapes by writing:

```
import COM.Bluehorse.shapes.*;
```

When you do this, you know that you are only getting the shapes classes—as opposed to, say, the shapes classes *plus* some application-specific classes. Only those classes in the shapes package are in the shapes directory.

Package Details

Creating a Package

Key Concept

To create a package, name the package at the top of the source file containing the package classes. Use the keyword package, followed by the name of the package.

A simple example of creating a package is:

```
package shapes;

// . . . class definitions . . .
```

The package keyword tells the Java compiler to assign the classes in that file to the named package—in this case, shapes.

You can have more than one file whose classes belong in the same package.

Tip

Package names determine a directory structure for compiled classes. For example, let's say we have two source files, Draw.java and Shapes.java. Draw.java contains an Applet subclass named Draw. Shapes.java defines two classes, Square and Circle. We assign the Square and Circle classes to the shapes package by using the package keyword. Figure 1-5 shows how Java would require the classes to be organized:

Figure 1-5
Organization of
Classes and Packages
in the File System

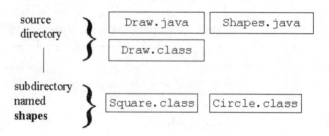

You can specify more levels of organization in your package by using subdirectories.

Tip

You specify each subdirectory using a dot (.), as in:

```
package Bluehorse.shapes;
```

If used with the classes we just discussed, this would require the directory structure shown in Figure 1-6:

Figure 1-6
Arrangement of
Classes and Packages
in the File System,
with Subdirectories

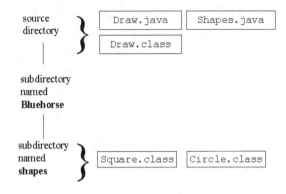

This would allow us to collect other packages under the top-level directory `Bluehorse`. For example, the `Bluehorse` directory could have the subdirectories `brushes`, `pens`, and `papers`, in addition to `shapes`. The Java class libraries are organized using subdirectores, with the `lang`, `util`, `io`, and other packages organized under the `java` directory.

The Sun Java Development Kit and other environments contain options to automatically place your package classes into the correct directories and subdirectories when they are compiled. With the JDK, you can use the –d option when you compile.

Tip

To use a class in a package other than the one in which it is defined, you must first import that class. You can import a class using the `import` statement, specifying the package the class is placed in.

Key Concept

To import a class named Circle in a package named `Bluehorse.shapes`, you can write:

```
import Bluehorse.shapes.Circle;
```

You can also import all of the classes in a package by using wild-card notation.

Tip

Here's an example of importing all the classes in `Bluehorse.shapes`
And as you saw, you can also fully qualify the class name, so that Java
knows where to find it when you reference it:

```
class SpecialCircle extends Bluehorse.shapes.Circle { . . . }
```

If you do not define a package for a source file, you can consider the
classes in that file to be in the same "default" package.

Exercise 1.3

Suppose you had a Circle class defined like this:

```
class Circle {
    double radius;
    double area() {
        return radius * radius * Math.PI;
    }
}
```

Place this class into a separate package. Add the appropriate access control keywords so that you can access this class from your default package
and create a new Circle instance, assign your new instance a `radius`
value, and display its area.

Exercise 1.4

Given a package named `COM.Company.utilities`, how would you import
a class in this package named Calculator? What would the structure be
for the directories and subdirectories that contained the Calculator class?

Class Keywords

Use the class modifiers `public`, `abstract`, and `final` appropriately.

Classes can be modified from their default state using any of three keywords: `public`, `abstract`, and `final`. As you've seen, the `public` keyword relates to access control; you'll see in a moment how the `abstract` and `final` keywords relate to your design.

public

If you import a package, you can only access those package classes that are declared to be `public`.

All of the classes you see in the Java APIs are declared `public`. Since each of these classes is defined in a different package from your application, declaring them `public` is the only way you can get at them.

abstract

If you have defined any methods as `abstract`, then you must define your class to be `abstract`, as well.

There's more information on overriding and overloading methods in Chapter 8, but let's talk about some object-oriented design aspects of methods here.

An `abstract` method consists of a method declaration without a body. That is, you define the keywords, return type, name, parameters, and the exceptions the method throws, but no instructions between a set of curly braces. Here's an example:

```
public abstract double area(double radius)
    throws IllegalGeometryException;
```

Since there is no code supplied for the `area()` method, the class itself cannot be instantiated. If it could be, then there is nothing stopping some other code from instantiating the class and invoking its `area()` method—but there are no instructions yet for `area()`. This flies in the face of Java's philosophy of doing its best to keep the programmer from making mistakes involving how the pieces fit together.

Why declare a method to be `abstract`? Can there possibly be a good reason for not providing any behavior at all and insisting that the class itself be abstract?

The reason has to do with design. Declaring a class to be `abstract` organizes your class hierarchy a certain way and forces a programmer using this class hierarchy to do things according to your understanding of the domain. For example, the `java.lang` package defines a class called Number. This class is abstract. This class defines the `abstract` methods `intValue()`, `longValue()`, `floatValue()`, and `doubleValue()`. The role of the Number class is to organize and unite a variety of "wrapper" classes into the same branch in the class hierarchy, and to specify what their interface will be. Concrete subclasses of Number are Integer, Long, Double, and Float. These subclasses implement the behavior for the `abstract` methods they inherit and make this behavior mean something specific to their class type.

The reason these methods are declared to be `abstract`, (rather than, for example, defining a method that returns a default value such as 0), is because the Number class is never intended to be instantiated. According to the design, it makes no sense to instantiate Number. The purpose of the subclasses is to put an object-oriented wrapper around a primitive data type that corresponds to the class name—`int`, `long`, `double`, or `float`. However, there is no generic `number` type. So making a Number object has no meaning.

Making Number `abstract` forces programmers to instantiate the classes that were intended to be instantiated. You can do the same thing in your design, so that programmers use your classes as you intended.

One of the benefits of this type of design—that is, of uniting the wrapper types under the same branch in the class hierarchy, even if you cannot instantiate the superclass—is that you can define an object reference to be the superclass type. Then, this object reference can refer to any subclass of that type.

For example, you can write something like:

```
Number n;
s = getInput();
if (isInteger(s))
    n = new Integer(s);
else if (isFloatingPoint(s))
    n = new Double(s);
```

The variable n can be used to invoke methods that are defined in Number, including Number's `abstract` methods that are implemented in the subclasses. Since Number defines `intValue()`, `longValue()`, `floatValue()`, and `doubleValue()`, we can invoke any of these methods using the variable n.

You can declare a class to be `abstract`, even if no methods are declared as `abstract`. Subclasses are automatically concrete. Two examples of this are Java's own Container and Component classes, defined in `java.awt`. Again, declaring the class as `abstract` forces programmers to instantiate subclasses of these classes. So, instead of allowing a programmer to instantiate Component, a programmer must instantiate Button, or Choice, or Checkbox, or some other subclass. However, an object reference of type Component can refer to any of these.

final

If you want to stop programmers from ever making a subclass of a particular class, you can declare that class to be `final`.

A `final` class makes all of its ~~variables and~~ methods `final` as well, since a `final` class cannot be extended.

As an example of a `final` class, the classes Integer, Long, Float, and Double are declared as `final`, so all of their methods are `final`, as well. None of these wrapper classes can be subclassed. If you would like to make your own type of wrapper, you must extend the class Number. Another commonly used class that's declared as `final` is String.

The `final` keyword optimizes your code and makes your design more secure.

First, let's look at optimization. When a variable is declared to be `final`, Java knows its value is a constant. A `final` variable must be initialized when it is declared, because it can never be changed later. Since this value is a constant, the compiler could feel free to optimize by replacing references to that variable with its constant value, eliminating the need to look up its value when it is referenced. As an example, the variables `PI` and `E` in the Math class in `java.lang` are defined as `final`.

When a method is declared to be final, Java knows that the method can never be overridden. A final method must be fully defined when it is declared—you cannot have an abstract final method, for example. Since Java knows the method can never be overridden by subclasses, the Java compiler can replace the call to the method with inline code if it wants. This eliminates all sorts of class look-ups to find the method in the class hierarchy and makes the method invocation much faster.

How about security? Declaring a method to be final is one way to guarantee that its contract—its published API—will never be violated. For example, the method getClass() in class Object is declared as final. No subclass can override this method so that it violates its contract and returns some other class type to hide its identity.

Exercise 1.5

Given the following class definition:

```
abstract class Shape {
    abstract double perimeter();
}
```

Create a subclass of Shape named 2DShape, and a subclass of 2DShape named Square. Like Shape, 2DShape should also be an abstract class, but Square should be concrete and should know how to calculate its perimeter. Define whatever instance variables you need for Square.

Exercise 1.6

Modify the classes you created above so that programmers cannot make subclasses of your Square class.

Ordering of a Java Source File

Distinguish legal and illegal orderings of top-level Java source file elements, including `package` declarations, `import` statements, public class declarations, and non-public class declarations.

Objectives

There are three basic entries that can be placed within a Java source file:

1. A `package` definition.

2. Any number of `import` statements.

3. Any `public` and non-`public` classes and interfaces.

If you include a `package` declaration, this must be the first thing to appear in a source file. Any `import` statements come next; you can have as many `import` statements as you'd like. After the `package` and `import` statements, you can define any classes and interfaces that you'd like.

Key Concept

In Sun's JDK, you can only define one `public` class. What's more, if you do define a `public` class, the source file must be named after the class. For example, if you are defining a `public` class named Earth, then the source file it is defined in must be named `Earth.java`.

Tip

Other Java development environments do not have this restriction of one `public` class per source file.

Exercise 1.7

What's wrong with this class file?

```
import java.util.*;
import java.awt.*;
package myUtils;

public class Util {
    public double avg(double a, double b) {
        return (a + b) / 2;
    }
}
```

Try compiling this file if you can't find the answer.

Variable and Method Keywords

Declare variables and methods using the private, protected, public, static, final, native, or abstract modifiers.

First, I'll present four keywords that are used with variables and methods. Then, I'll summarize the three access control keywords mentioned earlier in this chapter. I already covered the static, abstract, and final keywords when discussing class keywords. I'll summarize them here for class members and then move on to synchronized and native.

static

As I mentioned earlier, a static member belongs with the class.

A static variable always exists exactly once for a class, no matter how many instances are created.

A static method belongs with the class. Since a static method is not associated with a particular object, you cannot use this or refer to an instance member by name as you would from a non-static method.

abstract

An abstract method defines the method's signature, return value, and the exceptions it might throw, but does not define the code that implements the method.

If you define an abstract method, you must make that class abstract, as well.

final

A final member cannot be changed after it is defined. That means that a final variable is a constant, and a final method cannot be overridden by subclasses.

As I mentioned when describing what it means to declare an entire class to be `final`, the two benefits of a `final` method or variable are with security (enforcement of the API) and optimization (placing code inline). A `final` member provides these benefits on a member by member basis, rather than for the class as a whole.

synchronized

A `synchronized` method can only be invoked by one thread at a time. A `synchronized` method can belong to an object or a class. If a thread enters a `synchronized` instance method, no other thread can invoke any other `synchronized` instance method for that object. If a thread enters a `synchronized static` method, no other thread can invoke any other `synchronized static` method for that class.

There's much more information on `synchronized` methods in Chapter 11.

native

A `native` method is defined in a platform-dependent language—or at least, some language other than Java. I'll return to the topic of `native` methods in the second section of this book, because `native` methods appear mostly in the Developer exam.

Exercise 1.8

What is wrong with this class definition? Fix it so that it works when you invoke `main()`.

```
class Avg {
    public static void main(String[] args) {
        double a = 5.1;
        double b = 20.32;
        double c = 32.921;
        System.out.println(findAvg(a, b, c));
    }

    double findAvg(double a, double b, double c) {
        return (a + b + c) / 3.0;
    }
}
```

Access Control Keywords

Identify when variables and methods can be accessed based on access control keywords.

You've already seen a couple of tables regarding access control for class members. Here's a quick summary of these keywords. I'll follow this summary with a number of exercises involving access control.

If there are no access control keywords on a class, then only those classes defined in the same package can attempt to access members of that class. If there are no access control keywords on a member, then only those classes in the same package can access that member.

public

A public member can be accessed by any class that can access the member's class.

If a class in package number 1 wants to access the member of a class defined in package number 2, the class in package number 2 must be declared public so that the first class can get to it. Then, the first class can access any members that are declared as public.

private

You can restrict all access to a particular member from all classes except the class in which it is defined by using the keyword private on the member.

protected

A protected member can only be accessed by classes within the same package, or by subclasses in the same or different packages from the member's class.

Exercises

The following exercises deal with keywords that you can place on classes and class members.

Exercise 1.9

Imagine this hierarchy:

```
Tree (defines a protected instance variable named age)
Deciduous extends Tree
Evergreen extends Tree
Pine extends Evergreen
Forest
```

This hierarchy looks like this:

Figure 1-7
A Hierarchy of
Tree Classes

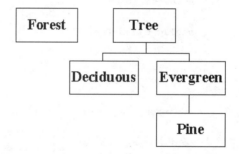

Now, create the following objects:

```
Deciduous d = new Deciduous();
Evergreen e = new Evergreen();
Pine p1 = new Pine();
Pine p2 = new Pine();
Forest f = new Forest();
```

Which objects can access the `protected` field in class Tree if all of these classes are defined as part of the same package? Which objects cannot access this `protected` field?

Exercise 1.10

What if each of the classes in Exercise 1.9—Forest, Tree, Evergreen, Deciduous, and Pine—were defined in different packages? Which objects could then access the Tree's protected field?

Exercise 1.11

What will happen when you first compile the file named Tree.java, and then compile the file named Forest.java, as presented below? If there is a problem, fix the code.

```
File Tree.java:

package Flora;

public class Tree {
    protected int age;
}
File Forest.java:

import Flora.Tree;

public class Forest {
    public static void main(String[] args) {
        Tree t = new Tree();
        System.out.println("The tree's age is " + t.age);
    }
}
```

Exercise 1.12

What will happen when you first compile the file named `Tree.java`, and then compile the file named `Forest.java`, as presented below? If there is a problem, fix the code.

```
File Tree.java:

public class Tree {
    protected/age;
}



File Forest.java:

public class Forest {
    public static void main(String[] args) {
        Tree t = new Tree();
        System.out.println("The tree's age is " + t.age);
    }
}
```

Exercise 1.13

Tie together the Violin and Guitar classes presented below with a superclass, and make the Violin class unable to be subclassed. Use Java's abstract and final keywords where appropriate.

```
class Violin {
    int numStrings;
    void play() {
        System.out.println("mmm");
    }
}

class Guitar {
    int numStrings;
    void play() {
        System.out.println("twang");
    }
}
```

Exercise 1.14

Change the following class definition for Employee. Restrict access to the Employee id to be read-only. (You can use a combination of a keyword on this variable and a new method to achieve this.) In addition, outside of this package, id should be able to be accessed by only the Employee class and Employee subclasses.

Maintain an id counter internally in the class. Start the id counter at 1 for the first employee, and for each new employee add 1 to the counter. Any class should be able to create a new employee—even classes in other packages. Use the keywords private, protected, public, and static, as necessary.

```
class Employee {
    int id;
    Employee(int id) {
        this.id = id;
    }
}
```

Exercise 1.15

Here is a small application to draw a square wherever the user clicks the mouse. When the user clicks in the applet, the applet detects this event and creates a new Square object, adding it to a Vector object. In the applet's paint() method, we enumerate through the Squares in the Vector and draw each one.

If you're not very familiar with graphical applications yet, don't worry too much about this exercise. If you feel comfortable with them, however, look over the code and then see if you can answer the questions that follow.

```
file name: Shape.java

package COM.Bluehorse.Shapes;

public abstract class Shape {
    Point loc;
    public abstract void draw(Graphics g);
}
```

Exercise 1.15 continued

```
file name: Square.java
package COM.Bluehorse.Shapes;
public class Square extends Shape {
   public void draw(Graphics g) {
      g.drawRect(loc.x, loc.y, 20, 20,);
   }
}


file name: DrawApplet.java

import java.awt.*;
import COM.Bluehorse.Shapes.*;

public DrawApplet extends java.applet.Applet {
   private Vector shapes = new Vector();
   public void paint(Graphics g) {
      for (Enumeration e = v.elements(); e.hasMoreElements(); )
{
         e.nextElement().draw();
      }
   }
   public boolean mouseUp(int x, int y, Event e) {
      v.addElement(new Square(x, y));
      repaint();
   }
}
```

Here are some questions regarding access between classes:

1. Is it possible for the mouseUp() method in DrawApplet to access the Square's loc field?
2. Is it possible for mouseUp() to access the Square's draw() method?
3. Could a subclass of DrawApplet, whose source is in the file DrawApplet.java, access DrawApplet's shapes field?

Exercise 1.16

Here are a few questions and thought experiments about combinations of keywords. If you're not sure of the answers, write some code and try to compile it.

1. Can an abstract method be final?
2. Can an abstract method be static?
3. Can you define a public protected field?

Casting Classes

You can cast one object type to another type.

If you cast up the hierarchy, you can assign an object to a superclass reference without casting.

For example, imagine these three simple classes:

```
class Parent {
    public static void main(String[] args) {
        Derived1 d1 = new Derived1();
        Derived2 d2 = new Derived2();
        Parent p = Parent();
        // we'll add code here. . .
    }
}

class Derived1 extends Parent { }

class Derived2 extends Parent { }
```

Let's replace the comment "we'll add code here" with some actual code. If we want to set d1 to p, that's no problem. All we need to do is write:

```
p = d1;
```

That's because we've cast up the hierarchy. All Derived1 objects are also of type Parent, so this assignment is perfectly legal.

Tip

Interestingly, this does not change the object type as far as invoking a method. The actual object type referenced by p is still of type Derived1. So, if Derived1 overrides a method in Parent, invoking that method using p (now pointing to a Derived1 object) will still invoke the version of that method in Derived1.

If you cast down the hierarchy, you must cast the class type.

If, instead of

```
p = d1;
```

we wrote

```
d1 = p;
```

the code would not compile. This kind of cast is somewhat similar to trying to assign a `float` value to an `int`. You are attempting to assign a value with more detail to a type that knows less detail.

   If we were dealing with `float` and `int`, we could cast the `float` to an `int` to make the compiler and runtime know that everything was okay and that we're aware of what we're doing. The same is true with classes—we can cast Parent to Derived1 and the code will compile.

```
d1 = (Derived1)p;
```

However, just because the compiler allows for the possibility that this is a legal cast, that does not mean that it actually is. Whether or not this is legal depends on what the object's type is at runtime. According to the code we've written, the object reference p refers to an instance of class Parent. Parent does *not* inherit from Derived1, so, at runtime, this code would throw a ClassCastException.

   If, instead, we had created a new object and assigned it to p like this:

```
                        Parent
Parent p = new Derived1();
```

Then this code:

```
d1 = (Derived1)p;
```

would both compile and run successfully.

You can only cast up and down the hierarchy—for example, you cannot cast between two classes that are siblings.

To illustrate this warning, you could not write:

```
d1 = d2;
```

or even

```
d1 = (Derived1)d2;
```

because d1 and d2 are not in the same branch of the class hierarchy. The compiler would complain that this is an invalid cast.

What's Not on the Test

By concentrating only on what is on the test, I've left out some very important topics. This section covers these topics so that you can get a complete snapshot of Java's object-oriented features.

Interfaces

For the programmer's test, the only interface you need to know about is the Runnable interface defined in `java.lang`. (We'll discuss this interface later in the book.)

An interface defines a set of `abstract` methods and class constants. In other words, as its name implies, an interface defines an *interface*, not an *implementation*. The implementation of an interface—that is, the behavior for the methods—is left to the class implementing the interface.

The need for an interface arose because Java only has single inheritance of implementation. This means that every class has exactly one superclass. If you want to inherit behavior from two classes, you just can't do it.

The reason for this restriction is purely one of eliminating complications. For example, imagine this class situation, shown in Figure 1-8, that arises in languages that allow multiple inheritance.

Figure 1-8
The Multiple
Inheritance
Diamond

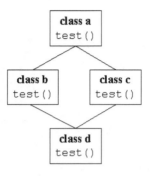

If we invoke d's `test()` method, and `test()` invokes `super.test()`, which method gets executed next—c's or b's? Maybe each gets executed once? What if each of these `test()` methods invoked its `super.test()` method—would that mean that a's `test()` method gets executed twice?

In Java, this confusion is not possible, since a class can only have one superclass.

Even though multiple inheritance of implementation is not allowed, a design based on multiple inheritance can be very useful. For example, imagine you are designing a forms package. You would like the user to drag and drop TextField, Checkbox, and Choice objects onto a form. You would like to identify your subclasses of these `java.awt` classes as being FormElements. In a multiple inheritance environment, you could design your classes like those in Figure 1-9.

Figure 1-9
A Form Builder
Application Design
using Multiple
Inheritance (You Can-
not Do This in Java)

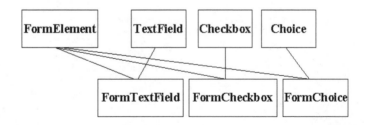

In this design, your own form objects inherit behavior from FormElement. In Java, even though you cannot pass an implementation to a subclass of another class, you can still pass an implementation to that class. The way you do that is by defining FormElement to be an interface. FormElement can still define a method, but instead of the `java.awt` subclasses inheriting an implementation, they only inherit a method signature. It is up to these subclasses to provide their own behavior for any methods defined by the interface. Figure 1-10 gives a sense of this relationship.

Figure 1-10
Inheriting an
Interface Only

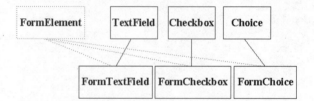

You define an interface similar to a class that defines only `abstract` methods and class constants. However, you do not have to use the `abstract` and `final static` keywords to define these things, since an interface assigns these keywords by default.

Here's an example of a FormElement interface

```
public interface FormElement {
    public int TEXT = 1;
    public int CHOICE = 2;
    public boolean mustAnswer();
    public String getResponse();
}
```

This interface defines two class constants, TEXT and CHOICE. It also defines two `abstract` methods, `mustAnswer()` and `getResponse()`.

Here is how you might implement an interface in the FormTextField class.

```
public class FormTextField extends java.awt.TextField
        implements FormElement {

    public boolean mustAnswer() {
        return true;
    }
    public String getResponse() {
        return getText();
    }
}
```

How to Clone Objects

There is no operator that allows you to make a direct copy of an object in memory. Instead, to make a copy of an object, you invoke its `clone()` method.

Not all classes allow their objects to be cloned. Only those that implement the Cloneable interface can be cloned.

An interesting thing about the Cloneable interface is that it does not define any methods that must be implemented. So why define an interface at all? Because defining your class as implementing an interface marks objects of that class as an *instance* of that interface. This means that we can use an interface as a kind of indicator of desired behavior. Before the Java runtime clones an object, it checks to see if the object's class implements the Cloneable interface. If it does, then the clone() method returns a clone of the object. Otherwise, the clone() method throws a CloneNotSupportedException.

The Java Virtual Machine does not call an object's constructor when you clone the object.

Tip

Exercise 1.17

The clone() method in Object is protected. What are the effects of making the Object's clone() method protected, if all classes inherit from class Object?

Exercise 1.18

What happens when you try to compile a Java source file containing the following code:

```java
class Tree {
    protected int age;
}


class Pine extends Tree implements Cloneable {
    Pine() {
        age = 2;
    }
}


class Maple extends Tree {
    public static void main(String[] args) {
        Pine p1 = new Pine();
        Pine p2 = p1.clone();
        System.out.println("Pine is " + p2.age);
    }
}
```

Static Initializers

A static initializer is defined using the keyword static, followed by a set of curly braces in which you can place code, as in:

```
static {
    System.out.println("The class is loading");
}
```

The Java Virtual Machine (JVM) executes all static initializers for a class when the class is first loaded. The JVM initializes any static variables and executes any static initializers in the order they are listed in the class.

Be careful to avoid dependencies between static initializers in different classes. There might be a dependency, for example, if a member variable or static initializer refers to variables or methods in another class. When the Java Virtual Machine comes across a reference to a class it has not yet loaded, the JVM stops loading the first class and attempts to load the second class. If that second class, in turn, refers back to the first, the member variables not yet initialized would have only their default values instead of the values assigned in their initialization statements. This might make your class behave in ways you had not expected.

Exercise 1.19

Use a static initializer to set a static array of three floating-point numbers to three random numbers between 0.0 and 1.0. You can acquire a random number of type double between 0.0 and 1.0 by writing:

```
Math.random();
```

(We'll cover arrays in depth in Chapter 4.)

Answers to the Exercises

Exercise 1.1

This is a classic example of knowing when to use 'is a' and 'has a'. The confusion comes into play with the fact that points, circles, and squares all have a position on the screen. Here is one way to do the hierarchy, where it looks as though you have pushed as much information up the hierarchy as possible:

Figure 1-11
An Awkward
Class Hierarchy—
Do You Agree?

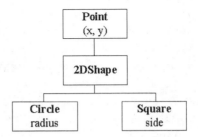

The problem here is not that 2D shapes such as circles and squares don't have a screen position—they do. The problem is that 2D shapes are not special kinds of points. In other words, points are not well represented as circles with a zero radius. This does not feel right or represent the situation as you think of it in the real world. Instead, it might make more sense to have the 2DShape class refer to a Point instance. In other words, a 2DShape 'has a' point—a position on the screen—but a 2DShape 'is not a' point.

Figure 1-12
A Better Class
Hierarchy

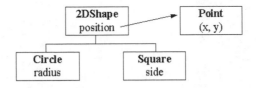

Exercise 1.2

There are many possible answers to this question. Here's one possible class hierarchy for coffee beans.

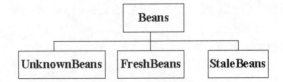

Before this discussion, you might have been tempted to say the shipment can be represented by an instance of class Beans. But when it is determined to be stale or fresh, what class would you use then? The instructions to this exercise state that the beans have some different characteristics and behavior depending on whether they're untested, fresh, or stale. You could simply keep a flag in the class itself that indicates state, but then you'd have to write an `if-else` or `switch-case` statement in the class to perform the correct behavior depending on whether the beans have been tested or not, and if they have been, what the outcome was. Using control flow to determine something that can be done using subclasses is a strong indication that you're not taking full advantage of object-oriented programming and that it's time for some reworking of your class hierarchy.

The hierarchy presented above will work fine, but in conjunction with another class. One way to make this work, for example, is to define a class named Shipment. The Shipment class can delegate its responses to the method calls that depend on its state to a Beans object reference. At first, the shipment is assigned an object of type UnknownBeans. Once the Shipment is tasted, its Beans object reference can be assigned a new object, of type FreshBeans or StaleBeans, as appropriate.

Now, the relationship is that Shipment 'has a' taste, and that taste is either unknown, fresh, or stale.

Exercise 1.3

You can modify Circle to place it into a package, like this:

```
package shapes;

public class Circle {
    public double radius;
    public double area() {
        return radius * radius * Math.PI;
    }
}
```

With everything `public`, classes outside of the package that Circle is defined in can now use the Circle class as before. Using Sun's JDK, if this is defined in a file named Circle.java, you can compile this by writing:

```
java -d . Circle.java
```

Here's how you can define a class to create a new Circle object:

```
import shapes.*;

class CircleTester {
   public static void main(String[] args) {
      Circle c = new Circle();
      c.radius = 10;
      System.out.println("area with radius = 10 is " + c.area());
   }
}
```

Exercise 1.4

You can import the class like this:

```
import COM.Company.utilities.Calculator;
```

The directory structure starts with COM at the top level. A subdirectory of COM is Company. A subdirectory of Company is utilities. In the utilities directory, you'll find the Calculator class.

Exercise 1.5

```
abstract class 2DShape extends Shape {
}
class Square extends 2DShape {
   double side;
   double perimeter() {
      return 4 * side;
   }
}
```

Exercise 1.6

All you have to do to stop programmers from making subclasses of a class is declare it using the `final` keyword. For the Square class, you could write:

```
final class Square extends 2DShape {
    double side;
    double perimeter() {
        return 4 * side;
    }
}
```

Exercise 1.7

A `package` declaration must come first in a source file, before any `import` statements or class definitions. The code presented in the exercise would cause a compile-time error.

Exercise 1.8

What's wrong here is that the `static` method attempts to invoke the non-static method named `findAvg()`. Since there is no instance of Avg to use to invoke `findAvg()`, this is a compile-time error. To fix this, we could either make `findAvg()` `static` or create an instance of Avg and use that when invoking `findAvg()`.

Exercise 1.9

The `protected` keyword is commonly defined as restricting access of a member to the same class or to a subclass of that class. However, `protected` is not as straightforward as that. Actually, within a package, any class can access any other class's `protected` field. So, all objects in this example—d, e, p1, p2, and f—can access any `protected` fields in Tree.

Exercise 1.10

Outside of the package a class is defined in, only subclasses can access a superclass's `protected` field. So: d, e, p1, and p2 could access the `protected` field; f could not.

If you have an object reference, say to object e, can the object p1 access e's `protected` field defined in Tree? The answer is yes. However, could e access p1's `protected` field defined in Tree? Here, the answer is no! The reason is that the object accessing the `protected` field must be of at least the type of the object reference. p1, a Pine, is of type e, an Evergreen, so it can access e's protected field. However, the reverse is not true. An Evergreen is not (always) a Pine, so e cannot access p1's `protected` field.

Similarly, p1 could not access d's `protected` field, since Pine does not inherit from Deciduous.

Exercise 1.11

The first file will compile fine, but when you try to compile Forest, the compiler will display a message indicating that Forest cannot access the `protected` field defined in Tree. A simple way to fix this problem is to make the age field `public`.

Another way is to define a `public` method that accesses the age field and returns its value. The Forest class can then invoke this `public` method from `main()`.

Exercise 1.12

Both files will compile fine and you can execute Forest's `main()` method without a hitch. It will access Tree's age field, even though it's `protected`, because Forest and Tree are in the same (default) package.

Exercise 1.13

```
abstract class StringedInstrument {
    int numStrings;
    abstract void play();
}

final class Violin extends StringedInstrument {
    void play() {
        System.out.println("mmm");
    }
}

class Guitar extends StringedInstrument {
    void play() {
        System.out.println("twang");
    }
}
```

Exercise 1.14

Here is one possible answer to this exercise:

```
public class Employee {
    private static int next_id = 1;
    private int id;
    public Employee() {
        id = next_id++;
    }
    protected int getId() {
        return id;
    }
}
```

Exercise 1.15

1. Is it possible for the `mouseUp()` method in DrawApplet to access the Square's `loc` field? No: Since `loc` is not defined with a `public` keyword, only those classes in the same package as the class defining `loc` can access this field.
2. Is it possible for `mouseUp()` to access the Square's `draw()` method? Absolutely. Both Square and `draw()` are defined with the `public` keyword, so any class in any package can invoke `draw()`.
3. Could a subclass of DrawApplet, whose source is in the file `DrawApplet.java`, access DrawApplet's `shapes` field? No. `shapes` is `private`, so only DrawApplet itself can access this field.

Exercise 1.16

1. Can an `abstract` method be `final`? No. An `abstract` method must be overridden by a subclass, but `final` methods cannot be overridden.
2. Can an `abstract` method be `static`? No. You cannot override a static method (think about it—there is no `this` or `super`, since there is no current object responding to a `static` method, so there's no way to invoke the superclass's behavior). Since you cannot override a `static` method, a `static` method cannot be abstract.
3. Can you define a `public protected` field? No. Only one access control keyword can be used at a time. (There is an oversight in earlier versions of Java where `protected private` was allowed, but it no longer is.)

By the way, you cannot define an `abstract` method to be `native`, either.

Exercise 1.17

Since Object is defined in a different package than your own (Object is defined in `java.lang`), declaring `clone()` to be `protected` puts some restrictions on which objects can request a `clone()` of which other objects. An object can only request a clone of another object whose class is the same type or subclass of the object being cloned. The idea is to only allow a method to request a clone of an object whose class is in the same branch of the class hierarchy as itself.

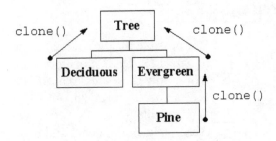

First of all, all objects can clone *themselves*. Beyond that, as indicated in the class hierarchy in Figure 1-14, some references to other object types that are allowed are:

- Pine objects can clone Evergreen or Tree objects.
- Evergreen objects can clone Tree objects.
- Deciduous objects can clone Tree objects.

This stops arbitrary objects, who have no relationship to each other, from cloning each other. For example, Deciduous objects cannot clone Evergreen objects, and no Tree object can clone a Forest object.

Exercise 1.18

The compiler issues an error because Maple is not in the same branch of the class hierarchy as Pine, clone() is protected, and class Object, which defines clone(), comes from a different package.

Exercise 1.19

Here is one way to define the array and static initializer (I have put them into a class called Example):

```
public class Example {
    public static double[] d = new double[3];
    static {
        for (int index = 0; index < d.length; d++)
            d[index] = Math.random();
    }
}
```

Review questions

Question 1: **What happens if you try to compile code that looks like this:**

```
class MyString extends String {
}
```

a) The code compiles successfully.
b) The code does not compile because you have not defined a `main()` method.
c) The code does not compile because String is `abstract`.
d) The code does not compile because String is `final`.

Question 2: **If you have this class definition:**

```
abstract class Shape {
    abstract draw();
}
```

What happens if you try to compile the following class definition?

```
class Square extends Shape {
}
```

a) Everything compiles succesfully.
b) Shape compiles, but Square does not compile.
c) Square compiles, but Shape does not compile.
d) Neither Shape nor Square compiles.

Question 3: **What happens if you try to compile the Shape and Square class from Question 2 if the Shape class is declared like this:**

```
abstract class Shape {
}
```

a) Everything compiles fine.
b) Shape compiles, but Square does not compile.
c) Square compiles, but Shape does not compile.
d) Neither Shape nor Square compiles.

Question 4: The following class definitions:

```
class Bridge {
    Road road;
}

class Road {
    String name;
}
```

represent

a) an 'is a' relationship
b) a 'has a' relationship
c) both
d) neither

Question 5: Specifying this line at the top of your source file:

```
package awt;
```

a) Results in a compile-time error because Java already defines an awt package.
b) Specifies that all of your classes in this file should go into Java's awt package.
c) Specifies that all of your classes in this file should go into your own awt package.
d) imports all of the classes in your own awt package.

Question 6: Given these two source files:

FormQuestion.java

```
package forms;

public class FormQuestion {
    int type;
}
```

Form.java

```
package forms;

class Form {
    int getType(FormQuestion question) {
        return question.type;
    }
}
```

What is the outcome of compiling FormQuestion.java and then Form.java?

a) Both compile successfully.
b) Neither compile successfully.
c) Only FormQuestion.java compiles.
d) Only Form.java compiles.

Question 7: What keyword can you give a class so that classes outside of the package this class is defined in cannot access the class?

a) don't give the class a keyword at all
b) private
c) final
d) protected

Question 8: To restrict access to a static member to the class itself:

a) use the `final` keyword
b) use the `private` keyword
c) do not use a keyword at all for the member
d) a `static` member cannot be restricted in this way

Question 9: Which of the following statements is false?

a) An instance method can be both `protected` and `abstract`.
b) A `static` variable can also be `final`.
c) A `static` method can also be `protected`.
d) A `static` method can also be `abstract`.

Question 10: By default—that is, without keywords—all classes can access all members except for those defined:

a) using the `final` keyword
b) using the `abstract` keyword
c) in another package
d) in the same package

Answers to the Review Questions

Question 1	d.	String is defined using the keyword `final`. Therefore, it cannot be subclassed, and the compiler will tell you that extending String is not allowed.
Question 2	b.	Square will not compile because it should either be declared as `abstract`, or it should implement the `draw()` method.
Question 3	a.	A subclass of an `abstract` class that does not declare any `abstract` methods is not `abstract` by default.
Question 4	b.	A Bridge 'has a' Road, represented by the instance variable `road` inside Bridge. Neither class extends another class (except for class Object, so in that sense, it does represent an 'is a' relationship).
Question 5	c.	The `package` keyword defines your own package for the classes in that file.
Question 6	a.	Both files compile successfully. Both classes were placed into the same package. Therefore, both classes can access each other and each others' members (as long as the accessed member is not `private`).
Question 7	a	The default access control for a class—that is, defining a class without a keyword—restricts other classes in other packages from accessing the class.
Question 8	b.	You can restrict access to a member by using the `private` keyword, regardless of whether that member is `static` or non-`static`.
Question 9	d.	A `static` method cannot be overridden: Therefore, it cannot be `abstract`.
Question 10	c.	All classes can access all members, by default, except for those defined in another package. To access classes and members in another package, those classes must be declared using the `public` keyword, and the members must also be declared `public` (or `protected`, if the accessing class is a subclass of the class defining the `protected` member).

Keywords

None.

Keywords are reserved words. You cannot use a reserved word as the name of a class, variable, or method.

You've no doubt seen all the keywords in Java in your travels through the language—or have you? This chapter makes sure you're familiar with Java's keywords by listing them all by category (under headings such as *exceptions*, *access control*, and so on) and by providing examples of how to use each of them.

What's on the Test

There are a few questions that make sure you're familiar with Java's keywords. We'll cover the keywords in slightly more depth here than you need for the test, but covering the keywords can provide you with a good perspective on the language as a whole and can help you determine which keywords you might have questions about.

Objectives for this Chapter

- Identify Java keywords from a list of keywords and non-keywords.
- State what each Java keyword is used for.

An Alphabetical List of All the Keywords

Identify Java keywords from a list of keywords and non-keywords.

Objectives

The three keywords in *italics* (`const`, `goto`, and `transient`) are reserved but currently unused in Java 1.0.2. The `transient` keyword is used in Java 1.1.

ABSTRACT	DOUBLE	INT	STATIC
BOOLEAN	ELSE	INTERFACE	SUPER
BREAK	EXTENDS	LONG	SWITCH
BYTE	FINAL	NATIVE	SYNCHRONIZED
CASE	FINALLY	NEW	THIS
CATCH	FLOAT	NULL	THROW
CHAR	FOR	PACKAGE	THROWS
CLASS	*GOTO*	PRIVATE	*TRANSIENT*
CONST	IF	PROTECTED	TRY
CONTINUE	IMPLEMENTS	PUBLIC	VOID
DEFAULT	IMPORT	RETURN	VOLATILE
DO	INSTANCEOF	SHORT	WHILE

For the rest of this chapter, I've divided the keywords into their logical categories and provided explanations for each one. Feel free to skim over these sections if this is mostly a review for you. You can reference this chapter later if you want to quickly look up a keyword or find an example of how to apply it.

State what each Java keyword is used for.

Organizing Classes

package   *specifies that classes in a particular source file should belong to the named package.*

You use the package keyword at the top of a source file, followed by the name of the package.

```
package shapes;
```

import   *requests the named class or classes be imported into the current application.*

Any number of import keywords can follow the package keyword. Each import statement specifies the name of a package to import.

```
import shapes.*;
```

Defining Classes

class   *defines a class: collection of related data and behavior that can also inherit data and behavior from a superclass.*

Define a class by writing the word class followed by the class name. The class definition follows within a set of curly braces.

```
class Circle
```

extends *indicate which class to subclass.*

Write the keyword extends after the class name if you would like to extend a class other than class Object.

```
class Circle extends Shape
```

Interfaces can extend other interfaces.

Tip

interface *defines class constants and abstract methods that can be implemented by classes.*

Specify an interface by writing the keyword interface followed by the interface name. The interface definition follows within a set of curly braces.

```
interface Editable
```

implements *indicates the interface for which a new class will supply methods.*

The implements keyword appears after the name of the superclass you are extending, or after the name of the class you are defining if you are simply extending class Object.

```
class Circle implements Editable
class Circle extends Shape implements Editable
```

Keywords for Classes and Members

public *means the class, method, or variable can be accessed from classes outside of the package in which they're defined.*

Place the public keyword in front of the class or member.

```
public Circle
public double radius;
public double area()
```

private *means only the class defining the method or variable can access it (classes cannot be private).*

Place the `private` keyword in front of the member.

```
private double radius;
private double area()
```

protected *means that when a class inside a package defines a member as protected, the only classes outside of the package that can access the protected member are subclass (classes cannot be protected).*

Place the `protected` keyword in front of the member.

```
protected double radius;
protected double area()
```

abstract *specifies the class cannot be instantiated directly.*

You must declare a class as `abstract` if:

- any of its methods are `abstract`
- it inherits from a class that defines `abstract` methods and does not implement them
- it extends an interface but does not implement its methods

Optionally, you can also decide you do not want other programmers instantiating your class and can declare your class to be `abstract`, even if your class does not contain any `abstract` methods.

The `abstract` keyword is placed in front of the class definition if the class is `abstract`, and in front of a method definition if the method is `abstract`.

```
abstract class Shape
abstract void draw()
```

static *indicates a member belongs with the class.*

Place the `static` keyword in front of the member.

Tip

By convention, access control keywords are placed first.

```
static double radius;
public static double area()
```

synchronized *indicates only one thread can access the synchronized methods for a particular object or class at a time.*

You can define a `synchronized` method by placing this keyword in front of the method.

```
synchronized void initCircle()
```

You can also define a `synchronized` block of code by writing the keyword `synchronized`, followed by an object or class that will be used to obtain the *monitor* or *lock* (there's much more information on threads and synchronization in Chapter 11).

```
synchronized (this) { }
```

volatile *tells the compiler a variable may change asynchronously due to threads.*

Declaring a variable to be `volatile` makes the compiler forego optimizations that might turn the variable into a constant and eliminate the possibility of it changing asynchronously.

```
volatile int numCircles;
```

final *means this variable or method cannot be changed by subclasses.*

A `final` member can be optimized by the compiler and turned into a constant if it is a variable and inline code if it is a method. A `final` method keeps programmers from changing the method's *contract*—its agreed-upon behavior.

```
public static final int RADIUS = 20;
final double area()
```

native *indicates a method is implemented using native, platform-dependent code (such as C code).*

The `native` keyword indicates the method is not written in Java but in some platform-dependent language.

```
native double area()
```

Simple Data Types

I'll discuss Java's data types in Chapter 5. Here's a quick list of all the primitive data types:

long is a 64-bit signed integer value
int is a 32-bit signed integer value
short is a 16-bit signed integer value
byte is an 8-bit signed integer value
double is a 64-bit floating-point value
float is a 32-bit floating-point value
char is a 16-bit Unicode character
boolean is a true or false value

Values and Variables

false is a Boolean value
true is a Boolean value
this refers to the current instance in an instance method

The keyword this is really a "magic" object reference that refers to the object responding to a method.

Tip

With this, you can pass the current object to another method or refer to an instance variable when a local variable might hide the instance variable.

```
addToList(this);
this.length = length;
```

super   *refers to the immediate superclass in an instance method.*

The keyword super is really a "magic" object reference that refers to an object responding to a method whose type is the superclass of the responding object. With super, you can pass a method call up the class hierarchy.

```
super.draw();
```

null   *represents a nonexistent instance.*

void   *indicates a method does not return a value.*

You can use void instead as the return type of a method to indicate the method does not return a value.

```
void draw()
void writeToScreen(String s)
```

Exception Handling

There's more explanation concerning these keywords in Chapter 8, which covers exception handling.

throw   *signals an exception has occurred.*

You must write a Throwable object following this keyword.

Typically, a new instance of an Exception class is created on the spot. Exception implements the Throwable interface.

```
throw new IOException();
```

try   *marks the stack so that if an exception is thrown, it will unwind to this point.*

The above explanation for try is a cryptic way of saying that you try to execute a block of code, and following the try block, you *catch* any exceptions that methods you invoked might have thrown. You can also execute a finally block following the try block (see below).

```
try { }
// followed by exception handling and/or a finally block
```

catch   *handles an exception.*

A catch block follows a try block. After the catch keyword, write the type of exception that your catch block will handle. This exception type is written in parentheses, similar to a method parameter.

```
// a try block precedes a catch block
catch (IOException x) { }
```

finally   *says "execute this block of code regardless of control flow statements".*

A finally block can follow a try block or a try/catch block.

```
// following a try or try/catch block
finally { }
```

throws   *indicates the types of exceptions a method is allowed to throw.*

Methods that might throw a *checked* exception must indicate the exception type with a throws clause in the method declaration.

Tip

Methods can optionally indicate they throw unchecked exceptions. Unchecked exceptions inherit from RuntimeException or Error.

```
void pauseGame(int seconds) throws InterruptedException { }
double area(String area) throws NumberFormatException { }
```

Instance Creation and Testing

new   *creates new instances.*

Following a new keyword, specify the class name you'd like to create an instance of, and supply the appropriate parameters for the constructor you want to invoke. The new keyword returns an object reference to the new object.

```
Circle c = new Circle();
Circle c = new Circle(40, Color.blue);
```

instanceof   *tests whether an instance derives from a particular class or interface.*

This keyword is really an operator that tests an object reference to see what it derives from. The instanceof operator will respond true if the object reference refers to an object that is an instance of the class being tested, if it is an instance of a subclass of that class, or if it is an instance of a class that implements the interface specified with this operator.

```
if (objRef instanceof Cloneable)
if (objRef instanceof Shape)
```

Control Flow

Java's control flow statements are similar to the control flow statements in other languages, such as C.

switch   *tests a variable.*

case   *executes a particular block of code according to the value tested in the switch.*

default   *means the default block of code executes if no matching case statement was found.*

break   *jumps out of the block of code in which it is defined.*

The switch-case construct is a convenient way to pick from a variety of possible values for an expression and take different action for each of them, rather than writing lots of nested if-else statements.

```
String nobelWinner = null;
switch (year) {
   case (1938):
      nobelWinner = new String("Enrico Firmi");
      break;
   case (1921):
      nobelWinner = new String("Albert Einstein");
      break;
   case (1903):
      nobelWinner = new String("Marie Curie");
      break;
   default:
      nobelWinner = new String("unknown");
}
```

for   *signifies iteration.*

A `for` statement contains three parts: initialization of the loop index, a test for halting the loop, and modification of the loop index. These are separated by semicolons. You can place more than one expression in any of these three parts by separating them with a comma.

continue   *continues with the next iteration of a loop.*

The `continue` statement can be a convenient way to skip over code and go on to the next loop iteration.

```
for (int index = 0; index < limit; index++) {
   if ((result = calculate(index)) == 0)
      continue; // loop back to the for loop
   // more code in this loop. . .
}
```

You can also use labels with a `continue` or `break` statement. Then, instead of continuing with the next loop iteration in the block where the `continue` is used, or instead of breaking out of the block the `break` is defined in, you can continue or break to the block defined by the label. There are examples of this in Chapter 7.

return   *returns from a method, optionally passing back a value.*

if tests   *for a condition and performs some action if true.*

else   *performs some action if an "if" test was false.*

```
String nobelWinner = null;
if (year == 1938)
   nobelWinner = new String("Enrico Firmi");
else if (year == 1921)
   nobelWinner = new String("Albert Einstein");
else if (year == 1903)
   nobelWinner = new String("Marie Curie");
else
   nobelWinner = new String("unknown");
```

do   *performs some statement or set of statements.*

while   *performs some action while a condition is true.*

To perform a block of code conditionally, you can use while without do, as in:

```
while (condition == true) {
   doThis();
}
```

To perform a block of code at least once, and thereafter conditionally, you can use while in conjunction with do:

```
do {
   doThis();
} while (condition == true);
```

Not Used Yet, But Reserved

You cannot use any of these words as identifiers, either, even though they are not yet defined or used by Java 1.0:

- const
- goto
- transient (this keyword is used in Java 1.1—see Chapter 18 for an explanation).

Exercises

Exercise 2.1

Sort the following list into reserved and non-reserved words.

- for
- do_while
- Integer
- int
- implements
- equals
- Object
- java
- switch
- break
- test
- code
- goto

Exercise 2.2

List all the keywords that can be used to define control flow statements.

Exercise 2.3

List the three keywords reserved by Java but not used in Java 1.0.

Answers to the Exercises

Exercise 2.1

Don't mistake class names for reserved words!

reserved words:

- for
- int
- implements
- switch
- break
- goto

non-reserved words

- do_while
- Integer
- equals
- Object
- java
- test
- code

Exercise 2.2

The keywords used with control flow statements are: do, while, if, else, for, break, continue, case, switch, default, and return.

Exercise 2.3

The three unused keywords are const, goto, and transient.

Review Questions

Question 1: Which word is not a Java keyword?

    a) `integer`
    b) `double`
    c) `float`
    d) `default`

Question 2: Which keyword is not used to control access to a class member?

    a) `public`
    b) `protected`
    c) `private`
    d) `default`

Question 3: Identify the keywords from this list:

abstract	class	object	reference
double	character	Boolean	this

    a) `abstract, class, object, double, this`
    b) `class, ` ~~`double`~~ `, this, ` *object*
    c) `abstract, class, double, this`
    d) `abstract, class, object, double, character, this`

Answers to Review Questions

Question 1   a.   The integer data types are `int`, `long`, `byte`, and `short`, but there is no integer type. (Integer, with a capital 'I', is a class name.)

Question 2   d.   The default keyword is used with `switch-case` statements.

Question 3   c.   The others (object, reference, character, and Boolean) are not keywords.

CHAPTER 3

Constructors

You should already know that you can use the new keyword to create a new object. Also, some of the examples in this chapter extend a class called Vector, defined in java.util. If you are unfamiliar with this class, you should take a moment to review this class' documentation in the API files.

In this chapter we'll look at constructors. Constructors are somewhat similar to methods. However, instead of directly calling a constructor, Java executes a constructor for you just after *Java* allocates the memory for your object, and after Java has set the object's instance variables to their initialization values.

As with methods (which are discussed in depth in Chapter 9), you can override and overload constructors. Java will invoke the constructor that corresponds to the parameters supplied with the new statement.

What's on the Test

The test covers all the basics of constructors. For example, you should know when you can use the default constructor and when you must create your own constructors. You should understand the flow of control with constructors—when your superclass' constructor is invoked for you, how you can invoke your superclass's constructor explicitly, and how to overload and override constructors.

Objectives for this Chapter

- Describe the default constructor.
- Identify situations when the default constructor is created for you and when it is not created for you.
- Overload and override constructors.
- Use this() and super() to invoke constructors in the current or parent class.

The Default Constructor

Describe the default constructor.

Identify situations when the default constructor is created for you and when it is not created for you.

If you do not define a constructor explicitly, Java defines one for you. This default constructor takes no arguments and invokes its superclass no-args constructor.

Here's a simple example for a class named Queue. This class is a subclass of Vector. (A queue stores values using a first-in, first-out strategy.)

```
class Queue extends Vector {
   void add(Object obj) {
      addElement(obj);
   }

   Object get() {          first
      Object obj = lastElement();
      boolean success = removeElement(obj);
      return obj;
   }
}
```

Given this class definition, you can create Queue objects by writing code like this:

```
Queue q = new Queue();
```

You can add() objects to and get() objects from this Queue object by invoking Queue's methods.

Defining a Constructor

Overload and override constructors.

This Queue class works fine except for one thing: it does not support two other constructors defined by Vector. These constructors are defined in the documentation within java.util (where Vector is defined) as:

```
public Vector(int  initialCapacity);
public Vector(int  initialCapacity, int  capacityIncrement);
```

These additional constructors *overload* the default Vector constructor.

As with methods, the Java Virtual Machine determines which constructor to execute by the arguments you supply when creating a new object.

If you do not *override* one of these overloaded constructors in the Queue class and try to create a Queue object like this:

```
Queue q = new Queue(100);
```

and you think that this would invoke the correct Vector constructor to set the initial capacity of this Queue/Vector, think again. The only constructor *Java* provides for you is the no-args constructor. So the above line wouldn't work with the code we've written so far—Java would say there is no constructor for Queue that takes an int as a parameter.

To make this work, you've got to write the appropriate constructor in the Queue class.

You can define a constructor for a class by writing any access control keywords, the class name, a set of arguments in parentheses, any exceptions the constructor might throw, and then the body of the constructor—just as you would for a method, except that you do not define a return value.

Constructors never return a value—if you specify a return value, Java will interpret your intended constructor as a method.

The constructor we need for Queue could take an int and invoke the corresponding constructor defined in Vector by using super():

```
Queue(int capacity) {
    super(capacity);
}
```

Now, the line of code:

```
Queue q = new Queue(100);
```

runs without a hitch. We could also write a constructor for Queue to handle the second Vector constructor—the one that takes two int parameters, an initial capacity and an increment.

This Queue class now works fine, except we can no longer create a Queue object the way we did before by writing:

```
Queue q = new Queue();
```

What gives? We've fixed one problem and created another.

The problem is that Java only supplies the default, no-args constructor if you do not define any other constructor.

Since we have now supplied a constructor that takes an int, Java does not define a no-args constructor for us.

The way around this problem is to supply a no-args constructor ourselves.

Here is a complete definition for our new Queue class:

```
class Queue extends Vector {

    Queue() {
        super();
    }

    Queue(int capacity) {
        super(capacity);
    }

    Queue(int capacity, int increment) {
        super(capacity, increment);
    }

    void add(Object obj) {
        addElement(obj);
    }

    Object get() {          first
        Object obj = lastElement();
        boolean success = removeElement(obj);
        return obj;
    }
}
```

Invoking Another Constructor

Use this() and super() to invoke constructors in the current or parent class.

If you do invoke another constructor directly, make that direct call as the first line of your constructor.

You can invoke one of the overloaded constructors by supplying the appropriate parameters in super(). Placing a call to super() in any line other than the first one results in a compiler error. If you do not invoke a superclass' constructor yourself, Java will attempt to invoke the no-args constructor in your superclass. If the superclass does not have a no-args constructor, the Java compiler will detect this situation if it can and issue a compiler error.

If the compiler doesn't detect this situation (because of classes loaded dynamically at runtime), Java will throw runtime exception when it encounters trouble.

In addition to invoking a superclass' constructor using super(), you can also invoke another constructor in the same class using this().

For example, let's say you want to define a constructor for Queue that takes an array of objects to place into the Queue, and you want to set the initial capacity of that Queue to the length of the array. You can write such a constructor like this:

```java
Queue(Object[] objs) {
    this(objs.length);
    for (int index = 0; index < objs.length; index++)
        addElement(objs[index]);
}
```

This constructor invokes a constructor in the same class that takes an `int` value (the constructor that takes the `int` value defines the initial capacity). The constructor then performs some additional processing to add the objects in the array to the Queue.

Exercise 3.1

Create a subclass of class Frame called MyFrame. Define MyFrame so that you can create a new MyFrame object with a title. The Frame class defines a constructor that takes a title as a String, as in:

```
Frame (String s);
```

(The Frame class is a real Java class defined in `java.awt`.)

Exercise 3.2

Here is a class named Bridge:

```
class Bridge {
   int length;
   Bridge(int length) {
      this.length = length;
   }
}
```

Modify this class definition to construct a new Bridge instance without explicitly supplying the Bridge's length, like this:

```
Bridge b = new Bridge();
```

Exercise 3.3

Given this class definition:

```
class Railroad {
   String name;
   Railroad() {
      System.out.println("I've been working on the railroad");
   }
   Railroad(String name) {
      this.name = name;
   }
}
```

How could you adjust the second constructor (the one that takes the String) most efficiently so that it also displays the message *I've been working on the railroad* when it is invoked?

Answers to the Exercises

Exercise 3.1

To create a class called MyFrame that defines a title, you've got to override the Frame's constructor that takes a String and pass that String object up to the Frame's constructor, like this:

```
class MyFrame extends Frame {
   MyFrame(String s) {
      super(s);
   }
}
```

Exercise 3.2

The no-args constructor is only supplied for you if you have not defined another constructor. In this case, since there is already another constructor, you've got to write the no-args constructor explicitly:

```
class Bridge {
   int length;
   Bridge(int length) {
      this.length = length;
   }
   Bridge() {
   }
}
```

You do not have to supply any code for this no-args constructor. The Java Virtual Machine will invoke your superclass' no-args constructor for you, and since `length` is already set to 0 as its default value, you do not need to initialize `length` in the constructor itself.

Exercise 3.3

You can invoke the no-args constructor in the Railroad class using `this()`, as in:

```
class Railroad {
   String name;
   Railroad() {
      System.out.println("I've been working on the railroad");
   }
   Railroad(String name) {
      this();
      this.name = name;
   }
}
```

Review Questions

Question 1:   What is the result of attempting to compile and run the following code?

```
class Ex {
    public static void main(String[] args) {
        Fx f = new Fx();
    }
    Ex(int i) {
    }
}

class Fx extends Ex {
}
```

a)   The code does not compile because the Ex class does not define a no-args constructor.
b)   The code does not compile because the Fx class does not define a no-args constructor.
c)   The code does not compile because there is no code in the Ex(int i) constructor.
d)   The code compiles and runs successfully.

Question 2:   What is the result of attempting to compile and run the following code?

```
class Ex {
    public static void main(String[] args) {
        Fx f = new Fx(5);
    }
    Ex() {
        System.out.println("Ex, no-args");
    }
    Ex(int i) {
        System.out.println("Ex, int");
    }
}
```

Question 2 continued

```
class Fx extends Ex {
   Fx() {
      super();
      System.out.println("Fx, no-args");
   }
   Fx(int i) {
      super(i);
      this();
      System.out.println("Fx, int");
   }
}
```

a) The messages "Ex, int," "Fx, no-args," and "Fx, int" appear in the standard output.
b) The messages "Ex, no-args," "Ex, int," "Fx, no-args," and "Fx, int" appear in the standard output.
c) The code does not compile because the Fx(int i) constructor is not defined legally.
d) The code does not compile because the Fx() constructor is not defined legally.

Question 3:   What is the result of attempting to compile and run the following code?

```
class Ex {
   public static void main(String[] args) {
      Fx f = new Fx(5);
   }
   Ex() {
      System.out.println("Ex, no-args");
   }
   Ex(int i) {
      System.out.println("Ex, int");
   }
}
```

Question 3 continued

```
class Fx extends Ex {
   Fx() {
      super();
      System.out.println("Fx, no-args");
   }
   Fx(int i) {
      this();
      System.out.println("Fx, int");
   }
}
```

a) The messages "Ex, int," "Fx, no-args," and "Fx, int" appear in the standard output.
b) The messages "Ex, no-args," "Fx, no-args," and "Fx, int" appear in the standard output
c) The code does not compile because the Fx(int i) constructor is not defined legally.
d) The code does not compile because the Fx() constructor is not defined legally.

Answers to the Review Questions

Question 1   a.   The default constructor in Fx will attempt to invoke a no-args constructor in Ex. Since Ex already defines a constructor, Java does not supply a no-args constructor by default. The compiler will catch this problem and complain.

Question 2   c.   The Fx(int i) constructor is defined like this:

```
Fx(int i) {
   super(i);
   this();
   System.out.println("Fx, int");
}
```

However, a direct call to a constructor must appear as the first thing in a constructor. While `super(i)` is first, `this()` is second, and `this()` is also a direct call to a constructor. This is illegal.

Question 3   b.   First, Java invokes the constructor `Fx(int i)`. This calls `Fx()`, which invokes the no-args superclass constructor `Ex()`. This writes "Ex, no-args" to the standard output. Then the `Fx()` no-args constructor continues, which writes "Fx, no-args" to the standard output. Then the Fx(int i) constructor continues, which writes "`Fx, int`" to the standard output.

Memory and Garbage Collection

It's useful to know that you can cast classes from one type to another. Some of the examples and exercises in this chapter define object references to be the superclass type of the actual object created, and some exercises also cast object references from one class type to another.

The `finalize()` method discussed here is declared as throwing an instance of type Throwable. Exception handling is discussed in Chapter 9, but knowing about exceptions and `try-catch` blocks can be useful in understanding `finalize()`.

The most important thing to know for this chapter is that you can either use one of Java primitive data types, or you can create your own type, which will be a class. When you instantiate a class, Java manages the memory for that instance.

Java manages your program's memory. This eliminates all manner of bugs that creep into programs built with languages where you must access and manage memory directly. Java's role in managing memory eliminates bugs involving:

- freeing memory too soon (resulting in a dangling pointer)
- not freeing memory soon enough or at all (resulting in a memory leak)
- accessing memory beyond the bounds of the allocated memory (resulting in using uninitialized values)

When you want to define a new data type, you define a new class. You allocate an instance of a class by using the new keyword. The new keyword returns an object reference. This object reference is essentially a pointer to the object in memory—except, in Java you cannot manipulate this object reference like a number. You cannot perform pointer arithmetic.

Objects are allocated from a garbage collected heap. You cannot directly alter the memory in this heap. You can only get at the objects in this heap by using object references. Since Java manages the heap, and since you cannot manipulate object references, you must trust the Java Virtual Machine to do what's right: free memory when it should, allocate the correct amount of memory when needed, and so on. But don't worry, the Java Virtual Machine is very good at its job—much better than any of us error-prone humans.

What's on the Test

There are few if any conceptual questions on the test concerning how Java manages the memory. Instead, most of the test questions are applied. If you can write a finalize() method, and if you can explain what method is invoked with different types of object references declared in different ways, you'll do fine. But the questions make you stay on your toes—sometimes the details can trip you.

Objectives for this Chapter

- Identify when an object referred to by a local variable becomes eligible to be garbage collected (in the absence of compiler optimization).
- Describe how finalization works and what behavior Java guarantees regarding finalization.
- Distinguish between modifying variables containing primitive data types and object references, and modifying the objects themselves.
- Identify the results of Java's "pass by value" approach when passing parameters to methods.

Garbage Collection

Identify when an object referred to by a local variable becomes eligible to be garbage collected (in the absence of compiler optimization).

Since Java manages the garbage collected heap, which is where all your objects live, you've got to trust Java to manage the memory for you. This includes believing that the Java Virtual Machine really will free memory you no longer need when it runs low.

An object becomes a candidate for garbage collection when your program can no longer reference it.

Here is an example. Say you allocate an object and only assign it to a method variable. When that method returns, there is no way for you to ever refer to that method variable again. Therefore, the object is lost forever. That means that when the method returns, the object is a candidate for garbage collection.

As another example, you might create an object, assign this object to an object reference, and then set this object reference to `null`. As soon as you lose the reference to the object, that object becomes a candidate for garbage collection.

Just because your program might lose a reference to an object does not mean that the *Java Virtual Machine* (hereafter called the JVM) will reclaim that object's memory right away, or even at all. The JVM will only perform garbage collection if it needs more memory to continue executing. For almost all simple programs, including the ones you've seen so far, the JVM doesn't even come close to running out of memory.

The reason the garbage collector does not reclaim memory as soon as it is available is that garbage collection takes time. If the garbage collector were continuously expunging allocated memory you could no longer access, it would seriously slow your program's execution.

There's no guarantee as to what order the garbage collector reclaims objects in. This allows the garbage collector to run as efficiently as possible.

Even though there is a new keyword, notice that you do not explicitly indicate how much memory to set aside. The JVM determines this for itself. The JVM determines the memory your object requires based on:

1. the amount of memory needed to maintain instance variables for the object, as well as
2. a standard overhead required by all objects.

What's more, even though Java supplies the keyword new, there is no corresponding delete or any other way to directly free memory. The way you indicate you are through with an object is to set its object reference to null or to some other object. Or, as mentioned, when a method returns, its method variables will no longer be valid, so the garbage collector also knows any objects referenced by method variables are candidates for garbage collection.

Even though you cannot free objects explicitly, you can directly invoke the garbage collector.

This will make the garbage collector run, which will reclaim candidates for garbage collection.

They way you run the garbage collector is to perform two steps:

1. Get an object that represents the current runtime.
2. Invoke that object's `gc()` method.

Here is a snippet that does this:

```
Runtime rt = Runtime.getRuntime();
rt.gc();
```

Exercise 4.2 asks you to work through an example of this.

Finalization

Describe how finalization works and what behavior Java guarantees regarding finalization.

In most situations, you'll never know when garbage collection has occurred. Java runs the garbage collecting process as a low-priority background thread. The garbage collector will run whenever memory gets low.

However, there is a way you can get into the act of garbage collection. If you want to perform some task when your object is about to go away, you can override a method called `finalize()`.

Java will invoke the `finalize()` method exactly once for every object in your program. `finalize()` is declared as `protected`, does not return a value, and throws a Throwable object.

Java invokes the `finalize()` method just before an object is about to be garbage collected. You might take advantage of this notification to clean up any resources that have been allocated outside this object. A classic example is a file that an object has opened that might still be open. The object can check to see if the file has been closed in `finalize()`, and if not, close the file.

While you can use `try` and `catch` blocks in `finalize()`, uncaught exceptions are ignored.

The official documentation says that `finalize()` will be run for all objects when the program exits. However, on some platforms and in earlier versions of Java, this was not always the case. Sometimes `finalize()` simply did not run unless the JVM ran out of memory or, if it did not, you explicitly invoked the garbage collector.

You can also invoke your own object's `finalize()` method. Typically, you would not invoke `finalize()` yourself, but would allow the JVM to do this for you. If you do invoke `finalize()`, remember that `finalize()` is declared as throwing a Throwable, and that it is declared as `protected`, so only objects with the proper access can invoke this method.

Always invoke your superclass's `finalize()` method if you override `finalize()`.

I made the above sentence a key concept rather than a tip because it's a very important rule. It's easy to forget that `finalize()` could be implemented in a superclass. Always be certain to invoke your superclass' `finalize()` method so that you don't break code you inherit from.

Since Java only invokes `finalize()` once per object, you should not resurrect an object in `finalize()`. If you did and the object was finalized again, its `finalize()` method would not get called. Instead, you should create a clone of the object if you really need to bring the object back to life.

Exercise 4.1

Write a class called Test whose objects write the message "We're in finalize" to the standard output when their `finalize()` methods are run.

Exercise 4.2

Given the code below for a class called GC, create a new Test object in GC's test() method and then make that object a candidate for garbage collection. Do this before the call to fullGC() in test().

When this code is working, running GC with the Test class you wrote should cause the message "We're in finalize" to appear in the standard output automatically, without you explicitly invoking finalize().

```
class GC {
    public static void main(String[] args) {
        GC gc = new GC();
        gc.test();
    }
    void test() {
        fullGC();
    }
    void fullGC() {
        Runtime rt = Runtime.getRuntime();
        long isFree = rt.freeMemory();
        long wasFree;
        do {
            wasFree = isFree;
            rt.gc();
            isFree = rt.freeMemory();
        } while (isFree > wasFree);

        rt.runFinalization();
    }
}
```

Accessing Members

Distinguish between modifying variables containing primitive data types and object references, and modifying the objects themselves.

Given an object reference, which variable you access and which method you invoke depend on different things.

The type of the object reference determines which variable you access. The type of the underlying object determines which method you invoke.

As an example, consider the following code:

```java
class Acc {
    public static void main(String[] args) {
        First s = new Second();
        System.out.println(s.var);
        System.out.println(s.method());
    }
}

class First {
    int var = 1;
    int method() {
        return var;
    }
}

class Second extends First {
    int var = 2;
    int method() {
        return var;
    }
}
```

What do you expect this program to display in the standard output? Notice that the variable s in main() is defined as an object reference for the First type, but we've actually allocated a new object of type Second, a subclass of First.

When we use s to access a variable, the type of s—in this case, First—is used to grab the variable. So, we access var from First, which is 1. So, in the first println() statement, 1 appears in the standard output.

When we use s to invoke a method, the type of the object referenced by s—in this case Second—is used to invoke the method. So, we invoke method() in Second, which accesses its local variable named var. This makes the second println() statement display 2 in the standard output.

What would happen if we changed the class definition of Second so that it no longer overrode `method()`? In that case, even though `s.method()` will look first in the Second class to access `method()`, the call will get passed up the class hierarchy. The `method()` that's defined in First will execute, which will access its local `var` variable, which is 1, so the second `println()` statement would display 1.

Exercise 4.3

> When you invoke a method given an object reference, is there a way to force the JVM to invoke the overridden method that's defined in that object's superclass, instead of invoking the method in the class type of the object itself? For example, given the classes First and Second defined in the previous section, is it possible to invoke `method()` defined in First, rather than `method()` defined in Second, given an object reference of type Second?

Passing Parameters to a Method

Identify the results of Java's "pass by value" approach when passing parameters to methods.

Java passes method parameters by value. This means that Java makes a copy of the parameter and passes this copy to the method.

For a primitive data type—such as an `int`, `float`, `boolean`, or `char`—the result of passing by value should be clear: anything that happens to that value inside the method does not affect the original value in the calling code.

Here's an example.

```
public class ch0401 {
    public static void main(String[] args) {
        double pi = 3.1415;

        System.out.println("before: pi is " + pi);
        zero(pi);
        System.out.println("after: pi is " + pi);
    }

    static void zero(double arg) {
        System.out.println("top of zero: arg is " + arg);
        arg = 0.0;
        System.out.println("bottom of zero: arg is " + arg);
    }
}
```

First we set a value for a variable named pi, and then we pass this value to a method that sets this value to 0. The value of pi gets to the method named zero() just fine, and zero() does its job of setting the value it receives to 0. However, zero() has received a copy. The original value of pi in main() is not affected.

The output from this program is:

```
before: pi is 3.1415
top of zero: arg is 3.1415
bottom of zero: arg is 0
after: pi is 3.1415
```

While the same *call by value* rule is in place when the argument is an object reference rather than a primitive data type, unraveling what's really going on involves some careful thinking.

Let's redo the above program, this time making the variable pi an object reference that refers to an instance of a class we'll create called Pi. This class will have one instance variable and will look like this:

```
class Pi {
    double value = 3.1415;
    public String toString() {
        Double d = new Double(value);
        return d.toString();
    }
}
```

By overriding the method toString(), we provide a way to place the object reference directly in a println() statement to display its value. You can use this trick in your own programs to help make your code easier to read and your objects easier to work with.

Tip

Let's rework the original program to use an instance of the Pi class instead of passing the value of pi directly as a double.

```
public class ch0402 {
    public static void main(String[] args) {
        Pi pi = new Pi();

        System.out.println("before: pi is " + pi);
        zero(pi);
        System.out.println("after: pi is " + pi);
    }
```

```
    static void zero(Pi arg) {
        System.out.println("top of zero: arg is " + arg);
        arg.value = 0.0;
        System.out.println("middle of zero: arg is " + arg);
        arg = null;
        System.out.println("bottom of zero: arg is " + arg);
    }
}
```

What do you expect the outcome of this program to be? To answer this question correctly, you need to have a picture in mind of what's going on in memory.

In main(), after creating the instance of Pi and assigning it to an object reference called pi, we have something like the following:

Figure 4-1
An Object Reference
Accessing an Object
in the Garbage
Collected Heap

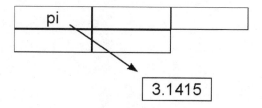

There's a chunk of memory somewhere that we refer to by using the name pi. This chunk of memory (which is four bytes long, to be exact) points to an object that's somewhere else in memory. Notice that an object reference like pi is a pointer, even though there is no way in Java to manipulate `pi` as if it were a pointer, as you can in C or C++. The object referenced by `pi` has an instance variable set to 3.1415, so that's how we've depicted it in the diagram.

As soon as we invoke the method named `zero()`, Java needs to keep track of another object reference—the method parameter (that is, the variable) we've named `arg`. The variable `arg` is completely separate from the variable `pi`, because parameters are passed by value, and so Java makes a copy of the variable. However, as with the `double` values in the previous example, the *contents* of each variable are the same. Hence, `arg` also points to the same object as `pi`.

Figure 4-2
Two Object References Pointing to the Same Object in the Garbage Collected Heap

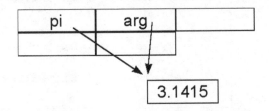

Now, if we use the variable `arg` to change the object, we change the object directly. The code, for example, sets `arg.value` to 0.

Figure 4-3
Changing the Same Object by Using the Second Object Reference

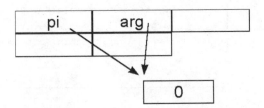

The final section of code in the method `zero()` sets the value of `arg` to `null`. This does nothing to the object itself or to any other object references—setting `arg` to `null` only changes the object reference named `arg`.

Figure 4-4
Setting One of the Object References to Null, but the Object is Untouched

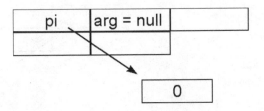

The variable `arg` loses its reference to the object, but the object itself is still intact. Also intact are any other references to the object. If `arg` were the only object reference to the underlying Pi object, then the object would become a candidate for garbage collection. However, arg is just a parameter, and there is another reference to the underlying object—the reference in the calling code.

The output of this code, then, looks like this:

```
before: pi is 3.1415
top of zero: arg is 3.1415
middle of zero: arg is 0
bottom of zero: arg is null
after: pi is 0
```

Exercise 4.4

Find a way to change the following code so that you can pass the values a, b, and c in test() to calc() and have calc() update these values and return them to test(). As they are currently defined, there is no way to pass a, b, and c to calc() and back because these are defined in primitive data types. Perhaps there is another data type you can pass to calc() so that this will work?

```java
class A {
    public static void main(String[] args) {
        A a = new A();
        a.test();
    }
    void test() {
        int a = 10;
        int b = 13;
        int c = 24;

        System.out.println("before: a = " + a);
        System.out.println("before: b = " + b);
        System.out.println("before: c = " + c);

        calc(a, b, c);

        System.out.println("after: a = " + a);
        System.out.println("after: b = " + b);
        System.out.println("after: c = " + c);
    }
    void calc(int a, int b, int c) {
        a *= 2;
        b *= 3;
        c *= 4;
    }
}
```

What's Not on the Test

Forcing Garbage Collection

Exercise 4.2 contained some code that used a Runtime object to force garbage collection. This is not something that is on the test, but it's useful to know how to do this.

There are four methods defined by Runtime that you can use to help keep track of and interact with the garbage collector.

- gc(): By the time this method returns, the Java Virtual Machine has performed garbage collection.
- runFinalization(): By the time this method returns, the Java Virtual Machine has run the finalize() method for all objects awaiting garbage collection whose finalize() methods have not yet been run.
- totalMemory(): This method returns an int containing the total amount of memory available in the Java Virtual Machine for allocating objects.
- freeMemory(): This method returns an int containing the total amount of free memory in bytes. Free memory is the amount of memory available for allocating objects. This amount will always be less than the value returned by totalMemory().

Answers to the Exercises

Exercise 4.1

You can write a Test class that overrides finalize() like this:

```
class Test {
   protected void finalize() throws Throwable {
      super.finalize();
      System.out.println("We're in finalize");
   }
}
```

Remember, as the text says, finalize() is declared as protected and throws a Throwable.

Exercise 4.2

Your test method in GC should now look like this:

```
void test() {
   Test t = new Test();
   t = null;
   fullGC();
}
```

Exercise 4.3

No. You can invoke super() from a method, but you cannot invoke a method defined in a superclass given only an object reference.

Exercise 4.4

One way to solve this problem is to create a new class that has three int values for a, b, and c, to pass an instance of this class to calc(), and have calc() operate on the instance variables of this object.

Another way is to create an array of int values and to pass the array to calc(). Remember, an array is an object, so you can pass the array to a method and if the method modifies the elements of the array, these changes will appear in the calling method's array as well.

Here is an example of this:

```
class B {
   public static void main(String[] args) {
      B b = new B();
      b.test();
   }
   void test() {
      int[] arr = {10, 13, 24};

      for (int i = 0; i < arr.length; i++)
         System.out.println("before: #" + i + " = " + arr[i]);

      calc(arr);
```

Exercise 4.4 continued

```
        for (int i = 0; i < arr.length; i++)
            System.out.println("after: #" + i + " = " + arr[i]);


    }
    void calc(int[] arr) {
        arr[0] *= 2;
        arr[1] *= 3;
        arr[2] *= 4;
    }
}
```

Review Questions

Question 1:   What would the result be in the standard output if you executed the class named Acc2, listed below?

```
class Acc2 {
    public static void main(String[] args) {
        First s = new Second();
        Second s2 = (Second)s;
        System.out.println(s2.var);
        System.out.println(s2.method());
    }
}

class First {
    int var = 1;
    int method() {
        return var;
    }
}

class Second extends First {
    int var = 2;
    int method() {
        return var;
    }
}
```

a) 2
2

b) 2
1

c) 1
2

d) 1
1

Question 2: How many objects are candidates for garbage collection by the end of the following code snippet:

```
String s = "kanga";
s = "kanga" + "roo";
int[] arr = {1, 4, 9, 25};
arr[3] = 16;
arr = new int[4];
s = null;
```

a) 1
b) 2
c) 3
d) 4

Question 3: Which answer defines a legal finalize() method?

a)
```
protected void finalize() {
    super.finalize();
    System.out.println("finalize");
}
```

b)
```
private void finalize() throws Throwable {
    super.finalize();
    System.out.println("finalize");
}
```

c)
```
protected void finalize() throws Throwable {
    super.finalize();
    System.out.println("finalize");
}
```

d)
```
void finalize() {
    super.finalize();
    System.out.println("finalize");
}
```

Question 4:   What happens if you attempt to compile and run this code:

```
class Clean {
    public static void main(String[] args) {
        Dirty d = new Dirty();
        d.finalize();
        d = null;
        Runtime r = Runtime.getRuntime();
        r.gc();
        r.runFinalization();
    }
}

class Dirty {
    protected void finalize() throws Throwable {
        System.out.println("Dirty finalization");
    }
}
```

a) The code will not compile because of a problem invoking `finalize()`.
b) The code will compile but will display nothing.
c) The code will compile and will display "Dirty finalization" once.
d) The code will compile and will display "Dirty finalization" twice.

Answers to the Review Questions

Question 1   a.   Since we cast the object reference s from a type First to type Second, we then access Second's var and method.

Question 2   c.   Let's take this line by line:

```
String s = "kanga";
s = "kanga" + "roo";
```

At this point, we have created two objects. The first String object contained the characters "kanga." The second contained the characters "kangaroo." Since we can no longer reference the first String object —we have reused the s object reference—this is the first object now available for garbage collection.

```
int[] arr = {1, 4, 9, 25};
arr[3] = 16;
```

At this point, we have created a new int array and accessed one of its elements.

```
arr = new int[4];
```

Now, we create a new int array and assign it to the object reference arr. Therefore, we lost track of the first array that contained 1, 4, 9, and 25. This is the second object that is now available for garbage collection.

```
s = null;
```

Setting s to null makes us lose the reference to the String containing "kangaroo." This object is now available for garbage collection, as well.

Question 3   c.   The finalize() method is protected and throws an object of type Throwable.

Question 4   a   The problem with invoking finalize() is that it is declared as throwing an object of class Throwable. That means the direct call to finalize() must be placed within a try-catch block. There's a full explanation of exception handling in Chapter 9.

CHAPTER 5

Data Types and Values

 It's helpful to know binary arithmetic and how to calculate powers of two. Other than basic multiplication, there are no other prerequisites for this chapter.

This chapter provides a review of Java's data types, how to use them, and what their default values are. As a bonus, we'll also look at some advanced features regarding arrays.

What's on the Test

The test will ask you to determine the upper and lower limits of the integer data types. You need to know what the default values are for these data types—and that leaving a method (or *local* or *automatic*) variable uninitialized is a compile-time error. You'll also have to work with char values a little and assign Unicode values to them.

There are a few questions about arrays, so I've included arrays in this section. This chapter offers a review of the easy questions as well as the tricky questions, such as:

- Do you know if there are default values for elements in an array, and if so, what they are?
- How can you use curly braces to initialize arrays? Can you define arrays of arrays whose columns are variable in length? If you hesitated before answering these questions, stay tuned.

Objectives for this Chapter

- Define the range of values for byte, short, int, long, and char.
- Construct literal char values using both quoted formats and Unicode escape sequences.
- Identify the default values of instance and static variables.
- Define arrays.
- Determine the default values for elements in an array.
- Use curly braces {} as part of an array declaration to initialize an array.

Data Types

Define the range of values for byte, short, int, long, and char.

Java has eight primitive data types:

Data Type	Size in Bits
byte	signed 8-bit integer
short	signed 16-bit integer
int	signed 32-bit integer
long	signed 64-bit integer
float	signed 32-bit floating-point
double	signed 64-bit floating-point
char	16-bit Unicode character
boolean	either true or false (special values built-in to Java)

You won't work with the floating-point types much on the test, so we'll concentrate on the integer, character, and Boolean types in this chapter.

Integer Values

The test only requires you to know the range of the integer and character data types. The integer types are easy to determine. They are:

largest positive integer value: $2^{(number\ of\ bits\ -\ 1)} - 1$

smallest negative integer value: $-2^{(number\ of\ bits\ -\ 1)}$

These values work out to the following:

Data Type	Maximum Positive Value	Minimum Negative Value
byte	$2^7 - 1$, or 127	-2^7 or -128
short	$2^{15} - 1$, or 32,767	-2^{15} or -32,768
int	$2^{31} - 1$, or 2,147,483,647	-2^{31} or -2,147,483,648
long	$2^{63} - 1$, or 9,223,372,036, 854,775,807L	-2^{63} or -9,223,372,036, 854,775,808L

The default value for any class variable or instance variable declared as a number is 0.

Character Values

Construct literal `char` values using both quoted formats and Unicode escape sequences.

A `char` variable can contain any Unicode character. You can use the escape sequence `'\udddd'` to represent any Unicode character, where d is a hexadecimal digit.

The ASCII characters are all found in the range `'\u0000'` to `'\u00ff'`.

The default value for any class variable or instance variable declared as a char is `'\u0000'`.

Don't confuse `'\u0000'` with a space character, which is `'\u0020'`.

Floating-point values are discussed in the section "What's Not on the Test," later in this chapter.

Default Values

Identify the default values of instance and static variables.

If you do not supply a default value for member variables, they take on the default values of zero, false, null, or '\u0000' for all numbers, Booleans, object references, and characters, respectively. Not defining a default value for a local variable results in a compile-time error.

The elements in arrays also take on these initial values. I'll talk about arrays in another page or two.

Literals

You can specify integer values in three bases: decimal, octal, and hexadecimal. To specify a decimal number (a number in base 10), just write the number in the usual way (for example, 123 and -403 represent integer numbers in base 10).

To specify an octal number (a number in base 8), put a leading 0 in front of it. To specify a hexadecimal number (a number in base 16), place a leading 0x in front of it.

For example, in base 10, the following values:

```
10
010
0x10
```

are equal to 10, 8, and 16, respectively.

By default, integer values are of type int, and floating-point values are of type double. However, you can force an integer value to be a long by placing an L after it. You can also force a floating-point value to be a float by placing an F after it.

Exercises

Exercise 5.1

What is the smallest integer data types you could use to hold:

- the number of letters in the alphabet
- the net worth of Bill Gates in U.S. dollars
- the number of pages in this book
- the number of people in the U.S.

Exercise 5.2

Write a program that displays the default values for each integer type.

Exercise 5.3

What is wrong with the following program? How would you fix this code?

```
class Test {
    public static void main(String[] args) {
        int index;
        boolean found;
        for (index = 0; index < 10 && !found; index++) {
            if (index > Math.PI) {
                System.out.println(index + " is greater than Pi");
                found = true;
            }
        }
    }
}
```

Arrays

Define arrays.

Arrays of data types can be declared by writing square brackets after the data type, as in:

```
int[] myIntArray;
```

or

```
MyClass[] myClassArray;
```

These two array declarations create variables whose types are an array of integers and an array of objects, respectively.

Arrays are objects. Use new to create the array and allocate the array to the appropriate size.

For example:

```
MyClass[] myClassArray = new MyClass[5];
```

allocates an array large enough to hold five elements. In this case, we have allocated an array of object references.

Determine the default values for elements in an array.

Java sets each element in an array to its default value when the array is created.

For `myClassArray`, defined above as an array of objects, each element is set to `null` when the array is first allocated.

For an array of `int` values, each element would be set to 0.

Something interesting about arrays in Java: since they are objects allocated at runtime, you can use a variable to set their length—something you cannot do in C/C++, for example, where you must lay out the memory for an array at compile time.

Rephrasing the tip above, an array's length can be determined at runtime. For example, you can write:

```
String[] attendees = new String[numAttendees];
```

The first element in an array is element 0. The last element is element length - 1.

Initializing an Array When it is Allocated

Use curly braces {} as part of an array declaration to initialize an array.

You don't have to use `new` explicitly to allocate and initialize an array. Instead, you can use curly braces to set its size and default values in one fell swoop.

You can create and initialize an array like this:

```
String[] movies = { "The Red Shoes", "Jeremiah Johnson", "Ninotch-
```

This allocates the `movies` array to three elements and initializes each element with a new String instance.

This works just as well with object references in place of string literals. For example, you can write:

```
String s1 = "The Red Shoes";
String s2 = "Jeremiah Johnson";
String s3 = "Ninotchka";

String[] movies = {s1, s2, s3};
```

This type of array initialization also works for primitive data types. For example, you can write:

```
int[] arr = {1, 2, 3};
```

to declare and allocate an array of three integers whose elements are 1, 2, and 3.

By the way, the array declaration

```
String movies[]
```

works just like

```
String[] movies
```

While the first version uses the same syntax as C/C++, the second version is preferred, because `String[]`, not `String`, is the data type of the variable `movies`.

Tip

You can find the length of an array—how many elements it was allocated to—by using the special array variable `length`, as in:

```
int numMovies = movies.length;
```

The curly braces used to initialize an array can only be used when the array is declared. That is, the curly braces can only be used as an initializer.

Warning

To illustrate the above warning, you cannot write something like this:

```
int[] arr = new int[5];
arr = {1, 2, 3, 4, 5}; // will not compile!
```

Instead, you must write:

```
int[] arr = {1, 2, 3, 4, 5}; // this will work fine
```

Exercise 5.4

Write a program that calculates the first ten squares (1, 4, 9, etc.) and places each entry in an array of integers. Then, create a new array and use curly braces to initialize the new array to the values in the old array. At the end of your program, write out all the entries in the second array to verify that your program worked. Be sure your array has 10 elements and that your squares range from 1 to 100.

What's Not on the Test

Arrays of Arrays

You can define an array of arrays by using multiple sets of square brackets. For example, a two-dimensional array could be declared like this:

```
int[][] chessBoard = int[8][8];
```

You can also use curly braces when declaring and initializing an array of arrays, as in:

```
double[][] identityMatrix = {
    { 1.0, 0.0, 0.0 },
    { 0.0, 1.0, 0.0 },
    { 0.0, 0.0, 1.0 }
};
```

So that this doesn't trip you up, take note: you can place a comma in the last line of a multi-array initialization, or not. There's no comma in the third line in the above array initialization. There is a comma in the third line of the initialization in the snippet below:

```
double[][] identityMatrix = {
    { 1.0, 0.0, 0.0 },
    { 0.0, 1.0, 0.0 },
    { 0.0, 0.0, 1.0 },
};
```

Either version will compile successfully.

Just as you might expect, you can find the length of each array within the array. For a two-dimensional array, you might think of the first entry as the row number and the second as a column. To find the number of columns for row 0 in a two-dimensional matrix called `catalog`, you can write:

```
catalog[0].length;
```

You can also allocate the length of each column one at a time. You can start by allocating the number of rows in an array. Let's say our catalog array is an array of string arrays.

```
String[][] catalog = new String[100][];
```

Notice that the number of columns is left undefined at first. This allows us to work with one column at a time, and each column in our array of arrays can be of variable length.

```
catalog[0] = new String[5];
catalog[1] = new String[10];
```

and so on. Then, we can refer to each element in the array by specifying its row and column. For example, the first element is:

```
catalog[0][0]
```

and we can set this to a String object, as follows:

```
catalog[0][0] = new String("shirt");
```

We can refer to other rows and columns as we'd like to.

Where Arrays Fit into the Class Hierarchy

If arrays are objects, what's their class type? And where do these classes fit into the class hierarchy?

Arrays follow a parallel hierarchy of the class types they hold. For example, if you have a class hierarchy involving Vehicle, Car, and Sports-Car that looked like what's in Figure 5-1:

Figure 5-1
A Hierarchy Involving
Three Classes

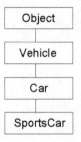

Then the hierarchy of arrays look like what's in Figure 5-2:

Figure 5-2
The Parallel Hierarchy
of Arrays

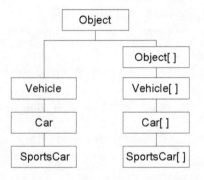

In other words, Vehicle[] is a sibling of Vehicle, Car[] is a sibling of Car, and SportsCar[] is a sibling of SportsCar. And, as the figure shows, Vehicle[] inherits directly from Object[], just as Vehicle inherits from Object. Of course, all arrays are objects, so Object[] in turn inherits from Object.

Floating-Point Arithmetic

Unlike integer data types, floating-point data types never throw an exception if some ill-defined state arises when performing arithmetic. For example, if you divide by 0 using integers, Java will throw an ArithmeticException. However, if you divide by 0 using floating-point types, Java assigns the value to infinity (of the appropriate sign matching the numerator). The class "wrapper" types Double and Float even define class constants called POSITIVE_INFINITY and NEGATIVE_INFINITY that you can use to acquire these values.

In fact, arithmetic with floating-point values will never throw an exception. If the result is not a number at all, the result is NaN. Here's a table that shows various outcomes with 0, finite values, and infinity.

x	y	x/y	x%y
finite	0.0	infinity	NaN
finite	infinity	0.0	x
0.0	0.0	NaN	NaN
infinity	finite	infinity	NaN
infinity	infinity	NaN	NaN

The sign of infinity depends on the signs involved in the arithmetic expression.

Any arithmetic expression involving NaN yields NaN.

Casting

You can not implicitly coerce a data type with greater accuracy into a data type with less accuracy. In fact, trying to do so results in compile-time error.

This means, for example, that you cannot write code that looks like this:

```
int i = 5;
byte b = i;
```

because an int holds larger numbers than a byte. An int is more accurate. The Java compiler will complain that these are incompatible types for the = operator, and that you need an explicit cast to convert the int into a byte.

The way to do this is to write:

```
int i = 5;
byte b = (byte)i;
```

The same is true with floating-point values. You cannot assign a `double` to a `float`, because a `double` is more accurate than a `float`. So, you must explicitly cast it.

Similarly, you cannot assign any kind of floating-point number to an integer type without an explicit cast.

Special Escape Sequences

No, this is not a reference to a film about Alcatraz. Java defines a number of escape sequences that allow you to work with non-printable characters. The following table shows what these are.

Escape sequence	Meaning	Unicode representation
\n	newline	\u000A
\t	tab	\u0009
\b	backspace	\u0008
\r	return	\u000D
\f	form feed	\u000C
\\	backslash	\u005C
\'	single quote	\u0027
\"	double quote	\u0022
\ddd	an octal char (each d is between 0 and 7)	
\udddd	a Unicode char (each d is between 0 and 9, A and F)	

Answers to the Exercises

Exercise 5.1

A byte holds values up to 127. It could hold the number of letters in the alphabet (26).

An int is not large enough to hold the net worth of Bill Gates (what is it now, around 16 billion dollars?). A long holds values up to 9,223,372,036,854,775,807. (However, if Microsoft stock splits a few more times...)

A short can hold values up to 32,767. This is large enough to hold the number of pages in this book. A byte would be too small.

An int can hold up to around 2 billion, which is enough to keep track of the number of people in the U.S. for some time to come. A short would be too small.

Exercise 5.2

Here is one possible solution to this exercise:

```
class Def {
   byte b;
   short s;
   int i;
   long l;
   public static void main(String[] args) {
      Def d = new Def();
      d.defaults();
   }

   void defaults() {
      System.out.println("default values:");
      System.out.println(b);
      System.out.println(s);
      System.out.println(i);
      System.out.println(l);
   }
}
```

Exercise 5.3

The method variable named found is not initialized before being used. This results in a compile-time error. You must set this variable to false for this program to compile and work as intended.

```
class Test {
    public static void main(String[] args) {
        int index;
        boolean found = false;
        for (index = 0; index < 10 && !found; index++) {
            if (index > Math.PI) {
                System.out.println(index + " is greater than Pi");
                found = true;
            }
        }
    }
}
```

The variable index is initialized in the for loop before it is referenced.
Exercise 5.4

One possible solution is:

```
class Squares {
    public static void main(String[] args) {
        int[] first = new int[10];
        for (int i = 1; i <= 10; i++)
            first[i-1] = i * i;
        int[] second = {first[0], first[1], first[2], first[3],
            first[4], first[5], first[6], first[7], first[8],
            first[9]};

        for (int i = 1; i <= 10; i++)
            System.out.println("entry " + i + " is " + second[i-1]);
    }
}
```

Review Questions

Question 1: The range of values for the integer data types is:

a) -2^{15} to $2^{15} - 1$
b) $-2^{(number\ of\ bits\ -\ 1)}$ to $2^{(number\ of\ bits\ -\ 1)}$
c) -2^{31} to 2^{31}
d) $-2^{(number\ of\ bits\ -\ 1)}$ to $2^{(number\ of\ bits\ -\ 1)} - 1$

Question 2: What are two ways to set a char variable named c to a blank space?

a) c = " " and c = ' '
b) c = " " and c = '\u0000'
c) c = ' ' and c = '\u0020'
d) c = " " and c = '\u0020'

Question 3: What is the result of trying to compile and run this program?

```
class Q3 {
   int instVar1 = 1;
   int instVar2;
   public static void main(String[] args) {
      int localVar = 3;      Q3 q = new Q3();
      System.out.println(instVar1 + instVar2 + localVar3);
   }
}
```

a) 4
b) 0
c) The code does not compile because localVar is not initialized correctly.
d) The code does not compile because instVar2 is not initialized at all.

Question 4: How can you initialize an array of three Boolean values to all true?

a) `boolean[] b = new boolean[3];`
b) `boolean[] b = {true, true, true};`
c) `boolean[3] b = {true, true, true};`
d) `boolean[] b = new boolean[3]; b = {true, true, true};`

Answers to the Review Questions

Question 1   d.   The range of values for an integer data type depends on the number of bits. For an `int`, which holds 32 bits, the range goes from -2^{31} to 2^{31} - 1. The number of bits is 8 for a `byte`, 16 for a `short`, 32 for an `int`, and 64 for a `long`.

Question 2   c.   A `char` value can be set using single quotes or the format `'\udddd'`. The value `'\u0020'` is a blank space.

Question 3   a.   This code compiles and runs successfully. An instance variable, such as `instVar2`, is set to 0 if it is not explicitly initialized.

Question 4   b.   This example shows how to use curly braces in an initializer to set the values for an array. (Since the default value for a `boolean` is `false`, answer *a* will not work).

CHAPTER 6

Operators

Prerequisites

Ah, the joys of binary arithmetic! If you want to see exactly what the bit-wise operators are doing, it's useful to be familiar with binary arithmetic and with Boolean logic.

There are lots of operators: most of them are quite simple. There are the standard arithmetic operators of +, -, *, /, and %. But there are also some others that you might feel a little less familiar with. Guess what? Those are the ones on the test! We'll cover them thoroughly in this chapter.

What's on the Test

The test covers the bit-wise operators. If you're like most programmers, you probably don't use these operators much on a day-to-day basis.

The bit-wise operators include:

1. right shift (>>),
2. left shift (<<), and
3. right shift, don't keep the sign bit (>>>).

There are also other bit-wise operators we'll cover in this chapter.

The test also makes sure you know how the operators used with objects and object references work. These include the +, ==, and instanceof operators. You should know the difference between == and equals() and which classes respond differently to equals() than class Object.

Objectives for this Chapter

- Apply the >> and << operators to a value and determine the result.
- Apply the >>> operator to a value and determine the result.
- Use the & and | operators and determine the results.
- Use the instanceof operator correctly.
- State the difference between the == operator and equals().
- Determine the result of applying the == comparison operator and the equals() method to instances of class String, Boolean, and Object.

The Bit Operators

Apply the >> operator to a value and determine the result.

The >> Operator

The >> operator shifts the bits in a number the specified number of places to the right.

For example, if you run the following program:

```
class Bit {
    public static void main(String[] args) {
        int i = 0x00000010;
        int ans;

        System.out.println("before: " + i);
        ans = i >> 1;
        System.out.println("after: " + ans);
    }
}
```

The result will be:

```
before: 16
after: 8
```

because the hex number 0x00000010 is 16 in base 10. The 32 bits representing this number are:

```
0000 0000 0000 0000 0000 0000 0001 0000
```

Shifting the bits once to the right yields the bit pattern:

```
0000 0000 0000 0000 0000 0000 0000 1000
```

which is the hex number 0x00000008, or 8 in base 10.

Negative numbers might yield results you did not expect, because the sign bit is moved to the right even though the number stays negative. Here's the simplest example. Running this program:

```
class Neg {
    public static void main(String[] args) {
        int i = 0x80000000;
        int ans;

        System.out.println("before: " + i);
        ans = i >> 1;
        System.out.println("after: " + ans);
    }
}
```

yields the following result:

```
before: -2147483648
after: -1073741824
```

The variable i is assigned the hex value 0x80000000, which, as a bit pattern, is:

```
1000 0000 0000 0000 0000 0000 0000 0000
```

Now, in Java's 2's complement notation, this is a negative number—the most negative an int can be. Java. You can see this in the result for i in the "before" printout: -2147483648, which matches the value in java.lang.Integer.MIN_VALUE. Then, moving this bit one to the right, but keeping the sign, yields the bit pattern:

```
1100 0000 0000 0000 0000 0000 0000 0000
```

which is the same as the base 10 number in the "after" printout.

The >>> Operator

Objectives

Apply the >>> operator to a value and determine the result.

To get around this strange "the sign bit both stays and moves to the right" syndrome, you can use the >>> operator instead. For example,

```
class Neg1 {
   public static void main(String[] args) {
      int i = 0x80000000;
      int ans;

      System.out.println("before: " + i);
      ans = i >>> 1;
      System.out.println("after: " + ans);
   }
}
```

yields the result

```
before: -2147483648
after: 1073741824
```

In other words, the bit pattern went from:

```
1000 0000 0000 0000 0000 0000 0000 0000
```

to

```
0100 0000 0000 0000 0000 0000 0000 0000
```

The >>> and >> operators yield the same results when the number is positive.

Tip

The << Operator

Apply the << operator to a value and determine the result.

Objectives

There is one more similar operator, the << operator, which moves all the bits to the left the indicated number of places. The result of applying this operator is straightforward, but you might wonder what happens when the bit pattern moves from

```
0100 0000 0000 0000 0000 0000 0000 0000
```

one step to the left, as in the program:

```
class Back {
   public static void main(String[] args) {
      int i = 0x40000000;
      int ans;

      System.out.println("before: " + i);
      ans = i << 1;
      System.out.println("after: " + ans);
   }
}
```

Does the number change sign? Yes, indeed. The printout reads:

```
before: 1073741824
after: -2147483648
```

What about moving the bit pattern

```
1000 0000 0000 0000 0000 0000 0000 0001
```

one to the left using the << operator? Does the number stay negative or become positive? It becomes positive! The bit that indicates the sign gets shifted out completely. The result is:

```
before: -2147483647
after: 2
```

The & and I Operators

Use the & and | operators and determine the results.

The operators & and | mean "bit-wise and" and "bit-wise or." These operators work on integers and yield integer results, not Boolean results.

These operators work on the individual bits in integers to combine them. The & operator turns bits on if both bits are on, and off if either or both bits are off. The | operator turns bits on if either or both bits are on, and off if both bits are off.

It's easier to look at a simple example than it is to comprehend these operators by reading about them. If you perform this operation:

```
1 & 2
```

the result is 0. You can see this clearly if you look at the bit patterns (we'll only look at the last 4 bits to make this easier to read):

```
0001 &
0010
- - - -
0000
```

However, if you perform the operation:

```
1 | 2
```

the result is 3. Here are the bits:

```
0001 |
0010
- - - -
0011
```

The & operator multiplies bit values; the | operator adds bit values.

Tip

Exercise 6.1

Write a class that stores two short integers in a single int variable. Write methods called putVar1(), putVar2(), getVar1(), and getVar2() to save and retrieve this value into the upper or lower half of an int.

You'll probably have to use the >> and << operators to make this work, as well as & and | to mask the bits when you set the int's value.

Testing for an Object's Class Type

Use the instanceof operator correctly.

Objectives

The operator instanceof tests to see whether a particular object is an instance of a class or a subclass of that class. It can also test whether an object's class or subclass implements an interface.

Key Concept

Here are some examples. Let's say you have the following code:

```
class Fruit { }
class Apple extends Fruit {
    public static void main(String[] args) {
        Apple a = new Apple();
        if (a instanceof Apple)
            System.out.println("A is for Apple");
        if (a instanceof Fruit)
            System.out.println("A is a Fruit");
        if (a instanceof Object)
            System.out.println("A is an Object");
    }
}
```

Running this code writes "A is for Apple", "A is a Fruit", and "A is an Object" to the standard output, because the instanceof operator returns true for each test.

Here's another example that deals with interfaces.

```
interface Fruit { }
interface Apple extends Fruit { }
class GrannySmith implements Apple {
    public static void main(String[] args) {
        GrannySmith gs = new GrannySmith();
        if (gs instanceof Apple)
            System.out.println("gs inherits from Apple");
        if (gs instanceof Fruit)
            System.out.println("gs inherits from Fruit");
    }
}
```

The strings "gs inherits from Apple" and "gs inherits from Fruit" appear in the standard output when you run this program.

Tip

Some compilers, such as Sun's JDK, will not allow code to compile if they can determine with the available classes that a particular object cannot possibly inherit from a class specified in instanceof.

Exercise 6.2

> Use the Apple and Fruit classes shown in the previous section (you can replace main() with your own code). Write a program that shows that an Apple array inherits from a Fruit array, that a Fruit array inherits from an Object array, and that an Object array inherits from Object.

Equals() and ==

State the difference between the == operator and equals().

Determine the result of applying the == comparison operator and the equals() method to instances of class String, Boolean, and Object.

The equals() method is used to test the value of an object. For example, do two object references refer to objects whose fields contain similar values? The == operator is used to test the object references themselves. For example, are two object references the same?

Identical object references can be in different variables.

By default, equals() returns true only if the objects reside in the same memory location—that is, if the object references are equal. So, by default, equals() and == do the same things. This will be the case for all classes that do not override equals().

The classes String, Wrappers, BitSet, Date, and File all override `equals()`. Each of these classes uses the data in its fields to determine whether the object represents the same thing.

- String objects are equal if they represent the same character strings.
- Wrapper objects—including Integer, Long, Float, Double, Character, and Boolean—are equal if they represent the same primitive data type.
- BitSet objects are equal if they represent the same sequence of bits.
- Date objects are equal if they represent the same date and time.
- File objects are equal if they represent the same path—not if they refer to the same underlying file. (The danger here is that the path name might be a relative path name. In that case, they might easily represent two different files in the system.)

You can override `equals()` for your own classes, just as the classes in the list above do, to perform whatever test for equality you feel is important.

Tip

Exercises

Exercise 6.3

Show that String objects and Date objects return `true` for `equals()` if they are created with the same data (the Date class is defined in `java.util`). What happens if you use the no-args constructor for Date and separate the creation of the Date objects by a few lines of code? Why aren't these Date objects equivalent, even though you supplied the same data—namely, no data at all—to the Date's constructor?

Exercise 6.4

Write your own `equals()` methods for the following two classes.

```
class Employee {
   private String id;
   Employee (String id) {
     this.id = id;
   }
}

class Movie {
   String name;
   boolean thumbsUp;
   int year;
}
```

What's Not on the Test

Here are the other operators that are taken for granted on the test:

+	addition
	(The + operator is overloaded for String objects to concatenate two Strings and return a new String.)
–	subtraction
*	multiplication
/	division
%	remainder

All of these operators can also take the form operator= (as in +=, -=, *=, /=, and %=).

Performing arithmetic with integers could cause Java to throw an exception. For example, dividing by 0 is illegal with integers. However, as I mentioned in the previous chapter on data types, floating-point numbers have values for infinity and not-a-number; using these operators with floating-point values never results in an exception.

There are two other bit-wise operators the test doesn't cover either. These are ~ (reverse bits) and ^ (exclusive-or).

Here's an example of the ~ operator:

```
class OtherOps {
   public static void main(String[] args) {
      int i = 0x80000000;
      System.out.println(i);
      i = ~i;
      System.out.println(i);
   }
}
```

The output from this program is:

```
-2147483648
2147483647
```

because each bit in the value 0x80000000, the most negative int value, is flipped, so that each 0 becomes 1 and each 1 becomes 0. This results in 0x7FFFFFFF, which is the most positive int value.

The ^ is an exlusive-or. That is, one or the other boolean conditions must true, but not both. Here's an example:

```
class Xor {
   public static void main(String[] args) {
      boolean t1 = true;
      boolean t2 = true;
      boolean f1 = false;
      boolean f2 = false;

      if (t1 ^ t2)
         System.out.println("both are true");
      if (t1 ^ f1)
         System.out.println("one is true");
      if (f1 ^ f2)
         System.out.println("neither are true");
   }
}
```

The output from this program is "one is true."

Answers to the Exercises

Exercise 6.1

Here is a class called Half that stores two short values in one int variable:

```
class Half {
    int value;

    void putVar1(short s) {
        value &= 0xFFFF0000;
        value |= s;
    }

    void putVar2(short s) {
        value &= 0x0000FFFF;
        value |= (s << 16);
    }

    short getVar1() {
        return (short)(value);
    }

    short getVar2() {
        return (short)(value >> 16);
    }
}
```

You can run a class such as Tester, listed below, to verify this class named Half is doing what it's supposed to:

```
class Tester {
    public static void main(String[] args) {
        Half h = new Half();
        h.putVar1((short) 100);
        h.putVar2((short) -91);

        System.out.println(h.getVar1());
        System.out.println(h.getVar2());
    }
}
```

Exercise 6.2

```
class Fruit { }
class Apple extends Fruit {
   public static void main(String[] args) {
       Apple[] a = new Apple[1];
       Fruit[] f = new Fruit[1];
       Object[] o = new Object[1];
       if (a instanceof Fruit[])
          System.out.println("a inherits from Fruit[]");
       if (f instanceof Object[])
          System.out.println("f inherits from Object[]");
       if (o instanceof Object)
          System.out.println("o inherits from Object");
   }
}
```

Exercise 6.3

```
import java.util.Date;

class Eq {
   public static void main(String[] args) {
       String s1 = new String("a");
       String s2 = new String("a");

       Date d1 = new Date();

       Date d2 = new Date(97, 2, 14);
       Date d3 = new Date(97, 2, 14);

       Date d4 = new Date();

       System.out.println(s1.equals(s2));
       System.out.println(d2.equals(d3));
       System.out.println(d1.equals(d4));
   }
}
```

This program displays "true, true, false." The reason why the two Date objects d1 and d4 are not equal is that the no-args Date constructor initializes the Date objects to the current date and time to the nearest millisecond. So, their internal data are different.

Exercise 6.4

```java
class Employee {
   private String id;
   Employee (String id) {
      this.id = id;
   }
   public boolean equals(Object obj) {
      if (obj instanceof Employee) {
         Employee e = (Employee)obj;
         if (e.id == id)
            return true;
      }
      return false;
   }
}

class Movie {
   String name;
   boolean thumbsUp;
   int year;
   public boolean equals(Object obj) {
      if (obj instanceof Movie) {
         Movie m = (Movie)obj;
         if (name.equals(m.name) && year == m.year)
            return true;
      }
      return false;
   }
}
```

Notice that we cast the object to the type being tested. Also, note especially the equals() test for Movie: the String object is tested using equals(), and the thumbsUp variable is not considered, since the movies might still be the same even if two different people rated them differently.

Review Questions

Question 1: What will be the result of this expression:

```
5 & 2
```

a) 0
b) 2
c) 5
d) 7

Question 2: What will be the result of this expression:

```
10 | 2
```

a) 0
b) 2
c) 10
d) 14

Question 3: What will happen when you attempt to compile and run the following code?

```
class Tree { }
class Pine {
  public static void main(String[] args) {
     Pine[] p = new Pine[1];
     if (p instanceof Tree[])
        System.out.println("p inherits from Tree[]");
  }
}
```

a) The compiler complains that Tree[ ] cannot inherit from Pine[ ].
b) The compiler complains that Pine[ ] cannot inherit from Tree[ ].
c) The program compiles and runs but does not display anything in the standard output.
d) The program compiles and runs and displays "p inherits from Tree[ ]" in the standard output.

Question 4: What is the result of invoking main() for classes A, B, and C?

```
class A {
   public static void main(String[] args) {
      Integer myInt = new Integer(5);
      Integer otherInt;
      otherInt = myInt;
      if (otherInt == myInt)
         System.out.println("equal");
      else
         System.out.println("not equal");
   }
}


class B {
   public static void main(String[] args) {
      Integer myInt = new Integer(5);
      Integer anotherInt = new Integer(5);
      if (anotherInt == myInt)
         System.out.println("equal");
      else
         System.out.println("not equal");
   }
}

class C {
   public static void main(String[] args) {
      MyClass mc1 = new MyClass(1);
      if (mc1.operatorEquals(mc1))
         System.out.println("equal");
      else
         System.out.println("not equal");
   }
}
```

Question 4 continued

```
class MyClass extends Object {
    int value;
    MyClass(int value) {
        this.value = value;
    }
    boolean operatorEquals(MyClass test) {
        return (this == test);
    }
}
```

a) A: equal; B: equal: C: equal
b) A: equal; B: not equal; C: equal
c) A: not equal; B: not equal; C: equal
d) A: not equal; B: not equal; C: not equal

Question 5:   What is the result of 0x800028FF >> 3?

a) 0x900005FF
b) 0x1000051F
c) 0x1000011F
d) 0x8000051F

Question 6:   What is the result of trying to compile and run the following program?

```
class Phone implements Cloneable {
    public static void main(String[] args) {
        Phone p = new Phone();
        if (p instanceof Object)
            System.out.println("Object");
        if (p instanceof Cloneable)
            System.out.println("Cloneable");
    }
}
```

a) The program does not compile.
b) The program compiles and runs and writes "Object" to the standard output.
c) The program compiles and runs and writes "Cloneable" to the standard output.
d) The program compiles and runs and writes both "Object" and "Cloneable" to the standard output.

Answers to the Review Questions

Question 1   a.   It's clear if you look at the bits:

```
101 &
010
- - -
000
```

Question 2   c.   The bits are:

```
1010 |
0010
- - - -
1010
```

Question 3   b.   When the compiler can figure out that an object cannot inherit from another object, it will not even compile the program. That's what Sun's JDK does in this case.

Question 4   b.   The only one that is not equal is class B, which checks for equivalence of object references. Since this check uses two different objects, the object references are different.

Question 5   d.   Translate the hexadecimal into a bit pattern to see this

```
0x800028FF is:
1000 0000 0000 0000 0010 1000 1111 1111
```

shifting each bit 3 positions to the right, and keeping the sign bit, yields:

`1001 0000 0000 0000 0000 0101 0001 1111`

or:

`0x9000051F`

Question 6   d.   The object referenced by `p` will return true to the `instanceof` test with Object and Cloneable.

CHAPTER 7

Control Flow

I only review the basics of Java's control flow keywords, I assume you are already familiar with implementing algorithms in Java. So, you should know the basic ways to loop and branch.

The basic control flow elements of looping and branching are similar to those in other programming languages. In fact, Java uses all of the same keywords as C/C++, with some minor modifications.

Most of this chapter reviews the basics of Java's control flow keywords. This chapter also covers the details (the differences between Java and C/C++) that might trip you up on the test.

What's on the Test

The test covers labels used with break and continue statements. You can use labels to break out of nested loops.

The test requires you to build simple loops and use if and switch statements. It also asks you questions about the legal arguments for loops, if, and switch statements.

There are a few questions about the logical-AND and logical-OR operators that require understanding their effects on control flow.

Objectives for this Chapter

- Write loops and nested loops using a loop counter.
- Use the break and continue keywords with and without labels.
- Write nested if-else and switch constructs.
- Identify the legal argument expression type for if and switch.
- Use the operators && and || and determine their effects on control flow statements.

Nested Loops

Write loops and nested loops using a loop counter.

A for statement defines a loop.

You can define a for loop like this:

```
for (initialization; termination; modification) { . . . }
```

Here is a common example:

```
for (index = 0; index < limit; index++) { . . . }
```

In this case, `index` is assumed to be an integer. However, it could also be a floating-point number, in which case the ++ operator would increment by 1.0, as you would expect.

Each of the three parts of the `for` loop—initialization, termination, and modification—can be made of multiple expressions, separated by commas. For example, you can write:

```
for (row = 0, col = 0; row < numRows; row++, col++) { . . . }
```

This loop could be used to look at the main diagonal in a square matrix, for example.

A `for` loop without any expressions loops forever.

The loop:

```
for ( ; ; ) { . . . }
```

is an infinite loop.

You can also define a loop variable within the initialization expression of a `for` loop. Java programmers do this all the time, because it is so convenient.

Here's an example:

```
for (int index = 0; index < limit; index++) { . . . }
```

A loop index created on the fly, as in the code snippet above, goes out of scope at the end of the loop.

An example of the above warning is the following, which is *not* legal:

```
for (int index = 0; index < limit; index++) {
   // do stuff here
}
System.out.println("The final value for index is " + index);
   // won't compile!
```

Loops can be nested. To loop through an array of arrays, you could write:

```
for (int row = 0; row < numRows; row++)
   for (int col = 0; col < numCols; col++)
      System.out.println(arr[row][col]);
```

Labels

Use the break and continue keywords with and without labels.

Objectives

You can assign a label to any line of code. You can then break or continue to that label.

Key Concept

A label is only useful with break and continue statements. Without a label, a continue statement continues with the next iteration of an inner loop, and a break statement stops its inner loop altogether.

Here's an example: we want to look over all the positions in a game board. If we see a mole, we want to bang it. After a swing of our mole bat, it's the next player's turn—we don't want to allow the user more than one swing of the mole bat per turn.

In the example below, the break statement doesn't quite do what we want:

```
for (int row = 0; row < 8; row++) {
   for (int col = 0; col < 8; col++) {
      if (moleAt(row, col)) {
         bangIt(row, col);
         break;
      }
   }
}
```

Unfortunately, the break statement only breaks out of the inner loop. The outer loop—the one going through the rows—keeps going, allowing the user to bang at more moles.

One way out of this predicament is to supply a label for the outer loop. We can then tie the break statement to the outer loop by using this label. Here's how we could update the code:

```
outer: for (int row = 0; row < 8; row++) {
   for (int col = 0; col < 8; col++) {
      if (moleAt(row, col)) {
         bangIt(row, col);
         break outer;
      }
   }
}
```

The appropriate, corresponding result would occur with a continue statement. By naming the outer loop, the continue statement would continue with the next iteration of the outer loop, rather than with the next iteration of the inner loop.

Exercise 7.1

Rewrite the following code snippet so that it uses both a label and a continue statement.

```
boolean[] inCheck = new inCheck[8];
for (int row = 0; row < 8; row++) {
   for (int col = 0; col < 8 && inCheck[row] == false; col++) {
      if (inCheck(row, col))
         inCheck[row] = true;
   }
}
```

Nested If and Else Statements

Write nested if-else and switch constructs.

if statements can be nested inside other if statements, just as for loops can be nested inside other for loops.

For example, you can write:

```
if (expression)
    statement
else if (expression)
    statement
else if . . .
```

There's a gotcha as far as nested if statements are concerned that can undermine the best laid plans: be sure that indentations of nested if-else statements don't cause you to mistake which else goes with which if.

As an example of this warning, check out the following snippet:

```
if (result >= 0)
    if (result > 0)
        System.out.println("positive");
else
    System.out.println("negative"); // wait a minute. . .
```

Yikes! Here's the same code written with different indentation so you can see what's really going on:

```
if (result >= 0)
    if (result > 0)
        System.out.println("positive");
    else
        System.out.println("negative"); // wait a minute. . .
```

So we'll get the message "negative" even if `result` is equal to 0. This is anything but good.

Tip

To help avoid these situations, you can use curly braces to delimit your blocks of code.

So, you can write:

```
if (result >= 0) {
    if (result > 0)
        System.out.println("positive");
} else
    System.out.println("negative"); // wait a minute. . .
```

Legal Values for If Statements

Objectives

Identify the legal argument expression type for `if` and `switch`.

Key Concept

The expression for an `if` and `while` statement must be a Boolean.

This is simple enough to remember, unless you're coming from an entrenched background in C. Then, you've got to write 10 times, so that you don't forget, "I will only use a Boolean in my `if` and `while` tests."

C programmers are familiar with using 0 and null to mean false. But in Java, you cannot coerce one to the other. Keep this in mind for the `||` and `&&` operators, as well. These operators combine Boolean arguments to achieve another Boolean.

Exercise 7.2

What's wrong with this class? Why won't it compile?

```java
class Exp {
    public static void main(String[] args) {

        int i = 10;
        int j = 12;

        if ((i < j) || (i = 3)) {
            System.out.println("hello");
        }

        System.out.println(i);

    }
}
```

Fix this code so that it works as intended.

Switch and Case Statements

A switch statement can be used to test a variable or expression and jump to a corresponding case statement containing a constant equal to that expression.

A switch statement takes the following form:

```java
switch (expression) {
   case constant:
      statements
   case constant:
      statements
   default:
      statements
}
```

A default statement is optional. If none of the constants in the case statements match the value of the variable in the switch statement, execution jumps to the default statement. If there is no default statement and none of the `case` statements match the `switch` expression, the `switch` block is, in effect, skipped altogether.

The expression in a `switch` statement must be of type `int` or `char`. The values in each case statement must be constants.

A `case` block will fall through to the `case` block that follows it, unless the last statement in a `case` block is a `throw`, `return`, or `break`. Often, you will write code that follows the same approach as the following snippet:

```
switch (season) {
    case 0:
        System.out.println("spring");
        break;
    case 1:
        System.out.println("summer");
        break;
    case 2:
        System.out.println("fall");
        break;
    case 3:
        System.out.println("winter");
        break;
    default:
        throw new IllegalSeasonException();
}
```

The `break` statements at the end of each `case` jumps control out of the `switch` to keep execution from flowing to the next, unrelated `case` statement.

If you want execution to flow from one case statement to the next, it is often a good idea to place a comment at the end of the case statement. That way it is clear to others looking at the code that the lack of a break statement is intentional.

Tip

As with `for` loops and `if` statements, you can also nest `switch` statements inside each other by placing a second `switch` statement within one of the case statements.

Tip

For example, you can follow this pattern:

```
switch (season) {
    case 0:
        System.out.println("spring");
        switch (month) {
            case 3:
                System.out.println("March");
                break;
            case 4:
                System.out.println("April");
                break;
            case 5:
                System.out.println("May");
                break;
        }
        break;
    case 1:
        System.out.println("summer");
        .
        .
        .
}
```

&& and ll

Use the operators && and || and determine their effects on control flow statements.

The operators && and || allow you to combine Boolean values for if and while conditions. The && operator means "logical-AND," and the || operator means "logical-OR."

The expressions are evaluated in order from left to right. As soon as the condition of the `if` or `while` clause is resolved, no more expressions for that condition are evaluated.

For example, in the `if` test:

```
if (5 > 3 || 2 < 1) ...
```

the second expression, 2 < 1, is never evaluated. Since 5 > 3 is known to be true before 2 < 1 is evaluated, the JVM already knows the entire if condition is true.

If, however, the test was:

```
if (5 > 3 && 2 < 1) ...
```

then if the first expression was true (which it is in this example), the second expression would be evaluated as well, because the entire `if` clause would only be true if both expressions were true. However, if the first expression was false, then the entire condition would be false; in that case, the second expression would not have to be evaluated.

Exercise 7.3

What will be the result of this program?

```
class Exp {
    public static void main(String[] args) {

        int i = 10;
        int j = 12;

        if ((i < j) || (i = 3) > 5) {
        }

        System.out.println("i is " + i);

    }
}
```

Run this code if it helps to see what's going on.

What's Not on the Test

While and Do-While Statements

The while and do-while statements are not covered very thoroughly on the test. Here's the basic idea behind them.

The while statement takes a boolean expression. The block of code after while is executed only if the expression is true:

```
while (expression) {
    // do this only if expression is true
}
```

If you want to always perform the block of code at least once, you can use a do-while statement, like this:

```
do {
    // do this at least once
} while (expression);
```

For example, you can write:

```
do {
    b = in.read();
} while (b != -1);
```

This code snippet reads at least one byte from the input stream, and stops reading when there are no more bytes.

Answers to the Exercises

Exercise 7.1

```
boolean[] inCheck = new inCheck[8];
rows: for (int row = 0; row < 8; row++) {
    for (int col = 0; col < 8; col++) {
        if (inCheck(row, col)) {
            inCheck[row] = true;
            continue rows;
        }
    }
}
```

Exercise 7.2

The expression

```
i = 3
```

in the `if` test is the problem. Even though this expression will never be evaluated (since `i` is less than `j`), `i = 3` does not yield a Boolean. In fact, its result is an integer—the value of `i`—which is set to 3. Since an integer is not a legal argument for the `||` operator, this code will not compile.

Exercise 7.3

This program writes "i is 10". Since the first expression in the `if` test:

```
(i < j)
```

is true, the second part of this test:

```
(i = 3) > 5
```

is not evaluated. If it were, the value of `i` would be set to 3.

Review Questions

Question 1:   The legal expression for an if statement is:

a) an integer
b) a `boolean`
c) a or b
d) neither of these

Question 2:   Given the following code snippet:

```
char c = 'a';
switch ( c ) {
   case 'a': System.out.println("a"); break;
   default: "System.out.println("default");
}
```

What will happen if you attempt to compile and run the code that includes this snippet?

a) The code will not compile because the switch statement does not have a legal expression.

b) The code will compile and run but nothing will be written to the standard output.

c) The code will compile and run and the letter "a" will be written to the standard output.

d) The code will compile and run and the word "default" will be written to the standard output.

Question 3:   Given the following code snippet:

```
int myInt = 3;
if ( myInt < 5 )
    if (myInt < 3)
        System.out.println("< 3");
else
    if (myInt > 2)
        System.out.println("> 2");
else
    System.out.println("other");
```

What will appear in the standard output?

a) "< 3"
b) "> 2"
c) "other"
d) nothing

Question 4:   What type of line of code can have a label?

a) any line of code
b) only lines of code associated with a loop (just before, at the loop, or just after)
c) only the line of code at the start of a loop
d) only the line of code defining the most outer loop

Answers to the Review Questions

Question 1 b.   An `if` statement only works with a `boolean`.

Question 2 c.   This is perfectly valid code and the letter "a" will appear in the standard output.

Question 3 b.   To see this, a better way to indent this code would be:

```
int myInt = 3;
if ( myInt < 5 )
    if (myInt < 3)
        System.out.println("< 4");
    else
        if (myInt > 2)
            System.out.println("> 2");
        else
            System.out.println("other");
```

Question 4 a.   Any line of code can be labeled.

CHAPTER 8

Exceptions

Prerequisites

You should be able to identify when a method throws an exception according to the method declaration.

You should also feel familiar with some of Java's common exceptions. You can look over the `java.lang` package for a rundown of some of these.

You should also know how to override methods in subclasses. Some of the examples in this chapter mention Runnable interface, as well as exceptions concerning input/output and threads. You don't have to fully understand threads and i/o to understand the discussion in this chapter. However, I have picked my examples because I assume ou already know the basics of Java programming, and these are more-or-less-real-world situations.

Java defines keywords and classes for exceptions, weaving exceptions right into the fabric of the language.

You can throw exceptions to signal errors. By handling exceptions, you can separate control flow involving error processing from control flow that occurs when everything proceeds as expected. Exceptions are an extremely flexible way to report and respond to errors. We'll cover the basics as well as the advanced aspects of exceptions in this chapter as they relate to the test.

What's on the Test

Most of the exception handling aspects of the test are straightforward, except for some of the rules regarding which exceptions a method can throw. You must know this rule cold to pick the right answer from the test question.

Objectives for this Chapter

- Determine the flow of control for try, catch, and finally constructions when execution proceeds normally, when an exception is thrown and caught, and when an exception is thrown but is not caught.
- Declare a method that might throw unhandled exceptions.
- Specify which exceptions a method can throw.
- Identify what exceptions may be legitimately thrown from an overriding method in a subclass.
- Write code to create and throw an Exception.

Exception Basics

Determine the flow of control for try, catch, and finally constructions when execution proceeds normally, when an exception is thrown and caught, and when an exception is thrown but not caught.

Are exceptions more effort than they're worth? What problem do exceptions solve?

When you write a program, you need some way to report and handle errors. In a language such as C, the typical way to do this is with return codes. However, return codes have a number of down sides. First, you've got to remember to check them and know which "magic numbers" mean what. Second, checking return codes inevitably leads to mingling error processing with normal processing, making your code more difficult to read and understand. And third, methods must pass back return codes to report an error to their caller.

All of this error handling "protocol" must be managed and verified by the programmer. There is no formal mechanism in place to make sure the programmer has checked return codes correctly.

Java's exception reporting and handling gets away from these problems. First, the language itself requires the methods to declare the exceptions they throw and to catch the exceptions a called method might throw, thereby formalizing exception handling. Along with this, exceptions are objects, not numbers, so their class names and any data they contain, such as strings, explains what they're all about without resorting to "magic numbers." Second, exception handling separates error processing from normal processing. Normal processing goes into a `try` *block; error processing goes into a* `catch` *block. Finally, exceptions can be passed on to their caller by declaring a method using the appropriate keywords; the language takes care of this chore for you.*

The idea in exception handling is that you try to execute a block of code, you catch any exceptions that were thrown, and you finally (always) do some cleanup.

The template to follow when invoking a method that might throw an exception is:

```
try {
    // . . . do something here that might cause an exception to be thrown
} catch (ExceptionType variable) {
    // . . . handle the exception
} finally {
    // . . . always do this
}
```

You can have multiple `catch` blocks, each `catch` block specifying its own ExceptionType in an order that always progresses from the most specific exception you wish to catch to the superclasses for these exceptions that you wish to catch.

Attempting to catch the superclasses first results in a compile-time error. For example, placing a `catch` block with type Exception before a `catch` block with type IOException results in a compile-time error.

If you know C++, you might have always wondered what the big deal is with Java and exceptions—after all, there are exceptions in C++, too.

The difference is that Java formalizes exceptions. In C++, exceptions are completely optional. In Java, you're forced to be very precise: methods must indicate which exceptions they throw in their declarations. Invoking methods that declare which exceptions they throw is not possible unless you catch these exception types. Java's insistence on a strict adherence to this protocol makes control flow for exceptions much more understandable and maintainable than when the exception policy is determined by individual programmers.

A method that might throw an exception must state this possibility in its method declaration.

Here's an example from a method defined by Java's Thread class named `sleep()`:

```
public static void sleep(long millis) throws InterruptedException
```

InterruptedException is a checked exception. This means any code invoking `sleep()` must be prepared to catch an InterruptedException.

What's a checked exception? There are two types of exceptions in Java: checked and unchecked. Checked exceptions must be caught (or rethrown—we'll get to that in a moment). Unchecked exceptions do not have to be caught. Whether a method is checked or unchecked depends on where the exception descends from in the class hierarchy.

Here's a diagram to help you see where checked and unchecked exceptions fit into the class hierarchy.

Figure 8-1
An Exception
Hierarchy

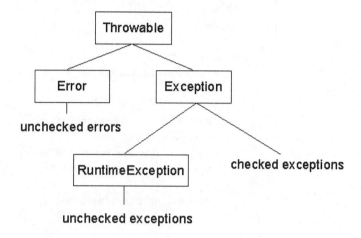

You should never throw an unchecked exception in your own code. All of your exceptions should be checked.

Tip

Exceptions and Errors both inherit from class Throwable, which allows an object to be thrown using the `throw` keyword and caught using the `catch` keyword. However, instances of class Error are unchecked. There's also a subclass of Exception called RuntimeException. Instances of RuntimeException and its subclasses are also unchecked. All other exception classes—namely, all other subclasses of class Exception—are checked.

You are not required to place calls to methods that throw unchecked exceptions in a `try`/`catch` block. However, it's often useful to do so anyway. For example, ArithmeticException is unchecked, but sometimes you want to handle this exception if it arises.

Tip

Let's go back to the `sleep()` method whose definition I've provided above. If you want to invoke `sleep()`, you must place this call in a `try`/`catch` block, like so:

```
class A implements Runnable {
   Thread t;
   public static void main(String[] args) {
      A a = new A();
      a.go();
   }
   void go() {
      t = new Thread(this);
      t.start();
      try {
         System.out.println("try");
         t.sleep(1000);
      } catch(InterruptedException e) {
         System.out.println("catch");
      } finally {
         System.out.println("finally");
      }
   }
   public void run() {
      while(true) {
         // . . . infinite loop . . .
      }
   }
}
```

This example shows the try/catch/finally blocks in action. If everything works smoothly when we invoke sleep() and it does not throw an exception, then the messages "try" and "finally" appear in the standard output. Otherwise, if sleep() does throw an InterruptedException, the messages "try," "catch," and "finally" appear. If sleep() throws an unchecked exception, such as an ArithmeticException, the messages "try" and "finally" appear—because there is no catch clause defined for an ArithmeticException.

Tip

You always need a try block to use catch or finally. With a try, you can (and must) use catch, or finally, or both. You cannot use a try block on its own.

Here's an example of using `try` and `finally` without a `catch` block at all:

```
try {
   if (result == 0) {
      doThis();
      return;
   } else {
      doThat();
      throw new MyException(); }
} finally {
   alwaysDoThis();
}
```

The `finally` block is always executed when it's a matter of control flow. In other words, if you use a `return` statement or throw an exception, or if you try to use a `break` statement to branch around a `finally` block, your efforts to thwart the `finally` statement will be to no avail. (The exercises for this chapter do ask you to identify a sure-fire way of avoiding `finally` by invoking a certain system method, but as long as the issue is one of control flow, `finally` cannot be avoided.)

Exercise 8.1

Rewrite this algorithm from a C method to use Java's exception handling. Then write the code, using an array as the return value.

method name: Roots

input: double a, double b, double c, a pointer to an array of two double values.

output: a boolean indicating success or failure

purpose: implements the quadratic equation

1. Find the value of b*b - 4 * a* c
2. If this result is negative, there are no roots. Return false.
3. If a is negative, also return false.
4. Otherwise, calculate (-b + this value) divided by 2 * a. Also calculate (-b - this value) divided by 2 * a. Place these results in the array referenced by the pointer and return true.

Rethrowing an Exception

Declare a method that might throw unhandled exceptions.

Objectives

Let's look at the idea of rethrowing an exception.

If you don't want to handle an exception yourself, you can let it go unhandled, meaning the exception will bubble up the call stack.

Key Concept

Here's an example. Notice that the method called doThis() is declared as throwing InterruptedException:

```
class A implements Runnable {
    Thread t;
    public static void main(String[] args) {
        A a = new A();
        a.go();
    }

    void go() {
        t = new Thread(this);
        t.start();
    }

    public void run() {
        try {
            doThis();
        } catch (InterruptedException e) {
            System.out.println("caught");
        }
    }
    void doThis() throws InterruptedException {
        t.sleep(2000);
    }
}
```

Even though do This() does not handle InterruptedException, some method in the call stack above the call to sleep() has got to. So, the method run() handles this exception.

You can also declare the `doThis()` method as in the following code snippet to achieve the same effect:

```
void doThis() throws InterruptedException {
    try {
        t.sleep(2000);
    } catch (InterruptedException e) {
        throw e;
    }
}
```

This version of `doThis()` explicitly rethrows the exception.

You can list more than one exception in the `throws` clause if you separate them with commas.

Tip

Exercise 8.2

Rewrite the following method so that instead of handling the exceptions itself, it rethrows the exceptions, putting responsibility on the caller to handle the exceptions.

```
int doDivision(InputStream in) {
    try {
        int c = in.readByte();
        return 100/c;
    } catch (IOException x) {
        return 0;
    } catch (ArithmeticException x) {
        return 0;
    }
}
```

Which Exceptions a Method Can Throw

Specify which exceptions a method can throw.

Objectives

A method can only throw those exceptions listed in its throws clause or subclasses of those exceptions. (A method can also throw any unchecked exception, even if it is not declared in its throws clause.)

Here's an example of throwing a subclass of an exception class specified in the throws clause.

```java
import java.io.IOException;

class Throw {
    public static void main(String[] args) {
        Throw t = new Throw();
        try {
            t.test(4);
        } catch (Exception e) {
        }
    }

    void test(int i) throws Exception {
        if (i == 0)
            throw new IOException();
    }
}
```

The `catch` clauses must match the exceptions listed in the `throws` clause, but the `test()` method can throw any subclass of an exception listed in its `throws` clause.

Exceptions in an Overriding Method in a Subclass

Identify what exceptions may be legitimately thrown from an overriding method in a subclass.

There's more on overriding methods in the next chapter, but we'll cover here how exceptions relate to overriding a method.

When you override a method, you must list those exceptions that the override code might throw. You can only list those exceptions, or subclasses of those exceptions, that are defined in the method definition you are inheriting from. (A method can also throw any unchecked exception, even if it is not declared in its throws clause.)

When you override a method in a subclass, you cannot add new exception types to those you inherit. You can choose to throw a subset of those exceptions listed in the method's superclass. However, a subclass further down the hierarchy cannot then re-list the exceptions dropped above it. For example, suppose you have the following hierarchy:

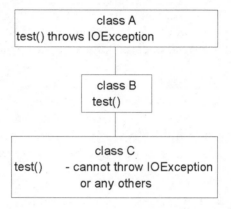

Class A defines a method named test(). Class B is a subclass of class A and overrides test(). Class C is a subclass of class B and also overrides test().

If class A indicates in its test() method that it throws an IOException, and class B does not, then class C cannot list IOException (or, in fact, any other exceptions if B does not also list any) in its throws clause.

In this example, the code will not compile. Even though the superclass, class A, lists IOException in its throws clause, class B does not. Since we create an instance of class B in main(), it is class B's exceptions that must match the catch clauses listed after the try:

```
import java.io.IOException;

class A {
   public static void main(String[] args) {
      B ref = new B();
      try {
         ref.test();
      } catch(IOException e) {
         // We can't catch something that's not thrown!
      }
   }
   void test() throws IOException {
      throw new IOException();
   }
}
```

continued

```
class B extends A {
    void test() {
    }
}
```

However, if we change `main()` so that it creates an instance of class A instead of class B, then this will compile and run fine.

This will also compile if the instance reference `obj` in `main()` is *declared* as type A. In that case, Java allows the possibility that this reference might really be of type A and the `catch` clause is fine.

If `test()` in class B invoked `super.test()`, then either `test()` in class B would have to indicate it throws an IOException, or the call to `super.test()` would have to be wrapped in a `try-catch` block.

Exercise 8.3

Take the above code and make the changes to it based on the possibilities listed above. First try to compile the code as is. Then, create an instance of class A; then declare the variable as class A. Finally, try to invoke `test()` in class A from class B using `super`. If the compiler complains at first, do what you have to do to get this working.

Creating and Throwing an Exception

Write code to create and throw an exception.

You can define your own exceptions simply by extending class Exception.

Typically, the class type is all you need to distinguish your exception from the others.

Tip

You can add behavior to your exception or take advantage of methods already defined in Exception and Throwable. You can also supply a string to the constructor when you create your new exception; this string can contain text detailing why the error occurred. You can retrieve this string from the exception object using getMessage().

The methods in Exception and Throwable are discussed in the section "What's Not on the Test."

To throw an exception, you simply create a new instance of the exception you want to throw and write it after a throw keyword. For example, to throw an exception named IllegalValueException (presumably a subclass of Exception), you can simply write:

```
throw new IllegalValueException();
```

As in the examples above, the method that throws this exception must indicate it throws an exception of this type in its throws clause.

Exercise 8.4

Rewrite the quadratic equation exercise so that you throw your own exception type. Indicate the cause of the exception when you create it, and display this cause in an error message. You can use the answer for Exercise 8.1 as a starting point if you'd like.

What's Not on the Test

Java's Exceptions

It's useful to be familiar with the most common Java exceptions. These exception classes are defined in the package they are most associated with. For example, IOException is defined in java.io; MalformedURLException is defined in `java.net`. Here are some exceptions that you might see or have to handle from time to time.

Checked Exceptions:

- `IOException` (defined in `java.io`): Signals that an error occurred when reading from or writing to a file. You'll have to handle this kind of exception often when you use stream methods.
- `FileNotFoundException` (defined in `java.io`): When you access a file, you must be prepared to handle this exception. Remember, just because you create a File object does not mean that the file exists.
- `MalformedURLException` (defined in `java.net`): When you create a URL, you must be prepared to handle this exception in case the URL string supplied is not valid.
- `InterruptedException` (defined in `java.lang`): When you put a thread to sleep or suspend a thread you've got to be ready to handle this exception; a sleeping thread or a suspended thread could be interrupted before its sleeping time elapses or before someone invokes `resume()` for the thread, in which case it will throw this exception.

Unchecked Exceptions:

- `ArithmeticException` (defined in `java.lang`): Whenever an illegal math operation takes place, such as an integer divide by zero, the Java Virtual Machine throws this exception.
- `NullPointerException` (defined in `java.lang`): If you try to invoke a method using a `null` object reference, you'll see this exception. This exception can creep into your code when you least expect it. For example, you might have set up two method calls like this:

```
int result = methodOne().methodTwo();
```

You expect `methodOne()` to return an object which you will use to invoke `methodTwo()`. However, if `methodOne()` returns `null`, attempting to invoke `methodTwo()` will throw a NullPointerException.

- `NumberFormatException` (defined in `java.lang`): If you are converting a String to a number, you've got to be prepared to handle this exception in case the String does not really represent a number.

There are, of course, many more exceptions that you'll probably come across in your travels as a Java programmer. But these give you a feel for what you'll find.

Using Methods Defined by Exception and Throwable

The most common way to use exceptions is to simply identify the exception that occurred by its class type. Most programmers only check whether the exception's class is IOException, ArithmeticException, and so on, and perform error handling in a catch clause appropriate for that class type.

However, an exception is also a wealth of information. Exceptions can be created with a descriptive String that explains why the exception occurred. You can access this String using getMessage(), which is implemented in Throwable—the superclass of Exception.

You can also print the stack to the standard output or standard error. This can help with debugging so that you can see exactly where the exception was thrown. You can do this by invoking printStackTrace() for the exception.

Answers to the Exercises

Exercise 8.1

method name: Roots

input: double a, double b, double c

output: an array of two double values (an object in Java)

throws: ArithmeticException (could throw a new exception you
defined yourself, called something like NoRootsException)

purpose: implements the quadratic equation

1. Find the value of b*b - 4 * a* c
2. If this result is negative, there are no roots. Throw the exception declared as part of this method.
3. If a is negative, throw the same exception.
4. Otherwise, calculate (-b + this value) divided by 2 * a. Also calculate (-b - this value) divided by 2 * a. Place these results in a new double array and return this array.

Here's what this code might look like. It contains a main() method so that you can run it and test the method.

```java
class Quad {
   public static void main(String[] args) {
      Quad q = new Quad();
      try {
         double[] answer = q.roots(1.2, 3.2, -4.0);
         System.out.println("The roots are " +
            answer[0] + ", " + answer[1]);
      } catch (NoRootsException x) {
         System.out.println("No roots exist");
      }
   }

   double[] roots(double a, double b, double c) throws NoRootsExcep-
tion {
      double[] result = new double[2];
      double temp = (b * b) - ( 4 * a * c);
      if (temp < 0)
         throw new NoRootsException();
      if (a < 0)
         throw new NoRootsException();
      temp = Math.sqrt(temp);
      result[0] = (- b + temp) / (2.0 * a);
      result[1] = (- b - temp) / (2.0 * a);
      return result;
   }

}

class NoRootsException extends Exception { }
```

If you threw something like ArithmeticException, that's fine for what you reviewed up to this point in the chapter. However, in general, you should not throw an unchecked exception (which is what ArithmeticException is). By creating your own exception type, as this chapter discusses towards the end, you can be very specific about what error occurred and you can make sure you throw a checked exception—an exception that must be handled.

Running the above Quad class' main() method yields the result:

```
The roots are 0.927443, -3.59411
```

To see an exception get thrown, try running with a equal to 0 or with b equal to 0 and a and c equal to something greater than 0.

Exercise 8.2

```
int doDivision(InputStream in) throws IOException, ArithmeticException {
    int c = in.readByte();
    return 100/c;
}
```

Exercise 8.3

Here was the original code, this time with line numbers:

```
1:   import java.io.IOException;
2:
3:   class A {
4:      public static void main(String[] args) {
5:          B ref = new B();
6:          try {
7:              ref.test();
8:          } catch(IOException e) {
9:              // We can't catch something that's not thrown!
10:         }
11:     }
12:     void test() throws IOException {
13:         throw new IOException();
14:     }
15: }
16:
17: class B extends A {
18:     void test() {
19:     }
20: }
```

First, compile the code as is. The JDK will complain about line 8 and will display the messsage:

```
Exception java.io.IOException is never thrown in the body of the
corresponding try statement.
```

Then, create an instance of class A instead of class B. To do that, change line 5 to read:

```
A ref = new A();
```

Now the code will compile and run successfully when you run class A's `main()` method.

Next, try changing line 5 to read:

```
A ref = new B();
```

The code will still compile and run successfully when you run class A's `main()` method.

Then, leaving the code defined as above—declaring the variable to be of class A but creating an instance of class B—add after line 18:

```
super.test();
```

When you try to compile this, the compiler will complain about the line you just added (now line 19), and will say:

```
Exception java.io.IOException must be caught, or it must be
declared in the throws clause of this method.
```

We can fix this—we have the technology. The simplest way to proceed is to indicate that `test()` as defined in class B also throws a `java.io.IOException`, just like `test()` in class A. So, we can change line 18 to read:

```
void test() throws IOException {
```

Now, we can compile and run this code just fine.

Exercise 8.4

Notice in this answer how NoRootsException must provide a constructor that passes the String argument to its superclass. This allows the new exception to be initialized with a string containing an explanation of what went wrong. This string can later be retrieved using `getMessage()`.

```
class Quad {
    public static void main(String[] args) {
        Quad q = new Quad();
        try {
            // WORKS double[] answer = q.roots(1.2, 3.2, -4.0);
            double[] answer = q.roots(1.2, 0.0, 2.1); // Produces exception
            System.out.println("The roots are " +
                answer[0] + ", " + answer[1]);
        } catch (NoRootsException x) {
            System.out.println("No roots exist: " + x.getMessage());
```

continued

```
        }
    }

    double[] roots(double a, double b, double c) throws NoRootsException {
        double[] result = new double[2];
        double temp = (b * b) - ( 4 * a * c);
        if (temp < 0)
            throw new NoRootsException("negative square root");
        if (a < 0)
            throw new NoRootsException("divide by zero");
        temp = Math.sqrt(temp);
        result[0] = (- b + temp) / (2.0 * a);
        result[1] = (- b - temp) / (2.0 * a);
        return result;
    }

}

class NoRootsException extends Exception {
    NoRootsException(String s) {
        super(s);
    }
}
```

Review Questions

Question 1:   Why is this code illegal?

```
class A {
    public static void main(String[] args) {
        try {
            System.out.println("hello");
        }
    }
}
```

a) You cannot have a `try` block without a `catch` and/or `finally`.

b) Code that does not throw an exception cannot be in a `try` block.

c) The method `main()` must always throw *something* if the `try` block is used without a `catch`.

Question 2: Analyze the following code and pick the best analysis from the ones presented below.

```
class A {
    public static void main(String[] args) {
        method();
    }
    static void method() throws Exception {
        try {
            System.out.println("hello");
        } finally {
            System.out.println("good-bye");
        }
    }
}
```

a) This code will compile and display both "hello" and "good-bye."

b) This code will do everything in choice a, but Java will then halt the program and report that Exception was thrown but not handled.

c) This code will not compile.

Question 3: What appears in the standard output if you run this program?

```
class A {
    public static void main(String[] args) {
        method();
    }
    static void method() {
        try {
            System.out.println("hello");
        } finally {
            System.out.println("good-bye");
        }
    }
}
```

a) "hello"

b) "good-bye"

c) "hello" followed by "good-bye"

Question 4: What appears in the standard output if you run this program?

```
class A {
    public static void main(String[] args) {
        method();
    }
    static void method() {
        try {
            System.out.println("hello");
            return;
        } finally {
            System.out.println("good-bye");
        }
    }
}
```

a) "hello"
b) "good-bye"
c) "hello" followed by "good-bye"

Question 5: What appears in the standard output if you run this program?

```
class A {
    public static void main(String[] args) {
        method();
    }
    static void method() {
        try {
            System.out.println("hello");
            System.exit(0);
        } finally {
            System.out.println("good-bye");
        }
    }
}
```

a) "hello"
b) "good-bye"
c) "hello" followed by "good-bye"

Question 6: What is the result of invoking B first with no command-line argument, and then with the command line argument "throw?"

```java
class B {
    public static void main(String[] args) {
        B b = new B();
        b.test(args);
    }

    void test(String[] args) {
        String s;

        if (args.length == 0)
            s = new String("don't throw");
        else
            s = args[0];

        try {
            method(s);
            System.out.println("no exception");
        } catch (MyException e) {
            System.out.println("caught");
        }
    }
    void method(String s) throws MyException {
        if (s.equals("throw"))
            throw new MyException();
        else
            return;
    }
}
```

a) The program prints "no exception" two times in a row.

b) First, the program prints "no exception." Then, the program prints "caught."

c) The program prints "caught" two times in a row.

Question 7: This question builds on Question 6, which defined a class called B. Given that class, why is it illegal to write a subclass of B like this?

```
class C extends B {

   public static void main(String[] args) {
      C c = new C();
      c.test(args);
   }

   void method(String s) {
      if (s.equals("yes"))
         throw new MyException();
      else
         return;
   }
}
```

a) When you override a method, you must also indicate the exceptions the overridden method will throw.
b) The subclass, C, cannot invoke `test()` without overriding it.
c) A subclass cannot define `main()` if its superclass also defines `main()`.

Question 8: This question also builds on class B, defined in Question 6. Is it legal to write a subclass of B (and new subclass of Exception) like this?

```
class C extends B {

   public static void main(String[] args) {
      C c = new C();
      c.test(args);
   }
}
```

Question 8 continued

```
    void method(String s) throws AnotherException {
        if (s.equals("yes"))
            throw new AnotherException();
        else
            return;
    }
}


class AnotherException extends Exception {
}
```

a) This code is legal.

b) This code is illegal because AnotherException is not declared correctly.

c) This code is illegal because the method you override cannot throw exceptions not declared by its ancestor's method.

Question 9: This question also builds on class B, defined in Question 6. Is it legal to write a subclass of B (and a subclass of MyException) like this?

```
class C extends B {

    public static void main(String[] args) {
        C c = new C();
        c.test(args);
    }

    void method(String s) throws AnotherException {
        if (s.equals("yes"))
            throw new AnotherException();
        else
            return;
    }
}


class AnotherException extends MyException {
}
```

a) This code is legal.

b) This code is illegal because AnotherException is not declared correctly.

c) This code is illegal because the method you override cannot throw exceptions not declared by its ancestor's method.

Answers to the Review Questions

Question 1	a.	Let's look at the two other choices.

- "Code that does not throw an exception cannot be in a `try` block." This is not true. You can have code that does not throw an exception within a `try` block. If you do, however you need a `finally` block following it.
- "The method `main()` must always throw *something* if the `try` block is used without a `catch`." Again, this is not true because you can use a `try` block with a `finally` block. No exceptions have to be involved in that case.

Question 2   c.   This code will not compile. Exception must be handled in `main()`, or `main()` must indicate that it throws an Exception.

Question 3   c.   Both "hello" and "good-bye" will appear in the standard output.

Question 4   c.   Both "hello" and "good-bye" will appear in the standard output. Even though the code in `try` issues a `return` statement, the `finally` block is still executed.

Question 5   a.   Only the word "hello" appears in the standard output. Why doesn't "good-bye" appear? Because this is not a control flow issue. We go from writing "hello" to invoking a method named `exit()` in the System class. The `exit()` method exits to the system. We never return to this method to reach the `finally` block. (Sneaky, I know.)

Question 6   b.   Run this to see the results in the standard output.

Question 7   a.   The overridden method in class C should be declared as follows:

```
void method(String s) throws MyException {
    if (s.equals("yes"))
        throw new MyException();
    else
        return;
}
```

Question 8   c.   The method you override can only throw exceptions that have been declared by the ancestor's method.

Question 9   a.   This is legal. A method you override can throw any exception declared by its ancestor's method or any subclass of one of these exceptions. In this case, AnotherException has been defined as a subclass of MyException, which class B's method named method() declares it is capable of throwing.

CHAPTER 9

Methods

You should already be familiar with defining simple methods and with the object-oriented concept of inheritance to tackle this chapter.

Methods encode behavior. You can define static methods, which belong to the class, and instance methods, which belong to objects created from the class. Generally, static methods access static data; instance methods access instance data.

Methods must be uniquely identified by name and signature—if there is more than one method with the same name, that method is said to be *overloaded*. Subclasses can *override* methods by defining their own method with the same name and signature as a method in any of its ancestors.

What's on the Test

The Programmer exam is big on overloading and overriding methods. While the concept is fairly straightforward if you're familiar with object-oriented concepts, the details can be tricky. There are rules you should know about when overloading and overriding methods you inherit. These rules will help you move quickly through questions on the test, and we'll cover them in this section.

Objectives for this Chapter

- Distinguish between overloaded and overridden methods.
- Identify legal return types for overloaded and overridden methods.
- Write code for an overridden method that uses the special reference `super`.
- State what occurs when you invoke an overridden method in a base class and a derived class.

Defining a Method

Here's a quick review on defining a method.

A method definition includes its access control keywords, keywords relating to its role in the class hierarchy, the type of its return value, name, parameters, and any exceptions it throws.

Access control keywords include `public`, `protected`, and `private`. These are discussed in Chapter 1.

Other keywords (mostly relating to a method's place in the class hierarchy) include `abstract`, `final`, `native`, and `synchronized`. These are also discussed in Chapter 1. (The keyword `native` is discussed in the second part of this book, when you'll prepare for the Developer exam.)

The return type can be any class type, any primitive data type, or `void`.

If the method throws any checked exceptions, these exception types must be listed in a `throws` clause after the method's signature. (You can also list any unchecked exceptions in the `throws` clause, if you wish.)

Here is a simple method definition:

```
void test() { }
```

This method does not use any keywords, does not return a value, does not take any parameters, and does not throw any exceptions.

Here is a complicated method definition:

```
public abstract synchronized Object test(String[] args, boolean var1)
    throws IOException, MyOwnException;
```

This method can be accessed by any other method that can access the class defining it, is `abstract` (and so does not provide a method body), is `synchronized` so that only one thread at a time can execute this and other instance methods, returns an instance of class Object, takes two parameters, and throws two exceptions. (This definition packs quite a wallop.)

Overloading a Method

Distinguish between overloaded and overridden methods.

Identify legal return types for overloaded and overridden methods.

You can overload a method by defining more than one method with the same name in the same class.

If you defined more than one method with the same name in the same class, Java must be able to determine which method to invoke based on the number and types of parameters defined for that method.

The return value does not contribute towards distinguishing one method from another; it does not affect which method Java invokes. The exceptions a method might throw also do not matter.

All that matters is that the method is sufficiently different in its parameters that the JVM can determine which method to invoke.

Here's a simple example of overloading a method named `test()`.

```
class Ex1 {
   public static void main(String[] args) {
      Ex1 e = new Ex1();
      e.test();
      e.test(1.0, 1);
   }
   void test() {
   }
   void test(double i, int j) {
   }
}
```

The JVM can easily determine which version of `test()` to invoke from `main()`. One version takes no parameters. The other takes a `double` and an `int`.

What if, instead of invoking the second version by writing:

```
e.test(1.0, 1);
```

we wrote

```
e.test(1, 1);
```

In other words, we have two `int` values. In this case, there's still no confusion. The JVM can also determine which version to invoke. It's a simple matter to coerce an `int` to a `double`. This code will compile and run successfully.

Here's an example that doesn't work. In this case, the methods are not different enough for the JVM to determine which one to invoke:

```
// THIS WILL NOT COMPILE!
class Ex2 {
   public static void main(String[] args) {
      Ex2 e = new Ex2();
      e.test(1, 1); // CONFUSION!
   }
   void test(int i, long j) {
   }
   void test(long i, int j) {
   }
}
```

This code won't even compile. The compiler will complain that the overloaded `test()` methods are too similar to each other to invoke using

```
e.test(1, 1)
```

However, there is nothing inherently wrong with the two `test()` methods. They are, in fact, different. If we changed the line where we invoke `test()` to clear up which one to call, then this code compiles and runs fine. We can do that, for example, by writing:

```
e.test(1L, 1);
```

Exercise 9.1

Write a class that defines two `static` methods. One should find the average for an `int` array, the other should find the average for a `double` array.

Overriding a Method

Write code for an overridden method that uses the special reference `super`.

Subclasses can override methods defined in their superclasses.

To pass the method invocation up the class hierarchy (that is, to pass the method call to your superclass so that its version of the method is also invoked), you can use the special object reference super.

This special object reference is an object whose type matches the superclass. Using super, an object can access the variables and methods defined by the superclass.

Here's a simple example of using super:

```
class Super {
    public static void main(String[] args) {
        Sub s = new Sub();
        s.test();
    }
    void test() {
        System.out.println("Superclass");
    }
}
class Sub extends Super {
    void test() {
        super.test();
        System.out.println("Subclass");
    }
}
```

This program writes "Superclass" followed by "Subclass" to the standard output. Here are some rules involving overriding methods.

Access Control

You cannot make a method in a subclass more private than it is defined in the superclass, though you can make it more public.

For example, given the following method:

```
class Super {           extn
  protected void test() {
  }
}
```

you cannot make the subclass look like this:

```
                extends Super
class Sub {
  private void test() {
    super.test();
  }
}
```

Other Keywords

A subclass may make an inherited method `synchronized`, or it may leave off the `synchronized` keyword so that its version is not `synchronized`. If a method in a subclass is not `synchronized` but the method in the superclass is, the thread obtains the monitor for the object when it enters the superclass's method. (There's more about threads in Chapter 12.)

You could also declare an inherited method to be `abstract`, but then there would be no way to get to the behavior in the hierarchy above the `abstract` declaration.

Why does an abstract method stop inheritance? Because you cannot invoke your superclass's behavior if your superclass defines the method to be abstract, since an abstract method does not define any behavior for the method. Hence, you cannot pass a method call up the class hierarchy beyond the abstract method declaration.

Also, as covered in Chapter 1, you cannot override a `final` method.

Return Types

Return types must match the overridden method in the superclass exactly.

Parameter Types

The parameters of the overridden method must match those in the super-class exactly.

Java does not coerce parameters, as it can do with overloaded methods.

Exceptions

A method in a subclass cannot add exception types to the exceptions defined in the superclass. However, it can leave off exceptions.

In the previous chapter, we covered exceptions in relation to overriding a method. Here's the key concept from that chapter that stated the rule:

When you override a method, you must list those exceptions that the override code might throw. You can only list those exceptions, or subclasses of those exceptions, that are defined in the method definition you are inheriting from. (A method can also throw any unchecked exception, even if it is not declared in its throws clause.)

Exercise 9.2

Create a subclass of Calculator called FancyCalculator that is able to provide all of Calculator's functions, plus "sin", "cos", and "tan". Here is the class definition for Calculator:

```
class Calculator {
    private String[] functions = {"+", "-", "*", "/", "="};

    String getFunctions() {
        String s = functions[0];
        for (int i = 1; i < functions.length; i++)
            s += ", " + functions[i];
        return s;
    }

}
```

Exercise 9.2 continued

You can use the following code to test the Calculator class and your new class:

```
class Tester {
    public static void main(String[] args) {
        Calculator c = new Calculator();
        System.out.println(c.getFunctions());

        FancyCalculator f = new FancyCalculator();
        System.out.println(f.getFunctions());
    }
}
```

The point of this exercise is to override a method and invoke the superclass' version of this method successfully.

Object References to Base and Derived Classes

State what occurs when you invoke an overridden method in a base class and a derived class.

A variable declared as an object reference for a certain class type can in fact hold an object reference for that class or an object reference for any subclass of that class.

For example, suppose you have two classes. One is named Base, and it derives directly from class Object. The other is named Derived, and it extends class Base.

You can create new classes and assign them to variables like this:

```
Base b = new Base();
Derived d = new Derived();
```

As you can see, the class type defines the type of object reference. But you can also define a new object and assign its reference to a variable like this:

```
Base b_d = new Derived();
```

Even though b_d is defined as a type of class Base, this type includes sub-classes of Base, such as class Derived. This has interesting effects when accessing data. For example, imagine we've defined the Base and Derived classes like this:

```
class Base {
    int i = 1;
}

class Derived extends Base {
    int i = 2;
}
```

Note that it's perfectly legal to have two different instance variables with the same name if they are defined in different two classes where one inherits from the other.

Tip

Which variable we access depends on the type of the object reference that the variable was declared to hold.

Key Concept

For example, if we accessed and displayed the values for i like this:

```
System.out.println(b.i);
System.out.println(d.i);
System.out.println(b_d.i);
```

what gets displayed depends on the object reference's declared type. The variable b is declared as a Base class. So, b.i accesses i in the Base class and displays "1." The variable d is declared as a Derived class. So, d.i accesses i in the Derived class, and displays "2."

The variable b_d is trickier. We have created an instance of the Derived class and assigned it to this variable. However, as our rule says, the variable that gets accessed depends on the *declared* type of the object reference, which in this case is Base. So, b_d.i accesses i in the Base class, and displays "1."

In contrast to which variable gets accessed, the method that gets invoked depends on the underlying object.

Imagine if our Base and Derived classes looked like this:

```
class Base {
    int i = 1;
    String test() {
        return "Base";
    }
}

class Derived extends Base {
    int i = 2;
    String test() {
        return "Derived";
    }
}
```

As you can see, the Derived class overrides the method `test()` defined in the Base class. Now, we create new instances as before:

```
Base b = new Base();
Derived d = new Derived();
Base b_d = new Derived();
```

This time, what happens when we invoke the `test()` method for each object reference and print the results, as in:

```
System.out.println(b.test());
System.out.println(d.test());
System.out.println(b_d.test());
```

The method that gets invoked depends on the *actual* type of the object itself, not on the *declared* type. So, `b.test()` invokes `test()` in the Base class, which displays "Base." `d.test()` invokes `test()` in the Derived class, which displays "Derived." And, following our rule, `b_d.test()` invokes `test()` in the Derived class, since that is the actual object assigned to the variable `b_d`.

Declaring Native Methods

You may have to identify how you declare a `native` method in the Programmer test. Here's an example:

```
public native void method();
```

A native method does not have a body, not even an empty set of braces.

Declaring a method to be `native` means that it is implemented in a language "native" to the platform you're running on. In other words, it is written in a language such as C and compiled for a particular platform.

Some rules for native methods: a native method can throw exceptions; a native method cannot be abstract.

Answers to the Exercises

Exercise 9.1

```
class Avg {

   static double avg(double[] arr) {
      double sum = 0.0;
      if (arr.length > 0) {
         for (int i = 0; i < arr.length; i++)
            sum += arr[i];
         sum /= arr.length;
      }
      return sum;
   }
}
```

continued

```
static int avg(int[] arr) {
    int sum = 0;
    if (arr.length > 0) {
        for (int i = 0; i < arr.length; i++)
            sum += arr[i];
        sum /= arr.length;
    }
    return sum;
}

public static void main(String[] args) {
    // Test the methods.
    int[] intArray = {1, 2, 3, 4, 5};
    double[] doubleArray = {10, 20, 30, 40, 50};
    System.out.println(avg(intArray));
    System.out.println(avg(doubleArray));
}

}
```

Exercise 9.2

Here is the new FancyCalculator class:

```
class FancyCalculator extends Calculcator {
    private String[] functions = {"sin", "cos", "tan"};

    String getFunctions() {
        String s;
        s = super.getFunctions();
        for (int i = 0; i < functions.length; i++)
            s += ", " + functions[i];
        return s;
    }
}
```

Review Questions

Question 1:   What is the result of trying to compile and run this program?

```
class Example1 {
   public static void main(String[] args) {
      Example1 e = new Example1();
      e.test(5);
   }

   int test(int i) {
      System.out.println("int");
      return 1;
   }

   void test(long i) {
      System.out.println("long");
   }

}
```

a)   The program does not compile because the compiler cannot distinguish between the two test() methods provided.
b)   The program compiles and runs but nothing appears in the standard output.
c)   The program compiles and runs and "int" appears in the standard output.
d)   The program compiles and runs and "long" appears in the standard output.

Question 2:   What is the result of trying to compile and run this program:

```
class Example1 {
   public static void main(String[] args) {
      Example1 e = new Example1();
      e.test(5, 5.0, 5L);
   }
```

continued

```
    void test(double a, double b, double c) {
       System.out.println("double, double, double");
    }

    void test(int a, float b, long c) {
       System.out.println("int, float, long");
    }

}
```

a) This code will not compile.
b) The code will compile and run and display "double, double, double."
c) The code will compile and run and display "int, float, long."

Question 3: What is the result of attempting to compile and run this program?

```
class Over {
   public static void main(String[] args) {
      Under u = new Under();
      u.test();
   }

   int test() {
      System.out.println("Over");
      return 1;
   }
}

class Under extends Over {
   short test() {
      super.test();
      System.out.println("Under");
      return 1;
   }
}
```

a) This code does not compile.
b) This code compiles and runs and displays "Over" followed by "Under."
c) This code compiles and runs and displays "Under" followed by "Over."

Answer to the Review Questions

Question 1   c.   The program compiles fine. When it runs, the word "int" appears in the standard output. Remember, the return type is not part of the signature of a method. An overloaded method can have different return types and the code will still be legal. Also, the Java Virtual Machine can determine which version to invoke because literals such as 5 are int values.

Question 2   b.   The second parameter is 5.0. Floating-point numbers in Java are double by default. So, even though the first and second parameters are int and long and match the second definition of test(), the second parameter would have to be coerced to a float. Java invokes the first version of test(), where no values have to be explicitlycoerced.

Question 3   a.   The compiler complains because the method in the subclass Under returns a different type than the method in the superclass. Unlike an overloaded method, the return type for an overridden method must match the superclass's return type for that method.

CHAPTER 10

The Math and String Classes

You should know how to invoke class methods and access class data.

The Math class contains lots of useful `static` methods for performing mathematical operations: finding the absolute value of a number, for example, or finding its square root.

The String class defines some `static` methods and lots of instance methods for working with character data within a String: finding the number of characters in a string, comparing to strings, and retrieving a character at a certain offset into the string, for example.

Both the Math class and the String class are defined in the package `java.lang`.

What's on the Test

The test requires you to identify certain methods in these classes and understand what they do. You should look those over here so that you don't get flustered on the test ("does `floor()` mean the next lowest integer or the next highest?").

Also, String objects are read-only. Once you set their data you can't change them. This has certain side effects which the test also asks you to identify.

Objectives for this Chapter

- Demonstrate the use of `static` methods defined in the Math class. These `static` methods include `abs()`, `ceil()`, `floor()`, `max()`, `min()`, `random()`, `round()`, `sin()`, `cos()`, `tan()`, and `sqrt()`.
- Write code that works with String instances, taking into account the fact that Strings are read-only.
- Identify legal operators for strings.
- Demonstrate the use of the following String methods: `length()`, `toUpperCase()`, `toLowerCase()`, `equals()`, `equalsIgnoreCase()`, `charAt()`, `concat()`, `indexOf()`, `lastIndexOf()`, `substring()`, `toString()`, `trim()`.

Math Methods

Demonstrate the use of static methods defined in the Math class. These static methods include `abs()`, `ceil()`, `floor()`, `max()`, `min()`, `random()`, `round()`, `sin()`, `cos()`, `tan()`, `sqrt()`.

The Programmer's test mentions these `static` methods defined in the Math class:

abs()

`abs()` returns the absolute value of a number.

This method is overloaded with four versions: the argument can be a float, double, long, or int. The types byte and short are coerced to an int if they are used as arguments. This method returns the same type as the argument supplied.

ceil()

ceil() finds the next highest integer.

The documentation says this method "returns the smallest (closest to negative infinity) double value that is not less than the argument and is equal to a mathematical integer." Let's unravel what this means with a simple example. Take a look at this program:

```
class M {
    public static void main(String[] args) {
        System.out.println(Math.ceil(9.01));
        System.out.println(Math.ceil(-0.1));
        System.out.println(Math.ceil(100));
        System.out.println(Math.ceil(Double.MIN_VALUE));
    }
}
```

When you run this, its output is:
```
10
0
100
1
```

The value Double.MIN_VALUE is the smallest possible positive number that a variable of type double can hold. The ceil() method went up to 1. If the number is an integer to begin with, it returns that integer. Otherwise, it goes to the closest integer, counting up.

floor()

floor() finds the next lowest integer.

This method does the opposite of ceil(). Its documentation reads: "returns the largest (closest to positive infinity) double value that is not greater than the argument and is equal to a mathematical integer." Let's run the same program that we just ran, this time changing ceil() to floor():

```
class M {
    public static void main(String[] args) {
        System.out.println(Math.floor(9.01));
        System.out.println(Math.floor(-0.1));
        System.out.println(Math.floor(100));
        System.out.println(Math.floor(Double.MIN_VALUE));
    }
}
```

The output is:
```
9
-1
100
0
```

max()

max() finds the maximum between two values.

max() is overloaded with versions for int, long, double, and float. This method simply returns the larger of the two values supplied.

min()

min() finds the minimum between two values.

min() is also overloaded with versions for int, long, double, and float. This method simply returns the smaller of the two values supplied.

random()

random() returns a random number—a double value—between 0.0 and 1.0.

You don't have nearly as much control over this random number as you do when you use the Random class and can seed the random number generator. If you want to seed the number or retrieve random numbers in different ranges, use the Random class.

round()

This method finds the closest integer to a float-point number.

There are versions of round() for double and float (of course, integer values don't need to be rounded).

For example, if you run this program:

```
class Round {
    public static void main(String[] args) {
        System.out.println(Math.round(9.01));
        System.out.println(Math.round(9.5));
        System.out.println(Math.round(-9.5));
        System.out.println(Math.round(-0.1));
        System.out.println(Math.round(100.0));
        System.out.println(Math.round(Double.MIN_VALUE));
    }
}
```

you get these results:

```
9
10
-9
0
100
0
```

As you can see, round() went up at .5 or above, and down when it the number was less than .5. So, for 9.5, the number was rounded to 10. At -9.5, the number was rounded up to -9.

sqrt()

sqrt() finds the square root of a number.

If the argument is "not-a-number" (NaN) or less than zero, the result of sqrt() is NaN.

sin()

sin() finds the sine of a number given the angle in radians.

If it's been a while and you don't remember, there are 2*pi degrees in a circle. For example, pi/2 radians equals 90 degrees.

cos()

cos() finds the cosine of a number given the angle in radians.

tan()

tan() finds the tangent of a number given the angle in radians.

Exercise 10.1

Using only the Math class, write a method that finds the maximum of two random numbers between 0 and pi. Then find the sine, cosine, and tangent of this number.

String Methods

Demonstrate the use of the following String methods: `length()`, `toUpper-Case()`, `toLowerCase()`, `equals()`, `equalsIgnoreCase()`, `charAt()`, `con-cat()`, `indexOf()`, `lastIndexOf()`, `substring()`, `toString()`, `trim()`.

String objects represent read-only character data. You must assign a value to the String when you create the String object; since String objects are read-only, you don't get a second chance to initialize one.

Strings have a privileged position in the Java world. All objects respond to `toString()`, which you can override to return a String representation of your object, and the + and += operators are overloaded for Strings.

The Programmer exam mentions these String methods:

length()

`length()` returns an `int` of the number of characters in this String.

toUpperCase()

toUpperCase() returns a new String object representing the upper-case equivalent of the String,

If the upper-case equivalent is not different from the original String, toUpperCase() returns the original object.

toLowerCase()

toLowerCase() returns a new String object representing the lower-case equivalent of the String.

If the lower-case equivalent is not different from the original String, toLowerCase() returns the original object.

equals()

equals() returns true if two String objects are the same lengths and contain the identical run of characters, taking case into account.

Note that String overrides the equals() method, which, by default, only returns true if the object references used with this method refer to the same underlying object. With String, completely different objects can make equals() return true.

Tip

equalsIgnoreCase()

equalsIgnoreCase() returns true if two String objects are the same lengths and contain the identical run of characters, not taking case into account.

In other words, with this method, a pair of corresponding characters are considered equal if the == operator returns true as they are; if the == operator returns true after they have both been made upper case; or if the == operator returns true after they have both been made lower case.

When this method runs, Java makes characters upper or lower case using a static Character method called toUppercase() or toLowercase().

Tip

charAt()

charAt() returns the character at the index position passed to this method.

Key Concept

The first character is at position 0. The last character is at position length() - 1. If you try to access a character outside the bounds of this String, this method will throw a StringIndexOutOfBoundsException.

This method returns type char.

indexOf(), lastIndexOf()

indexOf() finds the first occurrence of a character or substring. lastIndexOf() finds the last occurrence of a character or substring.

Key Concept

Both methods return the value -1 if they cannot find the character or substring; otherwise, they return the index where the character is, or the index where the substring starts, as appropriate.

There are four versions of each of these methods.

Arguments	Results
(int ch)	Finds the first occurrence of this character
(int ch, int fromIndex)	The index to start the search from
(String substring)	Finds the start of this substring
(String substring, int fromIndex)	The index to start the search from for the substring.

substring()

substring() returns a substring from the given String.

There are two versions of this method.

Arguments	Results
(int startIndex)	Returns a substring starting with startIndex and extending to the end of the String
(int startIndex, int endIndex)	Returns a substring starting with the startIndex and extending to—but not including—the endIndex

toString()

You can override toString() in any class so that instances of that class return a String representation of themselves. This is useful when you want to place an object directly in an expression that calls for a String, such as an argument to System.out.println().

For a String, toString() returns itself—the same object reference (of course, pointing to the same object) that was used to invoke this method.

trim()

trim() returns a new String object that cuts off the leading and trailing whitespace for the String for which this was invoked.

Java considers "whitespace" to be any character with a code less than or equal to '\u0020'. The character '\u0020' is the whitespace character.

String Operators

Write code that works with String instances, taking into account the fact that Strings are read-only.

Identify legal operators for strings.

You cannot overload operators in Java. If you do not have a C++ background, this doesn't mean much to you. But in C++, you can give an operator (such as + or *) a different meaning for a particular data type.

The only exception to this rule in Java is that Java itself overrides the + and += operators for Strings.

Of course, normally the + operator adds two numbers. When used with Strings, the + operator creates a new String object that's a combination of the Strings. For example:

```
String s = "hello," + " world";
```

results in the String s containing "hello, world." Strings also override the += operator, so that you can write:

```
String s = "hello,";
s += " world";
```

The + and += operators also work as you would hope when used with a String object and some other primitive data types, such as a number, boolean, or char.

For example, when used with a number:

```
String s = "Nine to " + 5;
```

The + operator results in s being set to the String "Nine to 5."

String Objects are Read-Only

String objects are read-only, while StringBuffer objects are read-write.

This means that if you perform some operation on a String—add characters to a String, say, using the + operator—the result is a *new* String, *not a modification* of the original String.

For example, imagine the following snippet:

```
String s = "Decaf";
s = s + " coffee";
```

Have we modified the original, underlying object after all? No. The + operator creates a new String object. In this case, we assigned it back to the object reference s. If we did not save the original reference in s (that is, the String object that only contained the string "Decaf,") we'll lose our handle on that object, and it will become a candidate for garbage collection.

Exercise 10.2

Write a standalone program that takes any number of command line parameters and displays the number of (naturally occurring) lowercase *e*s in all of them, combined.

What's Not on the Test

Other Math Methods and Constants

The Math class defines a number of other methods you might find useful. For example, in addition to the trig functions mentioned earlier, there are also methods for arc sine, arc cosine, and arc tangent. You can raise a number to a power by using:

```
Math.pow(number, power);
```

This raises the number to the specified power.

The Math class also defines constants for PI and E.

Other String Methods

concat()—This method concatenates a given string onto the end of the String object responding to this method. Of course, since Strings are read-only, the string passed as an argument is not really appended to the original String. Instead, concat() returns a new String.

startsWith()–endsWith() Returns a boolean indicating whether the String passed as the parameter is in the target String. The startsWith() method is also overloaded to start at an optional off-set into the String.

replace()—Returns a new String where all the occurrences of the first character passed as a parameter are replaced by the second parameter.

valueOf()—This static method is overloaded for the basic primitive data types, character arrays, and class Object. It returns a String represent-ing the value of the data type. For example, a boolean might be "true" or "false" and a float might be "3.14." Objects return their value for toString().

StringBuffer

If you want to alter the contents of a String—for example, if you want to read one character at a time from a source file or from the standard input and append the characters to what you've read so far—you probably want to use a StringBuffer object instead of a String.

The append() and insert() methods are overloaded to take every basic Java data type as well as character arrays and objects.

You can also do some interesting things to the characters in a String-Buffer such as reversing the characters by invoking reverse(), or chang-ing a particular character by using setCharAt().

StringBuffer does not inherit from String. If you want to use the string repre-sented by a StringBuffer object as a parameter to a method, for example (such as println()), you've got to obtain a String object from the String-Buffer object. You can do this by invoking toString().

Answers to the Exercises

Exercise 10.1

```
void exercise() {
    double d1 = Math.random() * Math.PI;
    double d2 = Math.random() * Math.PI;

    double m = Math.max(d1, d2);

    System.out.println(Math.sin(m));
    System.out.println(Math.cos(m));
    System.out.println(Math.tan(m));
}
```

Exercise 10.2

```
class ECounter {
    public static void main(String[] args) {
        String s;
        int index;
        int ecount = 0;
        for (int i = 0; i < args.length; i++) {
            s = args[i];

            index = 0;

            while ( (index = s.indexOf('e', index)) != -1) {
                index++;
                ecount++;
            }
        }

        System.out.println("There are " + ecount + " e's.");
    }
}
```

Review Questions

Question 1: **What Math methods, invoked like this:**

```
Math.method(x);
```

would return the value -5 given the value of x to be -4.5?

a) round()
b) ceil()
c) floor()
d) a, b, and c
e) a and c

Question 2: **What is possible output from invoking:**

```
Math.random();
```

a) 132.93
b) 0.2154
c) 29.32E10
d) all of the above

Question 3: **To find the square root of a number, you can use the Math method:**

a) srt()
b) sqrt()
c) squareRoot()

Question 4:   Given this line of code:

```
String s = "Penguin";
```

What will be assigned to c if you execute:

```
char c = s.charAt(6);
```

a)   'n'
b)   'i'
c)   nothing will be assigned because charAt() will respond with a
     StringIndexOutOfBoundsException.

Question 5:   What do you expect the output to be for the following program?

```
class Str {
   public static void main(String[] args) {
      String s = new String("HI");
      String t;
      t = s.toUpperCase();
      if (s == t)
         System.out.println("equals");
      else
         System.out.println("not equals");
   }
}
```

a)   "equals"
b)   "not equals"

Question 6: What do you expect the output to be for the following program?

```
class Str {
   public static void main(String[] args) {
      String s = new String("Hi");
      String t;
      t = s.toUpperCase();
      if (s == t)
         System.out.println("equals");
      else
         System.out.println("not equals");
   }
}
```

a) "equals"
b) "not equals"

Question 7: Imagine the following lines of code:

```
String s = "Hello,";
String t = s;
s += " world";
if (s == t)
   System.out.println("equals");
else
   System.out.println("not equals");
```

What gets written to the standard output?

a) "equals"
b) "not equals"

Answers to the Review Questions

Question 1	c.	Only `floor()` will go to the next lower number. Both `round()` and `ceil()` go higher—to -4.
Question 2	b.	`Math.random()` yields a result between 0.0 and 1.0.
Question 3	b.	(I made up the other method names).
Question 4	a.	The first index position is 0, so `charAt(6)` results in the 7th character in the string, which is 'n.'
Question 5	~~a.~~ b	Surprised? The method `toUpperCase()` returns the original string if the parameter is already in upper case. Hence the `==` operator yields `true` in this example.
Question 6	b.	As you would expect, `toUpperCase()` creates a new string containing "HI", and so the `==` operator yields ~~true~~ false in this example.
Question 7	b.	After these three lines of code execute, it might seem that we have modified the object reference s, and that t and s are still equivalent object references. However, this is not the case. The `+=` operator creates a new String object. The variables t and s now contain different references. The words "not equals" are written to the standard output.

CHAPTER *11*

Input/Output

You should know about exception handling and the try-catch-finally control flow mechanism to use the `java.io` classes effectively. Also, there are two interfaces in `java.io` that the file streams implement called DataInput and DataOutput. So, knowing how interfaces work is also useful in this chapter.

Java defines a wide variety of classes and methods in its `java.io` package that you can use to read from and write to streams of data. What is a stream? A stream is an ordered sequence of bytes that have a source or a destination. Destinations or sources can be files or Internet resources, for example.

There are different kinds of streams in Java. Some streams are associated with files and make it easy to read from or write to a file. Some streams can be chained together so that each type of stream adds its own processing to the bytes as they pass through the stream.

What's on the Test

The filter streams (FilterInputStream and FilterOutputStream) and the file streams (FileInputStream and FileOutputStream) are the key classes on the test. These descend from InputStream and OutputStream, which are abstract classes that declare basic methods for reading and writing bytes.

The stream classes work sequentially. To randomly access data, you can use the class RandomAccessFile. This class can read to and write from files.

In addition to reading and writing bytes, there are also questions concerning the file system. To work with the file system (such as navigating the file system and creating and deleting directories), you can use the File class.

Objectives for this Chapter

- Construct "chains" of InputStream and OutputStream objects using the subclasses of FilterInputStream and FilterOutputStream.
- Identify valid constructor arguments for FilterInputStream and FilterOutputStream subclasses.
- Read, write, and update files using FileInputStream, FileOutputStream, and RandomAccessFile objects.
- Describe the permanent effects on the file system of constructing and using FileInputStream, FileOutputStream, and RandomAccessFile objects.
- Navigate the file system using the File class.

The java.io Package

The top-level classes in the java.io package—InputStream and OutputStream, FilterInputStream and FilterOutputStream, FileInputStream and FileOutputStream, File, and RandomAccessFile—are all on the test. Here's a quick review of these classes.

There are three pairs of classes and interfaces to understand. Once you grasp where these are in the class hierarchy for the I/O classes, the rest of the classes fall into place. These three pairs of classes and interfaces are:

1. InputStream and OutputStream
2. FilterInputStream and FilterOutputStream
3. DataInput and DataOutput

InputStream and OutputStream

At the top level of the input/output hierarchy are the classes InputStream and OutputStream. These are `abstract` classes and define basic methods for working with streams of data, such as `read()`, `write()`, and `skip()`. They also declare a `close()` method to close the stream. Creating the object opens the stream.

These classes declare a few other methods. For example, InputStream declares a method called `available()` that tests to see whether any bytes are available to be read. OutputStream also declares a method called `flush()` which writes any bytes in a buffer to the stream.

Individual subclasses of InputStream implement the `read()` method for reading one byte at a time. Individual subclasses of OutputStream implement the `write()` method for writing one byte at a time.

Figure 11-1
InputStream and Out-
putStream are at the
Top Level

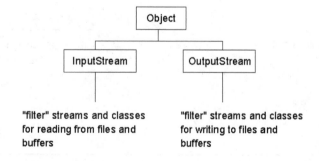

Subclasses of these top level `abstract` classes include classes for reading and writing to files, buffers, byte arrays, and more—most of which are *not* on the test, so don't panic. We'll cover the ones you need to know about in the first part of this chapter, and review the others in the section "What's Not on the Test."

FilterInputStream and FilterOutputStream

Construct "chains" of InputStream and OutputStream objects using the subclasses of FilterInputStream and FilterOutputStream.

Identify valid constructor arguments for FilterInputStream and FilterOutputStream subclasses.

Filter streams do things with the bytes read from or written to another stream.

The Filter stream classes are subclasses of InputStream and OutputStream. While some subclasses of InputStream and OutputStream can be used by themselves, FilterInputStream and FilterOutputStream and their subclasses are used with other stream objects.

Figure 11-2 shows a Filter stream attached to another stream which accesses a file. The Filter stream in this example is called a DataInputStream. The File stream is a FileInputStream.

Figure 11-2
A DataInputStream
Attached to a FileInputStream that Reads
from a File

When you create a Filter stream, you must specify the stream to which it will attach.

When you create a Filter stream object, you must pass an instance of an InputStream or OutputStream, as appropriate (depending on if you are creating a FilterInputStream or a FilterOutputStream), to the constructor. The Filter streams do not define a no-args constructor. This means they *must* be chained in some way—a Filter stream must reference either another Filter stream or an InputStream or OutputStream. (All Filter streams descend from either InputStream or OutputStream.)

A Filter stream processes a stream of bytes in some way. By "chaining" any number of Filter streams, you can add any amount of processing to a stream of bytes.

You can chain together as many Filter streams as you like. Each Filter stream in the chain continues adding processing to the bytes read from or written to a resource. In Figure 11-2, you can see that the DataInputStream knows how to work with Java data types; the FileInputStream only knows how to read individual bytes.

The first Filter stream in a chain must be associated with some underlying file or other resource to be created in the first place. Once the first Filter stream is created, other Filter streams can attach to that first Filter stream.

Figure 11-3 shows where the File streams and the Filter streams fit into the I/O hierarchy we started earlier.

Figure 11-3
File Streams and Filter Streams

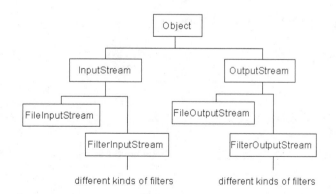

DataInput and DataOuput

DataInput and DataOutput are interfaces that declare methods for reading and writing Java's primitive data types—byte, short, int, long, float, double, char, and boolean.

It is up to the classes that implement this interface to supply the specific methods that fulfill these contracts.

There are three classes that implement the DataInput and DataOutput interfaces: DataInputStream, DataOutputStream, and RandomAccessFile.

Figure 11-4 shows where these classes are in the I/O class hierarchy and their connection to the DataInput and DataOutput interfaces.

Notice that RandomAccessFile implements both DataInput and DataOutput methods. RandomAccessFile objects can read from and write to files. That's why RandomAccessFile does not inherit from FileInputStream or FileOutput-Stream—it can do both (and remember, Java does not allow multiple inheritance of implementation).

Figure 11-4
Classes that Implement the DataInput and DataOutput Interfaces

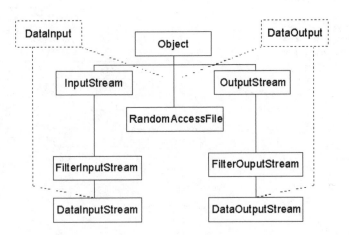

With these three cornerstones of the I/O hierarchy (InputStream and OutputStream, the Filter streams, and the DataInput and DataOutput interfaces), you can begin to make sense of the other I/O classes.

Let's sketch in the subclasses. Then, we'll move on and look at the File class, which you can use to navigate the file system.

Direct Subclasses InputStream and OutputStream

FileInputStream and FileOutputStream are used to read from and write to a file. FileOutputStream will also create the file you write to.

I have supplied examples of using FileInputStream and FileOutputStream later in this chapter.

In addition to FilterInputStream and FilterOutputStream, there are some direct subclasses of InputStream and OutputStream that you can instantiate. FileInputStream and FileOutputStream are really the only ones you need to use during the test. However, you should be able to identify the subclasses of FileInputStream and FileOutputStream. These are:

InputStream subclasses:

- SequenceInputStream
- StringBufferInputStream
- ByteArrayInputStream
- PipedInputStream
- FileInputStream

OutputStream subclasses:

- ByteArrayOutputStream
- PipedOutputStream
- FileOutputStream

Direct Subclasses of FilterInputStream and FilterOutputStream

The subclasses are on the test only to the extent that you need to know what makes a valid chain of Filter stream classes.

You should be able to identify the subclasses of FilterInputStream and FilterOutputStream. These are:

FilterInputStream subclasses:

- LineNumberInputStream
- BufferedInputStream
- DataInputStream
- PushbackInputStream

FilterOutputStream subclasses:

- PrintStream
- BufferedOutputStream
- DataOutputStream

Classes that Implement DataInput and DataOutput

There are three classes that implement the DataInput and/or DataOutput interfaces.

RandomAccessFile allows you to create, write to, and read from a file, with the ability to move the file pointer to any location within that file.

RandomAccessFile implements both DataInput and DataOutput. There's more on RandomAccessFile later in this chapter.

DataInputStream and DataOutputStream are Filter stream subclasses that add the ability to read and write Java's primitive data types.

DataInputStream and DataOutputStream implement DataInput and DataOutput, respectively.

The File Class

Navigate the file system using the File class.

Describe the permanent effects on the file system of constructing and using FileInputStream, FileOutputStream, and RandomAccessFile objects.

The File class is *not* used to create files. For that, you use ~~FileInputStream~~, FileOutputStream, or RandomAccessFile. (Creating files is discussed below.) With the File class you can delete and rename files, and you can also create directories. You can work with file names in a platform-independent way, test to see if a file exists, find information about a file node, delete and rename existing files, and create directories.

You can create a File object using one of three constructors. These constructors take:

1. a String containing a path name
2. a String containing a path name and a String containing a file name
3. a File representing a path and a String containing a file name

Notice that File does not define a no-args constructor.

The File class defines a static variable named separatorChar that contains the platform-dependent path separator—a back-slash for Windows, a colon for the Mac, and a forward-slash for UNIX. You can use this character to write platform-independent code that navigates the file system.

Here are some useful File methods.

Testing to See if a File Exists

Just because you can create a File object, it doesn't mean the file or directory exists.

To test to see if a File object refers to an existing file, you can invoke exists(), which returns true or false.

Finding Information about a File Node

The methods canRead() and canWrite() return boolean values that indicate whether the application can read from or write to the file. For example, a standalone application might be able to write to a file, while an applet, because of security restrictions, may not.

Another useful method is lastModified(). This method returns a platform-dependent value you can use to determine whether a particular file was created before or after another.

In other words, the return value from lastModified() is a relative time, not an absolute time.

Deleting and Renaming Files

While you cannot create files using the File class or a File object, you can use File methods to make a permanent change to the file system. For example, you can delete and rename files.

Invoke delete() to delete a file. This method returns a boolean indicating success or failure.

Invoke rename() to rename a file, and supply a File object that embodies the new name.

Creating Directories

You can also create directories using File. You can invoke the method mkdir() to create a directory specified by the File object. This method also returns a boolean indicating success or failure.

Navigating the File System

You can use the method getParent() to retrieve a String containing the name of the parent directory.

The methods getPath() and getName() return the directory structure for this File object and the file's name, respectively.

The method `getAbsolutePath()` returns the absolute path if this File object represents an absolute path.

If you use `getAbsolutePath()` and the File object does not represent an absolute path, this method makes one up! It returns the name of the current user directory with the file name concatenated to it.

Creating Files

While you can delete and rename files using a File object, you must use a stream object to create a file in the first place—either a FileOutputStream or RandomAccessFile object (a RandomAccessFile is a type of stream). Here's a very simple example of using a FileOutputStream to create a file, though this program does not do anything with the file it creates.

```
import java.io.*;

class A {
    public static void main(String[] args) throws Exception {
        FileOutputStream out = new FileOutputStream("A.test");
        out.close();
    }
}
```

This program creates an empty file called "A.test" in the same directory as this program. If you ran this program, you would see a file named "A.test" in the same directory as the program.

You can also pass the FileOutputStream constructor a File object, as in:

```
import java.io.*;

class A {
    public static void main(String[] args) throws Exception {
        File f = new File("hello.test");
        FileOutputStream out = new FileOutputStream(f);
        out.close();
    }
}
```

Exercise 11.1

Write a standalone program that takes a command line parameter and, after ensuring the file does not exist, creates a file with that name.

Writing To and Reading From Files

Read, write, and update files using FileInputStream, FileOutputStream, and RandomAccessFile objects.

Now to write to and read from this file. Here's another program that does just that:

```java
import java.io.*;

class A {
    static String fileName = "A.test";

    public static void main(String[] args) {
        try {
            FileOutputStream out = createFile();
            writeFile(out);
            readFile();
        } catch (IOException io) {
            System.out.println(io.getMessage());
        }
    }
    static FileOutputStream createFile() throws IOException {
        File f = new File(fileName);
        FileOutputStream out = new FileOutputStream(f);
        return out;
    }
    static void writeFile(FileOutputStream out) throws IOException {
        DataOutputStream ds = null;
        try {
            ds = new DataOutputStream(out);
```

continued

```
            ds.writeBytes("hello!");
        } finally {
            if (ds != null)
                ds.close();
        }
    }
    static void readFile() throws IOException {
        DataInputStream di = null;
        try {
            File f = new File(fileName);
            FileInputStream in = new FileInputStream(f);
            di = new DataInputStream(in);
            String s = di.readLine();
            System.out.println(s);
        } finally {
            if (di != null)
                di.close();
        }
    }
}
```

This example consists of three `static` methods in addition to `main()`. The first, `createFile()`, creates a new file and returns a FileOutputStream object so that we can write to it. The second, `writeFile()`, attaches a type of Filter stream—a DataOutputStream—to the FileOutputStream object, and uses the methods defined by DataOutputStream to write to our stream. The third, `readFile()`, creates a FileInputStream handle to the file, attaches a DataInputStream to it, and then uses the methods in DataInputStream to read from it.

Notice that I close the file very deliberately by placing the `close()` call inside a `finally` block so that it is always executed, even if one of the methods in the `try` block throws an exception. I also check to make sure the Filter object was created (in fact, the compiler insists upon it) before invoking `close()`.

Creating a FileOutputStream object creates the appropriate file. What if the file already exists? In that case, FileOutputStream recreates the file and writes to it again. (That is, FileOutputStream replaces the existing file.)

To append to a file instead of overwriting it, you need to use a RandomAccessFile object. RandomAccessFiles are described in the next section.

Exercise 11.2

Write a program that writes your phone number to a file. Don't write a String—write an int containing your seven digit number.

RandomAccessFile

RandomAccessFile objects do two things: they allow you to open a file as read-only or read/write, and they allow you to write to any location in the file, not just the beginning.

The downside of using a RandomAccessFile is that it does not inherit from InputStream or OutputStream. This means that you cannot use them in a chain, for example, with the Filter stream classes.

RandomAccessFile does at least implement the DataInput and DataOutput interfaces, so it does support all of the methods for reading and writing Java's primitive data types.

When you create a RandomAccessFile, you'll supply a mode as the second argument. This mode is a String that can be either "r" for read or "rw" for read/write. (The first argument is either a String containing the path and file name, or a File object.)

You can determine where the file pointer currently is, in bytes, by invoking getFilePointer(). The 0th byte is the first position in the file.

You can set the file pointer with seek(), passing this method the number of bytes to offset. And you can determine the length of the file with length().

Here's an example of appending to a file rather than overwriting it, as would happen if we used FileOutputStream in place of RandomAccessFile in the program that follows:

```java
import java.io.*;

class Ran {
    static String fileName = "Ran.test";

    public static void main(String[] args) {
        try {
```

continued

```
            sayHello();
            appendHi();
            readGreeting();
        } catch (IOException x) {
            System.out.println(x.getMessage());
        }
    }

    public static void sayHello() throws IOException {
        DataOutputStream ds = null;
        try {
            File f = new File(fileName);
            FileOutputStream out = new FileOutputStream(f);
            ds = new DataOutputStream(out);
            ds.writeBytes("hello!");
        } finally {
            if (ds != null)
                ds.close();
        }
    }

    public static void appendHi() throws IOException {
        RandomAccessFile out = null;
        try {
            File f = new File(fileName);
            out = new RandomAccessFile(f, "rw");
            out.seek(out.length());
            out.writeBytes(" hi!");
        } finally {
            if (out != null)
                out.close();
        }
    }

    public static void readGreeting() throws IOException {
        RandomAccessFile in = null;
        try {
            File f = new File(fileName);
            in = new RandomAccessFile(f, "r");
            String s = in.readLine();
            System.out.println(s);
        } finally {
            if (in != null)
                in.close();
        }
    }
}
```

The output from this program is a file named `Ran.test` that contains the following: *Data Output Stream*

```
hello! hi!
```

In addition, this program also writes these contents to the standard output.

If we used a ~~FileOutputStream~~ instead if a RandomAccessFile in the `sayHi()` method, the file would simply contain:

```
hi!
```

because "hello!" would have been overwritten. But we were able to append using a RandomAccessFile because RandomAccessFile objects don't recreate the file if it already exists, and we can set the file pointer exactly where we want it—in this case, to the end of the file.

You can also see that the first time we wrote to the file we used a FileOutputStream. It was only when we wanted to append that we needed a RandomAccessFile. We created the RandomAccessFile object using "rw" the first time, because we wanted to write to it. The second time, in `read-Greeting()`, we used "r", because we only wanted to read from the file.

Also notice how we used `readLine()` to read from the file. This method is declared in the DataInput interface, which RandomAccessFile implements.

Tip

As with the earlier example of working with files, we wrapped the `close()` call inside a `finally` block so that the file is always closed when we're done with it.

Exercise 11.3

Finish this program to first write the numbers 1, 3, and 5 to a file, leaving gaps for the even numbers. Then, on a second pass, write the numbers 2 and 4 in the proper gaps. Use the method declared by the DataOutput interface called `writeBytes()` to write out a String for "2" and 4" as appropriate.

Exercise 11.3 continued

```
import java.io.*;

class Gaps {
    public static void main(String[] args) throws Exception {
        File f = new File("Gaps.test");
        RandomAccessFile out = new RandomAccessFile(f, "rw");
        out.writeBytes("1 3 5");
        System.out.println("len is " + out.length());

        // Supply the missing code here to write out "2" and "4"
        // in the gaps in the character "1 3 5" already written to
        // the file.

        out.close();
    }
}
```

What's Not on the Test

There are a lot of I/O classes in the `java.io` package. As you've seen, only a handful of them are on the test. This section provides a quick review of what some of the other I/O classes are and what they do.

Figure 11-5
InputStream and Output-Stream Subclasses Not Fully Covered on the Test

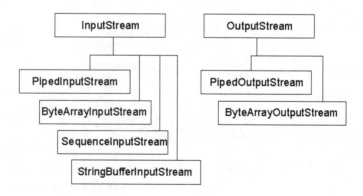

SequenceInputStream

This class enables you to read from a sequence of files. This class reads the first file until it comes to the end, then it reads the second, then the third, and so on.

StringBufferInputStream

This class allows you to read from a StringBuffer as you would from a file.

ByteArrayInputStream and ByteArrayOutputStream

These classes allow you to use byte arrays rather than a file as a stream.

PipedInputStream and PipedOutputStream

These classes allow you to associate an input file with an output file (or vice versa). This allows you to write to a PipedOutputStream, for example, and then turn around and read this data from a PipedInputStream.

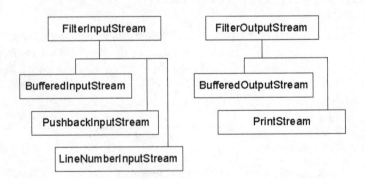

Figure 11-6
FilterInputStream and
FilterOutputStream
Subclasses Not Fully
Covered on the Test

LineNumberInputStream

LineNumberInputStream objects keep track of which line number is currently being read. You can retrieve the current line number using getLineNumber().

BufferedInputStream

Invoking a read method for a BufferedInputStream fills up the buffer and returns bytes from this buffer to the program doing the reading.

PushbackInputStream

This class reads a byte into a buffer and allows you to "return" the byte as "unread."

PrintStream

This class provides `print()` and `println()` methods for the basic primitive data types, as well as Object, String, and character arrays.

Tip

The `print(String)` and `print(char[])` methods are synchronized. This helps ensure that the contents of the String or character array they're printing will not change in the middle of the print.

BufferedOutputStream

This class allows you to write bytes to a buffer. Once the buffer is filled, its contents are written to the file.

FileDescriptor

There is one more way to create a FileOutputStream object, and that's by using a constructor that takes a FileDescriptor object. FileDescriptors represent an existing, open file. A FileDescriptor object is a handle to the open file, but it does not have any methods you can use other than a method called `valid()` that returns true if the file it represents exists and is open.

You can get a FileDescriptor object by invoking a FileOutputStream's or RandomAccessFile's `getFD()` method. It is sometimes necessary to use a FileDescriptor if you want to create another stream to an existing stream.

Here's the idea: you have an existing stream; you want to create another stream object that references the same underlying file. However, streams do not supply a method that allows you to retrieve the name of the underlying file. Nor do they supply a method that allows you to retrieve a File object for the underlying file. However, FileOutputStream and RandomAccessFile do supply the magical `getFD()` method.

So, if you do not know the File object or the file name the stream refers to, you must use the FileDescriptor object returned by `getFD()` to create your new stream.

(You can also create a new RandomAccessFile using a FileDescriptor.)

Answers to the Exercises

Exercise 11.1

```java
import java.io.*;

class NewFile {
    public static void main(String[] args) {
        if (args.length != 1) {
            System.out.println("Supply a file name.");
            System.exit(1);
        }

        try {
            File f = new File(args[0]);
            if (f.exists())
                System.out.println(args[0] + " already exists.");
            else
                new FileOutputStream(f);
        } catch (IOException io) {
            System.out.println(io.getMessage());
        }
    }
}
```

Exercise 11.2

```java
import java.io.*;

class Phone {
    static String fileName = "Phone.test";

    public static void main(String[] args) {
        try {
            FileOutputStream out = createFile();
            writeFile(out);
        } catch (IOException io) {
            System.out.println(io.getMessage());
        }
    }
```

continued

```
    static FileOutputStream createFile() throws IOException {
        File f = new File(fileName);
        FileOutputStream out = new FileOutputStream(f);
        return out;
    }
    static void writeFile(FileOutputStream out) throws IOException {
        DataOutputStream ds = null;
        try {
            ds = new DataOutputStream(out);
            ds.writeInt(5551212);
        } finally {
            if (ds != null)
                ds.close();
        }
    }
}
```

Exercise 11.3

The missing code is:

```
    out.seek(1);
    out.writeBytes("2");
    out.seek(3);
    out.writeBytes("4");
```

Review Questions

Question 1: What are valid parameters for the FilterInputStream constructor?

a) no parameter
b) InputStream
c) File
d) RandomAccessFile
e) DataInput
f) all of the above
g) a and b

Question 2:   To create a file you can use an instance of class:

a) File
b) RandomAccessFile
c) FileOutputStream
d) any of these
e) b and c

Question 3:   To create a new directory, you can use an instance of class:

a) File
b) RandomAccessFile
c) FileOutputStream
d) any of these
e) b and c

Question 4:   What will the result be of executing the following program:

```
import java.io.*;

class B {
   public static void main(String[] args) {
      try {
         File f = new File("B.test");
         FileOutputStream out = new FileOutputStream(f);
      } catch (IOException io) {
         System.out.println(io.getMessage());
      }
   }
}
```

a) It will throw an IOException which will be caught
b) It will run fine, but no file will result since nothing was written to it
c) It will run fine, the file "B.test" will exist after it runs, and the file's size will be 0

referred to by file

Question 5: **If file is an instance of a RandomAccessFile whose length is greater than 0, the line:**

```
file.seek(file.length() - 1);
```

will:

a) position the file pointer at the end of the file (after the last character)
b) position the file pointer just before the last character
c) will cause seek() to throw an IOException

Question 6: **You can attach a FilterOutputStream object to:**

a) An underlying file
b) Another FilterOutputStream object
c) A FilterInputStream object
d) all of these
e) a or b

Question 7: **To delete a file, you can use an instance of class:**

a) FileOutputStream
b) RandomAccessFile
c) File

Answers to the Review Questions

Question 1   b.   Only objects of type InputStream are valid parameters to pass to create a new FilterInput-Stream object.

Question 2   e.   RandomAccessFile and DataOutputStream will create a new file. File will not.

Question 3   a.   The File class contains a method called mkdir() that will create a new directory.

Question 4   c.   This is valid code and will run fine, creating an empty file called "B.test."

Question 5   b.   You can position the file pointer at the end of the file by setting it to `file.length()`.

Question 6   e.   A FilterOutputStream can be attached to any OutputStream subclass. This includes other filter streams as well as file streams.

Question 7   c.   You can use the `delete()` method defined in File to delete a file.

CHAPTER *12*

Threads

You should know how to handle exceptions before attempting to tackle threads, because a number of thread methods throw exceptions.

This chapter also illustrates threads using a couple of applets. The more you know about graphical user interfaces and applets, the better.

One of the coolest aspects to Java is its ability to easily perform multiple tasks concurrently. Java builds multitasking into its keywords and into its core set of classes. Such foresight not only makes multitasking easier, as an add-on class library might in C, but it also makes multitasking platform-independent, object-oriented, and part of the language itself.

Multitasking also helps make Java a natural language for the Internet. For example, your program can download a file in the background while running a Java applet in the foreground.

Java enables multitasking through the use of threads. Your program can create new instances of class Thread or subclasses of Thread to represent a thread of control. There is a thread life cycle that helps you keep track of what a thread is doing, there are keywords to coordinate among competing threads, and there are rules about scheduling threads and assigning priorities to them.

What's on the Test

The test covers four aspects to multitasking:

1. The basics of supplying behavior for a thread
2. Coordinating between threads using the synchronized keyword
3. Communicating between threads using the wait() and notify() methods
4. Scheduling threads

Objectives for this Chapter

- Subclass threads to provide their behavior.
- Implement the Runnable interface to provide the behavior of a thread.
- Start execution of a thread.
- Use the wait() method.
- Describe the interaction between a thread, the wait() method, and the object lock.
- Define the behavior of a thread which invokes the notify() or notifyAll() methods.
- Define the interaction between a thread, the notify() or notifyAll() methods, the object lock, and any thread that has invoked wait().
- Evaluate statements regarding thread scheduling.
- Demonstrate the use of the synchronized keyword to require a thread of execution to obtain an object lock prior to proceeding.
- Identify when conditions might prevent a thread from executing.

An Overview

Java builds multitasking right into its language keywords as well as into a core set of classes. Java represents a thread of execution using an instance of class Thread. Threads can run independently of each other, though they can also interact with each other. To help coordinate among threads, you can use the keyword synchronized.

A Java program runs until the only threads left running are daemon threads. The Java runtime consists of daemon threads that run your program. A Thread can be set as a daemon or user thread when it is created.

In a standalone program, your class runs until your main() method exits—unless your main() method creates more threads.

You can initiate your own thread of execution by creating a Thread object, invoking its start() method, and providing the behavior that tells the thread what to do. The thread will run until its run() method exits, after which it will come to a halt—thus ending its life cycle.

Telling a Thread What to Do

Start execution of a thread.

The only way to make a thread useful is to tell it what to do. The following example is *not* the way. There's nothing stopping you from creating a new Thread instance and invoking its start() method, like this:

```
Thread t = new Thread();
t.start(); // useless. . .
```

When you invoke a thread's start() method, the Java runtime will invoke the Thread's run() method. However, the Thread class, by default, doesn't provide any behavior for run(). This thread will end mighty quickly and will not have accomplished anything useful.

There are two ways to tell a thread what to do. You can subclass the Thread class and override the `run()` method, or you can implement the Runnable interface and indicate an instance of this class will be the thread's target.

Here's an example of each approach.

Subclassing Thread

Subclass threads to provide their behavior.

Subclassing the Thread class is easy.

When you subclass a Thread, you must override a method named `run()` to provide behavior for the thread.

Here's an example of a bouncing ball—it continuously reverses direction when it reaches the top or bottom of the screen. Figure 12-1 shows the ball somewhere in the middle of its travels up and down the applet.

Figure 12-1
A Screen Snapshot of
a Bouncing Ball

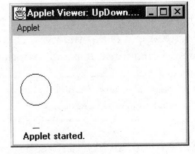

Here's the applet:

```
import java.awt.*;
import java.applet.Applet;
```

continued

```java
public class UpDown extends Applet {
    static int RADIUS = 20;
    static int X = 30;
    public int y = 30;

    public void init() {
        new BounceThread(this).start();
    }

    public void paint(Graphics g) {
        g.setColor(Color.blue);
        g.drawOval(X - RADIUS, y - RADIUS,
            2 * RADIUS, 2 * RADIUS);
    }
}

class BounceThread extends Thread {
    UpDown applet;
    int    yDir = +1;
    int    incr = 10;
    int    sleepFor = 100;
    BounceThread(UpDown a) {
        this.applet = a;
    }

    public void run() {
        while (true) {
            applet.y += (incr * yDir);
            applet.repaint();

            if (applet.y - UpDown.RADIUS < incr ||
                    applet.y + UpDown.RADIUS + incr >
applet.size().height)
                yDir *= -1;

            try {
                sleep(sleepFor);
            } catch (InterruptedException e) {
            }
        }
    }
}
```

It's often useful to tie the thread life cycle to the applet life cycle, so that when the applet goes away from the screen, the threads pause, and when the applet returns to the screen, the threads resume. In this applet, I've omitted these methods to isolate the run() method.

We'll tie threads to applets at the end of the chapter, in the section "What's Not on the Test," after you've learned more about the thread life cycle.

This applet creates a new thread and supplies a paint() method to draw a circle. The thread moves the circle's y value up and down, issuing a repaint and then going to sleep for 1/10 of a second. You'll learn about the sleep() method at the end of this chapter, but it should be fairly clear what it does: it puts a thread to sleep for a specified number of milliseconds. The thread reverses the direction it moves the ball's y value whenever the ball reaches the top or bottom of the applet's window. I've also taken the ball's (that is, the oval's) radius into account so that the ball appears to bounce off the inside edge of the applet.

The drawOval() method used by paint() draws an oval given the left and top of the oval, so I've offset where I draw the oval to take the radius into account.

Implementing Runnable

Implement the Runnable interface to provide the behavior of a thread.

Instead of creating a Thread subclass, we can write this code with only one class definition. We can accomplish this by implementing the Runnable interface and specifying our Java applet as the thread's target.

The Runnable interface can supply the behavior for a thread. This interface defines one method that must be implemented: run(). A Thread can look to its target—an object whose class implements Runnable—to find its run() behavior.

When the thread needs to invoke its `run()` behavior, we can make certain the thread knows to look to its target object for the `run()` method.

Here's an example of the same bouncing ball, this time implemented using the Runnable interface instead of a Thread subclass:

```java
import java.awt.*;
import java.applet.Applet;

public class UpDown extends Applet implements Runnable {
    static int RADIUS = 20;
    static int X = 30;
    public int y = 30;
    Thread t;
    public void init() {
        Thread t = new Thread(this);
        t.start();
    }
    public void paint(Graphics g) {
        g.setColor(Color.blue);
        g.drawOval(X - RADIUS, y - RADIUS,
            2 * RADIUS, 2 * RADIUS);
    }

    public void run() {
        int yDir = +1;
        int incr = 10;
        int sleepFor = 100;

        while (true) {
            y += (incr * yDir);
            repaint();
            if (y - RADIUS < incr ||
                    y + RADIUS + incr > size().height)
                yDir *= -1;

            try {
                t.sleep(sleepFor);
            } catch (InterruptedException e) {
            }
        }
    }
}
```

The Thread knows to look to its target because we have supplied a target object when we created the Thread instance.

We did this in the `init()` method with the line:

```
Thread t = new Thread(this);
```

In this case, we are indicating that the Applet object itself will be the target (that's why we used this). That's also why the Applet implemented the Runnable interface and supplied a run() method.

This version of UpDown is somewhat simpler than the first version. The run() method does not need to access the applet's instance or class variables through references anymore, since both run() and these variables are now defined in the same class definition. We do, however, have to keep track of the Thread instance, so that we can use this reference to invoke its sleep() method in run().

Exercise 12.1

Rewrite the following program to implement the Runnable interface rather than using a Thread subclass. This applet continually displays numbers in blue, one number per second. If the number is a prime, the applet displays the number in red.

Here is the code:

```
import java.awt.*;
import java.applet.Applet;

public class Ex1 extends Applet {
    Color        color = Color.red;
    int          candidate = 3;
    PrimeThread  prime;

    public void init() {
        prime = new PrimeThread(this);
        prime.start();
    }
```

continued

```java
    public void paint(Graphics g) {
        g.setColor(color);
        g.drawString(new Integer(candidate).toString(), 30, 40);
    }

}
class PrimeThread extends Thread {
    Ex1 target;

    PrimeThread (Ex1 target) {
        this.target = target;
    }

    public void run() {
        int candidate;
        for (candidate = 3; ; candidate++) {
            if (isPrime(candidate))
                target.color = Color.red;
            else
                target.color = Color.blue;

            target.candidate = candidate;
            target.repaint();

            try {
                sleep(1000);
            } catch (InterruptedException ie) {
            }
        }
    }

    public boolean isPrime(int number) {
        boolean isPrime = true;

        for (int i = 2; i < number - 1 && isPrime; i++) {
            if ( (number % i ) == 0)
                isPrime = false;
        }
        return isPrime;
    }

}
```

Thread Life Cycles

It's often useful to think of a thread as having a life cycle. Thread life cycle states take the descriptive names "new thread," "alive" (made up of two states, "runnable" "not runnable"), and "dead." These states are shown in Figure 12-2. We'll look at these states, because this progression makes clearer what happens to a thread in a program.

Figure 12-2
The States of a
ThreadLlife Cycle

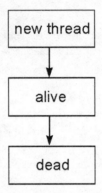

Creating a new Thread instance puts the thread into the "new thread" state. It's not "alive" until someone invokes the thread's start() method. The thread is then "alive" and "runnable" and will respond to the method isAlive() by returning true. The thread will continue to return true to isAlive() until it is "dead," no matter whether it is "runnable" or "not runnable."

Figure 12-3
A Thread that is
"Alive" can be
"Runnable" or "Not
Runnable"

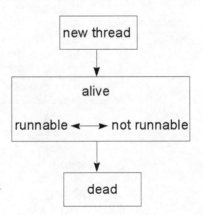

A thread can transition in and out of a "runnable" state by any number of incidents that fall under two broad categories:

1. scheduling
2. programmer control

We'll look at scheduling first, and then at programmer control.

Scheduling

Evaluate statements regarding thread scheduling.

Threads have priorities. The thread with the highest priority is the one that Java runs. All the other threads have to wait. If more than one thread has the same highest priority, Java will switch between them.

If two threads are "alive" with the same highest priority, the JVM switches between them, usually quickly enough so that you never realize they are alternating execute-sleep-execute-sleep cycles. Java will switch between any number of threads with the same highest priority.

The priority numbers for threads falls between the range of Thread.MIN_PRIORITY and Thread.MAX_PRIORITY. The default priority, Thread.NORM_PRIORITY, is typically midway between these two. New threads take on the priority of the thread that spawned them.

You can explicitly set the priority of a thread using setPriority(), and you can get the priority of a thread using getPriority().

As you might expect, if a thread is currently executing and you use set-Priority() to set a thread's priority to something less than it was before, the thread might stop executing, since there might now be another thread with a higher priority.

You can use priorities to help ensure your program responds to the user as expected. For example, let's say you are implementing a special kind of Web browser. You can set the thread to read the Web page over the Internet at a lower priority than a thread that responds to the user clicking the "stop" button. This way, your browser is likely to respond immediately when the user clicks "stop," rather than waiting until a large page is downloaded because the communication thread would not yield control.

The Java Virtual Machine determines the priority of when a thread can run based on its priority ranking, but that doesn't mean that a lower-priority thread will not run. This is important, because you should not rely on priorities to predict precisely what will occur in your program and when. For example, you should not rely on priorities to determine the correctness of an algorithm.

You don't have to rely on the Java Virtual Machine to switch between threads with the same priority. The currently executing thread can yield control by invoking `yield()`. If you invoke `yield()`, Java will pick a new thread to run. However, it is possible the thread that just yielded might run again immediately if it is the highest-priority thread.

Monitors and Synchronization

Demonstrate the use of the `synchronized` keyword to require a thread of execution to obtain an object lock prior to proceeding.

Working with concurrent threads sounds like a great idea, but we can create a many-headed monster if we're not careful. All these threads running about doing their own thing can get confusing, and threads might start to step on each others' toes. What if multiple threads need to change the same data? What if multiple threads each want to display something to the user? Will their efforts conflict with each other?

Here's an example of what might go wrong. Imagine an airline ticketing application. A ticket agent wants to assign a passenger to a seat. So he calls up a picture of a jet and looks at a map of the open seats. He looks for a minute or two until he spots a lovely window seat, 14A, then fills the passenger's request for a nice view and assigns the passenger to that seat.

In an application that uses only a single thread of execution, this works just fine. The ticket agent acts as the coordinator between multiple passengers who might request the same seat. For a multithreaded application, this has the potential for two passengers fighting over the same seat when they board the plane. (Perhaps you've seen this happening. Do you think their tickets were issued with a Java application? I think not.) The problem is that two separate threads might try to update the same data at once.

Here's a scenario. First, our ticket agent clicks a button to assign the passenger to the open seat. The thread of control used by this agent's program enters the method to update the seat. The method starts working with the data, finds the seat empty, and, having passed this test, is about to update the seat, when out of the blue...another ticket agent, working separately on another computer, oblivious of the first agent, does the same thing—clicks his button on his screen to assign his passenger to seat 14A. The thread of execution used by this second ticket agent interrupts the first thread (in this example) and performs its update. Then, the first thread regains access to the CPU and performs its update. Now, each agent has a ticket with that seat assignment. While the computer thinks only one person is assigned to the seat, each ticket agent has a printed ticket with an identical seat assignments.

To eliminate this type of problem, where one thread is interrupted in mid-step by another thread, Java provides a way to coordinate and synchronize between multiple threads. In fact, unlike other languages, Java builds this capability right into the language.

Each object and each class has a *monitor*. Threads can take temporary ownership of a monitor and release it later so that another thread can take temporary ownership of the same monitor. This is important as far as synchronizing between threads, because only one thread at a time can own a particular monitor.

By owning a monitor, a thread blocks all other threads from working with the other synchronized methods defined for an object or class that the monitor belongs to.

Let's take another look at the ticket reservation example and see what would have happened had the program used monitors. The first ticket agent clicks a button to assign a passenger to seat 14A. At this point, the program used by the first ticket agent would take control of the object's monitor that contained the method for updating the seat assignments—perhaps an instance of a class called SeatLayout or PassengerJet. Now, the second ticket agent clicks his button, but this time there's a slight delay.

His thread wants to take control of the monitor, but the thread cannot— another thread already owns it. So the second ticket agent's thread waits.

The first thread checks the seat 14A, finds it open, and performs the update. Then it exits, releasing the monitor. Now the second thread can have its turn. It takes control of the monitor, but when it goes to check 14A before the update, it finds the seat is already taken (which is exactly what we want). Now the ticket agent can assign the passenger to a different seat, and all is well again.

The way that a method takes control of an object's monitor is by entering a block of code or a method that's defined using the keyword synchronized.

There are three types of code that can be synchronized:

- class methods
- instance methods
- any block of code within a method

To declare a method to be synchronized, use the keyword synchronized when declaring the method, as in:

```
synchronized boolean reserveSeat(SeatID id) {
    // method body goes here . . .
}
```

Declaring a class method as synchronized is done similarly.

To declare a block of code as synchronized, use the keyword synchronized in front of that block. Then, in parentheses, indicate the object or the class whose monitor this code needs to acquire. Here's an example of synchronizing a block of code given an object reference called currentPlane:

```
boolean reserveSeat(SeatID id) {
    // method code can come before or after the block . . .

    synchronized (currentPlane) {
        // synchronized code goes here . . .
    }

    // method code can come before or after the block . . .
}
```

Using an object reference is appropriate in this example, where we only want one ticket agent assigning seats for a single plane—the plane they're currently working on—at one time.

Tip

Sometimes, it's appropriate to list a class after the synchronized keyword, such as when the code will change static data.

Using the synchronized keyword in a block of code takes the monitor from the class if it is a class method, or the object if it is an instance method.

Using the synchronized keyword guarantees that only one thread at a time will execute that object's or class' code.

If you have defined an instance method to be synchronized, any subclasses that override this method can be synchronized or not, according to their preference.

Tip

Synchronization stays in effect if you enter a synchronized method and call out to a non-synchronized method. So, if a subclass overrides a non-synchronized method and declares that method to be synchronized, the thread executing the synchronized method will continue to hold the monitor for an object, even if that method calls the non-synchronized superclass' method using super. The thread only gives up the monitor after the synchronized method returns.

Exercise 12.2

Variables cannot take the synchronized keyword. That means that, in the code below, even though one thread might be in the middle of updateBalance(), another thread might still come along and read the balance.

However, you can provide accessor methods for a variable and make that *accessor* method synchronized. Rewrite the following class so that its variable is (in effect) synchronized by defining a synchronized accessor method.

```
class Account {
   double balance;
   synchronized void updateBalance(double amount) {
      balance += amount;    }
   }
}
```

Programmer Control

You'll often see `run()` methods that loop forever, as in:

```
public void run() {
    while (true) {
        // do something continuously, like show an animation. . .
    }
}
```

Does this mean this thread can never die? That its life cycle is different? No. Because other events can transition the thread out of its "runnable," "not runnable," and even "alive" states.

One way to make a thread die is to invoke the thread's `stop()` method.

Two ways you can keep a thread alive and transition it between "runnable" and "not runnable" are:

- putting it to sleep and waking it up
- pausing it and resuming it

These both relate to one thread at a time; there is no communication between threads. You put one thread to sleep or wake it up; you pause one thread or resume that thread. Neither of these ways to control a thread are on the test. However, as always, the explanations for these methods are presented at the end of this chapter, because, as an expert, others will expect you to know them!

What *is* on the test is a third way to transition threads between "runnable" and "not runnable." However, unlike the two approaches listed above, this third way allows threads to interact with each other and provides some coordination between them. This third way uses the methods `wait()`, `notify()`, and `notifyAll()`.

Using wait(), notify(), and notifyAll()

Use the wait() method.

Describe the interaction between a thread, the wait() method, and the object lock.

Define the behavior of a thread which invokes the notify() or notifyAll() methods.

Define the interaction between a thread, the notify() or notifyAll() methods, the object lock, and any thread that has invoked wait().

Synchronization stops bugs from occurring where one thread changes the state of an object that another thread had depended on to be stable. However, synchronization does nothing as far as communicating between threads. Sometimes, you need a way for one thread to be informed of what another thread is doing. For example, thread number 1 might be waiting for thread number 2 to calculate some result. When thread number 2 achieves this result, it should be able to notify thread number 1 that it found the result thread number 1 was waiting for.

Java builds a wait-notify mechanism into the Object class. By using the methods wait(), notify(), and notifyAll(), any thread can wait for some condition in an object to change, and any thread can notify all threads waiting on that object's condition that the condition has changed and that they should continue.

Tip

A common scenario where this is useful is where one thread produces data for an object, and another thread is using the data in the object.

Here's a simple example of using wait() and notify(). The following applet, named ClickApplet, starts by creating a couple of ClickCanvas instances in its init() method. Each one of these special Canvas subclasses spawns a new thread in its constructor. The thread's run() method (supplied by ClickCanvas) waits on a condition. It starts waiting when it invokes wait(). The condition it's waiting to change is the boolean value defined in the applet named clicked.

As soon as clicked becomes true, the Canvas continues. How does the Canvas' thread know when the condition becomes true? The mouseDown() method in the applet, running in the user input thread, notifies the Canvas' thread that the condition has changed. It does this by invoking notify().

Here's the code.

```java
import java.awt.*;
import java.applet.*;

public class ClickApplet extends Applet {

    boolean clicked;
    int counter;

    public void init() {
        add(new ClickCanvas(this));
        add(new ClickCanvas(this));
    }

    public boolean mouseDown(Event e, int x, int y) {
        synchronized (this) {
            clicked = true;
            notify();
        }
        counter++;

        Thread.currentThread().yield();
        clicked = false;
        return super.mouseDown(e, x, y);
    }

}
```

continued

```
class ClickCanvas extends Canvas implements Runnable {
   ClickApplet applet;

   ClickCanvas(ClickApplet applet) {
      this.applet = applet;
      resize(30, 30);
      new Thread(this).start();
   }

   public void run() {
      while (true) {
         synchronized (applet) {
            while (!applet.clicked) {
               try {
                  applet.wait();
               } catch (InterruptedException x) {
               }
            }
         }
         repaint();
      }
   }

   public void paint(Graphics g) {
      g.drawString(new Integer(applet.counter).toString(), 10, 20);
   }

}
```

This applet counts the number of clicks the user makes in the applet. Of course, we could have simply made mouseDown() in the applet display the clicks and update the counter variable, but we want the above code to show how to coordinate between threads. Without wait() and notify() (or without a direct method call), there is no way for the ClickCanvas objects to know when to update their displays.

This applet exhibits some interesting behavior. Here's what it looks like when it starts:

Figure 12-4
ClickApplet When it
First Appears in the
Appletviewer

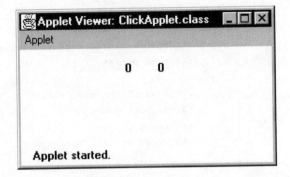

As the user starts clicking the applet, only one number in one ClickCanvas object updates at a time. Here are two screen shots showing successive clicks:

Figure 12-5
ClickApplet After
the First Click

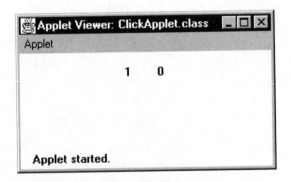

Figure 12-6
ClickApplet After the
Second Click

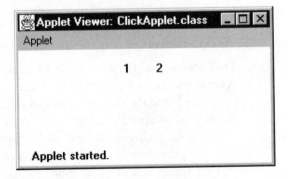

Why aren't both ClickCanvas objects updated at the same time? Why do they seem to leap-frog each other? Because we have only invoked `notify()`, rather than `notifyAll()`.

When the waiting thread pauses, it relinquishes the object's monitor and waits to be notified that it should try to reacquire it. It does this with a call to wait(). Notice that we indicate which object we're waiting on. In this case, we're waiting on the applet. Since we keep the applet in an instance variable named applet in the ClickCanvas object, we can wait on the applet object by writing:

```
applet.wait();
```

Tip

Generally, wait() is placed inside of a while clause. The idea is that just because a thread wakes up, the condition it's waiting on has not necessarily changed. So, this condition should be rechecked and the thread should wait again if necessary.

You'll also notice two other things about the call to wait(). First, it is placed inside of a try-catch block. The wait() method might throw an InterruptedException, so the code must be prepared to handle that. Second, wait() is placed inside a synchronized block. The wait() and notify() methods can only be invoked from synchronized code. The monitor that the block or method acquires for synchronization must belong to the object that the thread will wait on. In fact, if you try to invoke wait() on an object without owning the object's monitor, the Java runtime will throw an IllegalMonitorStateException.

Background

Placing the calls to wait() and notify() within synchronized code does two things. First, it guarantees that the currently executing code own the monitor, so that this code can give it up in the call to wait() or notify(). Second, it helps ensure the contents of the object being used to determine when the conditions are stable. For example, since a while loop surrounds the wait() call, it's important that the condition doesn't change to false before the code escapes the while loop after a notify() call.

The notify() method wakes up one thread waiting to reacquire the monitor for the object. The thread it awakens is generally the one that has been waiting the longest. If you know you only have one thread waiting on a condition, you can feel free to use notify(). Then, your application's behavior is predictable.

Just because the thread that `notify()` awakens is generally the one that has been waiting the longest, you should not rely on this for your algorithm to work. It is not guaranteed to awaken the longest-waiting thread; it is only most likely to awaken that one.

If you have more than one thread (or if there is the potential to have more than one thread) waiting on a condition, you should use `notifyAll()` instead of `notify()`. The `notifyAll()` method wakes up all threads waiting to reacquire the monitor for the object.

Exercise 12.3

Rewrite ClickApplet so that both threads are notified when the user clicks.

Why a Thread Might Not Execute

Identify when conditions might prevent a thread from executing.

Here is a list of reasons why a thread might be alive but still not run:

- The thread is not the highest priority thread and so cannot get CPU time.
- The thread has been put to sleep using the `sleep()` method.
- There is more than one thread with the same highest priority, and the Java Virtual Machine is switching between these threads; at the moment, the thread in question is awaiting CPU time.
- Someone has suspended the thread using the `suspend()` method.
- The thread is waiting on a condition because someone invoked `wait()` for the thread.
- The thread has explicitly yielded control by invoking `yield()`.

Exercise 12.4

or applications

> Write four applets, each one illustrating a different aspect from the above list of reasons why a thread might not run.

What's Not on the Test

As many questions as there might be on threads, multitasking is a big topic. Here are some of the more important aspects to threads that every Java expert should know about.

Other Ways to Pause and Restart a Thread

You can make a thread "not runnable" but keep it alive by using `suspend()` or `sleep()`.

When you `suspend()` a thread, you must invoke `resume()` for that thread to wake it up again. When you put a thread to `sleep()`, you put it to sleep for a specified number of milliseconds. When this time has elapsed, the thread wakes up and continues with what it was doing.

Tip

Putting a thread to sleep is a convenient way to slow down an animation. For example, rather than letting one frame move to the next in a blur, you could put a pause of _ of a second (for example), to help the user keep up with the animation.

Thread and Applet Life Cycles

In addition to these methods, there is another aspect to a thread's life cycle that's important, especially when dealing with applets. You should tie all of your threads' life cycles to the applet life cycle.

Here is a new version of the bouncing ball that is now tied to the applet life cycle. I've rewritten the version that uses a Thread subclass, but of course this would work just as well for the version that implements the Runnable interface. If the Web page containing the applet goes off-screen, the applet should stop, and that's what happens here. When the Web page comes back on-screen, the applet will start again.

Here's the new code:

```java
import java.awt.*;
import java.applet.Applet;

public class UpDown extends Applet {
    static int RADIUS = 20;
    static int X = 30;
    public int y = 30;
    BounceThread thread;

    public void init() {
        thread = new BounceThread(this);
    }

    public void start() {
        if (thread.isAlive())
            thread.resume();
        else
            thread.start();
    }

    public void stop() {
        thread.suspend();
    }

    public void destroy() {
        thread.stop();
    }

    public void paint(Graphics g) {
        g.setColor(Color.blue);
        g.drawOval(X - RADIUS, y - RADIUS,
            2 * RADIUS, 2 * RADIUS);
    }
}

class BounceThread extends Thread {
    UpDown applet;
    int    yDir = +1;
    int    incr = 10;
    int    sleepFor = 100;

    BounceThread(UpDown a) {
        this.applet = a;
    }
```

continued

```
    public void run() {
        while (true) {
            applet.y += (incr * yDir);
            applet.repaint();

            if (applet.y - UpDown.RADIUS < incr ||
                    applet.y + UpDown.RADIUS + incr >
    applet.size().height)
                yDir *= -1;

            try {
                sleep(sleepFor);
            } catch (InterruptedException e) {
            }
        }
    }
}
```

Other Thread Methods

Generally, a thread created by the user is a user thread. However, you can mark a thread as a daemon thread before you start it if you like by using setDaemon(). The Java Virtual Machine keeps running until all user threads have ended.

You can name threads using setName() or by supplying a name to the Thread's constructor. You can retrieve a thread's name using getName(). Naming a thread could be useful in identifying a particular thread if you are using more than one.

There is a static method named currentThread() that retrieves the currently executing thread. This allows you to put the current thread to sleep, for example, or to invoke some other method on it.

The stop() method is overloaded to take a Throwable parameter. If you invoke this version of stop(), the thread is halted and throws an instance of the Throwable class you supplied it.

The join() method waits for a thread to die before continuing. You might use join() to stop execution until a thread has completed its task.

You can treat threads as a set by using a ThreadGroup. The ThreadGroup class defines most of the methods that affect individual threads. By assigning a thread to a ThreadGroup when you create the thread, you can then affect many threads at once. For example, you can stop all threads in a Thread-Group from executing by invoking the ThreadGroup's stop() method.

Answers to the Exercises

Exercise 12.1

Here is one solution:

```java
import java.awt.*;
import java.applet.Applet;

public class Ans1 extends Applet implements Runnable {
    Color        color = Color.red;
    int          candidate = 3;
    Thread       prime;

    public void init() {
        prime = new Thread(this);
        prime.start();
    }

    public void paint(Graphics g) {
        g.setColor(color);
        g.drawString(new Integer(candidate).toString(), 30, 40);
    }

    public void run() {
        for (candidate = 3; ; candidate++) {
            if (isPrime(candidate))
                color = Color.red;
            else
                color = Color.blue;

            repaint();

            try {
                prime.sleep(1000);
            } catch (InterruptedException ie) {
            }
        }
    }

    public boolean isPrime(int number) {
        boolean isPrime = true;
```

continued

```
        for (int i = 2; i < number - 1 && isPrime; i++) {
           if ( (number % i ) == 0)
              isPrime = false;
        }
        return isPrime;
     }

  }
```

A common mistake in making this conversion is to forget to write `implements Runnable` in the class definition. If you forget this part, the compiler will complain about not finding a constructor matching the way you are trying to create the thread. The issue here is that the Thread constructor that takes a target for the `run()` method takes an instance of Runnable. Remember, an object of a class that implements an interface is considered an instance of that class. You can think of it like this: `instanceof` will return true for a class that implements an interface. So, if you forget to define your class (your applet, in this case) as implementing the Runnable interface, it won't match one of the Thread's constructors.

Exercise 12.2

```
class Account {
   private double balance;

   synchronized double getBalance() {
      return balance;
   }

   synchronized void setBalance(double newBalance) {
      balance = newBalance;
   }

   synchronized void updateBalance(double amount) {
      setBalance(getBalance() + amount);
   }
}
```

With this rewrite, no other thread can access the balance field (unless it circumvents the accessor method protocol) when the `updateBalance()` method is in the middle of altering its value.

Exercise 12.3

Simply change the call to `notify()` to `notifyAll()`. The rest of the applet stays the same.

Exercise 12.4

Here are four programs that illustrate the first four items from this list:

- The thread is not the highest priority thread and so cannot get CPU time.

```
class Ex1204a {
    public static void main(String[] args) {
        MyThread t1 = new MyThread(1);
        MyThread t2 = new MyThread(2);

        t1.setPriority(Thread.MAX_PRIORITY);
        t2.setPriority(Thread.MIN_PRIORITY);
        t1.start();
        t2.start();
    }
}

class MyThread extends Thread {
    int id;
    MyThread(int id) {
        this.id = id;
    }

    public void run() {
        for (int i = 0; i < 100; i++)
            System.out.println("My id is " + id);
    }
}
```

The output from this program is 100 lines of "My id is 1" and then, once that thread has completed, 100 lines of "My id is 2."

- The thread has been put to sleep using the sleep() method:

```
class Ex1204b {
    public static void main(String[] args) {
        MyThread t1 = new MyThread(1);
        MyThread t2 = new MyThread(2);

        t1.setPriority(Thread.MAX_PRIORITY);
        t2.setPriority(Thread.MIN_PRIORITY);

        t1.start();
        t2.start();
    }
}

class MyThread extends Thread {
    int id;
    MyThread(int id) {
        this.id = id;
    }

    public void run() {
        for (int i = 0; i < 100; i++) {
            if (id == 1 && i == 50) {
                try {
                    sleep(1000);
                } catch (InterruptedException x) {
                }
            }
            System.out.println("My id is " + id);
        }
    }
}
```

The output from this program is 50 lines of "My id is 1." Then, that thread goes to sleep, long enough (on my computer, at least) for the other thread to write out all of its lines ("My id is 2"). Then the first thread continues. With a shorter time, the sleeping thread would wake up and, with a higher priority than the currently running thread, get immediate access to the CPU and continue on.

- There is more than one thread with the same highest priority, and the Java Virtual Machine is switching between these threads; at the moment, the thread in question is awaiting CPU time:

```
class Ex1204c {
   public static void main(String[] args) {
      MyThread t1 = new MyThread(1);
      MyThread t2 = new MyThread(2);

      t1.other = t2;
      t2.other = t1;

      t1.start();
      t2.start();
   }
}

class MyThread extends Thread {
   int id;
   MyThread other;
   MyThread(int id) {
      this.id = id;
   }

   public void run() {
      for (int i = 0; i < 100; i++) {
         System.out.println("My id is " + id);
      }
   }
}
```

This program unpredictably alternates between displaying a few "My id is 1" messages and then a few "My id is 2" in the standard output.

- Someone has suspended the thread using the `suspend()` method:

```
class Ex1204d {
   public static void main(String[] args) {
      MyThread t1 = new MyThread(1);
      MyThread t2 = new MyThread(2);

      t1.other = t2;
      t2.other = t1;
```

```
        t1.start();
        t2.start();
    }
}

class MyThread extends Thread {
    int id;
    MyThread other;
    MyThread(int id) {
        this.id = id;
    }

    public void run() {
        if (id == 1)
            other.suspend();
        for (int i = 0; i < 100; i++) {
            System.out.println("My id is " + id);
        }
        if (id == 1)
            other.resume();
    }
}
```

This program displays all of the "My id is 1" messages first, because it suspends the other thread. Once this thread's run() method is about to end, it resumes the other thread, and it then displays all of its "My id is 2" messages.

Review Questions

Question 1: **If you would like to create a thread and supply a target that implements the Runnable interface, you can write:**

a) Thread t = new Thread(target);

b) Thread t = new Thread(); t.target = target;

c) Thread t = new Thread(); t.start(target);

Question 2: **Why might a thread be alive but not be the currently executing thread?**

a) It is the only thread currently running
b) It has been suspended
c) It has been resumed
d) It has been notified of some condition
e) All of the above

Question 3: **What may make this method throw an exception (other than InterruptedException) when it runs (if anything)?**

```
public void holdIt(Object ref) {
    synchronized (this) {
        try {
            ref.wait();
        } catch (InterruptedException x) {
        }
    }
}
```

a The call to wait() is not within a while loop
b) The holdIt() method must be synchronized
c) The current thread does not own the monitor it needs to invoke wait()
d) nothing is wrong with this method definition—it will run fine and will not throw an exception

Question 4: **If you have created two threads, one with a priority of Thread.MAX_PRIORITY and one with a normal, default priority, then which of these statements is true?**

a) The thread with the normal priority will definitely not run until the thread with the maximum priority ends
b) The thread with the normal priority will never run, even after the thread with the maximum priority ends
c) Neither of these statements is true

Question 5:   The `wait()` method is defined in class:

a) Thread
b) Applet
c) Object
d) Runnable

Question 6:   You can set a thread's priority:

a) When you first create the thread
b) At any time after you create the thread
c) both of these

Answers to the Review Questions

Question 1:   a.   You must supply the target for the thread when you create it.

Question 2:   b.   A suspended thread is not currently running and waits until it is resumed.

Question 3:   c.   The code synchronizes on `this`, but then invokes `wait()` for `ref`, which might be a different object. If it were a different object, the call to `wait()` would cause Java to throw an IllegalMonitorStateException.

To make this code hunky-dory, it could be written like this:

```
public void holdIt(Object ref) {
   synchronized (ref) {
      try {
         ref.wait();
      } catch (InterruptedException x) {
      }
   }
}
```

This time, the code synchronizes on the object `ref`, and then uses `ref` to invoke `wait()`.

Question 4:   c.   That's right. You should not rely on thread priorities for algorithm correctness. Even a thread with a lower priority may get some time to run. It will just get less time. But simply assigning one thread to the maximum priority and another thread to the minimum priority does not guarantee that the lower priority thread will not run. These priorities would just make one thread less likely to get access to the CPU, but it wouldn't stop it completely.

Question 5:   c.   All Objects can respond to `wait()`.

Question 6:   b.   You can set a priority for a thread using `setPriority()`. There is no constructor that takes a thread priority.

CHAPTER *13*

Graphical User Interfaces

You should already know the concepts behind building a graphical interface. For example, you should know how to design an event-driven program, where the program sets up a user interface and then waits for and responds to user input events.

You should also have experience using applets and graphical Java programs so that you've already seen components such as buttons, text fields, and check boxes and have a sense of what these do.

This chapter also assumes you can run an applet. If you'd like to review how to place an <applet> tag into an HTML page, check out Chapter 17.

"Graphical user interfaces" is a big topic. Entire books have been written on Java's Abstract Windowing Toolkit (AWT), which is the name of the package containing the classes you use to build graphical user interfaces. In this chapter, I'll review the basics of the AWT package as well as the advanced aspects you'll be expected to know for the test.

Until now, this book has, for the most part, separated issues of Java programming from issues relating to the user interface. To help make Java programming snippets clear, I have mostly used character-mode, stand-alone programs—as opposed to graphical, Web-based applets—to illustrate Java programming. In this chapter, we'll look exclusively at the classes and techniques of building graphical applications.

Exam number 310-020 has questions about Java 1.0.2, and exam number 310-022 has questions about Java 1.1. You should concentrate on learning the features specific to the release for which you plan to take the test.

In this chapter, I'll describe how to build a user interface up to handling events. There are some Component methods that are different in Java 1.0.2 and Java 1.1, and I'll point them out. It's important to note that all code is backwards compatible. However, code that uses features only found in Java 1.1 will of course only work in a Java 1.1 runtime environment.

The greatest area of change is with event handling. I've deferred the discussion about events to two follow-up chapters. Chapter 14 discusses how events work in Java 1.0.2. Chapter 15 discusses how events work in Java 1.1. You'll need to be familiar with both for the test.

What's on the Test

There are a lot of test questions relating to developing a user interface. You'll get a good sense of what you'll need to know as you look over the objectives for this chapter. You can group the aspects of creating a user interface into the following three categories:

1. Painting using low-level graphics methods
2. Creating and arranging a user interface
3. Responding to user input events

Painting using low-level graphics methods means overriding `paint()` and using a Graphics object to draw onto the screen.

Creating and arranging a user interface means, usually, overriding init() in an applet, or providing an init() method for a stand-alone program, creating the Components, and placing these Components into a Container using an appropriate Layout Manager. The test asks you to work with TextField, TextArea, and List Components, and FlowLayout, BorderLayout, and GridLayout Layout Managers.

Responding to user input events means, for Java 1.0.2, overriding the appropriate event method, accessing the fields in an Event object, and controlling how an event propagates up the Container hierarchy. For Java 1.1, it means specifying an object that acts as an event listener.

Objectives for this Chapter

- Implement the `paint()` method for Component classes.
- Describe the flow of control between the methods `repaint()` and `update()`.
- Use the following methods of the Graphics class: `drawString()`, `drawLine()`, `drawRect()`, `drawImage()`, `drawPolygon()`, `drawArc()`, `fillRect()`, `fillPolygon()`, `fillArc()`.
- Use Graphics methods in `paint()`.
- Obtain a Graphics object from an Image.
- Construct a TextArea and List that displays a specific number of lines.
- Construct a TextArea and TextField that displays a specific number of columns.
- Use of the Java 1.0.2 methods `show()`, `hide()`, `enable()`, `disable()`, `size()`, `setForeground()`, and `setBackground()` defined for the Component class.
- Use of the methods `add(Component)` and `add(String, Component)` for the Container class.
- List the classes in the `java.awt` package that are valid arguments to the `add()` methods and those that are not valid.
- Identify AWT classes which determine layouts for components with a container.
- Change the layout scheme associated with a Container instance.
- Identify the effects of BorderLayout, FlowLayout, and GridLayout.
- State strategies to achieve a dynamic resizing of a Component horizontally, vertically, both horizontally and vertically, and neither horizontally nor vertically.

- List the sequence of Component methods involved in redrawing where the drawing is initiated by both the programmer and the AWT package itself.
- Distinguish between methods invoked by the user thread and those normally invoked by AWT.

The Abstract Windowing Toolkit (AWT)

If you want to create a graphical user interface for your Java program, you've got to work with the java.awt package, referred to familiarly as AWT. This class library defines a slew of platform-independent classes that represent user interface elements.

I like to divide the classes in this package into three categories:

- *Components*, which are the things the user interacts with. Subclasses of Component includes List, TextField, TextArea. (It also includes Button, Checkbox, Choice, and more, but except in a small way, these Component subclasses are not on the test.)
- *Containers*, which are special types of Components that contain and arrange other Components.
- Other *helper classes*, such as Graphics, Color, and classes implementing LayoutManager, all of which are used by Components and Containers to draw and place things on the screen.

Figure 13-1 shows a hierarchy of the AWT Component and Container classes that are on the test. (Component and Container are both abstract classes, so they are shown with dashed edges.)

Figure 13-1
A Partial Component
and Container
Hierarchy

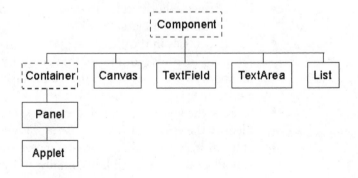

Figure 13-2 shows the three classes that implement the LayoutManager interface that are on the test.

Figure 13-2
Three LayoutManager
Classes

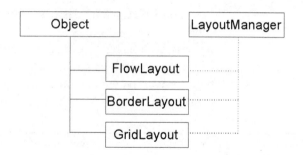

Figure 13-2
Three LayoutManager
Classes

Figure 13-3 shows the other AWT classes on the test.

Figure 13-3
The AWT Classes
Graphics, Color, and
Event

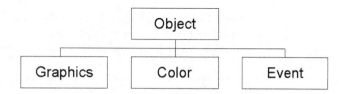

I'll talk about all of these types of classes and how they work in the course of this chapter. Naturally, this is not an exhaustive investigation into the AWT—I only dwell on those things on the test. However, with all the information discussed here, you'll still gain a very thorough understanding of the AWT.

A Quick Review of Applets

Java's Applet class is defined in the package `java.applet`, not in `java.awt`. However, the Applet class is a user interface component.

Applet descends from Panel. This means that Applets can do everything Panels can do (that is, they can contain a user interface), plus a little bit more.

That "little bit more" involves interacting with the Web browser. There are four life cycle methods that the browser (or appletviewer if you're running in a development environment) invokes at different stages of your applet's life.

- When the Applet instance is first instantiated, Java invokes the applet's `init()` method.
- When the Web page containing the applet is about to appear, Java invokes the applet's `start()` method.
- When the Web page is about to be replaced with another page, Java invokes the applet's `stop()` method.

Java can alternately call an applet's `start()` and `stop()` methods as the Web page containing the applet appears and is removed from the Web browser's display.

Tip

- When the Web page is removed from the browser's cache and the applet instance is about to go away, Java invokes the applet's `destroy()` method.

You can override any of these methods to support your own applet's behavior.

Typically, you would create a user interface in `init()`, pause and resume threads in `start()` and `stop()`, and halt threads in `destroy()`.

Tip

The paint() Method

Implement the paint() method for Component classes.

Objectives

Describe the flow of control between the methods `repaint()` and `update()`.

Objectives

The runtime environment tells every Component (and, naturally, every Container, because Container is a subclass of Component) when it is time to make something appear on the screen—that is, when to *redraw*. The runtime environment will tell a Component to redraw when it is *dirty*: when it has first appeared on the screen, when it is resized or its Container is resized, when something else on the screen (such as an overlapping window) that was covering the Component has gone away, or when the programmer has explicitly requested a redraw.

Java tells your Component to redraw by invoking its paint() method. The paint() method takes one parameter: an instance of class Graphics. You can use this instance to perform low-level drawing operations.

We'll take a look at the Graphics class in just a moment. The method declaration for paint() is:

```
public void paint(Graphics g)
```

You should put all of your drawing code into paint(), and no more than your drawing code. You want paint() to execute as quickly as possible. Don't put calculations into paint(), for example, or other things that will slow down the actual painting.

Repainting

List the sequence of Component methods involved in redrawing where the drawing is initiated by both the programmer and the AWT package itself.

Distinguish between methods invoked by the user thread and those normally invoked by AWT.

If you want to explicitly repaint a component, you should not call `paint()` directly. Instead, you should invoke your component's `repaint()` method.

The `repaint()` method is overloaded. The no-args version of `repaint()` does not cause your user interface to repaint right away. In fact, when `repaint()` returns, your component has not yet been repainted.: you've only issued a request for a repaint. However, there is another version of `repaint()` that requests the component be repainted within a certain number of milliseconds.

Tip

The `repaint()` method will cause AWT to invoke a component's `update()` method. AWT passes a Graphics object to `update()`—the same one that it passes to `paint()`. We'll cover the Graphics class in a moment. (For now, we're just getting the progression of repaint calls straight.)

The Graphics object that AWT hands to `update()` and `paint()` is different every time the Component is repainted.

Tip

When Java repaints on its own, such as when the user resizes an applet, the AWT does not invoke `update()`—it just calls `paint()` directly.

Warning

The `update()` method does three things in this order:

1. Clears the background of the object by filling it with its background color.
2. Sets the current drawing color to be its foreground color.
3. Invokes `paint()`, passing it the Graphics object it received.

Here is the sequence you should ingrain in your memory:

Figure 13-4
The Sequence of
repaint(), update(),
and paint()

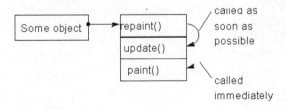

paint() and the Graphics Class

The `paint()` method takes an instance of the Graphics class. This object is a graphics context, platform-specific but with a platform-independent interface, that allows you to draw on the screen.

 The Graphics class defines lots of abstract methods for low-level drawing operations, such as drawing graphic primitives like lines and ovals, and setting drawing modes and colors. These abstract methods make the Graphics class an abstract class. Subclasses of Graphics implement the specific instructions that allow the graphics context to draw onto on-screen components or off-screen images. Most likely, you'll never see these Graphics subclasses, and you shouldn't care. They are platform-specific and depend on the operating environment your application is running in.

For example, running this program in Windows 95:

```java
import java.applet.Applet;
import java.awt.Graphics;

public class Gr extends Applet {
    public void paint(Graphics g) {
        System.out.println(g.getClass().getName());
    }
}
```

writes this class name to the screen:

```
sun.awt.win32.Win32Graphics
```

This program yields a different result when run on a Mac or under Solaris.

You can't write for this specific class, so it doesn't really matter what it is. Besides, all you care about as a Java programmer is the Graphics interface. That's what Java does well—hides the implementation of the specifics to let you concentrate on your application's design.

Drawing Using a Graphics Object

Use Graphics methods in paint().

Because Graphics is abstract, you cannot create a Graphics instance directly by invoking its constructor. When you draw inside of paint(), the AWT hands you a Graphics object to use. If you want to draw outside of paint(), you can get a Graphics object in one of two ways:

- If you already have some other Graphics object, you can create a copy of it using the create() method defined by Graphics.
- If you have a component and want a Graphics object for it, you can invoke the component's getGraphics() method.

Graphics objects have a state which includes its drawing color, paint mode, font, and clipping region. You can get and set any of these values.

The Graphics instance you receive in paint() is tied to the component responding to the paint() method. This means that any drawing you do using the Graphics class appears in the component.

Use the following methods of the Graphics class: drawString(), draw-Line(), drawRect(), drawImage(), drawPolygon(), drawArc(), fillRect(), fillPolygon(), fillArc().

The update() method and the paint() method are handed an instance of the Graphics class. Graphics defines lots of methods for drawing.

The Graphics methods use pixels as their units of measurement. Coordinates are also relative to the Component or Container they're displayed in. Horizontal (x) coordinates are measured from the left. Vertical (y) coordinates are measured from the top.

So, if a method calls for a baseline or corner point, you should supply measurements for that point as the number of pixels from the left and top edge of the window it is used in. Pixels are defined as `int` values.

Most of the methods in the Graphics class draw in the current foreground color. There's more information on color in the section "What's Not on the Test."

Tip

Following are some common Graphics methods you might use in `paint()`.

drawString()

This method draws the characters in a String object into the display. This method takes three parameters: String object (or string literal) to display and the baseline for the first character (the x and y coordinates for the first character).

Here is a classic example of using `drawString()` to create the "Hello, world" applet. The bottom, left of the "H" in "Hello, world" is at the x and y coordinates, which in this case is x=80, y=30.

```java
import java.awt.*;
import java.applet.*;

public class Str extends Applet {
    public void paint(Graphics g) {
        g.drawString("Hello, world!", 80, 30);
    }
}
```

The result in Windows 95 looks like this:

Figure 13-5
Using drawString()

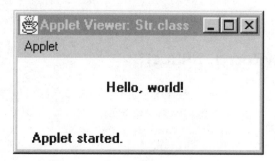

drawLine()

This method takes four parameters: the x, y location of the starting point, and the x, y location of the line's ending point. Here's an example of drawing a tic-tac-toe board.

```java
import java.awt.*;
import java.applet.*;

public class Tic extends Applet {
    public void paint(Graphics g) {
        g.drawLine(60, 5, 60, 175);
        g.drawLine(120, 5, 120, 175);
        g.drawLine(5, 60, 175, 60);
        g.drawLine(5, 120, 175, 120);
    }
}
```

The display looks like this:

Figure 13-6
Using drawLine()

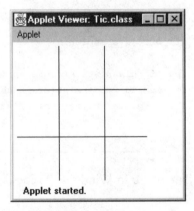

drawRect(), fillRect()

These methods draw a rectangle. The method `drawRect()` draws the outline of a rectangle; `fillRect()` draws a solid rectangle. Each of these methods take four parameters: the top, left corner of the rectangle, and the width and height of the rectangle. The left and right edges of the rectangle are at *x* and *x* + *width* respectively. The top and bottom edges of the rectangle are at *y* and *y* + *height* respectively.

Here's an example of drawing a variety of rectangles:

```java
import java.awt.*;
import java.applet.*;

public class Rect extends Applet {
    public void paint(Graphics g) {
        g.drawLine(60, 5, 60, 175);
        g.drawLine(120, 5, 120, 175);
        g.drawLine(5, 60, 175, 60);
        g.drawLine(5, 120, 175, 120);

        g.fillRect(80, 80, 20, 20);
    }
}
```

This code displays the following:

Figure 13-7
Using fillRect()

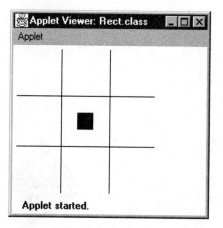

The drawOval() and fillOval() are very similar to drawRect() and fillRect(), except these draw ovals inside the rectangle defined by corresponding parameters to drawRect() and fillRect().

Tip

drawPolygon(), fillPolygon()

You can draw a shape with any number of sides using drawPolygon() or fillPolygon(). Each of these methods is overloaded. One version takes an array of x and y coordinates (int values) and the number of elements to use in the arrays. A second version takes a Polygon instance, which defines the x and y arrays as part of its instance data.

For example, the following code draws a wacky, five-sided shape:

```
import java.awt.*;
import java.applet.*;

public class Poly extends Applet {
    public void paint(Graphics g) {
        int[] xArray = {20, 60, 90, 70, 30};
        int[] yArray = {50, 4, 45, 90, 70};
        g.fillPolygon(xArray, yArray, 5);
    }
}
```

Here's what this code produces:

Figure 13-8
Using fillPolygon()

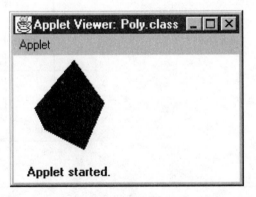

Notice how the last point connects back to the first.

drawArc(), fillArc()

These methods draw or fill an arc starting at a particular angle and moving counter-clockwise for the number of degrees you define. The 3 o'clock position is 0 degrees.

The documentation in Java 1.0.2 says that the x, y coordinate is the center of the arc, which is not correct; it is the top, left corner of the arc's bounding box.

To draw an arc, you supply:

- The arc's top, left corner as an x, y coordinate (similar to how you define a rectangle's top, left corner)
- The width and height of the arc (again, similar to how you define the width and height of an oval)
- The start angle
- The number of degrees to move along the arc (the end angle is *start angle + arc angle*)

For example, to draw the following arc:

Figure 13-9
Using drawArc()

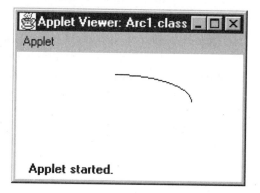

You could write code like the following:

```
import java.awt.*;
import java.applet.*;

public class Arc1 extends Applet {
    public void paint(Graphics g) {
        g.drawArc(20, 20, 150, 50, 0, 90);
    }
}
```

Notice that the x, y coordinates 20, 20 indicate the top, left of the bounding box of the arc. (Imagine continuing the arc so that it creates an oval. The left and top of the oval are at x=20, y=20.) Also, notice that 0 degrees is at the 3 o'clock position, and that we're moving counter-clockwise 90 degrees (one-quarter of the way around the oval).

Tip

You can also move in the negative direction, if you wish, so that you're moving clockwise around the oval, rather than counter-clockwise.

drawImage()

This method is overloaded to allow you a great deal of control over the way an image is displayed. The minimum parameters you need to supply are:

- An image to draw. This is an instance of the Image class.
- The x and y positions where the left and top corner of the image should appear.
- An image observer that communicates with the graphics system. This object helps notify the graphics system when the image is ready to be drawn—such as when it has been fully loaded over the Internet, for example.

There are also versions of drawImage() that specify a background color in which to draw transparent pixels (for example, when using a GIF image where you can define a particular pixel color to be transparent), and that specify height and width values for squeezing or stretching an image to fit a particular region.

To actually draw an image, you need to obtain an image object. I'll discuss that next.

Exercise 13.1

Write an applet to display a solid circle that fits perfectly inside the outline of a square.

The Image Class

Objectives

Obtain a Graphics object from an Image.

The Image class does not provide a constructor for specifying where an image will come from. Instead of creating an Image object using an Image constructor, you can obtain an image, typically by downloading it over the Internet by specifying a URL. (Of course, the URL can be a local URL.)

You can retrieve an image and obtain an Image object by invoking an Applet method named getImage(). This method takes a URL. (There is also an overloaded version that takes a URL and another String that is a relative address to the URL in the first parameter.)

Here's the idea behind getImage(): when this method returns, you have an Image object, but the data for the image is not necessarily immediately available. That is, this method returns right away, even if the image resource is located over the Internet on a Web server and must be downloaded.

When you invoke the Graphics method drawImage(), the image download begins. The object you specify as an ImageObserver keeps the Java graphics system up-to-date on the state of the download. When the ImageObserver sees that the download is complete, it notifies the graphics system that it can draw the image in its entirety.

ImageObserver is an interface. This interface is defined in the java.awt.image package. The Component class implements this interface, so any Component (such as the Applet itself) can be used as an ImageObserver.

Tip

You can also create an Image object, typically for use for as an off-screen buffer, by invoking the Component method createImage(). This method creates a new image to the given width and height. If you're using this new Image object as an off-screen buffer for rendering graphics that will appear in the Component object you're creating it from, you'll probably want to set this Image object's size to the same width and height as your component.

Once you have the Image object, you can obtain its Graphics object to use to draw to it by invoking its getGraphics() method.

Java Arranges Components within Containers

Objectives

List the classes in the java.awt package that are valid arguments to the add() methods and those that are not valid.

Creating a display using low-level graphics routines is fine, but at some point you'll probably want to create buttons, check boxes, and other standard user interface elements that the user can click, check, and so on. All of Java's user interface components are subclasses of the Component class.

We'll look at examples of creating Component objects in a moment. First, though, it's useful to know how you will arrange these Component objects in your application's display.

You add Component objects to Container objects using add(). The Container object knows how to contain objects and arrange the objects it contains.

First, you will probably have a Container object of some kind that will contain a Component. For example, a Window is a Container. Perhaps this Window object is referred to by the object reference window.

Second, you create a Component object, such as a Button, TextField, Checkbox, and so on. Let's say you assign the object reference for a Component object to a variable named component.

The way you add the component to the window is to write:

```
window.add(component);
```

Keep in mind that Container inherits from Component. Hence, Containers can contain Component objects as well as other Container objects.

Again, we'll look at Containers in more detail later in this chapter.

The Component Class and Three Subclasses

In this section, we'll create Component objects. Since the test has specific questions on TextArea, List, and TextField, those are the Component objects we'll look at in this section.

Construct a TextArea and List that displays a specific number of lines.

Construct a TextArea and TextField that displays a specific number of columns.

Identify the result of using a proportional font versus a fixed pitch font for a column in a TextArea and TextField.

TextArea

A TextArea object provides a window for the user to type into. When you create a TextArea object, you specify the number of lines that the text window can contain, and the number of columns of text it will contain.

The number of columns that a TextArea (or TextField) object can contain is only approximate.

There are four constructors for TextArea. The two you'll use the most specify the number of rows and columns for the TextArea. Their format is:

```
TextArea(int numRows, int numCols);

TextArea(String text, int numRows, int numCols);
```

The other two constructors are the no-args constructor and a constructor that simply takes a String parameter—the text to display in the TextArea object. Displaying a TextArea constructed without specifying the number of rows and columns will probably give you results you don't want, since the TextArea has not been sized properly.

Here's an example of a TextArea object that displays 3 rows of text and up to 10 columns:

```
import java.awt.*;
import java.applet.*;

public class TA1 extends Applet {
    public void init() {
        add(new TextArea(3, 10));
    }
}
```

This applet looks like what's shown in Figure 13-10 when it is first run.

Figure 13-10

A TextArea Set to 3
Rows and 10
Columns

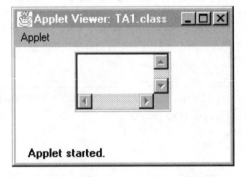

Figure 13-11 shows what happens as you start typing into the TextField.

Figure 13-11

Typing into the
TextArea Set to 3
Rows and 10
Columns

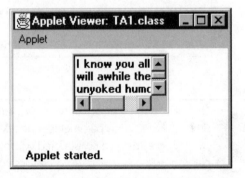

Even though the TextArea was only set to 3 rows and 10 columns, the user typed more text than could fit into this space. The TextArea displays little scroll bars when this happens so the user can get to the rest of the text. In this case, the user typed a speech from Henry IV, Part 1: "I know you all, and will awhile uphold the unyoked humor of your idleness."

Tip

If you want a TextArea (or a TextField) object to be used only to display text (if you want the user to be unable to edit the text in this object), you can invoke the method setEditable() and pass a value of false as the parameter.

TextField

Key Concept

A TextField object also provides a window for the user to type into, but it only allows the user to type one line. When you create a TextField object, you specify the number of columns in the TextField.

Warning

As with TextArea, you can also construct a TextField without specifying the number of columns. Again, this is probably not something you will want to do, because then you will not be in control of the size of the TextField.

Here is an example of creating a TextField that is 20 columns wide:

```java
import java.awt.*;
import java.applet.*;

public class TF1 extends Applet {
    public void init() {
        add(new TextField(20));
    }
}
```

Figure 13-12 shows what this looks like.

Figure 13-12
A TextField that is 20
Columns Wide

![Applet Viewer: TF1.class showing an empty text field]

Unlike with a TextArea, if you type more characters than can fit within the width of the TextField, no scroll bars appear. However, you can still use the arrow keys on the keyboard to move to the front or end of the text.

List

A List object presents a list of Strings that the user can select from. When you create a List, you indicate the number of lines the List will show at one time. If there are more items in the List than can be displayed, scroll bars appear to the right of the List so the user can scroll through the rest of the choices. You can also indicate whether the user may make multiple selections or just a single selection.

To create a List object containing a certain number of rows, use this constructor:

```
List(int numRows, boolean multipleSelections);
```

You can populate the List by invoking addItem(). For example, to create a List that shows 5 items at a time and allows the user to select multiple types of fish, you can write:

```
import java.awt.*;
import java.applet.Applet;

public class L1 extends Applet {
    public void init() {
        List l = new List(5, true);
        l.addItem("trout");
        l.addItem("salmon");
        l.addItem("snapper");
        l.addItem("bass");
        l.addItem("tuna");
        l.addItem("halibut");
        l.addItem("swordfish");
        add(l);
    }
}
```

This applet looks like Figure 13-13 when it first appears.

Figure 13-13
A List Displayed in an
Applet

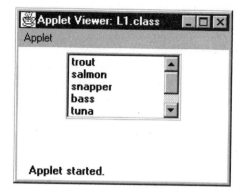

As the user interacts with it and selects multiple fish, the list might look like Figure 13-14.

Figure 13-14
The User Interacting
with a List that Allows
Multiple Selections

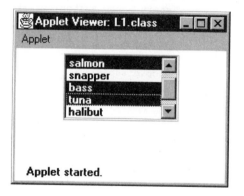

Exercise 13.2

Create and display a TextArea object that contains the text "To Whom It May Concern." The TextArea should be large enough to dash off a small note to someone. (You can decide what's large enough.)

Some Component Methods for Java 1.0.2

Use of the methods enable(), disable(), show(), hide(), size(), set-Foreground(), and setBackground() defined for the Component class.

enable/disable

You can use the `enable()` and `disable()` methods to make a component selectable or not by the user. Let's say you had two buttons that you wanted to make mutually exclusive. You could use `enable()` and `disable()` to turn them on and off—to make them selectable or not selectable—by the user. Here's an example of code that works with Java 1.0.2 as well as Java 1.1:

```java
import java.applet.Applet;
import java.awt.*;

public class Toggle extends Applet {
    Button start, stop;
    public void init() {
        start = new Button("start");
        stop = new Button("stop");

        start.enable();
        stop.disable();
        add(start);
        add(stop);
    }
    public boolean action(Event e, Object what) {
        if (e.target == start) {
            start.disable();
            stop.enable();
            return true;
        } else if (e.target == stop) {
            start.enable();
            stop.disable();
            return true;
        }
        return false;
    }
}
```

size/resize

The `size()` method retrieves the size of a Component. This method returns a Dimension object, which has two fields: `width` and `height`. The `resize()` method sets the size of a Component. There are two `resize()` methods: one takes a Dimension object; the other takes the width and height directly as `int` values.

Components that are within a Layout Manager (discussed later in the next section) that automatically sizes the Components they contain should not call `resize()` directly. Instead, the Layout Manager should take care of sizing the Component appropriately.

show/hide

The `show()` method makes a Component visible; the `hide()` method makes a Component invisible. The `show()` method is also overridden so that you can supply a `boolean` parameter to indicate whether to show the Component (if the parameter is `true`) or hide the Component (if the parameter is `false`).

One common place to use `show()` is when you create a standalone graphical application. Typically, your top-level Container is a Frame. To make the Frame appear, you've got to invoke it's `show()` method. Here's an example of using both `resize()` and `show()` to make a Frame take up space and appear on the screen:

```
import java.awt.*;

public class Fr extends Frame {
    public static void main(String[] args) {
        Fr fr = new Fr();
        fr.resize(220, 100);
        fr.show();
    }
}
```

Figure 13-15 shows what this simple program looks like when you run it.

Figure 13-15
A Simple Frame

setForeground/setBackground

The `setForeground()` and `setBackground()` methods are used to set the foreground and background color of a Component. These methods each take one parameter, an instance of class Color.

Some Component Methods for Java 1.1

Use of the methods `setEnabled()`, `setVisible()`, `setSize()`, `setForeground()`, and `setBackground()` defined for the Component class.

- The `setEnabled()` method replaces the `enable()` and `disable()` methods from Java 1.0.2. This method specifies whether a component can respond to the user.
- The `setVisible()` method replaces `show()` and `hide()` from Java 1.0.2. This method makes a component appear or disappear in the display.
- The `setSize()` method replaces `resize()` from Java 1.0.2. This method changes the width and height of a component. (You can use the method `getSize()` to retrieve a component's width and height.)
- The methods `setForeground()` and `setBackground()` are the same as they were in Java 1.0.2.

Let's turn our attention to color for a moment so you can see how to use these methods.

Color

Java provides a class named Color that you can use to specify colors for your interface. The Color class defines a whole bunch of `static` constants that contain instances of class Color already initialized to common colors.

Each constant is named after the color. To use red, for example, you can access `Color.red`. To use blue, you can access `Color.blue`. The colors Java makes available through the Color class are: black, blue, cyan, dark gray, gray, green, light gray, magenta, orange, pink, red, white, yellow.

Now, what if you want a different color? No problem! You can mix your own color out of red, green, and blue elements by creating a new Color instance and supplying the red, green, and blue values in the constructor. For example, you can use the constructor with this signature:

```
Color(int red, int green, int blue)
```

The red, green, and blue values range from 0 to 255. If all are set to 0, you get black. If all values are set to 255, you get white.

The Color class provides methods to convert between red, green, blue and hue, saturation, brightness if you'd rather work with the latter system. There are also methods for getting the red, green, and blue portions of a color.

For example, to set the foreground color to green for a Component referenced by the variable `component`, you can write:

```
component.setForeground(Color.green);
```

Layout Managers

Identify AWT classes which determine layouts for components with a container.

That Containers contain Components is all well and good, but how do Containers arrange the Components within them? The answer is that they hand off this chore to a layout manager.

Each Container has exactly one layout manager. The layout manager determines how to arrange the Components within a Container.

Whenever the Container or a Component within a Container changes in a way that might mean the layout needs to be updated—such as when the Container first appears on the screen, if new Components are added to a Container, if the Components within a Container change size, or if the Container itself is resized—the AWT invokes the Container's `invalidate()` method, followed shortly later by `validate()`. The `validate()` method in turn invokes that Container's `layout()` method. The Container's `layout()` method, however, does not figure out what to do on its own. This method asks its Container's layout manager what to do by calling the layout manager's `layoutContainer()` method. The `layoutContainer()` method takes the Container as an argument.

What is a layout manager, exactly? Any class that implements the LayoutManager interface. Java's five layout managers all inherit directly from class Object, but they implement the LayoutManager interface, which defines five `abstract` methods:

- `addLayoutComponent()`
- `layoutContainer()`
- `minimumLayoutSize()`
- `preferredLayoutSize()`
- `removeLayoutComponent()`

You will probably never invoke any of these methods directly, even if you implement your own layout manager instead of using one of the five that come with Java. (You'll usually find that one of Java's five layout managers works just fine.)

Instead of invoking a layout manager's methods yourself, Java's default Container methods invoke them for you at the appropriate times. Table 13-1 shows the connection between Container and layout manager methods.

Table 13-1
Container and Layout
Manager Methods

Container methods	Layout Manager methods
`add()`	`addLayoutComponent()`
`layout()`	`layoutContainer()`
`minimumSize()`	`minimumLayoutSize()`
`preferredSize()`	`preferredLayoutSize()`
`remove()` or `removeAll()`	`removeLayoutComponent()`

Using Layout Managers

Each type of Container comes with a default Layout Manager. I'll discuss the different ones in this section. Later, you'll review what the default Layout Managers are for the different Containers, and you'll review how to change the Layout Manager for a Container.

Identify the effects of BorderLayout, FlowLayout, and GridLayout.

State strategies to achieve a dynamic resizing of a Component horizontally, vertically, both horizontally and vertically, and neither horizontally nor vertically.

The five different layout managers are the classes FlowLayout, Border-Layout, GridLayout, CardLayout, and GridBagLayout. I'll discuss the first three in detail since these are the ones on the test. I'll explain the purpose of the other two in the section "What's Not on the Test."

FlowLayout

A FlowLayout object arranges components left to right and top to bottom, centering each line as it goes.

As new components are added to a Container with a FlowLayout, the FlowLayout positions each component on the same line as the previous one until the next component will not fit given the width of the Container. Then, the FlowLayout centers that row, starts a new row, and begins adding components to the new row. A FlowLayout lets each component be its preferred size and does not change the size of a component. (The same is not true for other Layout Managers, as we'll review shortly.)

The FlowLayout lets the component be its preferred size even if the component cannot fit in the width or height provided. For example, if a label or button contains text that makes it too wide to display in the Container, the component will be on its own row, and you'll see only the centered portion that fits in the Container's width.

Here's some code that illustrates this:

```java
import java.awt.*;
import java.applet.*;

public class Fit extends Applet {
    public void init() {
        add(new Label("Romeo, Romeo, wherefore art thou, Romeo?"));
    }
}
```

This places a very long label into an applet. However, if the HTML file that embeds this applet looks like this:

```html
<applet code=Fit.class width=50 height=50>
</applet>
```

then the label won't be fully seen. The applet will look like Figure 13-16:

Figure 13-16
A Label that Doesn't
Fit in the Width of
the Applet

If a Container using a FlowLayout is resized, all of the components inside it might need to be rearranged. This might very well mean the components end up in a different relationship to each other, depending on what now fits on each row. Where a text field, button, and choice might have been on the same row at first, resizing the Container to be smaller might force each component to be placed on its own row.

Figure 13-17 shows an example of a bunch of components first arranged one way, and then, when the applet is resized, Figure 13-18 shows how they look after the FlowLayout has rearranged them.

Figure 13-17
An Applet that Uses a
FlowLayout to
Arrange Components

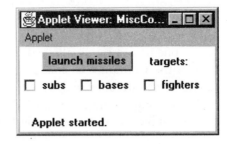

Figure 13-18
Resizing an Applet that
Uses a FlowLayout

Here's the code for this applet:

```java
import java.awt.*;
import java.applet.*;

public class MiscComponents extends Applet {
    public void init() {
        add(new Button("launch missiles"));
        add(new Label("targets: "));
        add(new Checkbox("subs"));
        add(new Checkbox("bases"));
        add(new Checkbox("fighters"));
    }
}
```

Tip

FlowLayouts are particularly useful for arranging a series of buttons to create a kind of menu, where each button is placed after the one before it.

BorderLayout

Use of the methods add(Component) and add(String, Component) for the Container class.

BorderLayout objects arrange components according to the directions "North," "South," "East," and "West." There's also an area for "Center," which includes any space left over from the other regions.

Components are rarely allowed to be their preferred size in a BorderLayout. If the Container is smaller than the components' preferred sizes, the components are squeezed. If the Container is larger, the components are stretched. For example, Figure 13-19 shows five Button objects arranged in a Container that uses a BorderLayout. This picture gives a better sense of the regions of a BorderLayout than words do. Notice that the "North" and "South" regions stretch all the way across the screen, while the "East" and "West" regions are positioned between the "North" and "South."

Figure 13-19
Five Buttons in a BorderLayout

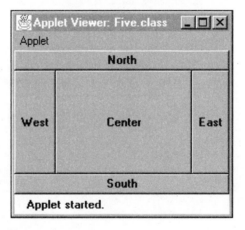

Here's the code for this picture:

```
import java.awt.*;
import java.applet.*;

public class Five extends Applet {
   public void init() {
      setLayout(new BorderLayout());
      add("North", new Button("North"));
      add("South", new Button("South"));
      add("East", new Button("East"));
      add("West", new Button("West"));
      add("Center", new Button("Center"));
   }
}
```

BorderLayout objects also have another limitation: you cannot display more than one component in a particular region. If you do add more than one to a region, only the last component you add will appear.

For example, if you try to add three Checkbox objects (though three buttons, three labels—three of anything have the same result) to the "North" of a BorderLayout, like this:

```
import java.applet.Applet;
import java.awt.*;

public class BorderOver extends Applet {
   public void init() {
      setLayout(new BorderLayout());
      add("North", new Checkbox("mouse"));
      add("North", new Checkbox("dog"));
      add("North", new Checkbox("cat"));
   }
}
```

the result is that only the last component is displayed, as shown in Figure 13-20:

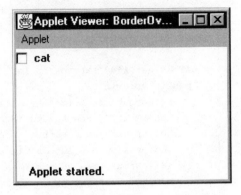

So what is a BorderLayout good for? Unlike a FlowLayout, a BorderLay-out is useful for making certain that components keep the same relation-ship to each other, even if the applet is resized. They also are excellent at arranging components along the top and bottom of a Container, which a FlowLayout cannot do.

If you want to show more than one component in a particular region of a BorderLayout, you can nest another Container inside the first Container.

For example, to place three buttons at the top of a Container and three at the bottom, you can place each set of three inside their own Container using a FlowLayout, and then place the two Containers inside the one using the BorderLayout. The code might look like this:

```java
import java.applet.Applet;
import java.awt.*;

public class Border extends Applet {
    public void init() {
        Panel p;

        setLayout(new BorderLayout());

        p = new Panel();
        p.add(new Button("dog"));
        p.add(new Button("cat"));
        p.add(new Button("mouse"));
        add("North", p);
```

continued

```
        p = new Panel();
        p.add(new Button("steak"));
        p.add(new Button("tuna"));
        p.add(new Button("cheese"));
        add("South", p);
    }
}
```

which would result in the display in Figure 13-21:

Figure 13-21
Panels Within a Bor-
derLayout

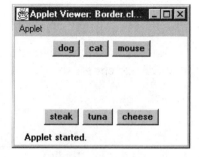

"North" and "South" components can be stretched horizontally—they fill up the space from the left to the right edge of the Container. "East" and "West" components can be stretched vertically—they fill up the space from the top of the "South" area to the bottom of the "North" area.

Adding a component to the center of the BorderLayout will make that component take up whatever space is left over in the center (if any). A "Center" component can be stretched both horizontally and vertically. The "Center" includes regions of the BorderLayout that are not used. For example, if nothing is placed in the "East" or "West," then the "Center" stretches all the way from the left edge of the Container to the right edge.

So which components can be stretched? Here's a division of the "stretchable" versus the "non-stretchable" components:

- *stretchable:* Button, Label, TextField ⟨partial lists⟩
- *non-stretchable:* Checkbox

Each component is placed within a different region of an applet that uses a BorderLayout. You can see the effect of stretching or not stretching based on the type of component.

Here's the code for this example:

```
import java.awt.*;
import java.applet.*;

public class Stretch extends Applet {
    public void init() {
        setLayout(new BorderLayout());
        add("East", new Button("East"));
        add("West", new Label("West"));
        add("North", new TextField("North"));
        add("South", new Checkbox("South"));
    }
}
```

The result is shown in Figure 13-22. Each component fills up its region of the screen, except for the checkbox in the south.

Figure 13-22
In a BorderLayout, Different Components Stretch or Don't Stretch Depending on their Type

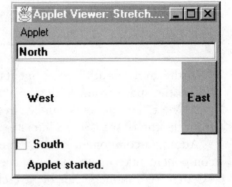

If you don't want the components right on top of each other, one of the constructors for BorderLayout allows you to specify the horizontal and vertical gaps that should be placed around the regions of the layout.

GridLayout

GridLayout objects allow you to specify a rectangular grid in which to place the components. Each cell in the grid is the same height as the other cells, and each width is the same width as the other cells.

Components are stretched both vertically and horizontally to fill the cell. The size of the cells is determine according to how many cells are requested in the Container given the Container's size.

When a GridLayout is first constructed, you must specify how many rows and how many columns the grid will have. Components are added to the GridLayout left to right and top to bottom. If more components are added than there are columns, the GridLayout keeps the same number of rows but adds the necessary number of columns.

For example, the following program causes the applet to be displayed with all six buttons on the same row:

```java
import java.applet.Applet;
import java.awt.*;

public class GridOver extends Applet {
    public void init() {
        setLayout(new GridLayout(1, 2));

        add(new Button("mouse"));
        add(new Button("dog"));
        add(new Button("cat"));
        add(new Button("elephant"));
        add(new Button("monkey"));
        add(new Button("giraffe"));
    }
}
```

This looks like what's shown in Figure 13-23:

Figure 13-23
A GridLayout Arranging Buttons in 1 Row

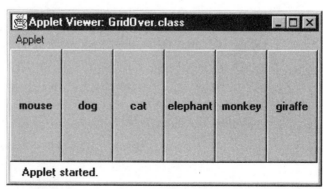

Changing the GridLayout to be created with 2 rows and 2 columns (instead of 1 row and 2 columns) makes GridLayout arrange the Button objects in 2 rows and 3 columns, like what's shown in Figure 13-24:

Figure 13-24
A GridLayout Arrang-
ing Buttons in 2 rows

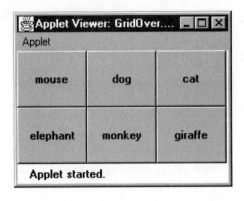

As with a BorderLayout, if you don't want the components right on top of each other, one of the constructors for GridLayout allows you to specify the horizontal and vertical gaps that should be placed around the cells of the layout.

Tip

CardLayout and GridBagLayout are discussed in the section "What's Not on the Test."

Default Layout Managers

Change the layout scheme associated with a Container instance.

Objectives

Since a Container class always has one layout manager associated with it, Container classes are defined with a default layout manager. These defaults are shown in Table 13-2:

Table 13-2
Containers and their
Default Layout
Managers

Container	Default Layout Manager
Frame	BorderLayout
Panel	FlowLayout
Dialog	BorderLayout
Window	BorderLayout

You can change a Container's layout manager to use a different kind by invoking setLayout().

One common technique is to create the new layout manager and set it at the same time, as in:

```
f.setLayout(new FlowLayout());
```

This creates a new FlowLayout object and assigns it as the layout manager for a Container object referenced by the variable f.

Exercise 13.3

Arrange two buttons that read "yes" and "no" at the bottom of an applet. Your applet should look something like what's in Figure 13-25:

Figure 13-25
Two Buttons in an
Applet

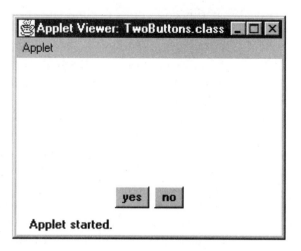

Here's a hint: making an applet look like this involves placing the buttons within their own Container, such as a Panel, and then placing the Panel into the applet. You'll see why if you try to place the buttons directly into the applet.

What's Not on the Test

Smoother Graphics

Tip

Because update() first clears the background, you'll sometimes find that your application flickers in a very unattractive way. To avoid this poor effect, you can override the normal update() method.

For example, imagine you are flipping between images in your applet and each image is the same size. If you allowed the standard update() to paint() sequence to occur each time you display a new image, the background of the image would "flash" and become the same color as the background before being replaced by the new image.

In your override, you can just call paint() directly, after setting the current foreground color:

```
public void update(Graphics g) {
    setColor(getForeground());
    paint(g);
}
```

What this code does is eliminate the call to fill the background in the background color. This eliminates the flash. If you sometimes want to perform the normal behavior, you can put a test in the update() method, and under normal conditions invoke your superclass' version of update(), but when you are just switching to a new image, you can branch to your flicker-free code.

There are a number of ways you can make your painting occur faster and more smoothly than by following what Java does by default. One of these ways is by overriding a method called update().

Even though all your drawing code goes into paint(), Java actually invokes update() first, due to a call to repaint(). The repaint() method invokes update() as soon as it can, which means that repaint() often returns before Java invokes update() and paint().

The update() method does three things:

1. Clears the Component of any drawing it contains (that is, it refreshes the background by redrawing the background in the background color).

2. Sets the current drawing color of the Component to be the Component's foreground color.
3. Invokes the Component's `paint()` method.

Normally, this sequence is exactly what you want. But sometimes, refreshing the background can cause your drawing to flicker: you're looking at your component, it redraws itself, you see a flash as the background is refreshed, and then it repaints itself.

You can eliminate this flicker by overriding `update()`. The `update()` method is simply:

```
public void update(Graphics g)
```

You can write a method that skips step 1 above by writing an `update()` method like this:

```
public void update(Graphics g) {
    g.setColor(foregroundColor());
    paint(g);
}
```

Other Types of Layout Managers

CardLayout

You can use CardLayout to present different screens to a user based on a stack of cards metaphor. You can flip to the first, next, or last card using methods defined by CardLayout. You can also go directly to a particular card, as long as you've named it, using a method named `show()`.

GridBagLayout

You saw how the GridLayout arranges components in a strict grid where each row and each column are the same size. Components can only occupy one cell.

GridBagLayout is much more complicated than that, and also much more flexible. With GridBagLayout, your rows and columns don't have to all be the same size. What's more, each component can occupy more than one cell.

Answers to the Exercises

Exercise 13.1

```
import java.awt.*;
import java.applet.*;

public class Drawing extends Applet {
    public void paint(Graphics g) {
        g.drawRect(5, 5, 50, 50);
        g.fillOval(5, 5, 50, 50);
    }
}
```

Exercise 13.2

```
import java.awt.*;
import java.applet.*;

public class ToWhom extends Applet {
    public void init() {
        add(new TextArea("To Whom It May Concern", 10, 30));
    }
}
```

Exercise 13.3

To place Components such as buttons along the bottom of an applet, you need a BorderLayout. However, to place two Buttons side by side, as in this applet, you need a FlowLayout. The trick here is to place the two Buttons inside a Panel. The default layout for a Panel is a FlowLayout. Then, you can place the Panel into the applet and replace the applet's layout manager to be a BorderLayout. That way, you can place this Panel containing the two Buttons at the bottom of the applet.

Here's a solution:

```
import java.awt.*;
import java.applet.*;

public class TwoButtons extends Applet {
    public void init() {
        Panel p = new Panel();
        p.add(new Button("yes"));
        p.add(new Button("no"));

        setLayout(new BorderLayout());

        add("South", p);
    }
}
```

Review Questions

Question 1: You should place all of your low-level graphics rendering code into:

a) `update()`
b) `paint()`
c) `init()`
d) `repaint()`

Question 2: The AWT passes your `paint()` method an instance of class:

a) Thread
b) Applet
c) Graphics
d) Component

Question 3: Given a Graphics object in the variable g, the method call:

```
g.drawRect(0, 10, 30, 40);
```

a) Draws the outline of a rectangle that is centered at x=0, y=10 and is 30 pixels wide and 40 pixels height.
b) Draws the outline of a rectangle whose top, left corner is at x=0, y=10 and whose bottom, right corner is at x=30, y=40.
c) Fills a rectangle with the foreground color where the rectangle's left edge is 0, top is 10, width is 30, and height is 40.
d) Draws the outline of a rectangle where the rectangle's left edge is 0, top is 10, width is 30, and height is 40.

Question 4: Here is some partial code for a `main()` method written in Java 1.0.2:

```
Frame f = new Frame("My frame");
f.resize(100, 100);
```

What line of code could you add to make this new Frame object appear on the screen?

a) `f.appear();`
b) `f.setForeground();`
c) `f.show();`
d) `f.enable();`

Question 5: To place a button at the bottom of a container, no matter how the user resized the container, it would be simplest to use what type of layout manager?

a) BorderLayout
b) GridLayout
c) FlowLayout
d) GridbagLayout

Question 6: You are porting code from Java 1.0.2 to Java 1.1. Instead of using `resize()`, you would like to use the Java 1.1 API. Which method should you use instead?

a) `size()`
b) `newSize()`
c) `reSize()`
d) `setSize()`

Question 7: To add a component referenced by `comp` to the center of a container using a BorderLayout and referenced by cont, you can write:

a) `comp.add("Center", cont);`
b) `comp.add(cont, "Center");`
c) `cont.add("Center", comp);`
d) `cont.add(comp, "Center");`

Question 8: The Code:

```
new List(10, true);
```

a) Creates a new list that is 10 columns wide and accepts multiple selections.
b) Creates a new list that is 10 rows tall and accepts multiple selections.
c) Creates a new list that can contain no more than 10 entries and accepts multiple selections.
d) Creates a new list that is 10 rows tall and only allows one entry to be selected at a time.

Answers to the Review Questions

Question 1   b.   All low-level drawing code should go into your `paint()` method.

Question 2   c.   You can use the Graphics object to perform low-level drawing operations.

Question 3   d.   The template is: `drawRect(left edge, top edge, width, height)`

Question 4   c.   The `show()` method in Java 1.0.2 makes a component appear.

Question 5   a.   With a BorderLayout, you could add the component to the "South," and that's where it would stay.

Question 6   d.   `setSize()` replaces `resize()` in Java 1.1.

Question 7   c.   `add()` is defined as a Container method. The placement of the component is the first parameter.

Question 8   b.   The first parameter is the number of rows to display without scrolling; the second parameter indicates whether or not to allow multiple selections.

CHAPTER *14*

Events in Java 1.0.2

You should be familiar with all of the topics in Chapter 13 before tackling this chapter.

In this chapter and the chapter that follows, I'll go over the basic idea behind event handling.

So far, we've created user interface components and placed them within containers. We can use layout managers to arrange these components in different ways, so our interfaces look pretty good at this point.

What remains? Creating a working user interface. That means detecting when the user has clicked a button or typed into a text field and responding appropriately.

What's on the Test

The test asks event questions related to two methods: `handleEvent()` and `action()`. These are the two most important event methods in Java 1.0.2, though there are others. There are also questions concerning the Event class itself and the fields in the Event class.

The biggest set of questions relates to how events propagate up the container hierarchy in Java 1.0.2. We'll look at this behavior and review this aspect of event handling.

Objectives for this Chapter

- Use the fields of the Event class to identify the target, mouse position, and nature and time of an event.
- Describe how TextField, Panel, and Canvas mouse and keyboard events appear at the methods `handleEvent()` and `action()`.
- State the role of the return value from the `handleEvent()` and `action()` methods.
- Identify why an event might be passed up a container hierarchy.
- Control propagation of an event up the container hierarchy using the return value from the `handleEvent()` or `action()` method.
- Determine when it is appropriate and inappropriate to call a superclass' `handleEvent()` and `action()` methods in subclasses Button, ScrollBar, List, TextField, and TextArea.

Java Tells You About Events

Whenever the user interacts with a Component, the AWT calls a method appropriate for that action and passes information regarding that action in an Event object.

Events Methods

Describe how TextField, Panel, and Canvas mouse and keyboard events appear at the methods `handleEvent()` and `action()`.

This section covers the Event methods for Java's Components in general. However, we'll look especially at TextField, Panel, and Canvas, since there are questions specific to these Components and Containers on the exam.

The handleEvent() Method

The primary event method that the AWT will always invoke for any event is handleEvent(), *which takes an Event instance as its argument.*

We'll discuss the Event class in just a bit. The Event instance that AWT passes to handleEvent() contains information about the location where the event occurred in the case of mouse events, the time the event occurred, and so on. For the moment, we'll concentrate on the methods that AWT invokes.

The Component class contains default behavior for handleEvent(), and what it does with the event depends on what kind of component it is and what the fields in the Event object are set to. The handleEvent() method will call one other event method each one defined by class Component. These other event methods—one of which will be called by handleEvent()—are:

- action()
- gotFocus() or lostFocus()
- keyDown() or keyUp()
- mouseEnter() or mouseExit()
- mouseMove() or mouseDrag()
- mouseDown() or mouseUp()

You can handle an event in handleEvent() *if you'd like to. However, a common approach is to wait for* handleEvent() *to perform its default processing and invoke one of these other, more specific event methods.*

Here are two examples of when the AWT invokes these other event methods.

1. A click down in a Container, such as an applet, will cause Java to first invoke handleEvent(), which will in turn invoke mouseDown().
2. A click down in a Component, such as a button, will cause Java to first invoke handleEvent(), which will in turn invoke action().

Typically, a Component will receive action(), or a focus or key method call. A Container will receive a mouse method call.

The action() Object

If the event implies action (for example, double-clicking the mouse or pressing *Enter*), the Components receive an action() invocation from AWT after handleEvent(). The action() method takes two parameters: the Event object passed to handleEvent(), and an object that gives some information about the action. The pattern for action() is:

```
public boolean action(Event e, Object what)
```

The type of object passed to action() as the second parameter (in the what parameter) depends on the event's target object.

Table 14-1 shows which object type the AWT passes as the action() when different Components are the target of the action() method.

Table 14-1
Component Targets and **action()** Objects

Component	action() object
Button	String
TextField	String (press return to get an action event)
Checkbox	Boolean
List	String (double-click to get an action event)
TextArea	String (press return to get an action event)
Choice	String
Panel	action not dispatched
Canvas	action not dispatched

Notice that Containers do not receive an `action()` event. Instead, they receive events such as `mouseDown()` or `mouseUp()`.

You can use the object passed to `action()` to determine what the user did. For example, for a Checkbox, the Boolean wrapper object is `true` if the Checkbox was selected and `false` otherwise. The String passed to `action()` for a TextArea or TextField contains the text the user typed. Similarly, a String passed to `action()` for a List contains the entry the user double-clicked.

The Event Class

Use the fields of the Event class to identify the target, mouse position, and nature and time of an event.

As part of invoking an event method, AWT passes along information about the event that occurred. This information arrives stuffed into an instance of class Event, which contains many fields.

Table 14-2 shows the Event fields and their meaning.

field name	type	meaning
Table 14-2 The Event Fields		
arg	Object	An object that depends on the target and type of the event. This is the same Object passed to `action()`.
clickCount	int	This field is only used for `MOUSE_DOWN` events. It contains the number of consecutive clicks the user made. Otherwise, it contains 0.
evt	Event	This refers to the next event if the events are placed into a linked list.
id	int	The identifier for this event. There is a large list of identifiers that's part of the Event's static data. The event identifiers include things such as `MOUSE_DOWN`, `GOT_FOCUS`, `SCROLL_PAGE_DOWN`, and `WINDOW_DESTROY`.

field name	type	meaning
key	int	The key the user pressed if this event is a keyboard event.
modifiers	int	The modifier keys include ALT, CONTROL, and SHIFT, and there are constants for these. They are masks—bit patterns—that can be combined using a bitwise-OR (the | operator) to see if the user held down any combination of these modifier keys.
target	Object	This Object refers to the Object where the event occurred.
when	long	The time stamp for this event. This can be used to determine whether a particular event occurred before or after another event.
x	int	The x coordinate of the event.
y	int	The y coordinate of the event.

Table 14.2
The Event Fields
(continued)

Event Propagation

Control propagation of an event up the container hierarchy using the return value from the handleEvent() or action() method.

Objectives

As you reviewed in the preceding sections, Components are placed within Containers. Containers can be placed inside other Containers. This arrangement of Components and Containers inside other Containers creates a "container hierarchy."

Each of the event methods returns a boolean value, and this boolean value relates directly to the container hierarchy.

false

If the return value from an event method is ~~true~~, the AWT dispatches the event method to the current object's Container. If the return value is ~~false~~, that's as far as the event goes.

Key Concept

As long as a Component returns false from an event method, indicating that the method did not handle the event, the event will continue to travel up the Container hierarchy until it reaches the top-level Container.

When an event propagates up the container hierarchy, its `target` field still references the Component or Container where the event originally occurred. Also, the `x` and `y` fields still contain the x and y position passed to the target. That is, the data in the Event object is not translated to the new Container in the hierarchy.

Exercise 14.1

Write an applet that writes the message "double-click" to the standard output whenever the applet detects double-clicks.

Exercise 14.2

Write an applet that displays all of the Event fields for `handleEvent()` for TextField, Panel, and Canvas objects added to an applet.

Exercise 14.3

Write an applet that increases its width and height by 5 pixels every time the user clicks, and decreases its width and height by 5 pixels every time the user clicks while holding down the *Shift* key.

Event Handling Strategies

Objectives

Identify why an event might be passed up a container hierarchy.

There are two approaches to handling events in Java:

1. Subclass each Component that you want to handle the event. This is technically more object-oriented—each Component knows how to handle itself. However, this could also lead to you developing many different types of classes.
2. Let a high-level Container handle the event when it propagates to it. The event method checks to see which Component is the target and takes the appropriate action. This is simpler to do in that you often only need to provide one subclass, which can often be the applet. However, it is less object-oriented in that you end up with a big case or switch statement to determine what to do.

Most developers go with an in-between strategy: they group Components in a Container placed within a top-level Container. This middle Container is then a custom subclass that handles the events for those Components inside it.

Key Concept

If an event is not handled in an event method, it should be passed up the container hierarchy.

For example, you might have code that draws a small dot wherever the user clicks. This code might look like the following:

```java
import java.awt.*;
import java.applet.*;

public class Circ extends Applet {
    public boolean handleEvent(Event e) {
        if (e.id == Event.MOUSE_DOWN) {
            Graphics g = getGraphics();
            g.drawOval(e.x - 5, e.y - 5, 10, 10);
            return true;
        }
        return false;
    }
}
```

Here's what this program looks like after the user has clicked a few times in the applet:

Figure 14-1
Making Circles

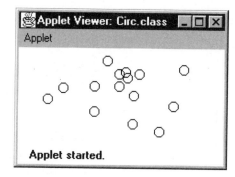

There are some important elements in this program you should take note of:

- We did not have a Graphics object to draw with in handleEvent(). So, we had to acquire one. We did this by invoking the Component method getGraphics().
- We used the e.id field to identify the type of event using the "magic number" stored in a static variable in the Event class (Event.MOUSE_DOWN). We could have also overridden mouseDown() instead of handleEvent(). That is probably preferable in this situation, but I wanted to show another aspect to handling events: returning true or false depending on whether the event method handled the event or not.
- If we handled the event, we returned true. If we did not handle the event, we returned false.
- We also used other Event fields, namely the e.x and e.y fields, to determine where the user clicked the mouse.

Determine when it is appropriate and inappropriate to call a superclass's handleEvent() and action() methods in subclasses Button, ScrollBar, List, TextField, and TextArea.

If the superclass provides some behavior for an event method, then rather than simply returning false or true if you do not handle the event, you should invoke the superclass' method and return its return value.

Miscellaneous Component Subclasses

Button

You can create a Button with or without a label. Here's an example of a Button that writes "clicked" to the standard output whenever the user clicks it:

```
import java.awt.*;
import java.applet.*;

public class B extends Applet {
    public void init() {
        add(new Button("click me"));
    }
    public boolean handleEvent(Event e)
        if (e.target instanceof Button)
            System.out.println("clicked");
        return super.handleEvent(e);
    }
}
```

Figure 14-2 shows what this looks like.

Figure 14-2
A Standard Button

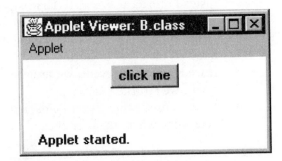

Choice

You can create a drop-down list of choices by creating a Choice object. Here's an example of code that creates a list of three choices:

```
import java.awt.*;
import java.applet.*;

public class Ch extends Applet {
    public void init() {
        Choice c = new Choice();
        c.addItem("white");
        c.addItem("wheat");
        c.addItem("rye");
        add(c);
    }
}
```

When this code first appears, it looks like Figure 14-3.

Figure 14-3
A Choice Object
When it First Appears

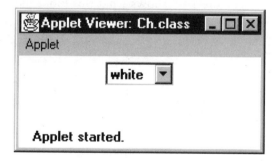

When the user selects it, the choices appear. This looks like Figure 14-4.

Figure 14-4
A Choice Object Displaying its Possible
Choices

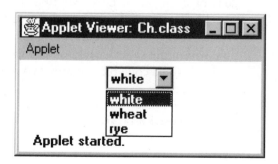

Checkbox

You can add a Checkbox object to a user interface with or without a label. For example, here's an applet that adds two Checkbox objects to the user interface:

```java
import java.awt.*;
import java.applet.*;

public class Two extends Applet {
    public void init() {
        add(new Checkbox("Eggs"));
        add(new Checkbox("Bacon"));
    }
}
```

Figure 14-5 shows what this looks like.

Figure 14-5

Two Checkboxes

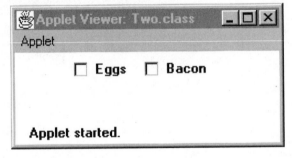

If you run this applet, you'll notice that these Checkboxes are independent of each other. If we wanted to create a mutually exclusive set of Checkboxes instead, we can create a CheckboxGroup and assign these Checkboxes to the same group. Only one Checkbox can be selected at a time within the same Checkbox group.

Here's some code that creates two mutually exclusive Checkboxes:

```java
import java.awt.*;
import java.applet.*;

public class Male extends Applet {
    public void init() {
        CheckboxGroup group = new CheckboxGroup();
        add(new Checkbox("male", group, false));
        add(new Checkbox("female", group, false));
    }
}
```

This applet looks like Figure 14-6 when it runs.

Figure 14-6
Mutually Exclusive
Checkboxes

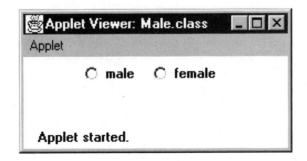

Notice that the mutually exclusive checkboxes (also known as "radio buttons") are round, while the non-mutually exclusive checkboxes are square.

Tip

At first, neither of the Checkboxes are selected. That's what the third parameter to the Checkbox constructor is for. If one of these started out as selected, then the third constructor parameter for that Checkbox would be set to `true`. Once the Checkboxes are displayed, selecting "male" deselects "female," and vice versa.

Answers to the Exercises

Exercise 14.1

```
import java.awt.*;
import java.applet.*;

public class D extends Applet {

  public boolean handleEvent(Event e) {
    if (e.clickCount == 2) {
      System.out.println("double-click");
    }
    return super.handleEvent(e);
  }

}
```

Exercise 14.2

```java
import java.awt.*;
import java.applet.*;

public class Handle extends Applet {
    Canvas c;
    TextField tf;
    Panel p;

    public void init() {
        c = new Canvas();
        c.resize(50, 50);
        c.setBackground(Color.blue);
        add(c);
        p = new Panel();
        p.setBackground(Color.red);
        p.resize(50, 50);
        add(p);

        tf = new TextField(10);
        add(tf);
    }


    public boolean handleEvent(Event e) {
        System.out.println("\n --- " + e.target.getClass() + " ---");
        if (e.target == p ||
            e.target == tf ||
            e.target == c)
        {
            System.out.println("arg is " + e.arg);
            System.out.println("click count is " + e.clickCount);
            System.out.println("evt is " + e.evt);
            System.out.println("id is " + e.id);
            System.out.println("key is " + e.key);
            System.out.println("modifiers are " + e.modifiers);
            System.out.println("target is " + e.target);
            System.out.println("when is " + e.when);
            System.out.println("x is " + e.x);
            System.out.println("y is " + e.y);
        }

        return super.handleEvent(e);
    }
}
```

Exercise 14.3

```java
import java.awt.*;
import java.applet.*;

public class Incr extends Applet {
    public boolean handleEvent(Event e) {
        if (e.id == Event.MOUSE_DOWN) {
            int incr = 5;
            if ((e.modifiers & Event.SHIFT_MASK) > 0)
                incr = -5;
            Dimension d = size();
            resize(d.width + incr, d.height + incr);

            return true;
        }

        return false;
    }
}
```

Review Questions

Question 1: To identify the object where an event first occurred from an event handler, you can look at which field in the Event object?

a) component
b) target
c) evt
d) id

Question 2: If the user hits the Enter key when typing in a TextField object, which event(s) does this TextField object receive by default?

a) handleEvent()
b) action()
c) both handleEvent() and action()
d) neither of these

Question 3:   What type of object is passed to a List object via `action()` as the second parameter when the user double-clicks?

a) List
b) the Lists' container
c) `Boolean`
d) `String`

Question 4:   The `handleEvent()` method takes which parameters?

a) Event and Object
b) Event
c) Object
d) Component

Question 5:   If you do not handle an event in `action()`, you should return:

a) `false`
b) `true`
c) `null`
d) 0

Answers to the Review Questions

Question 1   b.   The `target` field contains a reference to the original object where the event occurred.

Question 2   c.   The TextField object will first receive `handleEvent()`, followed by `action()`.

Question 3   d.   The second parameter is a String which contains the text in the list that the user double-clicked.

Question 4   b.   The handleEvent() method only takes one parameter: an instance of class Event. The `action()` method takes two parameters: An Event instance and another object.

Question5   a.   Returning `false` indicates to AWT that it should pass the event up the container hierarchy, which is what you want if you do not handle the event.

CHAPTER 15

Events in Java 1.1

You don't need to know the event handling model in Java 1.0.2 to pick up the event handling model in Java 1.1. However, this chapter does mention some of the differences in passing, so it can be useful to know the old approach.

Event handling in 1.1 is based on a set of interfaces, a basic understanding of what interfaces are all about is useful. Other than that, meeting the requirements for the prerequisites in Chapter 14—knowing all about the rest of building a graphical user interface—is also appropriate for this chapter.

The event handling model in the Abstract Window Toolkit (AWT) in Java 1.0.2 has a number of weaknesses addressed in Java 1.1. In general, these weaknesses concern a trade-off that version 1.0.2 forced you into. You either had to:

1. Override every component to make it do what you wanted, or
2. Brace a container against a flood of events and then sort through these events using a giant `switch` statement.

Neither approach is particularly compelling. The first is more object-oriented, but also a great deal of work. The second is easier, but anytime you use a `switch` statement, a little bell should go off in your thoughts somewhere to suggest that there's something un-object-oriented about the design, and that perhaps a different class hierarchy and design would make it go away.

In version 1.1, a different design and a different class hierarchy does in fact make the problem go away. Your whole design for your graphical user interfaces become much cleaner. This chapter explains why.

What's on the Test

You should understand the new event handling protocol. In particular, you should know how to register an event listener, how to implement a Listener interface, and how to extend an Adapter class.

Objectives for this Chapter

- Describe the event handling model in Java 1.1.
- Identify important events in the new AWTEvent hierarchy.
- Add a new Listener to a component's list of event listeners.
- Identify the important Listener interfaces.
- Implement a Listener interface.
- State the difference between low-level and semantic events.
- Extend an Adapter class.

A Quick Reminder of Events in 1.0.2

Components (such as buttons, lists, and text fields) are arranged inside of containers (such as panels and frames). Since the Container class inherits from the

Component class, container objects can also be embedded inside other containers. This nesting of components and containers within other containers is known as the *container hierarchy*. This hierarchy still exists in Java 1.1.

In Java 1.0.2, if an event (such as a mouse click) occurs over a particular component or container, the AWT invokes an appropriate event method corresponding to that mouse click, and passes that method an instance of class Event. The fields of this Event instance are set to a state that represents the event: the x, y coordinates where the event occurred, the time of the event, and so on.

If the method that AWT invokes does not handle this event, it will return `false`. If the method does in fact handle the event, it will return `true`. AWT uses this return value to determine what to do with the event. If the return value is `false`, AWT tries to find some other object that might want to handle this event. To accomplish this, it invokes the same event method in the object's container. If that method also returns `false`, AWT invokes the same event method in *that* object's container. AWT keeps passing the event up the container hierarchy until some container handles the method and returns `true`, or until the event reaches the top-level container and there's no container left to pass it to.

All of the methods in Java 1.0.2 continue to work in Java 1.1. However, you should be aware of two things. First, you should not mix and match the two different event handling protocols; use one or the other. Second, in some future release yet to be determined, the old event handling model will no longer be supported.

For now, if you compile a Java program using the 1.1 JDK but the program invokes methods and uses the design of Java 1.0.2, the compiler will issue a warning.

Design Goals for Events in Java 1.1

While the event scheme in Java 1.0.2 works for small applications and applets, it has a number limitations. First of all, it does not easily support large-scale applications with complex user interfaces. That's because you either have to override each component to allow it to perform its behavior, or, if you instead handle events in a container, you have to determine how you will handle every event that affects the components embedded in that container. Both approaches are inefficient.

Modern user interfaces also have other features that are not supported in Java 1.0.2. These features include scroll panes, the ability to cut to and paste from a clipboard, and mouseless operations. All of these are supported in Java 1.1.

In this chapter, we'll focus on event handling. This is the biggest change in the AWT in Java 1.1, and is the change that will most directly affect the way you write code.

An Overview

Describe the event handling model in Java 1.1.

So you can see where we're going, here's a quick overview of event handling in Java 1.1:

When the user interacts with a component, AWT notifies the component's listeners (if any) of the events they're interested in.

You can register your object as a listener interested in particular events by using methods such as addMouseListener() to get mouse events, or addActionListener() to get action events. There is a different method corresponding to the different types of events.

Objects that listen for events must conform to an interface appropriate for those events. Java defines a number of Listener interfaces you can implement in your own classes.

The New Event Classes

Identify important events in the new AWTEvent hierarchy.

In Java 1.1, the Java packages define many different event classes that represent specific types of events.

When you handled an event in 1.0.2, say in the `action()` method, you had to identify what kind of event your Event object represented based on an `int` (the old `id` field). That's not necessary with the new model. Instead, the event object will be a subclass of EventObject, and for user interface events, of AWTEvent. The specific type of event—a mouse event, a focus event, and so on (see Figure 15-1)—is now represented by a subclass of AWTEvent.

EventObject, which now stands at the top of the event hierarchy, is actually defined in `java.util`, not in `java.awt`. This is to make events more generic and not necessarily tied to the AWT. However, all of the events dispatched by AWT's components use event classes that are subclasses of AWTEvent, which is in `java.awt`.

Figure 15-1 shows the hierarchy of EventObject and AWTEvent classes that you'll work with.

Figure 15-1
The EventObject
Hierarchy

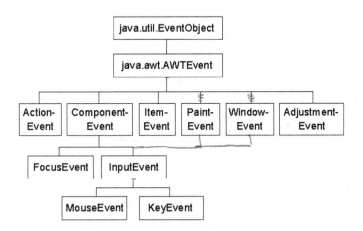

The AWTEvent objects your event handlers receive are tailored to the type of event they represent.

The AWT does not notify your event handler of every event that occurs over a component, as in the old days of 1.0.2. Now, AWT informs your event handler only about the events it is interested in.

Listening for Events

Add a new Listener to a component's list of event listeners.

The protocol of events propagating up the container hierarchy is history. Now, you explicitly indicate which objects should handle specific events that occur in a particular component.

You set up event handlers by telling a component which object will listen for the events it's interested in.

For example, let's say you have placed a button in your user interface, and you want your application to know when the user clicks this button. You need to perform the following steps in your code:

1. Define a class that implements a Listener interface. There are a variety of Listener interfaces, each one representing different types of events. For example, there's a MouseMotionListener that declares methods for handling mouse movements; there's a FocusListener that declares methods for reacting to a component acquiring or losing the focus. Figure 15-2 shows the hierarchy of the Listener interfaces.
2. Create an instance of this class.
3. Tell the component whose events you are interested in which types of events you are interested in, and which object will handle those events. You do this by invoking a method called addABCListener() and passing it the instance of your Listener class. There are different addABCListener() methods, where "ABC" in the method name is replaced by the type of listener you're adding to the component's list of listeners. So, to add an instance of MouseMotionListener called myMouseMotionListener to a component's list of listeners, you would write:

```
myComponent.addMouseMotionListener(myMouseMotionListener);
```

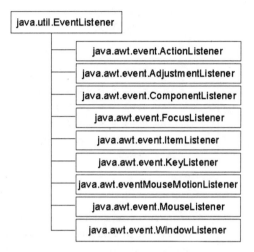

Figure 15-2
The Listener
Hierarchy

To get a flavor for this, here's a simple applet that draws scribbles by handling the MouseListener and MouseMotionListener events.

Tip

This program could also use an inner class (new in Java 1.1) to handle the events, rather than having the applet itself implement these interfaces. Or, it could define a separate class that only handled the events related to scribbling. Another possibility is for it to enable certain events and handle them directly without going through this Listener interface at all (we won't discuss that approach in this chapter). Let's start with this example and improve upon its design as we progress through this chapter.

```java
import java.awt.*;
import java.awt.event.*;
import java.applet.Applet;

public class Scribble extends Applet
    implements MouseMotionListener, MouseListener
{
    private int x;
    private int y;

    public void init() {
        addMouseListener(this);
        addMouseMotionListener(this);
    }
```

continued

```
public void mousePressed(MouseEvent e) {
    x = e.getX();
    y = e.getY();
}

public void mouseDragged(MouseEvent e) {
    Graphics g = getGraphics();
    int newX = e.getX();
    int newY = e.getY();
    g.drawLine(x, y, newX, newY);
    x = newX;
    y = newY;
}

// Left-over methods from the interfaces.
public void mouseMoved(MouseEvent e) { }
public void mouseClicked(MouseEvent e) { }
public void mouseReleased(MouseEvent e) { }
public void mouseEntered(MouseEvent e) { }
public void mouseExited(MouseEvent e) { }

}
```

Figure 15-3 shows what this looks like after a user has interacted with this applet for a bit.

Figure 15-3
Using the Scribble
Applet

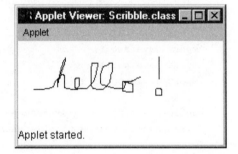

Applet Viewer: Scribble.class

Applet

hello !

Applet started.

As you can see, this applet doesn't remember the drawing the user has performed, so if the applet is resized, the `paint()` operation will make the scribble vanish like shaking an Etch-a-Sketch.

We imported an additional package, something new compared with Java 1.0.2. This new package is `java.awt.event`, which contains all of the event classes we need.

Notice how we had to implement stubs for `mouseMoved()`, `mouseClicked()`, `mouseReleased()`, `mouseEntered()`, and `mouseExited()`. We did not care about these events but were forced to implement them anyway. Why? Because the MouseListener and MouseMotionListener interfaces define all of these `abstract` methods. Sure, all we care about is `mousePressed()` and `mouseDragged()`, but if we didn't implement the others, our Applet subclass would be `abstract`.

Tip

Creating empty stubs seems like a waste of effort—if you are creating a class that only handles events, it is. There is a way around this problem; we'll look at that short-cut in a few pages. First, let's look at the Listener interfaces and the `addABCListener()` methods in more detail.

The Listener Interfaces

Objectives

Identify the important Listener interfaces.

The above program showed a way to detect mouse events. What other types of Listener interfaces are there?

The Listener interfaces are all defined in a package that's new in Java 1.1 called `java.awt.event`. They are presented here in alphabetical order.

Tip

I've also listed the methods that you must define if you implement one of these interfaces. You can refer to this list if you would like to implement one of these interfaces.

ActionListener

- `public void actionPerformed(ActionEvent e)`

AdjustmentListener

- `public void adjustmentValueChanged(AdjustmentEvent e)`

ComponentListener

- `public void componentHidden(ComponentEvent e)`
- `public void componentMoved(ComponentEvent e)`
- `public void componentResized(ComponentEvent e)`
- `public void componentShown(ComponentEvent e)`

FocusListener

- `public void focusGained(FocusEvent e)`
- `public void focusLost(FocusEvent e)`

ItemListener

- `public void itemStateChanged(ItemEvent e)`

KeyListener

- `public void keyPressed(KeyEvent e)`
- `public void keyReleased(KeyEvent e)`
- `public void keyTyped(KeyEvent e)`

MouseListener

- `public void mouseClicked(MouseEvent e)`
- `public void mouseEntered(MouseEvent e)`
- `public void mouseExited(MouseEvent e)`
- `public void mousePressed(MouseEvent e)`
- `public void mouseReleased(MouseEvent e)`

MouseMotionListener

- public void mouseDragged(MouseEvent e)
- public void mouseMoved(MouseEvent e)

WindowListener

- public void windowClosed(WindowEvent e)
- public void windowClosing(WindowEvent e)
- public void windowDeiconified(WindowEvent e)
- public void windowIconifiedClosed(WindowEvent e)
- public void windowOpened(WindowEvent e)

Implementing a Listener Interface

Implement a Listener interface.

You've already seen an example of the applet implementing a Listener interface. However, you can also define a class specifically for handling an event. Here's a trivial example so that you can see the mechanics of it. You'll see fuller examples in the exercises.

In this applet, we create a button named "Click me!" We also define a class called OurClickHandler that implements the MouseListener interface. In the applet's init() method, we add an instance of this class to the button's list of listeners by calling addMouseListener(). Then, when the user clicks this button, AWT routes all mouse events, including mouseClicked(), to our instance of OurClickHandler. There, we write a simple message to the standard output. Here's the code:

```
import java.awt.*;
import java.awt.event.*;
import java.applet.Applet;
```

continued

```
public class ClickApplet extends Applet {
   public void init() {
      Button b = new Button("Click me!");
      b.addMouseListener(new OurClickHandler());
      add(b);
   }
}


class OurClickHandler implements MouseListener {
   public void mouseClicked(MouseEvent e) {
      System.out.println("button clicked");
   }

   // Left-over interface methods.
   public void mousePressed(MouseEvent e) { }
   public void mouseReleased(MouseEvent e) { }
   public void mouseEntered(MouseEvent e) { }
   public void mouseExited(MouseEvent e) { }
}
```

Exercise 15.1

Create an applet that contains context-sensitive help messages. Do this in an applet that places three buttons along the top of the interface. These buttons should write their names to the standard output when clicked. You can use any names you'd like to for your buttons.

At the bottom of the applet, place a label. Whenever the user moves the mouse cursor over one of the buttons, display a simple message containing a few words in the label at the bottom of the applet that explains what will happen if the user clicks the button.

As an example, your applet might look like Figure 15-4.

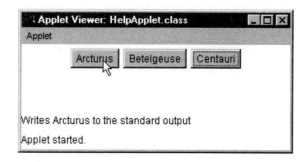

Figure 15-4
The Context-Sensitive
Help Applet

Semantic and Low-Level Events

State the difference between semantic and low-level and events.

It's convenient to separate the different types of events into two categories. You can think of these as semantic and low-level events.

There are three types of semantic events: action events, item events, and adjustment events.

Let's take a look at the different AWT components and see which semantic events they fire under what circumstances.

ActionEvent

AWT sends an ActionEvent object to any registered ActionListener objects when the user:

- clicks a button
- hits the Enter key when typing in a text field
- selects a menu item
- double-clicks a list item

ItemEvent

AWT sends an ItemEvent object to any registered ItemListener objects when the user:

- selects an item in a list
- selects an option from a choice box
- selects a menu item from a checkbox menu item
- clicks a checkbox

AdjustmentEvent

AWT sends an AdjustmentEvent object to any registered AdjustmentListener objects when the user:

- scrolls up, down, left, or right using a scroll bar
- scrolls up, down, left, or right using a scroll pane

AWTEvent Subclasses

So far, we've breezed over the AWTEvent subclasses so that you could see the overall architecture of event handling in 1.1. You know that you must implement a Listener interface if you are interested in a particular event, and you must register an instance of the class implementing this Listener interface as an event listener with the user interface component whose events you want to handle.

Now, let's back up just a bit and review the AWTEvent subclasses that AWT will pass your event handlers.

Even though Java 1.1 has done away with the single Event class that contained numerous int ids for the specific event the event object represented, Java 1.1 has not done away with event ids entirely. The problem is that there are so many events, it's not feasible to create AWTEvent subclasses that represent all of them. Instead, Java 1.1 defines AWTEvent subclasses for different *categories* of events. For example, the MouseEvent class is used when the user:

- clicks down on the mouse
- releases the mouse
- moves the mouse into or out of a component

Tip

If you need to identify which particular event occurred based on the MouseEvent object alone, you are back to using an int *id field to determine this. You would invoke the object's* getId() *method and then use constants defined in MouseEvent to identify the event. In this example, the constants you would check include* MOUSE_CLICKED, MOUSE_PRESSED, MOUSE_RELEASED, MOUSE_ENTERED, MOUSE_EXITED. *Different AWTEvent subclasses have their own constants. Many of these constants are presented in the section below on the AWTEvent subclasses. You can also review the APIs for a complete list. However, you generally won't need to do this. You can, instead, simply supply the appropriate event method and let AWT invoke this method for you.*

You can use methods in the AWTEvent subclasses to get specific information about the event. I have listed some of the important methods and constants for each type of event. (Refer back to Figure 15-1 for a class hierarchy of these classes.)

AWTEvent

This is the root of all AWT events and is defined in `java.awt`. All of its subclasses are located in `java.awt.event`.

ActionEvent

- `getModifiers()` returns an `int` whose bits match whether the user had selected the Shift, Alt or Control keys when the user generated this event.
- The constants `ALT_MASK`, `CTRL_MASK`, and `SHIFT_MASK` can be used with the | operator with `getModifiers()` to determine whether any of these special modifier keys were pressed when the user generated this event.

AdjustmentEvent

- `getAdjustable()` retrieves the object where this event originated. This object will be an instance of a class that implements the Adjustable interface.
- `getValue()` returns the current value in this adjustment event.

ComponentEvent

- getComponent() returns the component that triggered this event.

FocusEvent

This class simply defines some new constants (such as FOCUS_GAINED and FOCUS_LOST).

InputEvent

- getModifiers() returns an int representing the bit values that determine whether the user pressed the Alt, Control, or Shift keys when the user generated this event.
- getWhen() returns the time stamp for this event.

KeyEvent

- getKeyCode() returns an int value representing a key on the keyboard. This key may or may not generate a character—for example, the letter "a" does, but the F1 key does not.
- getKeyChar() returns a char of the character typed.

MouseEvent

- getClickCount() returns the number of times the user clicked the mouse to generate this event (that is, was this a double-click? A triple-click?).
- getX() returns the x coordinate of the mouse event.
- getY() returns the y coordinate of the mouse event.

ItemEvent

- getItem() returns the item where the event occurred.
- getItemSelectable() returns the object whose class implements the ItemSelectable interface where this event occurred.
- getStateChange() returns either SELECTED or DESELECTED, depending one whether the user just selected or deselected the item.

PaintEvent

Even though AWT passes this type of event to components, you should normally not listen for this type of event. Instead, you should override `paint()`, just as in Java 1.0.2.

WindowEvent

- `getWindow()` returns the window that generated this event.

Exercise 15.2

Write an applet that contains three text fields. These text fields should have a white background when the user is not interacting with them. Each text field should turn red when the user is about to enter data into it, and each should turn yellow if the user types an exclamation point (!). Once the user has finished typing, the text field should become white again.

Implement this by creating a special class that updates the text field's colors. This class should not be a subclass of TextField. Your application might look like what's shown in Figure 15-5.

Figure 15-5
An Applet with Colorful Text Fields

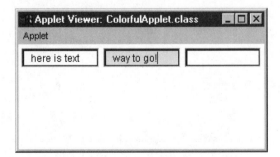

Extending Adapter Classes

Extend an Adapter class.

Sometimes it's not very convenient to implement a Listener interface. As you saw with the Scribble applet, you'll find that there are a number of methods that are simply stubs, doing nothing, cluttering up your source code. Rather than creating a bunch of useless no-op methods, you can extend a Java class that has already taken the trouble of doing this.

There's an Adapter class to match each interface. Each Adapter class defines no-op stubs for the methods declared in the corresponding interface.

For reference, here is the complete list of the Adapter classes:

- ~~ActionListener~~
- ~~AdjustmentListener~~ *Container Adapter*
- Component~~Listener~~ *Adapter*
- Focus~~Listener~~
- ~~ItemListener~~
- Key~~Listener~~
- Mouse~~Listener~~
- MouseMotion~~Listener~~
- Window~~Listener~~

Extending an Adapter class only makes sense when the object that will listen for and handle the event has no other responsibilities. If you want your applet to handle the event, as in the Scribble example, then it must implement the appropriate Listener interface, since Java does not have multiple inheritance of implementation.

Exercise 15.3

Rewrite Exercise 15.2 using an adapter class rather than implementing more than one Listener interface. If possible, eliminate the need to write no-op stubs.

Answers to the Exercises

Exercise 15.1

```java
import java.awt.*;
import java.awt.event.*;
import java.applet.Applet;

public class HelpApplet extends Applet {
    public void init() {
        Button b;
        Panel p = new Panel();
        setLayout(new BorderLayout());

        HelpLabel label = new HelpLabel();

        b = new Button("Arcturus");
        b.addMouseListener(label);
        p.add(b);

        b = new Button("Betelgeuse");
        b.addMouseListener(label);
        p.add(b);

        b = new Button("Centauri");
        b.addMouseListener(label);
        p.add(b);
        add("North", p);
        add("South", label);
    }
}

class HelpLabel extends Label implements MouseListener {

    public void mouseEntered(MouseEvent e) {
        Button b = (Button)(e.getComponent());
        String s = "Writes " + b.getLabel() + " to the standard output";
        setText(s);
    }
```

Exercise 15.1 continued

```
    public void mouseClicked(MouseEvent e) {
        Button b = (Button)(e.getComponent());
        System.out.println(b.getLabel());
    }


    // Left-over MouseListener methods.
    public void mousePressed(MouseEvent e) { }
    public void mouseReleased(MouseEvent e) { }
    public void mouseExited(MouseEvent e) { }


}
```

Exercise 15.2

```
import java.awt.*;
import java.awt.event.*;
import java.applet.Applet;

public class ColorfulApplet extends Applet {
    public void init() {
        for (int i = 0; i < 3; i++) {
            TFHandler tfHandler = new TFHandler();
            TextField tf = new TextField(10);
            tf.addFocusListener(tfHandler);
            tf.addKeyListener(tfHandler);
            add(tf);
        }
    }
}

class TFHandler implements FocusListener, KeyListener {

    public void focusGained(FocusEvent e) {
        e.getComponent().setBackground(Color.red);
    }
```

Exercise 15.2 continued

```
    public void focusLost(FocusEvent e) {
        e.getComponent().setBackground(Color.white);
    }


    public void keyTyped(KeyEvent e) {
        if (e.getKeyChar() == '!')
            e.getComponent().setBackground(Color.yellow);
    }


    // Left-over Listener events.
    public void keyPressed(KeyEvent e) { }
    public void keyReleased(KeyEvent e) { }
}
```

Exercise 15.3

The import statements and the Applet class are the same. Here is the new event handler.

```
class TFHandler extends KeyAdapter implements FocusListener {

    public void focusGained(FocusEvent e) {
        e.getComponent().setBackground(Color.red);
    }


    public void focusLost(FocusEvent e) {
        e.getComponent().setBackground(Color.white);
    }


    public void keyTyped(KeyEvent e) {
        if (e.getKeyChar() == '!')
            e.getComponent().setBackground(Color.yellow);
    }


}
```

Review Questions

Question 1: Given an object named `myHandler` whose class implements the FocusListener interface, how can you tell a `component` named component that `myHandler` should receive all focus events?

a) `component.add(myHandler);`
b) `component.addListener(myHandler);`
c) `addFocusListener(component, myHandler);`
d) `component.addFocusListener(myHandler);`

Question 2: Which messages will appear in the standard output whenever the user clicks the button named "Click me!" given the following code?

```java
import java.awt.*;
import java.awt.event.*;
import java.applet.Applet;

    public void init() {
        Button b = new Button("Click me!");
        b.addMouseListener(new OurClickHandler());
        add(b);
    }
}

class OurClickHandler implements MouseListener {
    public void actionPerformed(ActionEvent e) {
        System.out.println("button action");
    }

    public void mouseClicked(MouseEvent e) {
        System.out.println("button clicked");
    }

    // Left-over interface methods.
    public void mousePressed(MouseEvent e) { }
    public void mouseReleased(MouseEvent e) { }
    public void mouseEntered(MouseEvent e) { }
    public void mouseExited(MouseEvent e) { }
}
```

a) "button action"
b) "button clicked"
c) both "button action" and "button clicked"
d) neither of these messages

Question 3: **If you need to create a class that will handle key strokes as the user types, and if your new class will not need to extend any other class, you can:**

a) extend KeyAdapter to implement your new class
b) implement KeyListener
c) implement ActionListener
d) either a or b
e) either a, b, or c

Question 4: **AWT generates an action event for all of the following situations, except:**

a) the user clicks a list item
b) the user clicks a button
c) the user types text into a text field and hits enter
d) the user selects a menu item

Question 5: **To identify when the user has closed a window, you can implement which Listener interface?**

a) MouseListener
b) ActionListener
c) WindowListener
d) all of these

Answers to the Review Questions

Question 1   d.   Use `addABCListener()` to register a listener of type ABCListener with a component.

Question 2   b.   The message "button action" does not appear because the code never registers the instance of MyClickHandler as one of the button's ActionListeners (also, it does not declare that it implements the ActionListener interface).

Question 3   d.   Either extending KeyAdapter or implementing KeyListener are probably your best choices. An action event is only generated for a text field (for example) when the user hits Enter, and so is not best suited for processing keystrokes as the user types.

Question 4   a.   The user must double-click a list item to generate an action event. Single clicking a list item causes AWT to generate an item event.

Question 5   c.   WindowListener interface defines methods called `windowClosing()` and `windowClosed()` that you can override to detect when the user has closed a window.

CHAPTER 16

Passing Arguments to Programs

You need to know how to work with arrays to be able to pass arguments to programs. Also, since the main() method is defined as a public class method, it's useful to know the material from Chapter 1 that reviews what the access control keywords are all about and what a static method is.

This chapter reviews how to invoke a Java program from the command line and pass parameters to the program.

What's on the Test

There are a few questions on the exam that relate to creating a main() method and selecting arguments passed to main() from the command line.

Objectives for this Chapter

- Describe the role of a method.
- Write a main() method.
- Select specific command line elements from the arguments of the main() method using the correct array subscript value.

The main() Method

Describe the role of a main() method.

Write a main() method.

Unlike in C/C++ where you execute a file, in Java you run a program by passing a class name to the Java interpreter. When you invoke a stand-alone program, the Java runtime looks for that class' main() method.

The main() method must be declared as a public, static method that does not return a value and takes an array of String objects.

Here is the template for main():

```
public static void main(String[] args)
```

If the Java interpreter does not find a `main()` method that follows the above format, the interpreter won't run the class.

Some development environments, such as Metrowerks CodeWarrior, allow you to define a `main()` method that does not take any parameters. However, this is not the way things are done using the JDK, and the test is specific to the JDK.

The JDK will complain if you run a class whose `main()` method deviates from the standard declaration. The method must be `static`, since you have not yet created any instances of your class when you run your program. You cannot return a value to the operating system or Java interpreter. You cannot define a different argument. You can't even supply a subclass of String, because String is a `final` class and cannot be subclassed.

The exact order of the keywords `public` and `static`, and the way the String array is defined, is not strictly enforced. However, the accepted order for the keywords is to place `public` first, `static` second, and to define the String array using `String[]`.

For example, this is also a valid `main()` method:

```
static public void main(String args[]) { } // not the accepted way
```

However, the accepted way to write `main()` is:

```
public static void main(String[] args) { } // the accepted way
```

Command Line Arguments

Select specific command line elements from the arguments of the main method using the correct array subscript value.

Using the JDK, you can provide command line arguments for a standalone Java program. To do this, place the arguments after the program name when you invoke the Java interpreter.

For example, you can invoke a program called Flower, below, like this:

```
java Flower rose
```

This will pass the String "rose" to the `main()` method of the Flower class. The runtime will allocate a String array to the size of the number of command line arguments you supply (in this case, 1), allocate a String instance containing the command line argument, and place it into the array passed to `main()`.

For example, invoking the following Flower class' `main()` method using the command above:

```
public class Flower {
    public static void main(String[] args) {
        System.out.println("My favoriate flower is a " + args[0]);
    }
}
```

will result in the following output:

```
My favorite flower is a rose
```

Since this is an array, and since in the program we don't know for certain that the user has supplied a command line argument, we could get into trouble. We can't just go around accessing elements from an array beyond the bounds of an array—Java will throw an ArrayIndexOutOfBoundsException.

Taking the previous tip to heart, before using elements out of the `args` array in `main()`, it's a good idea to first check the length of the `args` array to make sure it contains what you think it contains. Here's a new version of the Flower class that does this in its `main()` method:

```
public class Flower {
    public static void main(String[] args) {
        if (args.length == 0)
            System.out.println("I like all flowers");
        else if (args.length == 1)
            System.out.println("My favorite flower is a " + args[0]);
        else {
            System.out.print("My favorite flowers are " + args[0]);
            for (int i = 1; i < args.length - 1; i++)
                System.out.print(", " + args[i]);
            System.out.println(" and " + args[args.length-1]);
        }
    }
}
```

When run with commands like this:

```
java Flower
java Flower violet
java Flower violets roses daffodils
```

This prints:

```
I like all flowers
My favorite flower is a violet
My favorite flowers are violets, roses, and daffodils
```

Exercise 16.1

Write a main() method that displays the command line arguments you pass to a program in reverse order.

When main() Ends

When main() ends, that may or may not be the end of the program. The JVM will run until the only remaining threads are daemon threads—it will run until all of the user threads have died. If main() does not spawn any more threads, then the program will end when main() ends. However, if main() creates and starts a new thread, then even when main() comes to an end, the JVM may continue executing to support these other threads.

What's Not on the Test

Even though there may be a question or two that mentions that the JVM runs until all user threads have died, the test does not cover how to set a thread to be a user thread or a daemon thread.

By default, a thread is a user thread if it was created by another user thread, and it is a daemon thread if it was created by another daemon thread. This means that, by default, all threads that you create in your program will be user threads.

If you create and display a user interface element from main(), such as a frame, your program will continue to run even after main() ends, because user interface elements have their own user thread associated with them to handle user input. Once the user closes this frame, though, the program will end (if this is the last remaining user thread).

To explicitly set whether a thread is a user thread or a daemon thread, you can use the Thread method setDaemon() and pass it a boolean. To test whether a thread is a daemon thread or a user thread, you can use the Thread method isDaemon(), which returns an appropriate boolean.

Answers to the Exercises

Exercise 16.1

```
class Reverse {
   public static void main(String[] args) {
      System.out.println("The parameters in reverse order are:");
      for (int i = args.length - 1; i >= 0; i--) {
         System.out.print(args[i] + " ");
      }
      System.out.println("");
   }
}
```

If you run this program like this:

```
java Reverse My name is Barry
```

it will display

```
The parameters in reverse order are:
Barry is name My
```

Review Questions

Question 1: Which of these defines a valid `main()` method?

    a) `public static void main(String args[]) { }`
    b) `public static void main(String[]) { }`
    c) `public static void main(String[] args);`
    d) `public static void main(args) { }`

Question 2: How can you access the word "kiss" from the following invocation of `main()`:

java lyrics a kiss is but a kiss

    a) `args[0]`
    b) `args[2]`
    c) `args[4]`
    d) `args[5]`
    e) `args[6]`
    f) b and e

Question 3: The Java Virtual Machine will run until:

    a) `main()` ends
    b) the only threads left are user threads
    c) the only threads left are daemon threads
    d) a or c, whichever comes first

Answers to the Review Questions

Question 1   a.   A String array can be defined by placing the square brackets after the variable name. The other possible main definitions are not valid.

Question 2   d.   The String array starts at 0. So, `args[0]` would be "a", `args[1]` would be "kiss", and so on, up to `args[5]`, which is also "kiss". (Remember, `lyrics` is the name of the class to run.)

Question 3   c.   The JVM will run until all user threads die and the only threads left are daemon threads.

CHAPTER 17

Embedding Applets into Web Pages

This chapter does not go into how to write applets: that's covered as part of the user interface discussion in Chapter 13. You should already know how to put together a basic applet so that, in this chapter, you can tailor it based on applet parameters.

Just as you can pass command-line arguments to a stand-alone application, you can also pass arguments to a Web-based applet. With foresight on the part of the programmer, this allows non-programmers to control the behavior of an applet. Non-programmers can treat the applet more like any other Web-based resource that contains some values they can tweak to control its appearance or behavior. The difference in the behavior of the applet can range from displaying different text to performing a different calculation. I'll show you a few examples in this chapter.

What's on the Test

The test asks you to write a `<param>` tag so that you pass a parameter to an applet. It also asks you to retrieve a parameter. You should know the basics of the `<applet>` tag, as well.

Objectives

- Write HTML code to embed an applet in a Web page.
- Use the `<applet>` tag to specify the width and height of the applet.
- Supply parameter values to the applet within the `<applet>` tag.
- Read the values of parameters specified in an `<applet>` tag and use them in an applet.

The Simplest HTML File

Write HTML code to embed an applet in a Web page.

Use the <applet> tag to specify the width and height of the applet.

First, we'll look at how you embed an applet in an HTML page. You've no doubt done this already in your Java career, but let's review for the test.

To run an applet, you need to embed a reference to the compiled applet in an HTML file. You can then view the HTML file in a Java-enabled Web browser, or in a development tool such as the JDK's appletviewer.

You use the <applet> tag to embed an applet within a Web page.

Here's the simplest HTML file you can write to reference an applet (in this case an applet with the compiled class file named `Metric.class`). It contains three keywords in the `<applet>` tag:

```
<applet code=Metric.class width=200 height=100>
</applet>
```

The `code` keyword identifies the compiled class file containing the applet. In this example, this file is relative to the IP address and directory containing the HTML file in which this reference is embedded. However, this value can also be an absolute path name, so that a Web page can contain an applet found anywhere on the Web.

If the applet is loaded relative to the page, there are two things that can change the base location. The first is if the HTML file itself contains a <base> tag—this tag specifies where to look for the applet class. The second is if the <applet> tag contains the codebase keyword. The codebase keyword is described in the next section.

The two other keywords you must have inside an `<applet>` tag are `width` and `height`. These specify the size of the screen, in pixels, that the browser or appletviewer should use to display the applet. The browser or appletviewer sizes the applet itself to the size indicated by these keywords.

Be aware that since you are specifying the height and width in pixels, different screens will display the applet differently, according to their own, unique resolutions.

Passing Parameters to an Applet

Supply parameter values to the applet within the <applet> tag.

The conventional way to pass a parameter to an applet is to use the <param> tag, using one <param> tag per parameter. (Each <param> tag can only takes one parameter.)

Each parameter value can be retrieved by the applet as a String, using methods defined in class Applet.

If you want to pass a different type of value, such as an int or a boolean, you must convert it from a String, most likely by using a wrapper class.

Any number of <param> tags can be placed between the <applet> and </applet> tags. The <param> tag uses two keywords: name, to name the parameter, and value, to give it a value. An example of the <param> tag is:

```
<param name=state value=Hawaii>
```

If you'd like a parameter value to contain spaces, you should place this value within quotes.

For example, to supply a parameter value that's really two words, you can write:

```
<param name=state value="New Mexico">
```

However, it never hurts to include quotes, even for a single word, as in:

```
<param name=state value="California">
```

Retrieving Parameters

Read the values of parameters specified in an <applet> tag and use them in the applet.

You retrieve the value of a parameter using the getParameter() method defined by the Applet class. This method returns a String containing the value of the parameter, or null if the parameter was not defined at all.

Most programmers don't realize that you can actually retrieve the parameters in the <applet> tag itself using getParameter(). Here's an example:

```java
import java.applet.Applet;

public class Tag extends Applet {
   public void init() {
      System.out.println(getParameter("code"));
      System.out.println(getParameter("width"));
      System.out.println(getParameter("height"));
   }
}
```

Here's an HTML file we can use to run this applet:

```html
<applet code=Tag.class width=200 height=100>
</applet>
```

The output from this program in the standard output is:

```
tag.class
200
100
```

You can even put your own parameters right into the <applet> tag, rather than the <param> tag. For the sake of convention, you shouldn't do this—but it works. For example, if you run this program:

```java
import java.applet.Applet;

public class Tag extends Applet {
   public void init() {
      System.out.println(getParameter("code"));
      System.out.println(getParameter("width"));
      System.out.println(getParameter("height"));
      System.out.println(getParameter("extra"));
   }
}
```

using this HTML file:

```
<applet code=Tag.class width=200 height=100 extra=Thea>
</applet>
```

the result in the standard output is:

```
Tag.class
200
100
Thea
```

However, the reverse is not true. You cannot place a width value within a
<param> tag, like this:

```
<applet code=Tag.class height=100>
<param name=width value=200>
</applet>
```

If you do, the appletviewer or Web browser won't run the applet and
will complain that the <applet> tag was not written properly.

Exercises

Exercise 17.1

Write an <applet> tag to embed an applet named Example into a Web
page and to size this applet to be 500 pixels wide and 200 pixels tall.

Exercise 17.2

Write an init() method that checks for a parameter named "button"
and creates a button with that name that prints that string to the standard output. If no parameter is defined, give the button any name
you'd like.

Customizing an Applet

To put this all together, the purpose of passing parameter values to an applet is to allow an applet to be used for many slightly different purposes. The applet will always do the same thing—for example, it might display text that runs across the page like a stock ticker, or display a sequence of images fast enough to animate them. But with applet parameters, the specifics can change—the text an applet displays can be different text, and the images that compose the animation can be different images.

This ability to customize allows you to reuse an applet without programming. As an example, here's an applet that can convert inches to centimeters. You can see what this look like in Figure 17-1. Here's the code:

```java
import java.awt.*;
import java.applet.Applet;

public class Metric extends Applet {
    TextField tf;
    TextField tf2;
    double    convFactor;
    String    toUnits;
    String    fromUnits;

    public void init() {
        String factor = getParameter("factor");
        fromUnits = getParameter("from");
        toUnits = getParameter("to");
        if (fromUnits == null || toUnits == null || factor == null) {
            fromUnits = "inches";
            toUnits = "cm";
            convFactor = 2.56;
        } else {
            try {
                convFactor = new Double(factor).doubleValue();
            } catch (NumberFormatException e) {
                fromUnits = "inches";
                toUnits = "cm";
                convFactor = 2.56;
            }
        }

        add(new Label("Convert " + fromUnits + " to " + toUnits + ":"));
```

```
        tf = new TextField(10);
        add(tf);

        tf2 = new TextField(20);
        tf2.disable();
        tf2.setBackground(Color.gray);
        add(tf2);
    }
    public boolean action(Event e, Object what) {
        if (e.target == tf) {
            String s = tf.getText();
            try {
                double d = new Double(s).doubleValue();
                double result = d * convFactor;
                String toEntry = new Double(result).toString();
                tf2.setText(toEntry + " " + toUnits);
            } catch (NumberFormatException x) {
                tf2.setText("Please enter a number.");
                tf.setText("");
            }
            repaint();
            return true;
        }
        return false;
    }
}
```

If you run this applet using an HTML file that does not specify any parameter values, such as:

```
<applet code=Metric.class width=266 height=72>
</applet>
```

Then you will see an applet that allows you to convert inches to centimeters. This applet will look like Figure 17-1 once you interact with it.

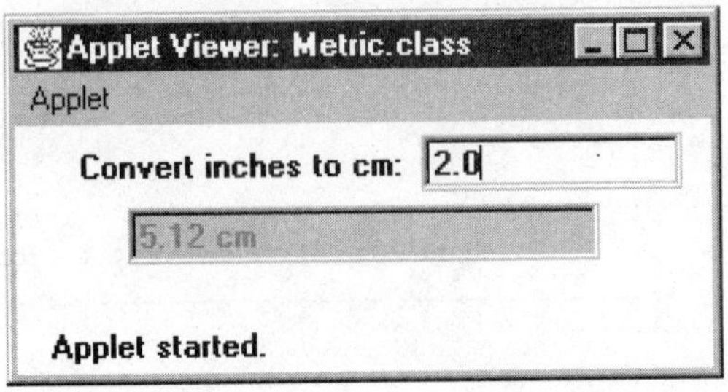

Figure 17-1
The Metric Applet
with its Default Values

However, this applet can convert from any unit to any other unit, and it's a simple matter to let users know how to embed this conversion applet into their own HTML pages. All they have to do is provide three <param> tags. These tags should be named from, to, and factor, and their values control what the applet displays (the order of these tags does not matter). For example, when run with the following HTML file:

```
<applet code=Metric.class width=266 height=72>
<param name=from value=miles>
<param name=to value=kilometers>
<param name=factor value=1.6>
</applet>
```

this applet appears like the screen shot in Figure 17-2 once you type in a number to convert:

Figure 17-2
The Metric Applet
Customized for Miles
and Kilometers

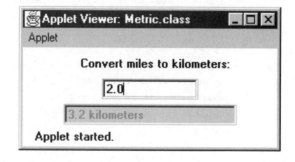

Now, you're able to convert between miles and kilometers without any programming.

What's Not on the Test

getParameterInfo()

If you'd like to make your applet self-documenting, you should override this method. This method returns an array of String arrays. Each entry in the array lists a parameter that this applet accepts, its legal values, and a description of what this parameter does. For example, here's a valid method definition:

```
public String[][] getParameterInfo() {
    String[][] info = {
            {"planet", "String", "the name of a planet"},
            {"conversion", "double", "weight conversion factor"},
            {"metric", "boolean", "metric if true, else english"}
            };
    return info;
}
```

Supplying a getParameterInfo() method allows others using your applet to determine how to embed the applet within an HTML page. With the code above, a programmer could invoke getParameterInfo() for an applet named PlanetWeight (for example) and determine that it takes three parameters: the name of a planet, a conversion factor for calculating your weight based on your earth weight, and whether the units are metric or english.

From this, the programmer could determine that a valid HTML file for embedding this applet could be:

```
<applet code=PlanetWeight.class width=200 height=100>
<param name=planet value=Mars>
<param name=conversion value=.31>
<param name=metric value=false>
</applet>
```

Advanced Keywords

There are a number of additional keywords for the <applet> tag that you might not be as familiar with. These are codebase, name, align, vspace, and hspace.

Use the codebase keyword to change the location where applet resources, such as images and sound files, are located. Applet resources include the applet itself. This value can be an absolute or a relative path. If the value for codebase is relative and a <base> tag is not defined, the value is relative to the HTML document's URL. If the value for codebase is relative and there is a <base> tag defined, the value is relative to the path in the <base> tag.

If the applet wants to access the document's URL, all it has to do is invoke the method getDocumentBase(), which returns a URL instance representing the document's URL. (There's also a method called getCode-

`Base()`, which returns a URL instance representing the URL the applet class came from.)

The `name` parameter names an applet. You can gain access to another applet in the same environment by retrieving an AppletContext object for the applet (which represents the environment in which the applet is running) and then invoking `getApplet()`, passing it the name of the applet you want to find.

The `align` keyword can take the values `left`, `right`, `top`, `texttop`, `middle`, `absmiddle`, `baseline`, `bottom`, or `absbottom`. These values determine where the applet is displayed on the page.

The keywords `vspace` and `hspace` specify the space around the applet. The `vspace` and `hspace` values are used only when the `align` attribute is `left` or `right`.

Answers to the Exercises

Exercise 17.1

```
<applet code=Example.class width=500 height=200>
</applet>
```

Exercise 17.2

Here's the code:

```java
import java.awt.*;
import java.applet.*;

public class MyButtonApplet extends Applet {
    public void init() {
        String s = getParameter("button");

        if (s == null)
            s = new String("giraffe");

        add(new MyButton(s));
    }
}
```

continued

```
class MyButton extends Button {
   MyButton(String s) {
      super(s);
   }
   public boolean action(Event e, Object what) {
      System.out.println(getLabel());
      return super.action(e, what);
   }
}
```

When this runs with the following HTML file (where a `<param>` tag is not defined):

```
<applet code=MyButtonApplet.class width=230 height=100>
</applet>
```

This applet looks like Figure 17-3.

Figure 17-3
The Default Button in
MyButtonApplet

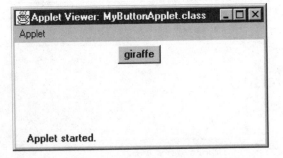

Clicking on the **giraffe** button writes the word "giraffe" to the standard output.

When you supply the following HTML file, however (where a `<param>` tag is now defined):

```
<applet code=MyButtonApplet.class width=230 height=100>
<param name=button value=elephant>
</applet>
```

Then the **giraffe** button is replaced with an **elephant** button, and clicking on this button writes the word "elephant" to the standard output.

Review Questions

Question 1: To specify a parameter in an `<applet>` tag named `lastname` that contains the value "Einstein," you could write:

    a)   `<param name=lastname value="Einstein">`
    b)   `<param name=lastname value=Einstein>`
    c)   either a or b

Question 2: To retrieve a parameter named `lastname`, you could write code for your applet that looked like:

    a)   `String s = getName("lastname");`
    b)   `String s = parameter("lastname");`
    c)   `String s = getParameter("lastname");`

Question 3: If you tried to read a parameter value and a parameter with that name was not defined in the `<applet>` tag:

    a)   The runtime would throw an exception
    b)   The parameter's value would be `null`
    c)   The parameter's value would be an empty string

Answers to the Review Questions

Question 1	c.	A parameter value can have quotes or not, depending on your preference. If the value contains spaces, however, it must be placed within quotes.
Question 2	c.	The method `getParameter()` retrieves a parameter value given a parameter name.
Question 3	b.	The method `getParameter()` returns `null` if a parameter with the given name is not defined.

Java 1.1

You should know how to embed an applet in a Web page, how to read and write data using streams, and how to create user interface components.

I'll discuss additional Java 1.1 features, including Java Database Connectivity and Remote Method Invocation, in Chapter 21. In this chapter, we'll go over some of the simpler features new to Java 1.1. You'll find that many of these are related and build on each other. For example, serialization and JAR files enable Java Beans; serialization uses the new `transient` keyword; and inner classes help with implementing the new Event model.

What's on the Test

Exam 310-022, which tests your knowledge of Java 1.1, is the latest addition to Java certification. It's important to be familiar with the concepts in this chapter to take and pass this test successfully. It's important to be familiar with these newer Java features before taking the exams.

Objectives for this Chapter

- Define inner classes.
- Use JAR files.
- Read objects from streams and write objects to streams using serialization.
- State what reflection is used for.
- Turn your AWT classes into Java Beans.

Inner Classes

In Java 1.0.2, you can only define a class at the "top level," as part of a package.

In Java 1.1, you can define classes inside other classes.

If you define an inner class at the same level as the enclosing class' instance variables, the inner class can access those instance variables—no matter what their access control (even `private`)—just as a method can access the variables of the class it is defined in. If you define an inner class within a *method*, the inner class can access the enclosing class' instance variables and also the local variables and parameter for that method.

If you do reference local variables or parameters from an inner class, those variables or parameters must be declared as `final` to help guarantee data integrity. (A new feature in Java 1.1 is that parameters and local variables can now be declared `final`.)

Creating inner classes allows you to better organize your classes in tune with your program. For example, if a class is really only used by one other class, that class can be placed within the class that refers to it. In a sense, the first class owns the helper class.

Here's an example (you already saw this program in Chapter 11). This applet displays a new number every second. It displayed prime numbers in red, and non-primes in blue:

```java
import java.awt.*;
import java.applet.Applet;

public class Ex1 extends Applet {
    Color        color = Color.red;
    int          candidate = 3;
    PrimeThread  prime;

    public void init() {
        prime = new PrimeThread(this);
        prime.start();
    }

    public void paint(Graphics g) {
        g.setColor(color);
        g.drawString(new Integer(candidate).toString(), 30, 40);
    }

}

class PrimeThread extends Thread {
    Ex1 target;

    PrimeThread (Ex1 target) {
        this.target = target;
    }

    public void run() {
        int candidate;
        for (candidate = 3; ; candidate++) {
            if (isPrime(candidate))
                target.color = Color.red;
            else
                target.color = Color.blue;
```

continued

```
        target.candidate = candidate;
        target.repaint();

        try {
            sleep(1000);
        } catch (InterruptedException ie) {
        }
    }
}

public boolean isPrime(int number) {
    boolean isPrime = true;

    for (int i = 2; i < number - 1 && isPrime; i++) {
        if ( (number % i ) == 0)
            isPrime = false;
    }
    return isPrime;
}

}

public boolean action(Event e, Object what)
```

Let's take this applet and turn PrimeThread into an inner class. When we do this, we'll no longer have to keep tabs on the applet itself in the target variable. Now, PrimeThread, as an inner class, can directly reference its enclosing class' variables and methods:

```
import java.awt.*;
import java.applet.Applet;

public class Ex2 extends Applet {
    Color         color = Color.red;
    int           candidate = 3;

    public void init() {
        new PrimeThread().start();
    }
```

continued

```java
    public void paint(Graphics g) {
        g.setColor(color);
        g.drawString(new Integer(candidate).toString(), 30, 40);
    }

    class PrimeThread extends Thread {

        public void run() {
            for ( ; ; candidate++) {
                if (isPrime(candidate))
                    color = Color.red;
                else
                    color = Color.blue;

                repaint();

                try {
                    sleep(1000);
                } catch (InterruptedException ie) {
                }
            }
        }

        public boolean isPrime(int number) {
            boolean isPrime = true;

            for (int i = 2; i < number - 1 && isPrime; i++) {
                if ( (number % i ) == 0)
                    isPrime = false;
            }
            return isPrime;
        }
    }
}
```

We can go even further and move this class definition into the applet's init() method so that the new class is declared right before we create an instance of it, just as we might declare a variable right before its use:

```java
import java.awt.*;
import java.applet.Applet;

public class Ex3 extends Applet {
    Color          color = Color.red;
    int            candidate = 3;

    public void init() {

        class PrimeThread extends Thread {

            public void run() {
                for ( ; ; candidate++) {
                    if (isPrime(candidate))
                        color = Color.red;
                    else
                        color = Color.blue;

                    repaint();

                    try {
                        sleep(1000);
                    } catch (InterruptedException ie) {
                    }
                }
            }

            public boolean isPrime(int number) {
                boolean isPrime = true;
                for (int i = 2; i < number - 1 && isPrime; i++) {
                    if ( (number % i ) == 0)
                        isPrime = false;
                }
                return isPrime;
            }
        }

        new PrimeThread().start();
    }

    public void paint(Graphics g) {
        g.setColor(color);
        g.drawString(new Integer(candidate).toString(), 30, 40);
    }

}
```

Where you define your class is in part a matter of style. You should define your classes where they make the most sense in your design.

Tip

Anonymous Classes

You can also define an anonymous class—a class without a name.

Key Concept

What does this mean? If we were to rewrite the prime number applet to define PrimeNumber as an anonymous thread, we could rewrite the `init()` applet like this:

```
public void init() {
    Thread t = new Thread() {
        // The old PrimeThread definition goes here . . .
    };
    t.start();
}
```

As you can see, the `new` expression states that it is creating an instance of class Thread. Actually, it's creating a subclass of Thread that we have not named, though we have supplied a definition for this subclass.

Note also the ending semicolon for anonymous class. The anonymous class is defined like a statement, so it needs a semicolon at the end.

Anonymous classes are great if you have a very simple class that's pretty much self-documenting because of the straightforward code and familiar context. This might not necessarily be the case with the PrimeThread class we were working with. In that case, an inner class with a name might be a better choice. The exercises coming up show where you might want to use an anonymous inner class.

Tip

Some Rules for Inner Classes

If you'd like to refer to the current instance of the enclosing class, you can write:

```
EnclosingClassName.this
```

If you need to refer to the inner class using a fully qualified name, you can write:

```
EnclosingClassName.InnerClassName
```

If your inner class is not defined as static, you can only create new instances of this class from a non-static method.

Anonymous classes cannot have constructors. Java invokes their super-class' constructor implicitly.

Exercise 18.1

In this exercise, you'll update a program written in Chapter 15 (where we reviewed Java's 1.1 event handling) to use inner classes.

First, start with this simple applet:

```
import java.awt.*;
import java.awt.event.*;
import java.applet.Applet;

public class ClickApplet extends Applet {
   public void init() {
      Button b = new Button("Click me!");
      b.addMouseListener(new OurClickHandler());
      add(b);
   }
}

class OurClickHandler implements MouseListener {
   public void mouseClicked(MouseEvent e) {
      System.out.println("button clicked");
   }

   // Left-over interface methods.
   public void mousePressed(MouseEvent e) { }
   public void mouseReleased(MouseEvent e) { }
   public void mouseEntered(MouseEvent e) { }
   public void mouseExited(MouseEvent e) { }
}
```

Turn OurClickHandler into an inner class.

Then, make it an inner class defined within the `init()` method.

Then, make it an anonymous class.

One question you might have is, how do you implement an *interface* as an anonymous class? You cannot use `implements` with an anonymous class. Try your solution, and if you have questions check out the answer at the end of the chapter.

JAR Files

Something that many Java programmers have griped about is the need to establish a new network connection for every class downloaded into a client's Web browser. Even if the Java classes themselves are small, it takes a few seconds to establish each connection. For an applet containing a dozen classes, this might mean a minute of download time—not counting anything other than the connection handshaking!

In Java 1.1, instead of placing all of your class files on the server individually, you can define a JAR file. JAR stands for "Java Archive."

A JAR file can contain all the resources that are part of an applet: class files, images, and sounds. Since all of these applet resources are contained in a single file, the browser only needs to establish one connection with the server to slurp up the entire application at once. This greatly helps improve performance.

JAR files are also useful for packaging your files for distribution. For example, as you'll learn about at the end of this chapter, you can write Java Beans, which are reusable components you can use to program graphically. You can distribute your Java Beans in a single JAR file.

Creating a JAR File

The 1.1 JDK comes with a utility called `jar` that creates JAR files.

Tip

If you type `jar` at the command line, this tool will provide documentation on how to use it.

You specify any options, the name of the JAR file, and then the files you'd like to place inside it. The options you'll probably use the most are shown in the following list.

option	use
c	create a new archive
x	extract the files from the archive
t	view the table of contents
f	specify the archive's file name
O	don't use zip to compress the file (this allows you to place the JAR file in a directory in your classpath)

For example, to create a new archive named `Jungle.jar` and add two files named `Panther.class` and `Leopard.class` to this archive, you could write:

```
jar -cf Jungle.jar Panther.class Leopard.class
```

Directories are processed recursively.

Specifying a JAR File in a Web Page

Java defines a new tag in 1.1 named `archive` that you can use to specify an archive file. The file is defined relative to the HTML page. You still need to define a `code` parameter to identify the applet class, even if the applet class is actually part of the JAR file and is no longer a separate file on the Web server. Here's an example:

```
<applet code=ExampleApplet.class
  archive="jars/example.jar"
  width=230 height=110>
</applet>
```

This applet tag defines a JAR archive in the `jars` directory under the directory containing the HTML page. The class `ExampleApplet.class` could be in the JAR file or not; the Web browser will download the entire JAR file and look for the classes it needs there. If it cannot find them, it will go back to the server and look for them individually.

Also, be certain to specify the `-f` option when you look at the table of contents or extract the files. So, to extract `example.jar`, you can write:

```
jar -xf example.jar
```

Serializing Objects

In Java 1.0.2, you could read and write Java's primitive data types using classes that implemented the DataInput and DataOutput interfaces. If you wanted to read and write objects, you had to implement your own protocol.

In Java 1.1, you can now read and write objects as well as primitive data types, using classes that implement ObjectInput and ObjectOutput. These two interfaces extend DataInput and DataOutput to read or write an object. ObjectInputStream and ObjectOutputStream implement these interfaces.

Key Concept

Figure 18-1 shows where these new `java.io` classes fit into the class hierarchy.

Figure 18-1
New Object Stream
Classes

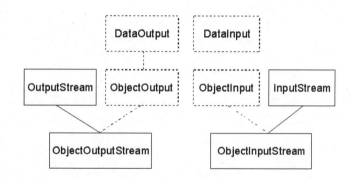

If a class implements the Serializable interface, then its public and protected instance variables will be read from and written to the stream automatically when you use ObjectInputStream and ObjectOutputStream.

If an instance variable refers to another object, it will also be read or written, and this continues recursively.

If the referenced object does not implement the Serializable interface, Java will throw a NotSerializableException.

The Serializable interface serves only to identify those instances of a particular class can be read from and written to a stream. It does not actually define any methods that you must implement.

Class Object does not implement Serializable, but lots of its subclasses do. For example, String, Date, and Number all implement Serializable, so it's very easy to read and write objects of these types. Many other basic object types implement this interface as well. However, if you inherit directly from class Object and want to read and write your object using streams, make sure your new class implements Serializable.

Here's an example of reading and writing a String and a URL object to a file:

```java
import java.io.*;
import java.net.URL;

public class Wr {
    private static final String FILE = "example";
    public static void main(String[] args) {
        write();
        read();
    }
```

continued

```java
    private static void write() {
        try {
            FileOutputStream f = new FileOutputStream(FILE);
            ObjectOutput s = new ObjectOutputStream(f);
            s.writeObject("My home page is: ");
            s.writeObject(new URL("http://www.learnjava.com"));
            s.close();
        } catch (IOException x) {
            System.out.println(x.getMessage());
        }
    }

    private static void read() {
        try {
            FileInputStream f = new FileInputStream(FILE);
            ObjectInput s = new ObjectInputStream(f);
            String text = (String)(s.readObject());
            URL url = (URL)(s.readObject());
            System.out.println(text + url);
            s.close();
        } catch (IOException x) {
            System.out.println(x.getMessage());
        } catch (ClassNotFoundException x) {
            System.out.println(x.getMessage());
        }
    }
}
```

This program uses ObjectInputStream and ObjectOutputStream to read from and write to the file. Notice that Java takes care of handling the details of the data to read and write for each object.

Tip

If you create your own class and want to keep certain data from being read or written (sensitive runtime information such as a password would be one example), you can declare that instance variable using the `transient` keyword (new in Java 1.1). Java skips any variable declared as `transient` when it reads and writes the object following the Serializable protocol.

Exercise 18.2

> Create a class called MyStrings that contains two Strings in a Vector. Initialize the two String objects in this Vector. Create a main() method that writes an instance of this class to a file and reads it back again. How should you declare MyStrings? Do you need to do anything special to write the Vector or the String objects in the Vector to make them read and write correctly?

Keywords

I've already covered the points in this section in the other sections, but I wanted to be sure you saw them in case you're just skimming this chapter.

You can now use the transient keyword for instance variables. Instance variables that are transient will not be serialized.

You can now use the final keyword for local variables and parameters. Local variables and parameters must be declared final if they are used by an inner class as well as in the enclosing class.

Reflection

Java needed a way to determine at runtime how an object was defined and what an object was capable of. With this information, it becomes possible to present a graphical user interface for manipulating the fields and behavior of Java Beans, and it allows the classes in the java.io package to read and write objects using streams.

By making the ability to determine how an object is built available as an API, all programs—not just the Java Virtual Machine—can discover what an object can do at runtime and adapt themselves to that.

Using the Reflection API, a program can determine a class' accessible fields, methods, and constructors at runtime.

Java now defines a package called `java.lang.reflect`. This package defines classes called Field, Method, and Constructor. While only the JVM can create a new instance of these classes, you can still get hold of an instance of these classes to determine what a class can do. You do this by obtaining a Class object representing the object's class by invoking `getClass()`, and then using methods defined for Class objects (such as `getFields()`, `getMethods()`, and `getConstructors()`) to retrieve arrays of the Field, Method, and Constructor objects, as appropriate. Each of the entries in the array contains an instance of one of these classes, which describes the name, access control, keywords, and other information for the entry.

In addition to simply finding out how an object's class is defined, with Field, Method, and Constructor instances you can also get and set field values, invoke methods, and create new instances. This allows you to write sophisticated programs such as debugging tools and other applications that adapt to the loaded classes. It also allows Java to implement serialization and Java Beans, which I briefly describe next.

Beans

No matter what you've heard or what it seems like from the hype, Java Beans are really quite simple to understand, even from a programmer's perspective.

Java Beans are reusable software components that developers program and manipulate visually using application builders.

If you've been programming in Java for a while, you'll find that Java Beans are easy to create. At its simplest, you can create a Java Bean just by following a naming convention. (I discuss that naming convention again in Chapter 23, under the general category of good programming practice, but this "good programming practice" has definite effects in relation to creating a Bean.) You can provide as much programming power for a Bean as you feel is best.

A Java Bean is capable of introspection at design time.

This means that a development environment can determine what a Bean is capable of and display options appropriate for that Bean. Just so you get the idea, when you drop a Bean into an application development environment that knows how to work with Beans, that development environment will display a palette of options for the Bean, allow you to set its options and change how it responds to events, and offer a way to trigger its behavior. The development environment lets you do all this graphically, through menus and palettes associated with the Bean. The development environment knows how to do this because of *introspection*—the development environment can determine what you, the developer using a Bean to build an application, can tinker with. An end user won't see these pathways into the heart of the Bean—only a developer will. Once the developer likes the way the Bean behaves, he can save the Bean to preserve its state and use that customized Bean as part of his application.

Beans can be arbitrarily complex—they can range from sliders to real-time data collection utilities to word processors. Beans don't have to be graphical when they run; they only have to be graphical when you design with them in an application development tool.

Beans are wonderful to work with, but not everything should be a Bean. If it is not useful to tinker with an object that's part of your program by using a mouse, or if it is extremely awkward to manipulate this object graphically when you program with it, it might be better if your creation were just a plain old class with an API that programmers work with by writing code. Of course, your Bean can have both types of programming interfaces (graphical and programmatic) if you'd like.

Properties

You change properties from a properties list and assign actions to events. If you follow a few simple naming conventions, you can have the Java Beans development environment do a great deal of the work for you as far as allowing the user to change a Bean's properties.

A Java Beans development environment identifies properties based on the pattern setProperty(), getProperty(), and isProperty() (for boolean types) within a class.

The environment knows that setX() and getX() methods indicate that the Bean developer wants to enable developers using this Bean to get and set the property named in this method (the X property, in this example). The development environment creates an interface of the appropriate data type to allow the developer using this Bean to do this and adds this interface to the property sheet.

If you have defined a boolean property, you can also write a method called isX() to retrieve the value of this property.

In all, there are four different types of patterns:

- What we just covered above is a *simple property*.
- You can also define an *indexed property*, which is similar, but uses arrays. The get and set properties take an additional parameter: an index into the array.
- A *bound property* notifies other objects when their values change. A bound property fires a PropertyChanged event that others can listen for.
- A constrained property lets other objects accept or reject a change in this property value. An object can reject a change by throwing a PropertyVetoException.

Constrained properties should also be bound.

Events

A Java Beans development environment identifies which events a developer can program for a Bean based on the pattern addListenerType() and removeListenerType() within a class.

The Bean itself should maintain a Vector that keeps track of the listeners for that event type. To inform a listener of an event, loop through the vector and dispatch an event to each listener.

You should clone the vector of listeners and dispatch events to objects referenced from the clone.

Customizer, PropertyEditor, and BeanInfo

You can create a customized property sheet for your Bean by implementing the Customizer interface. This interface consists of the methods addPropertyChangeListener() and removePropertyChangeListener(). You should keep track of the listeners in a vector in your Bean.

You can implement the PropertyEditor interface to create a customized property editor.

You can implement the BeanInfo interface to provide specific information about properties, methods, and events.

Instead of implementing BeanInfo, you can also extend SimpleBeanInfo, which is an adapter class.

Persistence

Once you've customized a Bean in a development environment, you'll want to save it. Java Beans achieve persistence through serialization.

A Bean must be serializable.

A Java Bean development environment can save the application the developer is building by writing out the objects in its construction area. It does this by using serialization, so all Beans must implement the Serializable interface.

Displaying a Bean

You should at least override the method `getMinimumSize()` (which returns a Dimension object) so that your Bean will be large enough to see when you place the Bean in a Bean-enabled development environment.

You should also override `paint()` if you want to make your Bean's display to do something special.

Distributing your Bean

Beans come packaged in JAR files. You should create a JAR file for your Bean's classes and resources to distribute your Bean. A Bean-enabled development environment will know how to work with your Bean's JAR file.

Exercise 18.3

In this exercise you'll create your own Bean. If you have the Bean Developer's Kit (the BDK) or some other Bean-enabled development environment, and if you can create a make file that tags this class as a Bean, you can then see your Bean in action. However, this exercise only asks you to write the code, not work with any particular development environment or create make files for a particular make command or operating environment.

Create a Bean called **Clicker** that is 100 pixels by 100 pixels. The programmer manipulating this Bean in a development environment should be able to set the Bean's background color, and the programmer should also be able to make something happen when the user clicks the Bean.

Answers to the Exercises

Exercise 18.1

Here's the original program, now with an inner class:

```java
import java.awt.*;
import java.awt.event.*;
import java.applet.Applet;

public class ClickApplet1 extends Applet {
    public void init() {
        Button b = new Button("Click me!");
        b.addMouseListener(new OurClickHandler());
        add(b);
    }

    class OurClickHandler implements MouseListener {
        public void mouseClicked(MouseEvent e) {
            System.out.println("button clicked");
        }

        // Left-over interface methods.
        public void mousePressed(MouseEvent e) { }
        public void mouseReleased(MouseEvent e) { }
        public void mouseEntered(MouseEvent e) { }
        public void mouseExited(MouseEvent e) { }
    }
}
```

And here's how we can place the class within the `init()` method itself, bringing it very close to where the instance is used:

```java
import java.awt.*;
import java.awt.event.*;
import java.applet.Applet;

public class ClickApplet2 extends Applet {
    public void init() {
        Button b = new Button("Click me!");
```

continued

```
        class OurClickHandler implements MouseListener {
          public void mouseClicked(MouseEvent e) {
            System.out.println("button clicked");
          }

          // Left-over interface methods.
          public void mousePressed(MouseEvent e) { }
          public void mouseReleased(MouseEvent e) { }
          public void mouseEntered(MouseEvent e) { }
          public void mouseExited(MouseEvent e) { }
        }

        b.addMouseListener(new OurClickHandler());
        add(b);
      }

    }
```

As for the anonymous interface implementation, you just write it as if it were an instance of an interface—of course, this is not possible. What's really happening is that Java extends class Object and implements the interface. Here's a solution:

```
import java.awt.*;
import java.awt.event.*;
import java.applet.Applet;

public class ClickApplet3 extends Applet {
  public void init() {
    Button b = new Button("Click me!");
    b.addMouseListener(myClickHandler());
    add(b);
  }

  private MouseListener myClickHandler() {

    return new MouseListener() {

      public void mouseClicked(MouseEvent e) {
        System.out.println("button clicked");
      }
```

Exercise 18.1 continued

```
        // Left-over interface methods.
        public void mousePressed(MouseEvent e) { }
        public void mouseReleased(MouseEvent e) { }
        public void mouseEntered(MouseEvent e) { }
        public void mouseExited(MouseEvent e) { }
    };
  }
}
```

Similarly, it's easy to rewrite the first program in Chapter 15 (`Scribble.java`) so that the adapter classes are inner classes or even anonymous classes.

You could also extend MouseAdapter here; the returned anonymous class would start out:

```
    return new MouseAdapter() { . . . }
```

Exercise 18.2

All we need to do is declare MyStrings to be Serializable. That will ensure its instance data gets written correctly. The Vector class is already Serializable, as is the String class, so these references will be written just fine as they are when Java encounters them (when writing out MyStrings):

```
import java.io.*;
import java.util.Vector;

public class MyStrings implements Serializable {

  private static final String FILE = "test";

  private Vector v = new Vector();

  public static void main(String[] args) {
    MyStrings ms = new MyStrings();
    ms.v.addElement("porcupine");
    ms.v.addElement("turpentine");
    write(ms);
    read();
  }
```

continued

```
    private static void write(MyStrings ms) {
        try {
            FileOutputStream f = new FileOutputStream(FILE);
            ObjectOutput s = new ObjectOutputStream(f);
            s.writeObject(ms);
            s.close();
        } catch (IOException x) {
            System.out.println(x.getMessage());
        }
    }

    private static void read() {
        try {
            FileInputStream f = new FileInputStream(FILE);
            ObjectInput s = new ObjectInputStream(f);
            MyStrings ms = (MyStrings)(s.readObject());
            System.out.println(ms.v.elementAt(0));
            System.out.println(ms.v.elementAt(1));
            s.close();
        } catch (IOException x) {
            System.out.println(x.getMessage());
        } catch (ClassNotFoundException x) {
            System.out.println(x.getMessage());
        }
    }

}
```

Exercise 18.3

```
import java.awt.*;
import java.awt.event.*;
import java.io.Serializable;
import java.util.Vector;

public class Clicker extends Component
    implements Serializable, ActionListener
{
    private Vector listeners = new Vector();
```

Exercise 18.3 continued

```
   public void setBackground(Color c) {
      super.setBackground( c );
      repaint();
   }

   public Color getBackground() {
      return super.getBackground();
   }

   public synchronized void addActionListener(ActionListener a) {
      listeners.addElement(a);
   }

   public synchronized void removeActionListener(ActionListener a) {
      listeners.removeElement(a);
   }

   public void actionPerformed(ActionEvent e) {
      Vector targets;

      synchronized (this) {
         targets = (Vector)listeners.clone();
      }

      ActionEvent actionEvt = new ActionEvent(this, 0, null);
      for (int i = 0; i < targets.size(); i++) {
         ActionListener target =
(ActionListener)targets.elementAt(i);
         target.actionPerformed(actionEvt);
      }
   }

   public Dimension getMinimumSize() {
      return new Dimension(100, 100);
   }
}
```

Review Questions

Question 1: If you define a class that implements the Serializable interface, but this class defines an instance variable whose value you do not want to read or write, what keyword can you use so that the value is not read or written?

   a) `transient`
   b) `private`
   c) `final`
   d) do not supply a keyword

Question 2 How can you rewrite the following two classes so that the second becomes an inner class of the first? (The resulting program should still work like the original.)

```
class First {
   public static void main(String[] args) {
      new Second().sayGoodnightGracy();
   }
}

class Second extends First {
   void sayGoodnightGracy() {
      System.out.println("Goodnight, Gracy");
   }
}
```

a)

```
class First {
   public static void main(String[] args) {
      System.out.println("Goodnight, Gracy");
   }
}
```

b)

```
class First {
   public static void main(String[] args) {
      new First() {
         void sayGoodnightGracy() {
            System.out.println("Goodnight, Gracy");
         }
      };
   }
}
```

c)

```
class First {
   public static void main(String[] args) {
      new Second().sayGoodnightGracy();
   }

   class Second extends First {
      void sayGoodnightGracy() {
         System.out.println("Goodnight, Gracy");
      }
   }

}
```

d)

```
class First {
   public static void main(String[] args) {
      new First().test();
   }
```

```
void test() {
   new Second().sayGoodnightGracy();
}

class Second extends First {
   void sayGoodnightGracy() {
      System.out.println("Goodnight, Gracy");
   }
}
}
```

Question 3: To reference a JAR file from a Web page, you can use the keyword:

a) jar
b) class
c) archive
d) java-archive

Question 4: Which lines of code successfully writes a string to a file named "test"?

a)

```
FileOutputStream f = new FileOutputStream("test");
ObjectOutput s = new ObjectOutputStream(f);
s.writeObject("Announced by all the trumpets of the sky. . .");
```

b)

```
ObjectOutput f = new ObjectOutputStream("test");
FileOutputStream s = new FileOutputStream(f);
s.writeObject("Announced by all the trumpets of the sky. . .");
```

c)

```
ObjectOutput s = new ObjectOutputStream("test");
s.writeObject("Announced by all the trumpets of the sky. . .");
```

Question 5: You can allow developers to get and set a variable named `maxValue` in an object from within a Java Beans-enabled application development environment by:

a) Defining `maxValue` to be public.
b) Defining a pair of methods named `getMaxValue()` and `setMaxValue()`.
c) Defining special Field objects to represent `maxValue`.
d) Making certain the class defining `maxValue` is Serializable.

Answers to the Review Questions

Question 1	a.	The `transient` keyword is new in 1.1 and stops an instance variable from being written to a stream.
Question 2	d.	Only this programs defines an inner class that keeps the output of the original code. Answer c does not work because you cannot define an inner class within a `static` method if the inner class is not also declared as `static`.
Question 3	c.	The `archive` keyword identifies a JAR file relative to the HTML page.
Question 4	a.	First you create a FileStream. Then you associate an ObjectStream with it. Then you write your objects.
Question 5	b.	By following this naming protocol, the Java Beans environment will allow the developer to get and set the value.

Developer Certification Study Guide

CHAPTER 19

Creating Clean APIs

Starting with this chapter, this book assumes you know the basics of Java programming. You should know how to create classes, implement methods, and define variables.

At this point, you've reviewed all of the basics of the Java language. If you've already taken the Sun Certified Java Programmer test and passed, congratulations!

If you've tried the test and failed, use the experience to focus your studying on those areas you were least certain about. Use this book's objectives to help you, and work through all the exercises. Make up your own test questions based on the samples in this book and what you can remember from the exams. Sometimes you'll come up with a question that you stump yourself with! Now's the time to do so, because you can look up the answer and write programs to verify your answers, before you get into the testing room.

The fun part comes after you've passed the Programmer exam. After you've fought through the 70 questions on the first test, it's time become a Sun Certified Java Developer.

Developer certification involves two stages: completing a programming assignment (which is really the heart of it), and then answering questions about your design. Since the programming assignment is the focus, the chapters in this section will concentrate on the skills you need to complete this assignment. In this part of the book, you'll work on expanding your basic programming knowledge and learning how to implement what you know to write sophisticated programs.

What's on the Programming Assignment

The assignment is graded partly on good object-oriented programming technique, especially concerning clarity of design. It's important to use abstract classes, interfaces, and packages correctly.

Objectives for this Chapter

- Define abstract classes where appropriate.
- Use interfaces where appropriate.
- Arrange classes into packages.
- Create well-defined APIs for your classes.

Abstract Classes

Define abstract classes where appropriate.

We've already covered `abstract` classes briefly at the end of Chapter 1, but I wanted to say a word about their role in building an API.

Defining an `abstract` class forces you and other developers to make clear choices.

The big difference between an `abstract` class and a superclass that defines no-op stubs for its methods is that the `abstract` class forces you and other programmers to use your set of APIs in a particular way. While a programmer can directly instantiate a concrete superclass, a programmer has no such option with an `abstract` class; she must either instantiate a predefined subclass or create her own subclass to instantiate.

This can help clarify your design. For example, imagine a class called Transaction that is to be used in a home banking application. This class has two subclasses: Deposit and Withdrawal. It might make no sense to create an instance of Transaction—a customer doesn't generically announce to a bank teller, "I want to make a transaction," but rather, "I want to make a withdrawal," or "I want to make a deposit." (If a customer does say "I want to make a transaction," the teller will ask him to clarify his intentions.)

You can make your desire for programmers to use only a Deposit or Withdrawal class clear in your design by making Transaction `abstract`. Now, programmers using your APIs know your intention—you would like them to be specific about the type of transaction they want to perform.

You know that if you define any `abstract` methods, you need to make the class abstract. What if you don't have any `abstract` methods but you still want to make the class `abstract`? You can do this—just use the `abstract` keyword for the class. Then, any subclasses are automatically concrete classes (unless, of course, they in turn are declared as `abstract`).

Interfaces

Use interfaces where appropriate.

Interfaces define constants and method signatures. Interfaces are not like abstract classes where all of the methods are declared as abstract—interfaces are not classes. Instead, they define, as their name implies, an interface for you to implement.

So what good are they? Why not just define methods in a class rather than fooling around with interfaces? The answer is that interfaces clean up your APIs.

Interfaces allow you, as the developer, to make clear to other developers which sets of behavior belong together. Interfaces also help you enforce the proper use of your API.

Grouping Behavior

Identifying related behavior in one place is ideal for an interface. You can find a great example of this in Java 1.1, where interfaces identify related event methods. As one example, an interface called FocusListener defines focusGained() and focusLost(). It's clear that the API expects developers to supply behavior for these two methods to be able to handle focus events.

Enforcing Your API

Since Java can identify classes that implement interfaces by using instanceof, interfaces can also *enforce* an API. Continuing with the FocusListener example, you must use an object whose class provides the methods focusGained() and focusLost() when you want to handle focus events. To handle focus events, you must register your object as a focus listener by using addFocusListener(). By declaring the parameter in this method to be an instance of type FocusListener, the Java Virtual Machine, compiler, and language, working in conjunction, will not let you pass an object whose class does not implement both methods.

Identifying Intent

Interfaces can also be used to *tag* a class. For example, the Cloneable interface does not declare any method; there's nothing for implementers to implement. Instead, any class identified as an `instanceof` Cloneable lets the Object class' `clone()` method know that this class can be cloned. The Cloneable interface merely identifies the developer's intent; it does not make the developer implement any behavior.

Exercise 19.1

> Imagine that you have developed a class named Tester that tests other objects. Perhaps it has a `testObject()` method that, given the name of the object to test, invokes that object's `test()` method and displays the String result in the standard output.
>
> Naturally, you would like to use any kind of object with your Tester class. How can you define your API so that this will all work well and be as self-documenting as possible?

Packages

Arrange classes into packages.

Creating packages can help you clean up your APIs in two important ways:

- You can better restrict access to methods and variables.
- You can define subsystems.

Creating Packages

Chapter 1 already covered how to create packages and place classes inside them. Here's a quick review.

To tell the compiler the classes in a particular source file belong in a package, write the keyword `package` as the first line in your source file, followed by the package name, as in:

```
package MyUtils.MyPackage;
```

To import `public` classes defined in other packages, specify which packages or specific classes you want to import by writing the keyword `import` followed by the package or class names, as in:

```
import MyUtils.MyPackage.Average;
import MyUtils.OtherPackage.*;
```

Tip

Java will expect your packages to be in a directory structure where each dot (.) defines a new subdirectory.

Restricting Access

Here's a quick review of restricting access to members.

First of all, as we reviewed in Chapter 1, only a `public` class can be accessed outside of the packages it is defined in.

As you also know, there are four ways to specify access control for a class member: you can use the keyword `public`, `protected`, or `private`, or you can leave off an access control keyword and accept the default—`public` and `private` have the same effect regardless of whether or not the classes you've defined are in the same package. However, `protected` and the default are greatly affected by multiple packages.

If all of your classes are in the same package (including the default package), they can access each others' members as long as those members are declared as `protected` or have no access control specifier (or are declared as `public`).

Sometimes this is what you want. For example, a small class that contains some simple utility methods only meant for use by other classes in its package could restrict outside classes from invoking these methods by leaving off any access control keywords. But keep in mind that a lack of access control keywords should never stem from laziness; it should be your design intent. If it is appropriate only for the class defining a member to access that member, make that member `private`.

If it is possible that some other package will define a subclass for a class you have defined, and in general you would like subclasses of your class to be able to access specific members in your class, you can give those specific members the `protected` keyword.

Defining Subsystems

Packages clean up your design by allowing you to think of your application as a collection of cooperating *subsystems*. You can think of a subsystem as a collection of related classes that accomplish a specific design goal—that fill in one box in a drawing of your application's architecture.

For example, imagine you are creating a database client/server application. You might have a database, a database server, a TCP/IP component that runs on the client side, and a user interface for the client. Perhaps the actual data in the database contains information on birds: their songs, migration paths, and egg colors. If you can generalize the pieces of your application, you could conceivably define four different subsystems which fit the boxes shown in Figure 19-1:

Figure 19-1
The Four Pieces of a
Hypothetical Database Client/Server
Application

In Java, you can define each of these subsystems by creating classes and placing them into packages. Each package would represent one subsystem.

Packages allow you to conceive of your application as a machine constructed out of "tinker-toys." On your next project, if you need a database server and a TCP/IP client that, this time, accesses a database of baseball cards, you can just use these packages as-is and plug them into your new application, which might look like Figure 19-2:

Figure 19-2
A New Application
using Old Packages

You can place your applet or the class with the `main()` method in a package, as well as any other classes (rather than letting it be placed in the "default" package). Most programmers don't do this, but this can help keep your class files organized. If you place a class defining `main()` called MyClass into a package named MyPackage, for example, you can invoke it by writing:

```
java MyPackage.MyClass
```

Exercise 19.2

Consider these two classes, currently defined in the same source file:

```
class Transaction {
   Amount amount;

   void process() {
   }
}

class Amount {
    int dollars;
    int cents;
}
```

Place each of these classes into a different package so that they can still access all of the same fields and methods they can access now. Call the first package `banking` and the second package `currency`.

Defining Access Methods

Create well-defined APIs for your classes.

Rather than allowing other classes to access a class' member variables directly, you should make those members `private` and supply access methods.

For example, this class allows anyone to get and set its instance variables:

```
public class Circle {
   public Point position;
   public int radius;
   public boolean canDelete;
   public boolean canMove;
}
```

This might seem okay, but perhaps you want to make sure the radius is never set to a negative number. What then? What if you want to make canMove and canDelete read-only? With the above definition, you're stuck.

The better way is to provide getter and setter methods for these values. Here's a new class definition that implements the new requirements listed in the previous paragraph. It's a little longer, but it's much more flexible. It also uses a new Exception subclass called IllegalGeometryException:

```
public class Circle {
   private Point position;
   private int radius;
   private canDelete;
   private canMove;

   public Point getPosition() {
      return position;
   }

   public void setPosition(Point p) {
      position = p;
   }

   public int getRadius() {
      return radius;
   }

   public void setRadius(int r) throws IllegalGeometryException {
      if (r < 0)
         throw new IllegalGeometryException();
      radius = r;
   }
```

continued

```
    public boolean getMove() {
        return canMove;
    }

    public boolean getDelete() {
        return canDelete;
    }

}
```

Defining access methods for getting and setting values for your classes is good programming practice. First, only allowing other classes to use access methods hides your class' implementation and makes these other classes much less dependent on your class' data layout.

For example, let's go back to the Circle class we defined above. If you decided to change canMove and canDelete into bit flags, your interface would not have to change at all. getMove() and getDelete() would still return boolean values. However, rather than returning the value of a boolean field, your method would perform the appropriate & operation to mask the irrelevant bits.

Second, you can ensure an object's data integrity. Instead of allowing a class to assign arbitrary values to a field, a setter method can verify that the new value makes sense. If it doesn't, it can fix the problem and possibly throw an exception to inform the caller that the operation did not take place—and maybe present an indication of why. That's what we did with the radius for the Circle class. Similarly, a getter can make certain that data is in a valid and consistent state before returning this data to the caller.

Third, you have more control over the data in a multithreading environment. For example, you can make your access methods synchronized, so that one thread is not getting or setting the data while another thread manipulates it elsewhere.

Tip

For example, what if you have a field that contains a Vector object, but some methods might change the values in the Vector? If you want to ensure that no thread in a multithreaded environment accesses the Vector while it's being used, you can make the methods that manipulate the Vector as well as the access method synchronized.

Fourth, you can make a value read-only or write-only if you desire by only defining a getter or setter. We did this above with the `canMove` and `canDelete` fields—perhaps they are dependent on the mode the application is in and cannot be set directly.

Tip

You can also define a method called `isProperty` if the property is read-only and this approach makes sense for your code. For example, I could have defined the methods `isMovable()` and `isDeletable()` instead of `getMove()` and `getDelete()`, but I chose not to because I'm not convinced that "movable" and "deletable" are real words (I know, details, details…).

Java 1.1 has introduced many getter and setter methods that used to have other inconsistent names or that used to be variables programmers could access directly. You should make sure your own APIs are as clean as Java's.

Exercise 19.3

Consider two class definitions:

```
public class Employee {
    int employeeNumber;
    Amount salary;
}

class Amount {
    int dollars;
    int cents;
}
```

Our intent is to assign an employee number for each employee when the Employee object is created, and we want to number our employees sequentially. Also, we've created an Amount class to eliminate possible problems with rounding as far as dollars and cents goes.

Here are three possible problems with these classes. First, anyone can set the employee number. This could lead to errors if the numbers are repeated. Second, anyone can access the Employee salary and set the cents amount to something greater than 99. Third, anyone can set either the dollars or cents amount to less than 0.

Modify these classes to clean up their APIs and eliminate these problems.

Answers to the Exercises

Exercise 19.1

You can define an interface, perhaps named CanBeTested, that declares a
test() method, as in:

```
public interface CanBeTested {
    String test();
}
```

Your Tester class can then require an object in its parameter list for
testObject() that requires an instance of CanBeTested:

```
public class Tester {
    public void testObject(CanBeTested obj) {
        System.out.println(obj.test());
    }
}
```

Now, looking at testObject(), it's clear you can only use the Tester class
if you have an instance of CanBeTested, which means implementing the
CanBeTested interface for the classes you wish to test, which means defining a test() method which testObject() will invoke.

Exercise 19.2

Here is the first source file, which we would call Transaction.java:

```
package banking;

import currency.Amount;

public class Transaction {
    public Amount amount;

    public void process() {
    }
}
```

Here is the second source file, which we would call `Amount.java`:

```
package currency;

public class Amount {
   public int dollars;
   public int cents;
}
```

There's a cleaner way to write these interfaces, and that involves using getters and setters, which the next exercise explores.

Exercise 19.3

Another possible solution would be to throw exceptions if the new Amount values were illegal, and to carry over any cents value in excess of 99 into the dollars field:

```
public class Employee {
   private static nextNumber;

   private int employeeNumber;
   private Amount salary;

   public Employee() {
      employeeNumber = nextNumber++;
   }

   int getEmployeeNumber() {
      return employeeNumber;
   }

   Amount getSalary() {
      return salary;
   }
}

class Amount {
   private int dollars;
   private int cents;

   int getDollars() {
      return dollars;
   }
```

Exercise 19.3 continued

```
    void setDollars(int d) {
        if (d >= 0)
            dollars = d;
    }

    int getCents() {
        return cents;
    }

    void setCents(int c) {
        if (c >= 0 && c <= 99)
            cents = c;
    }
}
```

Review Questions

Question 1: If you define an interface without any method declarations:

a) By default, all classes that implement that interface are abstract.
b) All classes that implement that interface are concrete (that is, they can be instantiated).
c) It is illegal to define an interface without any method declarations.

Question 2: What kind of methods can be accessed by classes in the same package? (For this question, pick all the answers that apply.)

a) public
b) protected
c) private
d) those using the default access control

Question 3: Which statements about the package keyword are true? (For this question, pick all the answers that apply.)

a) It must be placed at the top of the source file.
b) It must follow immediately after the `import` statements.
c) Only `public` classes can be placed into a package.
d) You can have more than one source file whose classes are put into the same package.

Question 4: To make salary in the following class definition read-only:

```
class Employee {
    double salary;
}
```

a good approach would be to:

a) Make the Employee class `private`.
b) Make salary `protected`.
c) Make salary `private` and define a method called `getSalary()`.
d) Make salary `private` and define methods named `getSalary()` and `setSalary()`.

Answers to the Review Questions

Question 1	b.	An interface without any method declarations can be used to tag classes.
Question 2	a, b, d.	Private methods can only be accessed by the same class that defines them. Other than that, any class in the same package can access the other methods.
Question 3	a, d.	The package statement must appear before the `import` statements. Any type of class (or interface) can be placed into a package.
Question 4	c.	First of all, there is no such thing as a `private` class. Also, making `salary` `protected` doesn't make it read-only. Making it `private` and providing a getter method (not a setter method too!) does the trick.

CHAPTER 20

Advanced Graphical
User Interfaces

You should know all of the basics
of creating a user interface before
reading this chapter.

If you've been reading this book
straight through, you've already
read Chapters 13, 14, and 15, where
we discussed the basics of creating a
graphical user interface. With that
knowledge, you can probably fish
around in the APIs for the methods
you need, piece together more complicated user interfaces, and add the
little flourishes that will make your
interface behave exactly as you
would like.

However, there's no need to waste your time through trial and error. This chapter helps point you in the right direction when building advanced graphical user interfaces.

What's on the Programming Assignment

Imitating a typical real-world situation, the programming assignment requires you to create a graphical user interface that exactly matches a set of specifications. The assignment provides diagrams that show you how the user interface should look when it first appears, and how it should look if the user enlarges the enclosing frame.

To meet the specifications, you've got to create a hierarchy of containers within other containers, using a combination of different layout managers. You've also got to know how to change components after they've been displayed on the screen.

The programming assignment is a standalone graphical application. This means that there is no appletviewer or Web browser to create an enclosing frame for you. You need to know how to write your own.

Objectives for this Chapter

- Use layout managers to size and space components as you intend.
- Embed layout managers within other layout managers to achieve sophisticated effects.
- Set fonts and colors for your components.
- Change a component after it has been displayed.
- Place user interface elements within top-level frames.

This chapter uses the APIs from Java 1.0.2, but I have included in the tips how to update the code to Java 1.1.

Mix and Match!

Use layout managers to size and space components as you intend.

Embed layout managers within layout managers to achieve sophisticated effects.

We briefly looked at how components are sized back in Chapter 13. However, our objective then was to understand enough to pass the programmer's test. Now, our objective is a little broader: to use the proper layout manager in the proper way to achieve a specific look.

You can create arbitrarily complex arrangements in your user interface by nesting layout managers.

Here are some scenarios.

Let's say you want to arrange five buttons along the top of an applet. You might want these five buttons in any number of appearances:

- All with a width equal to the widest button
- Each only as large as necessary to contain its label
- Centered, left aligned, or right aligned
- Centered but equal in width

and so on. Achieving the look you want involves two things:

1. Using the right layout manager to stretch or not stretch the buttons as appropriate, and
2. Using the right *combination* of layout managers so that the buttons are aligned and arranged correctly in relation to each other.

Using One Layout Manager

Let's look at the simplest situations first: using one layout manager to achieve the button layouts. A BorderLayout is not the best choice to use directly for laying out five buttons—each region ("North," "South," and so on) can only contain one component, so the look of all five regions being used by five buttons is unusual. This arrangement is shown in Figure 20-1.

Figure 20-1
Five Buttons
Arranged in a Border-
Layout

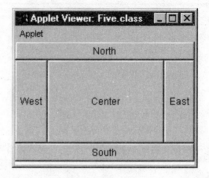

Each button expands to fill up its region. In particular, the "North" and "South" buttons expand horizontally, while the "East" and "West" buttons expand vertically. The "Center" button takes up the remaining space.

The code for this (which you saw back in Chapter 13) is:

```java
import java.awt.*;
import java.applet.*;

public class Five extends Applet {
    public void init() {
        setLayout(new BorderLayout());
        add("North", new Button("North"));
        add("South", new Button("South"));
        add("East", new Button("East"));
        add("West", new Button("West"));
        add("Center", new Button("Center"));
    }
}
```

A GridLayout also is likely to not be what you want, if a GridLayout is the only layout manager you're using. For example, arranging five buttons in a grid that is 1 row by 5 columns looks like Figure 20-2.

Figure 20-2
Five Buttons in a
GridLayout

As you can see, the buttons are all equally sized and take up the full region of the grid cell. The code is:

```
import java.awt.*;
import java.applet.*;

public class GridFive extends Applet {
   public void init() {
      setLayout(new GridLayout(1, 5));
      add(new Button("First"));
      add(new Button("Second"));
      add(new Button("Third"));
      add(new Button("Fourth"));
      add(new Button("Fifth"));
   }
}
```

You can also create the GridLayout using a constructor where you define space around the cells. For example, creating the GridLayout with this line of code:

```
setLayout(new GridLayout(1, 5, 10, 0));
```

creates the display in Figure 20-3.

Figure 20-3
A GridLayout with
Space Around
Each Cell

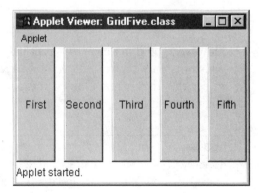

Tip

If there were multiple rows, we could also specify a vertical gap. In the snippet above, we pass 0 to the constructor for GridLayout for the vertical gap, since we have only one row.

A FlowLayout will arrange the buttons first left to right, and then, as it runs out of room on each row, top to bottom. The buttons take on their natural size. By default, each row is centered, as in Figure 20-4.

Figure 20-4
A FlowLayout
Arranging Five
Buttons

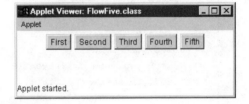

Here's the code that produced Figure 20-4:

```
import java.awt.*;
import java.applet.*;

public class FlowFive extends Applet {
    public void init() {
        setLayout(new FlowLayout());
        add(new Button("First"));
        add(new Button("Second"));
        add(new Button("Third"));
        add(new Button("Fourth"));
        add(new Button("Fifth"));
    }
}
```

However, you don't have to accept that each row is centered. You can use the constants `FlowLayout.LEFT`, `FlowLayout.CENTER`, and `FlowLayout.RIGHT` to set the alignment. One of the constructors allows you to pass in this alignment value.

You can also specify horizontal and vertical gaps between components and rows by invoking the constructor that takes three parameters: the alignment, the horizontal gaps, and the vertical gaps.

Tip

For example, creating the FlowLayout with this line of code:

```
setLayout(new FlowLayout(FlowLayout.LEFT));
```

creates the display shown in Figure 20-5.

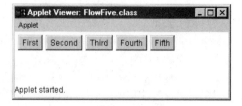

Figure 20-5
A FlowLayout
Arrangement where
the Components are
Left-Aligned

As you can see, there's only so much you can achieve when you use layout managers one at a time. The power comes in using them in combination.

For example, to arrange the five buttons along the bottom of an applet and make them left-aligned, you can write the following code:

```java
import java.awt.*;
import java.applet.*;

public class FlowFive extends Applet {
   public void init() {
      Panel p = new Panel();
      p.setLayout(new FlowLayout(FlowLayout.LEFT));
      p.add(new Button("First"));
      p.add(new Button("Second"));
      p.add(new Button("Third"));
      p.add(new Button("Fourth"));
      p.add(new Button("Fifth"));

      setLayout(new BorderLayout());
      add("South", p);
   }
}
```

In this code, we first place the buttons into a Panel object that uses a FlowLayout to left-align them. Then, we add the Panel object to the applet, which uses a BorderLayout. This program produces the display shown in Figure 20-6.

Figure 20-6
Using BorderLayout
and FlowLayout
Together

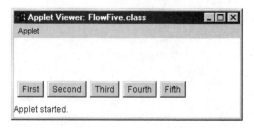

What if you wanted to make each button the same size, but still align them on the left at the bottom of the applet? Then you'd have to use three layout managers in combination. That's no problem at all; just think through your design carefully so that it all comes together in the end.

First, you want to size all the buttons to be the size of the largest one (you can use a GridLayout to achieve this effect). Then, you want to align this group of buttons on the left (you can use a FlowLayout to accomplish this). Finally, you want the left-aligned buttons on the bottom of the applet (naturally, you use a BorderLayout to make this happen).

Figure 20-7 shows the layout you're shooting for.

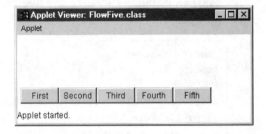

Figure 20-7
A Layout Involving
Three Layout
Managers

And here's the code:

```
import java.awt.*;
import java.applet.*;

public class FlowFive extends Applet {
    public void init() {
        Panel p1 = new Panel();
        p1.setLayout(new GridLayout(1, 5));
        p1.add(new Button("First"));
        p1.add(new Button("Second"));
        p1.add(new Button("Third"));
        p1.add(new Button("Fourth"));
        p1.add(new Button("Fifth"));

        Panel p2 = new Panel();
        p2.setLayout(new FlowLayout(FlowLayout.LEFT));
        p2.add(p1);

        setLayout(new BorderLayout());
        add("South", p2);
    }
}
```

The examples so far have involved buttons, because it's clear where the layout managers are placing each one. You can achieve the same effects with the other components. Button, Label, TextField, TextArea, Choice, and List will all stretch in GridLayout and BorderLayout regions. Checkbox will not.

Exercise 20.1

Create a user interface that looks like the display shown in Figure 20-8.

Figure 20-8
An Interface with a
Text Area and Two
Rows of Options

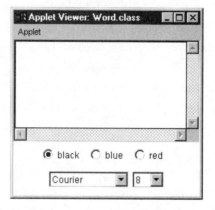

This is the interface for a word processing application. There are two rows of options on the bottom of the applet. The first row contains checkboxes indicating possible text: black, blue, and red. Notice that these are evenly spaced in their row. Naturally, they should be mutually exclusive. The second row offers a list of font types (Courier, Helvetica, and Times Roman) and point sizes (8, 10, and 12). Notice that these are centered.

The text area should take up the rest of the applet. It should be 60 columns wide and 10 rows high. (It's not necessary to make this applet functional now.)

Changing Your Look

Set fonts and colors for your components.

Just because you've displayed a component doesn't mean it's out of your hands entirely. As long as you can find it through an object reference, you can continue to change its appearance.

Text

One common task is to change the text in a label. For example, you might have a label that displays a status message.

You can use the method setText() to change what a Label object displays and pass this method a new String to use.

Updating a label or a button can be tricky in certain situations. If the label is in a BorderLayout in the "North" or "South" region, it will already be stretched to its widest and you won't have to concern yourself with the label's size. However, if the label is in a flow layout, the label will not change its size if the new text is longer than the old text. This can cause your new text to be clipped.

If your label won't stretch because it is in a flow layout, but it won't display any text initially, you may want to create the label with some blank spaces. That way, when you do place text into it, the label is already sized large enough to contain the text.

Tip

Font and Color

Here are some important classes and methods to keep in mind regarding changing the appearance of a component:

The Font class defines a font. To define a new Font object, you supply the font name, font style (from a set of constants defined by the Font class), and the size of the font. You can then set the font used by a component by invoking setFont() and passing your new Font object.

Courier is a proportional font, which means that each letter's width is the same. It's convenient to use a proportional font when you want your text to line up with text in other lines (such as in a text area or list).

You can use setForeground() to set the text color for components. You can also use setBackground() to set the component's background color. Pass both of these methods a Color object. Almost always, you will use a predefined Color object referenced from the Color class, such as Color.blue, Color.red, or Color.gray, to name three colors. Many common colors are represented as static variables like this in the Color class.

Replacing a Component

If you'd like to remove a component from a container, all you have to do is invoke remove() and pass this method the object reference of the component you want removed.

You can even add a component by invoking add() at any time—not just when you initially build your user interface. Invoking remove() and add() back-to-back can replace a component. However, there are a number of gotchas.

First of all, you may have to force the user interface to lay itself out again after you've tinkered with it. You can do this by invoking validate().

Second of all, and perhaps most importantly, you have to be aware of the order in which you added components to your container. If you are attempting to replace the third button in a grid that is 2 rows by 3 columns, you can't just remove the third button and replace it by invoking add(). That would cause the new button to be added to the end of the grid.

Instead of using add() and only passing the component to add, you can use an overloaded version of add() that also takes a position index indicating where it should be added to the container. So, to replace the third button in this scenario, you can write:

```
remove(oldButton);
add(newButton, 2); // 0 based
```

Sometimes, if you want to replace components in a panel or replace the text in a choice or list, the best way to achieve a smooth look is to create a new component or set of components, and then replace the ones on-screen—rather than changing the on-screen components as you go, which can cause the display to look messy while the change is taking place.

Exercise 20.2

Extend the applet you wrote in Exercise 20.1 so that the text in the text area matches the selections in the options on the bottom two rows.

Working with Frames

Place user interface elements within top-level frames.

If you climb the container hierarchy to the top, you'll always find a Frame.

All components must ultimately be contained inside a Frame. You can either create this enclosing Frame yourself, or, in the case of an applet, you might use the Frame the appletviewer or Web browser provided for you.

It's important to know that you need a top level Frame for a number of reasons:

- If you want to display a window separately from your applet, perhaps outside of the Web browser, you'll need to create a Frame to contain this separate window.
- If you don't create an applet, you must create a Frame for any standalone graphical user interfaces you create.
- You need a Frame to show dialogs and, in Java 1.0.2, to change the mouse cursor.

Tip

Java 1.1 allows you to change the mouse cursor on a component-by-component basis.

Let's start our work with Frames by looking at a snippet (which we'll improve upon) to display a standalone, graphical user interface contained in an object reference named `panel`:

```
Frame f = new Frame();
f.add("Center", panel); // BorderLayout is the default for Frames
f.pack();
f.show();
```

Let's nit-pick this snippet for a moment. First of all, the Frame's title will say "Unknown," because we haven't explicitly supplied our own title. Second of all, the application won't close or exit when the user clicks the **Close** button in this Frame. In fact, in Windows and Solaris, the user has to use **Control-C** in the window the user launched this program from to end it. That's not exactly a graceful user interface.

Closing the Frame

We can fix the lack of a title in the Frame by passing one to the Frame's overloaded constructor. But the inability to exit when the user clicks the **Close** button can best be fixed in Java 1.0.2. by subclassing Frame.

You can use this template for a Frame subclass, based on the Java 1.0.2 event handling API:

```
import java.awt.*;

/**
 * The top-level frame for the user interface.
 * This class gives the ui a home and knows how to exit gracefully.
 */
public class TopFrame extends Frame {

   /** Construct a frame with a title. */
   public TopFrame(String s) {
      super(s);
   }
```

continued

```
/** Handles the user clicking the close icon. */
public boolean handleEvent(Event e) {
    if (e.id == Event.WINDOW_DESTROY) {
        hide();
        dispose();
        System.exit(0);
    }
    return super.handleEvent(e);
}

}
```

Tip

You should always hide the window first before disposing of it. The `hide()` method removes the frame from the screen; `dispose()` frees any resources associated with that window. (`System.exit()` ends the current run of the Java Virtual Machine and returns control to the native operating system.)

Tip

To make the Frame close in Java 1.1, you don't need to subclass Frame at all. You can simply provide a WindowListener for the Frame and handle the `windowClosing()` event, like this:

```
import java.awt.Window;
import java.awt.event.WindowAdapter;
import java.awt.event.WindowEvent;

/**
 * This handler helps a window (such as a top-level Frame)
 * exit gracefully.
 */
public class WindowCloser extends WindowAdapter {
    public void windowClosing(WindowEvent e) {
        Window w = e.getWindow();
        w.setVisible(false);
        w.dispose();
        System.exit(0);
    }
}
```

Then, add an instance of this class to the window listeners for the window or frame you want to be able to close. For example, if your Frame is in a reference named `topFrame`, and your instance of WindowCloser is in a reference named `closer`, you can write:

```
topFrame.addWindowListener(closer);
```

Making an Applet a Standalone Application

If you would like to turn an applet into a standalone application so you can run it outside of a Web browser (free of many security requirements related to accessing servers and the file system), you can write a main() method for your applet. That way, you can invoke it from the command line.

To make this work, you've got to handle the chores that the Web browser used to handle.

Key Concept

As far as Java is concerned, a Web browser's chores include:

1. Creating an instance of your applet.
2. Making sure your applet progresses through its life-cycle—especially so that it creates and arranges its user interface components. (If your applet creates a user interface in init(), make sure any frame you write that replaces the applet also invokes init().)
3. Creating a top-level frame for your applet and placing your applet in this frame.
4. Setting this frame to its appropriate size. (You can either set the frame's size directly—using resize() in Java 1.0.2 or setSize() in Java 1.1—or you can invoke pack() to "shrink-wrap" the frame around your user interface.)
5. Making this frame appear on the screen. (You can accomplish this by invoking your frame's show() method in Java 1.0.2, or setVisible(true) in Java 1.1.)

Exercise 20.3

Take the word processing applet you wrote in Exercises 20.1 and 20.2 and add a main() method to this applet so that it can run as a standalone application.

Answers to the Exercises

Exercise 20.1

This code contains a few instance variables in preparation for making this interface operative:

```java
import java.awt.*;
import java.applet.Applet;

public class Word extends Applet {
    private TextArea area;
    private Choice fonts;
    private Choice sizes;

    private String currentFont = "Courier";
    private int currentSize = 8;
    private int style = Font.PLAIN;
    private Color currentColor = Color.black;

    public void init() {
        setLayout(new BorderLayout());

        area = new TextArea(10, 60);
        area.setFont(new Font(currentFont, style, currentSize));
        area.setForeground(currentColor);
        add("Center", area);

        Panel p = new Panel();
        p.setLayout(new GridLayout(2,1));

        Panel firstRow = new Panel();
        CheckboxGroup group = new CheckboxGroup();
        firstRow.add(new Checkbox("black", group, true));
        firstRow.add(new Checkbox("blue", group, false));
        firstRow.add(new Checkbox("red", group, false));
        p.add(firstRow);

        Panel secondRow = new Panel();
        fonts = new Choice();
        fonts.addItem("Courier");
        fonts.addItem("Helvetica");
        fonts.addItem("Times Roman");
        secondRow.add(fonts);
```

Exercise 20.1 continued

```
        sizes = new Choice();
        sizes.addItem("8");
        sizes.addItem("12");
        sizes.addItem("16");
        secondRow.add(sizes);


        p.add(secondRow);


        add("South", p);
    }


}
```

Exercise 20.2

```
import java.awt.*;
import java.applet.Applet;

public class Word extends Applet {
    private TextArea area;
    private Choice fonts;
    private Choice sizes;

    private String currentFont = "Courier";
    private int currentSize = 8;
    private int style = Font.PLAIN;
    private Color currentColor = Color.black;

    public void init() {
        setLayout(new BorderLayout());

        area = new TextArea(10, 60);
        area.setFont(new Font(currentFont, style, currentSize));
        area.setForeground(currentColor);
        add("Center", area);

        Panel p = new Panel();
        p.setLayout(new GridLayout(2,1));
```

Exercise 20.2 continued

```
        Panel firstRow = new Panel();
        CheckboxGroup group = new CheckboxGroup();
        firstRow.add(new Checkbox("black", group, true));
        firstRow.add(new Checkbox("blue", group, false));
        firstRow.add(new Checkbox("red", group, false));
        p.add(firstRow);

        Panel secondRow = new Panel();
        fonts = new Choice();
        fonts.addItem("Courier");
        fonts.addItem("Helvetica");
        fonts.addItem("Times Roman");
        secondRow.add(fonts);

        sizes = new Choice();
        sizes.addItem("8");
        sizes.addItem("12");
        sizes.addItem("16");
        secondRow.add(sizes);

        p.add(secondRow);

        add("South", p);
    }

    public boolean action(Event e, Object what) {
        if (e.target instanceof Checkbox) {
            Checkbox c = (Checkbox)(e.target);
            String s = c.getLabel();
            if (s.equals("black"))
                currentColor = Color.black;
            else if (s.equals("blue"))
                currentColor = Color.blue;
            else
                currentColor = Color.red;
        }

        else if (e.target == fonts) {
            currentFont = fonts.getSelectedItem();
        }
```

Exercise 20.2 continued

```
    else if (e.target == sizes) {
        switch (sizes.getSelectedIndex()) {
            case 0: currentSize = 8; break;
            case 1: currentSize = 12; break;
            case 2: currentSize = 16; break;
        }
    }

    area.setFont(new Font(currentFont, style, currentSize));
    area.setForeground(currentColor);

    return super.action(e, what);
}

}
```

Exercise 20.3

You can use the TopFrame class provided in the text. Here's how you can write a main() method for the Word applet:

```
public static void main(String[] args) {
    Word w = new Word();
    w.init();
    TopFrame frame = new TopFrame("Word processor");
    frame.add("Center", w);
    frame.pack();
    frame.show();
}
```

Review Questions

Question 1: How can you display three labels that line up top to bottom along the right hand side of an interface and are sized equally?

a) Place the labels into a GridLayout.
b) Place the labels into a BorderLayout.
c) Place the labels in a container that uses a BorderLayout, and then place this container into another container that uses a GridLayout.
d) Place the labels in a container that uses a GridLayout, and then place this container into another container that uses a BorderLayout.

Question 2: To force a layout manager to re-layout the components in a container, you can invoke the container method named:

a) `validate()`
b) `repaint()`
c) `layout()`
d) `update()`

Question 3: To set the text color for a component, you can use the component method:

a) `setColor()`
b) `setFont()`
c) `setForeground()`
d) `setBackground()`

Question 4: What is the cleanest way to make a window vanish permanently in Java 1.0.2?

a) invoke `dispose()`
b) invoke `hide()`
c) invoke `dispose()` and then `hide()`
d) invoke `hide()` and then `dispose()`

Question 5: What method can you invoke for a Frame enclosing a user interface so that it fits perfectly around that interface?

a) `resize()`
b) `size()`
c) `pack()`
d) `show()`

Answers to the Review Questions

Question 1   d.   You can place the components first into a container using a GridLayout that is 3 rows by 1 column. Then, you can place this container into another container using a BorderLayout on the "East" side.

Question 2   a.   The `validate()` method forces a layout manager to lay out the components again.

Question 3   c.   `setColor()` sets the drawing color, `setFont()` changes the font type, and `setBackground()` sets the background color. `setForeground()` changes the text color.

Question 4   d.   You should always hide the window before disposing of it to make sure the interface looks clean.

Question 5   c.   The `pack()` method makes the Frame shrink or expand as necessary to contain the interface.

CHAPTER 21

Accessing Databases

Once again, this chapter assumes you have a firm grasp of all of Java's basics. In particular, I'll use the classes from `java.io` and `java.util` in my examples.

The programming assignment will ask you to access a database. This database could be as simple as a RandomAccessFile, and the class that accesses the database could simply reads lines from the file; each line would represent a record.

Even though you might develop your own mini-database application for the exam, in real life there's a better way: you can use Remote Method Invocation and Java Database Connectivity. Both of these features are built into Java 1.1. We'll review them here.

No matter what method you need to implement on the exam concerning the database, there are some concepts you should know that will help you think through your design. These include how to query a database, how to allow your database to maintain its integrity as different clients attempt to read from and write to it at the same time, what database designers mean when they talk about 2-tier and 3-tier designs, and how to address concerns regarding efficiency.

What's on the Programming Assignment

The original version of the developer's programming assignment involves accessing a database, possibly on a remote machine, using TCP/IP to communicate over the network. It also requires you to implement an application-level protocol for the client and server to communicate with each other. The client and server send Java primitives, such as opcodes, strings, and integers to each other over the network. A class on the back end accesses a RandomAccessFile containing database records.

The first part of this chapter reviews some concepts that can help you understand this architecture. Future versions of the programming assignment may involve JDBC and RMI. And regardless of exactly what is part of the programming assignment and exams, when you become certified in Java 1.1 others will expect you to know this advanced information. So, this chapter reviews these concepts and APIs.

Objectives for this Chapter

- Implement a simple database using a RandomAccessFile and a class to read from and write to this file.
- Describe how to make a database server thread-safe, so that multiple clients can access it at the same time.
- Describe an n-tiered client/server architecture.
- Define a remote object and access it from another JVM using Remote Method Invocation.
- Use JDBC to access a database via ODBC.

Roll-Your-Own Databases

Implement a simple database using a RandomAccessFile and a class to read
from and write to this file.

Performing database programming in Java can be quite easy for simple
programs. At its most basic, all you need is a random access file, a
method to read from the file, and a method to write to the file. Each line
that you read and write can be one record.

As with any database, you first need to determine the record format.
You should have a unique key for each record to search for specific
records in the database.

For example, let's say you want to keep a database of employees. You
can track these employees by social security number. If you hire poets,
you might have the following list:

```
432-82-3212          e e cummings
092-55-3923          John Haines
932-11-5930          Alfred Tennyson
```

Such a list would represent a table. Each row in the table is a record. A
record is made up of fields that keep track of different data types.

A database consists of a collection of tables. For this simple example, we
only have one table in our database.

By reading and writing rows to a file, we can read and write records for
our database.

Which field should we use as our key? It might seem we could use
either field, but really, only the social security field will be unique. While
we could easily have two employees named John Smith at our company,
their social security numbers would still be unique.

To assist with our home-grown database, we might write a class called EmployeeRecord that looks like this:

```
public class EmployeeRecord {
    private String ssn;
    private String name;

    public EmployeeRecord(String ssn, String name) {
        this.ssn = ssn;
        this.name = name;
    }

    public String getSsn() {
        return ssn;
    }

    public String getName() {
        return name;
    }
}
```

Now that we know what each record will look like, we can define a RandomAccessFile object to act as our database. For example, we could write the following code:

```
import java.io.*;

public class DB {
    private static final String FILE_NAME = "test.db";
    private RandomAccessFile file;
    private File test;
    private boolean open;

    public DB() throws IOException {
        try {
            test = new File(FILE_NAME);
            file = new RandomAccessFile(FILE_NAME, "rw");
            open = true;
        } catch (IOException x) {
            close();
            throw x;
        }
    }
```

continued

```java
    public void close() {
        if (open) {
            try {
                file.close();
            } catch (IOException x) {
                System.out.println(x.getMessage());
            } finally {
                open = false;
            }
        }
    }

    public void finalize() throws Throwable {
        close();
        super.finalize();
    }

    public void rewind() throws IOException {
        file.seek(0);
    }

    public boolean moreRecords() throws IOException {
        return (file.getFilePointer() < file.length());
    }

    public EmployeeRecord readRecord()
        throws IOException, EOFException
    {
        String ssn = file.readUTF();
        String name = file.readUTF();
        EmployeeRecord record = new EmployeeRecord(ssn, name);

        return record;
    }

    public void writeRecord(EmployeeRecord record)
        throws IOException
    {
        file.seek(file.length());
        file.writeUTF(record.getSsn());
        file.writeUTF(record.getName());
    }

}
```

This class is not appropriate to use with multiple clients. We'll discuss how to update this class so that it is safe for multiple clients in a moment.

Warning

This class lets us create an object that can access a file called test.db. This file will hold records of type EmployeeRecord. You can see that it knows how to open the file when it's created, and it closes the file if someone invokes its close() method. It also closes the file, if necessary, when the object is garbage collected, because it overrides finalize().

This class provides a way for other objects to use it to read all of the records. Other objects can rewind the file and then keep on checking if there are more records before reading the next one. New records are appended to the end of the file.

If we wanted to be able to delete records in this database file, one way to proceed would be to prefix each record with a flag that indicated whether that record was active or deleted. To delete a record, then, we would simply change its flag. Periodically, we could copy the database to a new file to get rid of deleted records, thereby keeping them from clogging up the database.

Tip

Accessing Databases from Multiple Clients

Describe how to make a database server thread-safe, so that multiple clients can access it at the same time.

Objectives

We can create a server class that would allow any number of clients to access this database over a network using TCP/IP. Our architecture would look like Figure 21-1.

Figure 21-1
A Server Providing
Multiple Clients
Access to a Database

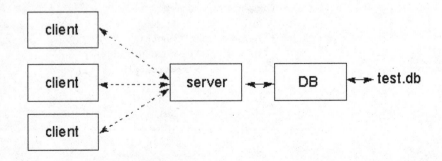

We'll look at how to implement a TCP/IP server capable of handling multiple clients in Chapter 22.

For now, the issue we're concerned with is what happens if multiple clients are manipulating the database at the same time. What if one client is deleting a record while another client is attempting to read from the database? How can we prevent the clients from interfering with each other?

To keep clients from working on the same record and to keep the database from becoming corrupted, it's important to make the methods that access and change records synchronized. Every method—except, perhaps, for the constructor and finalize()—would be a candidate for becoming synchronized. All you need to do is place the synchronized keyword in front of the method's return type, and voila! The class is thread-safe.

Two-Tiered and Three-Tiered Architectures

Describe an n-tiered client/server architecture.

Objectives

We have looked at Figure 21-1 but we have not indicated which machines any of these objects are running on. We could assume that clients connect directly to the machine where the database resides. This is fine, but this is not always the case in the real world. Often, client/server architectures are really client/client/server, or *3-tiered*.

This kind of arrangement, where one machine talks to another which talks to another, can go on indefinitely. You can have an n-tiered architecture, where n is essentially any number.

Tip

For example, perhaps our physical architecture actually looks like Figure 21-2. Here, there are three different groups of machines. There is a client group, which represents the first tier. There is a server, which represents a middle tier, and there are database engines, which represent the third tier, or the back end. Each box in this diagram could represent a different machine, but because we think of the roles that each machine plays, we think of this as 3-tiered: client, to server, which in turn is a client to the database engines.

Figure 21-2
A 3-Tiered Design

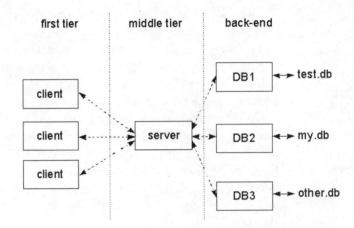

This kind of design has a number of interesting aspects. First, it is easily extendible. Our server can act as a gateway to any number of other servers or database engines. The client never has to know that data is coming from 2, 3, or 101 different databases. This means that our server is acting as a kind of gatekeeper. It can establish security precautions, business rules, and can force clients to access data a particular way. What's more, the middle tier, where the server lives, and the back end, where the databases reside, can maintain a very high-speed connection. This helps with performance. By contrast, a different architecture might involve the clients talking over a slower network, such as a dial-up network, with each individual database.

Using Java 1.1 APIs

To help implement this kind of architecture, Java 1.1 comes with a set of APIs that helps remove you from the low-level chore of creating your own special database and implementing your own application-level protocol used to communicate over TCP/IP networks. These new APIs provide two new features: Remote Method Invocation (RMI), and Java Database Connectivity (JDBC). We'll review each of these over the remainder of this chapter.

Remote Method Invocation

Define a remote object and access it from another JVM using Remote Method Invocation.

When communicating via TCP/IP, the applications themselves must define the protocol of bytes to pass back and forth. This can be difficult to work with and is definitely error prone. Passing bytes over a network also runs counter to Java's philosophy of helping the programmer concentrate on the application code rather than the protocol details. By providing an API to invoke methods in objects in other JVMs, Java frees you from this chore. Using RMI, you can invoke remote methods and work with remote objects as if they were defined locally in the same application.

You can use RMI to call methods in other Java applications running in different JVMs, where the JVMs are possibly running on different hosts.

You can call a method on a remote object once you have a reference to the object. Often, you can get a reference to a remote object as a return value from some other RMI call, but to get your first remote object to begin using RMI, you use a bootstrap naming service provided by RMI.

Figure 21-3 shows the basic concept behind RMI. An object in one application, perhaps on a client machine, invokes a method in another application running on a completely different machine, perhaps on a server. The client can pass parameters and even get a return value. RMI uses object serialization to pass parameters and return values between applications. (We covered serialization in Chapter 18.)

Figure 21-3
Invoking Remote
Objects Using RMI

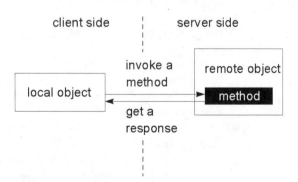

Once you establish a connection to an object in another program, you can invoke methods on that object as if that object were running in the same program as your own. However, for this to work, everything must be defined and set up just right.

Defining a Remote Interface

You need to define an interface for the remote object.

Here are the first steps you need to take to define a remote class:

1. Define an interface that declares the methods that objects will be able to invoke using RMI.
2. Throw RemoteException from the methods that objects will be able to invoke using RMI.

The local object will use this interface to determine what it can do with the remote object. This interface must inherit from another interface called Remote. In the example that we'll pursue here, we'll create a class called DBServer that works with our original DB class. We will define DBServer so that we can invoke methods on its objects remotely:

```
package server;

import java.rmi.RemoteException;
import java.rmi.Remote;
import java.io.IOException;
import java.io.EOFException;

public interface DBInterface extends Remote {
   void close()
      throws RemoteException;
   void rewind()
      throws RemoteException, IOException;
   boolean moreRecords()
      throws RemoteException, IOException;
   EmployeeRecord readRecord()
      throws RemoteException, IOException, EOFException;
   void writeRecord(EmployeeRecord)
      throws RemoteException, IOException;
}
```

Each method must declare that it throws a RemoteException, in addition to any other application-specific exceptions you would like it to throw.

RemoteException indicates that something went wrong in the communication between the local and the remote object.

Defining a Remote Class

Your remote class must extend RemoteObject and implement your remote interface.

To define a remote class, you should complete the following steps:

1. Extend the RemoteObject class or one of its subclasses, such as UnicastRemoteObject.
2. Implement the remote interface you defined for your remote class' methods.
3. Define a constructor that throws RemoteException.
4. Create and install a security manager.
5. Register the first object others will access via RMI by defining it in RMI's bootstrap naming service.

You start defining your remote class by extending RemoteObject or a subclass of RemoteObject such as UnicastRemoteObject.

Extending UnicastRemoteObject is a common approach when you are implementing a class whose objects will not be replicated across multiple servers.

You also need to implement the interface that defines your remote methods. You might start by writing:

```
public class DBServer extends UnicastRemoteObject
    implements DBInterface
{
}
```

Your class would go on to implement all of the methods declared in the interface. In our example, this would involve forwarding the method calls to DB, which we looked at earlier in this chapter. I did rewrite DB a little so that its definition started like this:

```
package server;

import java.io.*;

public class DB {
   private RandomAccessFile file;
   private boolean open;

   public DB(String fileName) throws IOException {
      file = new RandomAccessFile(fileName, "rw");
      open = true;
   }
```

The rest of this class is the same.

Here's what DBServer looks like:

```
package server;

import java.io.*;
import java.rmi.*;
import java.rmi.server.*;

public class DBServer extends UnicastRemoteObject
   implements DBInterface
{
   private static final String FILE_NAME = "test.db";
   private DB db;

   public DBServer() throws RemoteException, IOException {
      db = new DB(FILE_NAME);
   }
   public synchronized void close() throws RemoteException {
      db.close();
   }

   public synchronized void rewind()
      throws IOException, RemoteException
   {
      db.rewind();
   }
```

continued

```java
public synchronized boolean moreRecords()
   throws IOException, RemoteException
{
   return db.moreRecords();
}

public synchronized EmployeeRecord readRecord()
   throws IOException, EOFException, RemoteException
{
   return db.readRecord();
}

public synchronized void writeRecord(EmployeeRecord record)
   throws IOException, RemoteException
{
   db.writeRecord(record);
}

public static void main(String[] args) {

   // Create and install a security manager
   System.setSecurityManager(new RMISecurityManager());

   try {
      DBServer dbServer = new DBServer();

      Naming.rebind("//myhost/DB", dbServer);
         // located on the same machine as the client

      System.out.println("DBServer bound in registry");
   } catch (Exception e) {
      System.out.println("DBServer err: " + e.getMessage());
      e.printStackTrace();
   }
}

}
```

Your class can define methods not declared in your remote interface, but these other methods cannot be invoked from client-side objects—the client can only invoke those methods that are defined in the interface. Also, one reason why it's necessary to create a special server class that interfaces with the DB class, rather than just interfacing directly with DB, is that interface methods cannot be synchronized.

The class you define that implements the remote interface must define its own constructor. The default no-args constructor won't do, because the object's constructor must declare that it throws a RemoteException.

Your remote class must also create and install a security manager and, as with this DBServer object, register itself with the bootstrap naming service.

You can create and install a new security manager quite easily by writing:

```
System.setSecurityManager(new RMISecurityManager());
```

A security manager must be running because RMI will be loading classes over the network. Just as with Java applets, Java takes a conservative approach and does not trust the classes that come from anywhere other than the local machine. Java insists that a security manager is up and running to make sure that the classes coming in over the network don't do anything malicious.

Registering an object with the bootstrap naming service is also fairly simple. We can create the new object and register it with these two lines of code:

```
DBServer db = new DBServer();
Naming.rebind("//myhost/DB", db);
```

This says we're going to identify our DBServer object via the String that looks like a URL: "//myhost/DB". This URL allows the client to identify this object later.

You also need to make sure your remote object gets exported. If you extend a class such as UnicastRemoteObject, this will be done for you. This is because UnicastRemoteObject exports the object in its constructor, which is invoked with an implied call to super(). By exporting your object, you start it listening for incoming calls on an anonymous port.

Tip

If you do not extend UnicastRemoteObject, you must export your object yourself. You can do this by invoking `UnicastRemoteObject.exportObject()`.

To pass parameters or return values that are objects, they must be serializable. This means that we have to make EmployeeRecord serializable,
since it is a return value for one of the methods we've defined. (We don't
have to register EmployeeRecord in the bootstrap naming service, because
it will be returned. However, we have to make it a remote object just like
DBImplementation by defining a Remote interface, and so on. The client
also will need to import EmployeeRecord so that it can use it.)

Key Concept

You must also create a stub and a skeleton for your remote object. A stub
represents the remote object on the client side. The skeleton represents the
remote object on the server side.

I'll review how Java uses these in just a moment. You can use the RMI
compiler named `rmic` that comes with the JDK to accomplish this. Figure
21-4 shows where we are so far.

Figure 21-4
Creating the Remote
Class and Skeleton

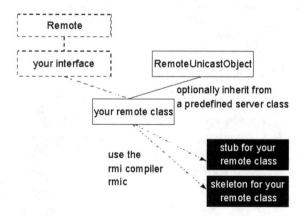

Invoking Remote Objects

Figure 21-5 shows what we've accomplished so far on the server side
(we'll get to the client side next).

Figure 21-5
The Server-Client Connection Via Stubs

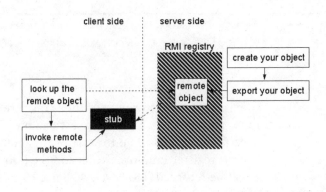

We've reviewed how to create an object and export it to the registry. Now we'll look at the client side. Calling a method in a remote object from the client side is simple and can be performed in two steps:

1. Obtain a reference to the remote object.
2. Invoke a method in the remote object.

You can obtain a reference by using the `static` method `lookup()` in the Naming class and passing it the same URL you used to register your remote object. This method returns a reference to the remote object—actually, the stub representing the remote object—which you can cast to the interface type you want to use.

Do not cast the remote object to the object type! Remember, you can only invoke methods that are declared in the remote interface. The stub returned declares those methods in the interface. Also, don't forget to import the interface to refer to it.

Once you acquire the stub representing the remote object, you can invoke methods for this object just as if it were a full-blown object residing locally on your machine as part of your local application.

Here's an example of a client that accesses a remote object:

```
package client;

import java.rmi.*;
import java.io.*;
import java.net.MalformedURLException;
import server.DBInterface;
import server.EmployeeRecord;
```

continued

```java
public class DBClient {
    public static void main(String[] args) {
        EmployeeRecord record;

        try {
            DBInterface db =
              (DBInterface)Naming.lookup("//myhost/DB");

            record = new EmployeeRecord("123-45-6789", "William Blake");
            db.writeRecord(record);

            record = new EmployeeRecord("000-11-2222", "John Dunne");
            db.writeRecord(record);

            db.rewind();
            while (db.moreRecords()) {
                record = db.readRecord();
                System.out.println("Ssn: " + record.getSsn());
                System.out.println("Name: " + record.getName());
            }

        } catch (MalformedURLException e) {
            error(e);
        } catch (NotBoundException e) {
            error(e);
        } catch (RemoteException e) {
            error(e);
        } catch (EOFException e) {
            error(e);
        } catch (IOException e) {
            error(e);
        }
    }

    private static void error(Exception e) {
        System.out.println("DBClient exception: " + e.getMessage());
        e.printStackTrace();
    }

}
```

Stubs and Skeletons

Java communicates between the local object and remote object via a stub and a skeleton. For all appearances, the client program might think it has actually acquired a direct reference to the remote object residing on the remote server. But Figure 21-6 shows what is going on under the covers. In reality, the client is communicating with a stub that represents the remote object on the local machine. The stub performs the network operations to communicate with the skeleton on the remote machine; the skeleton then talks to the remote object.

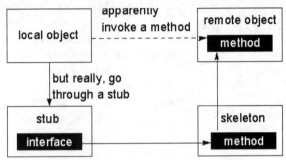

Figure 21-6
Invoking a Remote
Method Via Stubs
and Skeletons

The stub is the client-side representation of the remote object. It defines an interface declaring the methods that the local object can invoke.

When the server-side object responds, the flow of control goes back through the skeleton, which handles the network communication to get back to the stub, where the return values or exceptions are passed back to the local, client-side object.

Getting Things Going

To use RMI, you must start the bootstrap registry before you do anything. You must do this even before starting the server class.

To start the RMI registry, you can execute a command from your operating system's command line named `rmiregistry`.

You can then start the server, specifying `java.rmi.registry.code-base=URL` (the URL should include a trailing /), of course replacing URL with your own URL, so that clients can use the URL to find the stubs in the registry.

Finally, you can start your clients.

You need to have an HTTP server running on the remote machine.

Exercise 21.1

Develop a class that can be accessed remotely. This class should be named NYSE and should respond to a method called `dowJonesAvg()` to return a `double` value. This object will not be replicated across multiple servers.

JDBC

Use JDBC to access a database via ODBC.

JDBC provides an interface to databases. JDBC allows Java programs to access data residing in databases on servers and use that data in the client applet.

JDBC allows you to write programs in Java that access any database that can be queried using SQL (Structured Query Language).

Does this mean you have to know SQL? Unfortunately, the answer is "yes." JDBC does not put any restrictions on the SQL statements you can send to the database.

Tip

A variety of vendors are working on simpler ways to access databases that use JDBC themselves but do not require the programmer to know SQL.

To send SQL statements from a Java client, you need to know the APIs in the JDBC classes. These JDBC classes issue the SQL queries, passing your applet the data they retrieve.

JDBC is good at performing three important tasks as part of accessing data on a server: It can:

1. establish a connection with a database
2. send SQL statements
3. process the results

JDBC is a low-level API because you must issue SQL statements directly. If you want to work at a higher level, you can write an API with method names like `getEmployees()`, `setSalary()`, and so on, and have these methods make the translation into the SQL statements that you need.

The Need for Drivers

JDBC interacts with a driver that performs the database-specific connections from the general SQL and JDBC methods. Figure 21-7 shows the connections between a client applet and a back-end database using JDBC.

Figure 21-7
Accessing a Database
from an Applet
Using JDBC

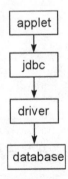

All drivers contain a `static` initializer that creates a new instance of itself and registers itself with the DriverManager when it's loaded.

You can force a class to be loaded by using the `static` method `forName` defined in the class Class. For example, your client might include this line of code:

```
Class.forName("bluehorse.db.Driver");
```

To define a `static` initializer in the driver itself that registers the new driver object, you can write:

```
static {
    Driver d = new Driver();
    DriverManager.registerDriver(d);
}
```

Using ODBC

There are already a great number of drivers for databases. However, since Java and JDBC are relatively new, most of these drivers conform to a protocol called ODBC, or Open Database Connectivity. Does JDBC start from scratch, then, and require a programmer to toss all of this existing work into the recycling bin of history?

No! While JDBC can interact directly with SQL databases if there's a driver written for it in Java, JDBC can also be used in conjunction with ODBC, which then goes off and interacts with SQL databases. JDBC can interact with ODBC by using what's known as a JDBC-ODBC bridge.

This allows you to take two approaches to interacting with a database: you can write a driver that takes JDBC calls and performs the SQL calls to the database, or you can use an ODBC driver that already does this and connect JDBC to ODBC using a JDBC-ODBC bridge. Figure 21-8 shows what this looks like.

Figure 21-8
Accessing a Database
Using the JDBC-
ODBC Bridge

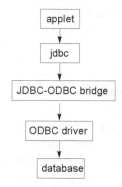

The ODBC driver will be native to the platform it's running on. However, using JDBC to access ODBC allows your applet to remain platform-independent while still taking advantage of ODBC.

Opening a Connection to a Database

To open a connection to a database, follow these steps:

1. Load the database driver (which causes it to create an instance of itself and register itself with the DriverManager).
2. Invoke the DriverManager method getConnection() and identify the database driver you will use to connect to the database, the database file name, and optionally as a user ID and password.

Here's how you can load the JDBC-ODBC bridge that comes with Sun's version of Java:

```
Class.forName("sun.jdbc.odbc.JdbcOdbcDriver");
```

You identify the driver and database file by using a special kind of URL. There are three parts to this special URL:

- The jdbc prefix (this is known as the *protocol*).
- An indication of which driver to use to access the database (this is known as the *subprotocol*).
- The database file name.

Here is a URL you might use to access a database called BaseballCards using the JDBC-ODBC bridge:

```
String url = "jdbc:odbc:BaseballCards";
DriverManager.getConnection(url, "userID", "passwd");
```

Interacting with a Database

Once you've established a connection with the database, you can send it SQL statements and get results.

There are three different types of Statement classes. You can use instances of these classes to send SQL statements to a database. These classes are:

- Statement: sends simple SQL statements with no parameters.
- PreparedStatement (extends Statement): sends precompiled SQL statements.
- CallableStatement (extends PreparedStatement): executes a database procedure.

There are also two different types of methods you can use to send these SQL statements: executeQuery() and executeUpdate(). Which method you use depends on what type of SQL statement you create. The following table shows you which statement you would use with which method, and what that statement does.

SQL statement	Method	What this SQL statement does
SELECT	executeQuery()	Finds records in a database given criteria to look for.
INSERT	executeUpdate()	Inserts a single record into a table.
UPDATE	executeUpdate()	Updates fields in a table.
DELETE	executeUpdate()	Deletes records matching a criteria.
CREATE TABLE	executeUpdate()	Creates a new table.
DROP TABLE	executeUpdate()	Removes a table.

The Select statement returns a ResultSet object containing the results of the search. You can use ResultSet methods to iterate over the results. The other SQL statements generally return a result indicating success or failure.

Tip

While statement objects are closed automatically by the garbage collector, you should close them yourself as soon as you're done using them to help Java to optimize its memory management chores.

An Example of Using ODBC with Microsoft Access on Windows 95

The following code is one specific example of using JDBC and the JDBC-ODBC bridge. The trouble with any example is that it will be specific for the database and platform you're running in. However, it still might be useful to see a working example, even if your environment is not the same as this one.

I started by creating a very simple database in Microsoft Access. This consisted of a single table and three entries. You'll see when you get to the sample programming assignment in Chapter 27 what this database is supposed to represent (passengers assigned to airplane seats). Figure 21-9 shows what this single table looks like.

Figure 21-9
A Simple Table in a
Database

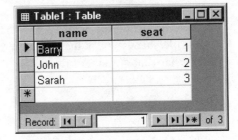

I then acquired and installed the ODBC System Administrator from Microsoft. This is free from Microsoft's Web site. I specified my database in this system administrator software as a system data source that used the Microsoft Access ODBC driver.

Then I wrote the code to access this database via JDBC:

```java
import java.net.URL;
import java.sql.*;
import sun.jdbc.odbc.*;

class JdbcExample {

    public static void main(String[] args) {

        if (args.length == 0) {
            System.out.println("java JdbcExample <url>");
            System.exit(1);
        }

        try {
            Class.forName("sun.jdbc.odbc.JdbcOdbcDriver");
            Connection con = DriverManager.getConnection(args[0]);

            Statement stmt = con.createStatement();
            ResultSet rs =
                stmt.executeQuery("SELECT name, seat FROM Table1");
```

continued

```
        while (rs.next()) {
            String name = rs.getString("name");
            int    seat = rs.getInt("seat");

            System.out.println(name + " " + seat);
        }

        stmt.close();
        con.close();

    } catch (Exception x) {
        System.out.println(x.getMessage());
        x.printStackTrace();
    }
  }
}
```

The JDBC-ODBC bridge translates JDBC method calls into ODBC function calls. It allows JDBC to leverage the database connectivity provided by the ODBC driver that already knows how to work with Microsoft Access.

I ran this program by using this command:

```
java JdbcExample jdbc:odbc:mydb.mdb
```

(mydb.mdb was the name of my Access file.) This program ran, established the connection with the database, read the records in Table 1, and displayed the names and seat assignments in that database:

```
Barry    1
John     2
Sarah    3
```

Exercise 21.2

- Establish a connection to a database file named "thisdb" located on the machine "remote" under the directory "top/db".
- Execute the SQL statement "INERT INTO Table1 (name, seat) VALUES('Greg', 5)".
- Perform any cleanup to complete this connection.

Answers to the Exercises

Exercise 21.1

First, here is the interface. Remember that it has to extend Remote.

```
import java.rmi.RemoteException;
import java.rmi.Remote;

public interface NYSEInterface extends Remote {
    double dowJonesAvg() throws RemoteException;
}
```

Now, here is the NYSE class. Notice that it has to define a constructor that throws RemoteException. This is true even if you only need a no-args, default constructor.

```
import java.rmi.*;
import java.rmi.server.*;

public class NYSE extends UnicastRemoteObject
    implements NYSEInterface
{

    public NYSE() throws RemoteException {
    }

    public double dowJonesAvg() throws RemoteException {
        double avg = 0.0;

        // FIND THE AVERAGE

        return avg;
    }

}
```

Exercise 21.2

1. Establish a connection to a database file named "thisdb" located on the machine "remote" under the directory "top/db".

```
Class.forName("sun.jdbc.odbc.JdbcOdbcDriver");
Connection con =
    DriverManager.getConnection("//remote/top/db/thisdb");
```

2. Execute the SQL statement "INERT INTO Table1 (name, seat) VALUES('Greg', 5)".

```
Statement stmt = con.createStatement();
int result = stmt.executeUpdate(
    "INERT INTO Table1 (name, seat) VALUES('Greg', 5)");
```

3. Perform any cleanup to complete this connection.

```
stmt.close();
con.close();
```

Review Questions

Question 1: **You can make an object that reads and writes records from a database safe for multiple clients by:**

a) Declaring its methods to be `synchronized`.
b) Declaring the method as throwing a RemoteException.
c) Implementing the Remote interface.
d) Closing the file on `finalize()`.

Question 2: To create an object that others can access remotely, you must implement which interface?

a) Clonable
b) Throwable
c) RemoteObject
d) Remote

Question 3: All methods in a remote interface must:

a) not return a value
b) throw a RuntimeException
c) throw a RemoteException
d) be static methods

Question 4: When an applet obtains a reference to a remote object, that reference is:

a) a stub representing the object
b) a copy of the object
c) a direct reference to the object
d) an instance of RemoteObject

Question 5: You can load Sun's JDBC-ODBC bridge by invoking:

a) Class.forName()
b) DriverManager.getConnection()
c) executeQuery() given a Statement object
d) you don't have to do anything to load the JDBC-ODBC bridge

Question 6: A JDBC-style URL follows the format:

a) jdbc:subprotocol
b) jdbc:subprotocol:SQL statement
c) jdbc:subprotocol:database file name
d) jdbc:protocol:subprotocol

Answers to the Review Questions

Question 1   a.   By synchronizing the methods that access and update a database file, multiple clients can work with the object responsible for this file at the same time.

Question 2   d.   You must implement the Remote interface. Typically, you extend the Remote interface by defining an interface specific to your application. Then, you implement this new interface. Ultimately, however, your new remote class is an `instanceof` Remote.

Question 3   c.   All methods that you want to invoke remotely must declare that they throw a RemoteException.

Question 4   a.   When you find an object on a remote JVM, RMI passes back a stub representing the object.

Question 5   a.   `Class.forName()` loads a class. (Database drivers should register themselves with the DriverManager when they load.)

Question 6   c.   An example of a JDBC-style URL is:
`jdbc:odbc:mydb`

In this example, `odbc` is the subprotocol, and `mydb` is the name of the database file.

Network Programming

Prerequisites

I assume you are familiar with the basic concepts of client/server computing in this chapter. (It's also useful to have written an Internet-based application, though I do go over all the basic topics you'll need to know to complete the developer programming assignment.)

This chapter calls upon your full knowledge of Java, from multithreading to exception handling to graphical user interfaces.

With Java, network programming is—dare I say it—*fun*. The package `java.net` contains a few classes that hide what's happening at the Transport Control Protocol/Internet Protocol (TCP/IP) layer and make programs that communicate over the Internet relatively easy to write. However, to use these classes effectively, you've got to know how TCP/IP works, what sockets are, and the strategies for writing a client/server application. We'll review all of these topics in this chapter.

What's on the Programming Assignment

The developer assignment requires you to write a client/server application. The client and server talk to each other using TCP/IP. You will pass data between the client and server using sockets.

Objectives for this Chapter

- Describe what IP addresses are and how they work.
- State why TCP makes it possible to send streams of data over the Internet.
- Identify what a socket is and what it represents.
- Identify the classes in `java.net` used to communicate via TCP/IP.
- Use Java to establish network connections.
- Write a client/server application.
- Write a server that can handle more than one client.

A TCP/IP Primer

Describe how IP addresses work.

State the reason why TCP makes it possible to send streams of data over the Internet.

The programming assignment for the Developer exam requires you to understand TCP/IP. If you're a little fuzzy on these protocols, or are not quite sure what this acronym even stands for, have no fear. I'll cover them in this section, and you'll even write your own simple client/server programs using TCP/IP in the exercises.

TCP/IP stands for *Transport Control Protocol/Internet Protocol*. TCP and IP are really two different protocols, but together they define the way things work on the Internet.

The Internet Protocol (IP) identifies computers on the Internet. Computers are identified by a four byte value.

This four byte value is often called a "dotted octet," because this number—the IP address—is written in a form like this:

    206.26.48.100

Given this number, one computer on the Internet can find and identify another computer. That's the Internet Protocol.

Since it's not always easy to remember numbers like this, these numbers are often mapped to human names, called domain names, such as java.sun.com. There are special servers on the Internet that perform this mapping, called Domain Name Servers. If you ask your Web browser to connect to www.javasoft.com, for example, it finds a Domain Name Server, looks up its dotted octet, and connects to that machine.

Before we look at how that connection occurs, let's look at the other protocol—Transport Control Protocol, or TCP.

TCP enables you to treat any Internet resource as a stream. It does this by guaranteeing two things:

1. Data sent to a particular machine arrives at that machine.
2. If the data sent to a particular machine had to be divided into smaller pieces and sent separately, all of these pieces are reassembled on the receiving end in the correct order.

Here's an example of why this is important and how it's used. Let's say you are about to send a memo to your boss asking for a raise. You've stated all the important reasons why you deserve a raise. Since you're thorough, the message is quite long. You want to make certain your boss knows each and every reason why you're worth more than his penny-pinching mind currently comprehends.

You hit **"send"** on your email program. The email program wants to send this out over the Internet to the IP address you've specified. But it can't. Why? Because the message is too big! You were too thorough. Does the email program ask you to rewrite your message and state your reasons in 50 words or less? No! It takes matters into its own hands. It divides the message you wrote into lots of smaller messages, each one small enough to travel over the Internet. This first step is shown in Figure 22-1.

Figure 22-1
Preparing to Send a Message Over the Internet

Because of TCP, each piece contains a header that indicates where it's going and identifies its place in the sequence to be received. Each piece of the message—each *packet*—goes out into the Internet. (For the sake of completeness, here's a simple definition of the Internet: a network of networks that relies on TCP/IP.) As each packet travels from computer to computer—from node to node—on its way to its IP destination, perhaps not all pieces of this monster message go the same way. Perhaps some pieces get rerouted. Perhaps a machine in the stepping stones across the net goes down after sending packet 16 but before sending packet 17. TCP/IP still works its magic—the pieces of your message still arrive at their correct destination—but now they start arriving in a different order from the order you sent them. This is shown in Figure 22-2.

Figure 22-2
Packets Don't Have to Take the Same Route to their Destination

Naturally, you don't want any arguments left out because it didn't arrive. And you don't want your email in a jumbled order when your boss looks at it. You want to keep your argument cogent and focused, building to a crescendo by the time you ask for a raise at the end.

This is where TCP kicks into high gear. Not only have all your message pieces arrived (guaranteed delivery), but now they are reassembled into the correct order. Once the pieces are reassembled, they're accepted by your boss' email program. Your boss now has an impressive piece of email to read. This is illustrated in Figure 22-3.

Figure 22-3
Packets are
Reassembled into
their Proper Order

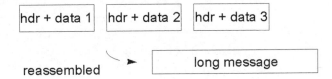

reassembled

long message

Ports and Sockets

Identify what a socket is and what data it represents.

This is fine as far as it goes, but I left out one crucial step: how does the computer receiving the email message know that this message *is* an email message? What if there is also a Web server on your boss' machine, serving up pages to the people in your group? How can the Web server and the email program both be running at the same time and paying attention only to the data meant for them when they're both talking TCP/IP? After all, both programs are running on the same machine, and that machine has only one IP address.

The solution to this riddle is that there is one more piece of information that distinguishes where the data should go. That piece of information is a *port number*.

Each server program listens to a different port. There are 2 to the 16th different ports, and each is assigned a number.

By convention, these numbers are divided into two groups:

- Port numbers below 1024 are reserved for well-known system uses, such as Web protocols, email, ftp, and so on.

- Port numbers above 1024, up to 2 to the 16th minus 1 (because port numbers start at 0), are all yours, and you can assign your own programs and services to these port numbers.

So, the email program is listening to one port, and the Web server is listening to another port. Email might arrive looking for port 25 (which is the port usually associated with SMTP, or Simple Mail Transfer Protocol), while requests for Web pages might arrive looking for port 80 (which is the port usually associated with HTTP, or HyperText Transport Protocol). Each server only listens for data arriving on its particular port. Figure 22-4 gives a sense of this.

Figure 22-4
Server Software
Listening to
Specific Ports

This combination of IP address and port number uniquely identifies a service on a machine.

This service could be a server program, such as a Web server. Client programs also listen to a particular port for data from the server. Just as the client uses this combination of IP address and port to send data to the server, the server also uses this combination of IP address and port to send data back to the client.

Such a combination of IP address and port is known as a socket.

A socket identifies one end of a two-way communication. When a client requests a connection with a server on a particular port, the server identifies and keeps track of the socket it will use to talk to the client.

Tip

This might help explain how a server can keep track of and talk to multiple clients at once. Even though the server is communicating over the same port with many clients, it uses sockets (remember, port + IP address) to determine the destination and source of that communication. The server keeps track of each client's socket. The server knows data arriving on one socket comes from a different client than data arriving on another socket. The server knows that it can respond to a client by passing data back to that client's socket.

Figure 22-5 gives a sense of the role that sockets play in this client/server communication. (We'll look at exactly what's happening on the server side regarding port numbers shortly.)

Figure 22-5
Sockets Uniquely
Identify the End
Point of a Two-Way
Communication

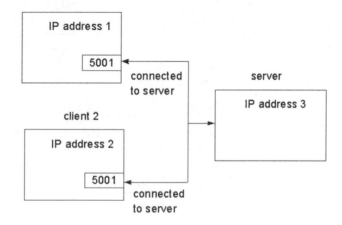

Streams

Key Concept

With IP addressing, TCP's guaranteed delivery and sequencing of data, and with sockets to identify the end points of two-way communications, data passing over the Internet can be treated by an application as a stream.

In other words, you can read from a socket just as if you were reading from a file, because TCP ensures that all the data sent from the machine on the other end of the Internet connection is received in order. TCP hides the fact that the data is arriving via the Internet and, at the level of the public interfaces declared by Java's Stream classes, makes the data indistinguishable from data read from a local file.

You can attach a Stream class to a socket and read from it or write to it just as you learned about in Chapter 11. We'll look at some examples in a moment.

Designing Servers and Clients

To develop an application that communicates over the Internet, you'll develop a server and a client. The server listens for connections on a particular port; when it receives a connection, it obtains a socket to use for the communication and begins a dialog with the client at the other end of that socket. The client initiates the connection and communicates with the server via a socket representing that server.

A classic design for a server is one that runs forever, listening for connections with clients, and then taking part in a dialog with the client (by reading data from the client and writing data to the client, as appropriate).

Figure 22-6 shows the basic steps that a client and server take in communicating with each other.

Figure 22-6
The Basic Interaction between a Server and a Client

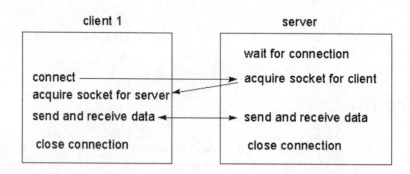

Handling Multiple Clients

As long as the server only uses a single thread, other clients attempting to communicate with the server wait in a queue until the server is through with its current client and closes its connection with that client. If you only anticipate having one client communicate with the server, then the possibilities of other clients waiting in a queue is not a concern. If you might have multiple clients talking to the server, you need a design that can handle this situation.

Regardless of whether the communication between the server and client is lengthy or relatively short, there's really no need to fear implementing a server that can handle more than one client. In Java, with its ability to easily implement multithreading, synchronize between multiple threads, and work directly with sockets, it's quite straightforward to create a multithreading server.

You might wish to implement a server that follows the basic flow chart shown in Figure 22-7:

Figure 22-7
A Basic Flow Chart for a Multithreading Server

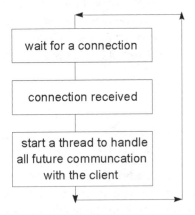

Threads introduce new wrinkles to the server.

The first wrinkle you might want to iron out is making the server thread-safe.

For example, let's say the server is accessing a database. If one thread is reading from the database at the same time that another thread is writing to it, clearly this is trouble. Fortunately, it's simple to lock the dependent methods in Java by declaring them to be `synchronized`. You'll see an example of a working server in a few more pages.

That's great as far as interacting with the database. But how does the server keep track of multiple clients? How does the server know which data read from a port goes with a particular thread? The answer is that TCP/IP takes care of this data routing for you, and TCP is the protocol layer below sockets—which you probably won't ever have to deal with *directly* if you program in Java.

Remember, sockets encode both the port number and the IP address. This means each client is uniquely identified. When a server accepts a connection, it acquires the client's socket. From then on, all data received from or sent to the client is read from or written to this socket. The TCP protocol below the socket layer ensures the data sent from a particular client goes to the correct socket in the correct server thread.

Because the server uses a socket to interact with the client, the server is born ready for multithreading.

Tip

Assigning each socket communication with a client to its own thread also has the great benefit that if something goes terribly wrong with the communication between the server and a particular client, only the thread that's dealing with that client will be in trouble (and possibly end with an exception); the rest of the server will continue chugging along.

Client Issues

Let's look briefly at some design issues involving the client. Here are some questions you might want to think about for your client. Your answers will depend on the needs of your particular client application.

If the client sends a request to the server and the server takes some time to answer it, will the user interface "freeze" because it is waiting for a response from the client, or will it continue working? If the user interface continues working, what will happen if the user then issues another request? Should this second request supersede the first one?

You have a number of strategies in implementing your client, and the right approach will take into account lots of factors that depend on your particular situation. You've got to decide how sophisticated to make your user interface, and whether that sophistication is worth the price of increased development and maintenance. Here are some possible strategies for you to contemplate:

- Block all user input until (and hopefully when!) the server responds. You might want to change the cursor to a busy cursor during this communication time.
- Spawn a separate thread to communicate with the server. When the server responds, have that thread invoke a method that updates the user interface appropriately. Work at recovering gracefully if the user interface changes before the server responds.

- Spawn a separate thread that displays a modal dialog that allows the user the option of canceling the communication with the server. The modal dialog should disappear when the server does respond. Because it is modal, it will keep the user from altering the user interface if communication with the server is still taking place.

Two other important considerations in writing a client/server application are:

1. Does the server need to save state for each individual client, or will all clients manipulate the same data source on the server? If the server needs to save state for each client, it will either need objects that store the relevant information, or better (in case the connection is dropped prematurely), a file where it can keep the information for the various clients (or perhaps the server can keep one file per client).

2. Does the server communicate with each client independently of the others, or will the server broadcast information to all the clients connected to it? If the clients are operating independently of each other, the server does not need to keep track of each thread in the server. However, if the server will broadcast information to all connected clients (as in a multi-client chat program), the server will need to keep some kind of list of the threads handling communication with the various clients.

The Networking Package

Identify the classes in `java.net` used to communicate via TCP/IP.

Java makes working with TCP/IP easy, because it has built-in support for these protocols. Java provides this support in the form of classes.

In particular, you'll find that three classes are particularly useful for this kind of low-level communication. They are:

- InetAddress
- Socket
- ServerSocket

InetAddress

The InetAddress class encodes an IP address. You obtain InetAddress objects not by creating them with a constructor, but by calling one of three static methods defined by InetAddress.

One of these is called getByName(). This method takes a String object that contains the IP address either as a dotted octet or as its Domain Name Server equivalent. You can create a new InetAddress object either with this line of code:

```
InetAddress ipAddress = InetAddress.getByName("206.26.48.100");
```

or with this one:

```
InetAddress ipAddress = InetAddress.getByName("java.sun.com");
```

You can obtain the IP address of the machine which your code is running on by writing:

```
InetAddress ipAddress = InetAddress.getLocalHost();
```

This creates an InetAddress object that represents the local machine.

The InetAddress class defines two instance methods: getAddress(), which returns an array of four bytes, and getHostName(), which returns a String. Each returns the IP address. getAddress() returns the dotted octet, while getHostName() returns the name found in the Domain Name Server.

You'll see next how you can use an InetAddress object to create a socket used to communicate with another computer over the Internet.

Socket and ServerSocket

The Socket class defines a socket—one end of a two-way communication.

You need an IP address and a port to create a Socket object. Here's an example:

```
InetAddress ipServer = InetAddress.getByName("java.sun.com");
Socket s = new Socket(ipServer, 5001);
```

The first line obtains the IP address of the server. The second line creates a socket connected to that server if it's listening to port 5001 for client connections. This constructor establishes a dedicated connection between the local machine and the server. Figure 22-8 shows the first step in this process.

Figure 22-8

The Client Requests a Connection with a Server

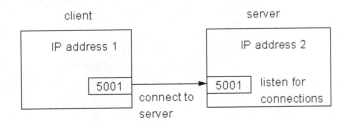

 For this constructor to work, the server must already be waiting for clients to connect to it. The server first creates a ServerSocket object listening on a specified port:

```
ServerSocket serverSock = new ServerSocket(5001);
```

Then, the server waits for clients to connect to it by executing:

```
Socket sock = serverSock.accept();
```

 The accept() method waits until a client connects with the server.

At this point, the accept() method does something very interesting: it tells the client that it should use a different port to continue the communication. This is shown in Figure 22-9.

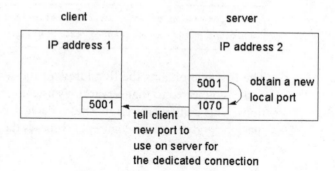

Figure 22-9
The Server Obtains
a New Local Port
and Tells the Client
What it is

For example, the server might obtain a new, free port to use to communicate with the client whose number is 1070. The client now communicates using local port 5001 and remote port 1070 (the remote port is the server's port from the client's point-of-view). Similarly, the server communicates using local port 1070 and remote port 5001 (the remote port is the client's port from the server's point-of-view). The server needs to obtain a new port so that it can continue to listen for other clients trying to connect to it on port 5001. This is shown in Figure 22-10.

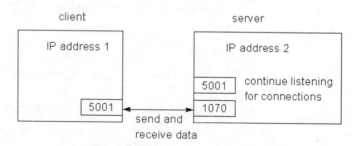

Figure 22-10
The Server and Client
Can Now Have a
Dedicated Connection

All you need to know as an application programmer is the original port that the server is listening to: the port that the server and client agree to use for their dedicated connection is not something you need to decide on. Java's classes will handle this detail for you. In fact, if you do not invoke `getLocalPort()` and `getPort()` on the sockets you create to identify the local and remote ports, respectively, you'll never realize that ServerSocket's `accept()` method has reassigned the server's port for you.

This is really just background information—you won't have to deal with these ports directly, other than knowing which port the server is listening to initially. But it's useful to know what's going on under the hood.

There are other constructors, as well, for both ServerSocket and Socket. For example, you can specify the local port as a different number from the remote port. For example, perhaps you want your socket's local port to be 3333, but you still want to connect to the server listening to port 5001. You can create your socket and connect to the server by writing:

```
Socket sock = new Socket(ipServer, 5001, ipLocal, 3333);
```

By default, the ServerSocket object you create will accept connections with up to 50 clients. You can also create a ServerSocket where you indicate this limit directly. For example, you can write:

```
ServerSocket serverSock = new ServerSocket(5001, 25);
```

This server socket can only accept up to 25 simultaneous connections. If a 26th client tries to connect to it, the server socket refuses the connection.

Internet Streams

At this point, once you've established a dedicated connection between client and server, you can use everything you're familiar with from the review of streams in Chapter 11.

For example, you can acquire an InputStream object that has a socket as its source. Then, you can create a new Filter stream object and attach it to this InputStream. You might create a new DataInputStream object and use it to read bytes from the socket. Here's a code snippet that does this.

Let's say you have a Socket object in the variable sock. You can get an InputStream object by writing:

```
sock.getInputStream();
```

From this, you can create a DataInputStream by passing this value to its constructor. You might write this all in one line of code:

```
DataInputStream remoteIn = new DataInputStream(sock.getInput-
```

You can then use remoteIn to read from the socket and receive data from the machine you're connected to. For example, to read an integer, you can write:

```
int myInt = remoteIn.readInt();
```

To send data, you need to acquire an output stream for the client by using the method getOutputStream():

```
DataOutputStream remoteOut =
    new DataOutputStream(sock.getOutputStream());
```

You can then use remoteOut to write to the socket and send data to the machine you're connected to. For example, to write the number 5, you might write:

```
remoteOut.writeInt(5);
```

You've got to be sure to handle all of the exceptions appropriately. In particular when reading and writing using streams, you need to wrap your read() and write() calls in try–catch blocks and be prepared to catch IOException.

Tip

Of course, you need to read and write according to a protocol that both the server and client know how to speak. When your client reads, the server better send you something. Similarly, when your client writes, the server better try to read it. There are some read() methods that will time out if nothing appears. However, if you don't use these, read() will block forever until data finally arrives.

Warning

When your protocol is clearly established and you're reading and writing in the right sequence, you'll find that you're communicating over the Internet with just a few lines of code.

Once you have completed your connection, you should close any streams you've created. After this, you should close the socket connection. You can invoke close() for both a stream and a socket to accomplish this.

Tip

Client-Server Examples

You've learned the basics of TCP/IP, seen the design issues and approaches for servers and clients, and learned about the networking classes available in Java to help you work with TCP/IP. Now, let's look at how to write a client/server application in Java by writing two types of chat programs.

In the first program, we'll write a simple chat program that connects one computer with another and passes messages back and forth. In the next program, we'll write a server that allows any number of clients to connect to it. In this second version, the server will broadcast each message it receives from a client to all other connected clients.

These servers do not require synchronization. To see how to synchronize between multiple clients, work through the practice programming assignment for the Developer exam, located in Chapter 27.

You'll find that you've seen some of this code in the snippets presented in the chapter so far. Now, you'll see these snippets as part of a working program.

Writing a Single-Client Server in Java

Use Java to establish network connections.

Write a client/server application.

Let's take a look at how the single-client chat program works. You can launch this program from the command line; it runs as a stand-alone graphical application, not as an applet. If you specify no command-line arguments, it's launched as a server, waiting for a connection from a client. You can also launch it as a client by specifying the name of the host to connect to. If you are running both the client and the server on the same machine, you can pass it the name "local." In other words, this program can act as either the client or the server, depending on whether or not you have supplied a command line parameter.

When you first launch the program as a server (without a command line parameter), by typing:

```
java SingleChat
```

it will appear as in Figure 22-11:

Figure 22-11
The SingleChat Application Launched as a Server

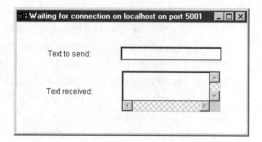

Then, when you launch the program as a client (by specifying the host where the server is already running), by typing:

    java SingleChat local

the new program runs and displays the user interface shown in Figure 22-12:

Figure 22-12
The SingleChat Application Launched as a Client with a Server Already Running

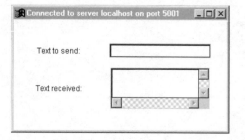

These two graphical user interfaces look mighty similar; the difference is in the title of the frame (and what went on behind the scenes, which we'll look at in a moment). Notice the title of the client states that it has connected to the server named "localhost." In the meantime, the title of the server application changed to indicate it has "Accepted connection from localhost."

Now whenever one person types text into the field labeled "Text to send" and hits **enter**, the text is sent over the network connection using TCP/IP to the other version of SingleChat it is connected with. This is shown in Figure 22-13 and Figure 22-14. The first figure shows text being typed into the "Text to send" text field. Then, after the user hits **enter**, the text is sent to the other SingleChat application. The text is received and displayed in the "Text received" text area shown in the second figure.

Figure 22-13
Text Typed into the
"Text to Send"
Text Field

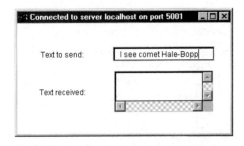

Figure 22-14
Text Received and
Displayed in the "Text
Received" text Area

So how does this work? Let's look at the basic architecture first. Then I'll present the entire source code, and then we'll examine the lines of code specific to TCP/IP.

The SingleChat class is a Panel. It creates a Frame in main() so that it can appear on the screen. It lays out its user interface using a GridBagLayout.

SingleChat invokes one of two methods, client() or server(), depending on whether or not the user has supplied a command line parameter. Without a parameter, it runs as a server. With a parameter, it runs as a client, and the server's name is passed to client().

The server() method waits for a connection. When a client connects to it, it obtains a socket for the client and spawns a thread that loops forever. This thread listens to this socket for data sent by the client.

The client() method tries to establish a connection with the server given the name of the machine the server is running on. Once it establishes this connection, it obtains a socket for the server and spawns a thread that loops forever. This thread listens to this socket for data sent by the server.

When the user hits the **enter** key in the text field labeled "Text to send," the application gets the text in this text field and writes it to the socket it obtained when the two applications connected. When data arrives on the socket, as monitored in the thread that's continually looping, the application takes this text and displays it in the text area labeled "Received text."

Here is the complete code listing. It weighs in at under 200 lines of code, including comments:

```java
import java.io.*;
import java.net.*;
import java.awt.*;

/**
 * SingleChat -- A chat program between a server and one client.
 *
 * To run as a server, do not supply any command line arguments.
 * SingleChat will start listening on the default port, waiting
 * for a connection:
 *    java SingleChat
 *
 * To run as a client, name the server as the first command line
 * argument:
 *    java SingleChat bluehorse.com
 * or
 *    java SingleChat local           // to run locally
 */

public class SingleChat extends Panel {
    Socket      sock;
    TextArea    receivedText;

    private GridBagConstraints c;
    private GridBagLayout       gridBag;
    private Frame               frame;
    private Label               label;
    private int                 port = 5001;    // The default port.
    private TextField           sendText;
    private DataOutputStream    remoteOut;

    public static void main(String args[]) {
        ExitFrame f = new ExitFrame("Waiting for connection...");

        String s = null;
        if (args.length > 0)
            s = args[0];

        SingleChat chat = new SingleChat(f);
        f.add("Center", chat);
        f.resize(350, 200);
        f.show();
```

continued

```
        // Make the connection happen.
        if (s == null)
            chat.server();
        else
            chat.client(s);

    }

    public SingleChat(Frame f) {
        frame = f;

        // Build the user interface.
        Insets insets = new Insets(10, 20, 5, 10); // bot, lf, rt, top
        gridBag = new GridBagLayout();
        setLayout(gridBag);

        c = new GridBagConstraints();

        c.insets = insets;
        c.gridy = 0;
        c.gridx = 0;

        label = new Label("Text to send:");
        gridBag.setConstraints(label, c);
        add(label);

        c.gridx = 1;

        sendText = new TextField(20);
        gridBag.setConstraints(sendText, c);
        add(sendText);

        c.gridy = 1;
        c.gridx = 0;

        label = new Label("Text received:");
        gridBag.setConstraints(label, c);
        add(label);

        c.gridx = 1;

        receivedText = new TextArea(3, 20);
        gridBag.setConstraints(receivedText, c);
        add(receivedText);
```

continued

```
    }

    // As a server, we create a server socket bound to the specified
    // port, wait for a connection, and then spawn a thread to
    // read data coming in over the network via the socket.

    private void server() {
        ServerSocket serverSock = null;
        try {
            InetAddress serverAddr = InetAddress.getByName(null);

            displayMsg("Waiting for connection on " +
                    serverAddr.getHostName() +
                    " on port " + port);

            // We'll only accept one connection for this server.
            serverSock = new ServerSocket(port, 1);
            sock = serverSock.accept();

            displayMsg("Accepted connection from " +
                    sock.getInetAddress().getHostName());

            remoteOut = new DataOutputStream(sock.getOutputStream());
            new SingleChatReceive(this).start();

        } catch (IOException e) {
            displayMsg(e.getMessage() +
                ": Failed to connect to client.");
        } finally {
            // At this point, since we only establish one connection
            // per run, we don't need the ServerSocket anymore.
            if (serverSock != null) {
                try {
                    serverSock.close();
                } catch (IOException x) {
                }
            }
        }
    }

    // As a client, we create a socket bound to the specified port,
    // connect to the specified host, and then spawn a thread to
    // read data coming coming in over the network via the socket.
```

continued

```
    private void client(String serverName) {
        try {
            if (serverName.equals("local"))
                serverName = null;

            InetAddress serverAddr = InetAddress.getByName(serverName);
            sock = new Socket(serverAddr.getHostName(), port, true);
            remoteOut = new DataOutputStream(sock.getOutputStream());

            displayMsg("Connected to server " +
                        serverAddr.getHostName() +
                        " on port " + sock.getPort());

            new SingleChatReceive(this).start();

        } catch (IOException e) {
            displayMsg(e.getMessage() +
                ": Failed to connect to server.");
        }
    }


    // Send data out to the socket we're communicating with when
    // the user hits Enter in the text field.
    public boolean action(Event e, Object what) {

        if (e.target == sendText) {
            try {

                // Send it.
                remoteOut.writeUTF(sendText.getText());

                // Clear it.
                sendText.setText("");

            } catch (IOException x) {
                displayMsg(x.getMessage() +
                    ": Connection to peer lost.");
            }

        }

        return super.action(e, what);
    }
```

continued

```
    void displayMsg(String s) {
        frame.setTitle(s);
    }

    protected void finalize() throws Throwable {
        try {
            if (remoteOut != null)
                remoteOut.close();
            if (sock != null)
                sock.close();
        } catch (IOException x) {
        }
        super.finalize();
    }

}

/** So that we can exit when the user closes the frame. */
class ExitFrame extends Frame {
    ExitFrame(String s) {
        super(s);
    }

    public boolean handleEvent(Event e) {
        if (e.id == Event.WINDOW_DESTROY) {
            hide();
            dispose();
            System.exit(0);
        }
        return super.handleEvent(e);
    }
}

/*
 * SingleChatReceive takes data sent on a socket and displays it in
 * a text area. This receives it from the network.
 */
class SingleChatReceive extends Thread {
    private SingleChat chat;
    private DataInputStream remoteIn;
    private boolean listening = true;
```

continued

```java
    public SingleChatReceive(SingleChat chat) {
        this.chat = chat;
    }


    public synchronized void run() {
        String s;
        try {
            remoteIn = new DataInputStream(chat.sock.getInputStream());

            while (listening) {
                s = remoteIn.readUTF();
                chat.receivedText.setText(s);
            }

        } catch (IOException e) {
            chat.displayMsg(e.getMessage() +
                ": Connection to peer lost.");

        } finally {
          try {
             if (remoteIn != null)
                remoteIn.close();
          } catch (IOException x) {
          }
        }
    }
}
```

Here are the key lines of code as far as TCP/IP is concerned.

server()

First, here is how the `server()` method works. The two lines that actually wait for a client to connect to it and then accept this connection are:

```java
    ServerSocket serverSock = new ServerSocket(port, 1);
    sock = serverSock.accept();
```

The constructor for ServerSocket takes a port number and, optionally, the number of connections to allow at one time. The default is 50; in this version of the chat program, we only allow one connection from one client. In the next version, we'll allow multiple clients to be connected to the server simultaneously.

The ServerSocket's `accept()` method waits for a connection from a client. When it accepts a connection and returns, it passes back a Socket object that represents the client.

Before these two lines, this method simply acquires the machine name that this server is running on so that it can display this to the user. After these two lines, it formats and displays a message containing the client's name. It then acquires a stream to use to write to the socket and starts a thread going that waits for data coming in on this socket.

client()

The two lines that connect with the server are:

```
InetAddress serverAddr = InetAddress.getByName(serverName);
sock = new Socket(serverAddr.getHostName(), port, true);
```

`serverName` is a String that represents the IP address (either the dotted octet or the Domain Name Server name) where the server is running. If this name is `null`, then `getByName()` returns the name of the local machine. When the constructor for the socket returns, you will have obtained a socket you can use to communicate with the server.

The third parameter passed to this constructor is a `boolean` that indicates whether this socket will be used like a stream to read and write data. In this case it will be, so it is set to `true`.

In Java 1.1, this Socket constructor has been deprecated (it is in the process of being phased out). Now, all Socket objects are stream sockets. It's perfectly fine to create the new socket only using the first two parameters and leave off `true` as the third parameter.

As we covered already, the actual remote port number that this socket contains will be a port the server has decided it will use to establish the dedicated connection with the client. As I indicated earlier, this is a detail that is handled by Java classes, though it is useful to keep this in mind while trying to understand what is going on.

Before these two lines, this method sets the serverName String to null if the name is "local," so that the Java methods will work with the local host. After these two lines, it formats and displays a message containing the server's name. It then acquires a stream to use to write to the socket and starts a thread that waits to process data arriving on this socket.

action()

When the user types some text into the text field labeled "Text to send" and hits **enter**, the application finds out about it in action(). Since we have already acquired a DataOutputStream object, we can use any DataOutputStream method and write the data to the socket. From there, Java handles the TCP/IP and makes sure the data goes out over the network and finds its destination.

run() for *SingleChatReceive*

The first thing this method does is acquire a DataInputStream object with the line:

```
DataInputStream remoteIn =
    new DataInputStream(chat.sock.getInputStream());
```

We reference this socket via the SingleChat object, since SingleChatReceive is a different class from SingleChat.

Then, this thread loops forever, reading text from the socket and displaying it in the text area.

Cleaning Up

You'll notice that this application is very careful to clean up after itself. If we fall out of the listening loops, or if this object is finalized, it first closes the streams and then closes the sockets.

Writing a Multi-Client Server in Java

Write a server that can handle more than one client.

The SingleChat server is a little bit unusual in that it only communicates with one client during its life. Let's write a server that accepts connections from multiple clients.

When one client sends the server a message, the server will broadcast this message to all clients attached to it. As with the single chat application, we'll look first at how it works. Then, we'll look at the basic architecture, view the source code, and examine the lines of code that make this a good multi-client, multithreaded server.

For this application, it was easier to write two different programs. One program is the server, which runs as a standalone character-mode program. (It doesn't really have much of an interface at all.) The other program is a client program that looks and acts very similar to the client program we looked at already.

When you launch the server (called MultiChatServer) by typing:

java MultiChatServer

at the command line, the program writes the following messages to the screen:

Hit control-c to exit the server.

Waiting for first connection on localhost on port 5001

At this point, it's ready for clients to connect to it. There is a hard limit in the code of 50 clients, set somewhat arbitrarily, with the intent of ensuring the server doesn't get swamped with requests. Otherwise, the server might get bogged down with keeping track of lots of network connections and performance could become slow. The server will run forever, until the user hits **Control-C** to actually break out of the program with this interrupt.

Once the server is running, the user can launch clients—any number theoretically, but up to 50 in this case—that connect to the server. To launch a client for this multi-chat application, specify two command line parameters: the name of the person taking part in the chat session, and the name of the host where the server is running. As before, you can type **local** to run locally, with the server and the client on the same machines. The name of this program is MultiChat. For example, you might type:

java MultiChat Shakespeare local

This will launch the client, this time putting the user's name in the title of the frame. Other clients can also connect to the same server. Now, when the user types into the text field labeled "Text to send" and hits **enter**, all other clients connected to the server will receive that message, with the client's name also displayed as a prefix, as in:

Shakespeare: If music be the food of love play on.

This identifies whom this message came from.

Now, here's the architecture. The server loops forever, waiting to accept connections from clients. When a client does connect with the server, the server acquires a stream to use to write to the socket and saves this stream in a list. It then creates a new thread that will handle all future communication with the client. It passes the client's socket to the thread and this output stream, since the thread will use this socket to communicate with the client. The server also passes the server instance to the thread, because the thread will later need to invoke some server methods.

Tip

Even if multiple clients can connect with the server, there might not be a need to keep track of all of the currently connected clients in a list in the server. If the clients do not need to interact with each other, the server can just spawn a new thread that handles the connection with the client, independently of the other client-handling threads. It is only because each client's message is broadcast to all the other clients that the server must keep track of all of the clients in this application.

The thread that interacts with the client also loops forever, waiting to receive data from the client. When it receives a message from the client, it invokes a method called broadcast(). This method loops through the different client output streams and sends the message to each of them.

After setting up the user interface, the client establishes a connection with the server and starts a thread that will listen for messages from the server.

This thread listening for server messages loops forever. When it receives a message, it displays it in the text area labeled "Received text." Whenever the user types into the text field labeled "Text to send" and hits **Enter**, the action() method sends this text to the server (where it gets broadcast to all other clients connected to the server).

Now that you've gotten an overview of the architecture for both the client and the server, let's look at the source code.

There are two separate source files for this application—one representing the server, and one representing the client. After each listing, I'll go over the lines of code you need to pay particular attention to.

First, here's the server:

```java
import java.io.*;
import java.net.*;
import java.util.Vector;
import java.util.Enumeration;

/**
 * MultiChatServer -- A chat program between any number of clients.
 *
 * The server acts as the central clearing house of all messages.
 * To run as a server, do not supply any command line arguments.
 * MultiChat will start listening on the default port, waiting
 * for a connection:
 *
 *    java MultiChatServer
 */

public class MultiChatServer {
    private int       port = 5001;    // The default port.
    private boolean   listening = true;
    private Vector    clients = new Vector();

    public static void main(String args[]) {
        System.out.println("Hit control-c to exit the server.");
        new MultiChatServer().server();
    }

    // As a server, we create a server socket bound to the specified
    // port, wait for a connection, and then spawn a thread to
    // read data coming in over the network via the socket.

    private void server() {
        ServerSocket serverSock = null;

        try {
            InetAddress serverAddr = InetAddress.getByName(null);

            System.out.println("Waiting for first connection on " +
                    serverAddr.getHostName() +
                    " on port " + port);
```

continued

```
                // Accept up to 50 connection at a time.
                // (This limit is just for the sake of performance.)
                serverSock = new ServerSocket(port, 50);

        } catch (IOException e) {
            System.out.println(e.getMessage() +
                ": Failed to create server socket.");
            return;
        }

        while (listening) {

            try {
                Socket socket = serverSock.accept();
                System.out.println("Accepted connection from " +
                    socket.getInetAddress().getHostName());
                DataOutputStream remoteOut =
                    new DataOutputStream(socket.getOutputStream());
                clients.addElement(remoteOut);
                new ServerHelper(socket, remoteOut, this).start();

            } catch (IOException e) {
                System.out.println(e.getMessage() +
                    ": Failed to connect to client.");
            }
        }

        if (serverSock != null) {
            try {
                serverSock.close();
            } catch (IOException x) {

            }
        }
    }

    synchronized Vector getClients() {
        return clients;
    }
```

continued

```
    synchronized void removeFromClients(DataOutputStream remoteOut) {
        clients.removeElement(remoteOut);
    }

}

/*
 * ServerHelper handles one client. The server creates one new
 * ServerHelper thread for each client that connects to it.
 */
class ServerHelper extends Thread {
    private Socket sock;
    private DataOutputStream remoteOut;
    private MultiChatServer server;
    private boolean listening = true;
    private DataInputStream remoteIn;

    ServerHelper(Socket sock, DataOutputStream remoteOut,
        MultiChatServer server) throws IOException
    {

        this.sock = sock;
        this.remoteOut = remoteOut;
        this.server = server;
        remoteIn = new DataInputStream(sock.getInputStream());
    }

    public synchronized void run() {
        String s;

        try {
            while (listening) {
                s = remoteIn.readUTF();
                broadcast(s);
            }

        } catch (IOException e) {
            System.out.println(e.getMessage() +
                ": Connection to peer lost.");
```

continued

```
        } finally {
           try {
              cleanUp();
           } catch (IOException x) {
           }
        }
     }


     // Send the message to all the sockets connected to the server.
     private void broadcast(String s) {
        Vector clients = server.getClients();
        DataOutputStream dataOut = null;

        for (Enumeration e = clients.elements(); e.hasMoreElements(); ) {
           dataOut = (DataOutputStream)(e.nextElement());

           if (!dataOut.equals(remoteOut)) {

              try {

                 dataOut.writeUTF(s);

              } catch (IOException x) {
                 System.out.println(x.getMessage() +
                    ": Failed to broadcast to client.");
                 server.removeFromClients(dataOut);
              }
           }
        }
     }


     private void cleanUp() throws IOException {
        if (remoteOut != null) {
           server.removeFromClients(remoteOut);
           remoteOut.close();
           remoteOut = null;
        }a

        if (remoteIn != null) {
           remoteIn.close();
           remoteIn = null;
        }
```

continued

```
        if (sock != null) {
            sock.close();
            sock = null;
        }
    }


    protected void finalize() throws Throwable {
        try {
            cleanUp();
        } catch (IOException x) {
        }

        super.finalize();
    }
}
```

server()

This time, we allow up to 50 clients to connect to the server. We accomplish this with the following line of code:

```
serverSock = new ServerSocket(port, 50);
```

Then, the server loops forever (until the user hits Control-C). At each iteration in the loop, the server waits to accept a connection with a client:

```
Socket socket = serverSock.accept();
```

If the clients were operating independently of each other (for example, in a database server), the server could simply spawn a new thread to handle all future communication with that client, handing that thread the socket it just acquired. However, in this program, we need to keep track of all of the clients connected to the server—that's how we'll know who to broadcast the message to.

So, we create a DataOutputStream object, save this object in a list of all the other client DataOutputStreams, and then start our new thread, which we've called ServerHelper. Now, ServerHelper will handle all future communication with the client—but it will turn to this list of output streams to broadcast any messages it receives from the client it's handling:

```
DataOutputStream remoteOut =
    new DataOutputStream(socket.getOutputStream());
clients.addElement(remoteOut);
new ServerHelper(socket, remoteOut, this).start();
```

run()

The run() method in ServerHandler loops forever, simply reading data from the socket and broadcasting it to other clients also connected to the server.

```
while (listening) {
    s = remoteIn.readUTF();
    broadcast(s);
}
```

broadcast()

This method simply enumerates over the list of clients connected to the server, and as long as the DataOutputStream object in this list is not from the client that sent the message, it writes the message to that client.

cleanUp()

As always, we're very careful to close all the streams and sockets when we're through with them.

The Client

Now, here's the client (it's very similar to the SingleChat program in many ways):

```
import java.io.*;
import java.net.*;
import java.awt.*;
```

continued

```java
/**
 * MultiChat -- A chat program between any number of clients.
 *
 * To run as a client, supply two parameters:
 *   1. The name of the person to identify this user
 *   2. the name the server:
 *      java MultiChat Spielberg bluehorse.com
 * or
 *      java MultiChat Spielberg local       // to run locally
 */

public class MultiChat extends Panel {
    TextArea   receivedText;
    Socket     sock;              // The communication socket.
    private GridBagConstraints c;
    private GridBagLayout       gridBag;
    private Frame               frame;
    private Label               label;
    private int                 port = 5001;  // The default port.
    private TextField           sendText;
    private String              hostname;
    private String              username;
    private DataOutputStream    remoteOut;

    public static void main(String args[]) {
        if (args.length != 2) {
            System.out.println("format is: java MultiChat <username> <hostname>");
            return;
        }

        ExitFrame f = new ExitFrame(args[0]);

        MultiChat chat = new MultiChat(f, args[0], args[1]);
        f.add("Center", chat);
        f.resize(350, 200);
        f.show();

        // Make the connection happen.
        chat.client();

    }
```

continued

```java
public MultiChat(Frame f, String user, String host) {
    frame = f;
    username = user;
    hostname = host;

    // Build the user interface.
    Insets insets = new Insets(10, 20, 5, 10); // bot, lf, rt, top
    gridBag = new GridBagLayout();
    setLayout(gridBag);

    c = new GridBagConstraints();

    c.insets = insets;
    c.gridy = 0;
    c.gridx = 0;

    label = new Label("Text to send:");
    gridBag.setConstraints(label, c);
    add(label);

    c.gridx = 1;

    sendText = new TextField(20);
    gridBag.setConstraints(sendText, c);
    add(sendText);

    c.gridy = 1;
    c.gridx = 0;

    label = new Label("Text received:");
    gridBag.setConstraints(label, c);
    add(label);

    c.gridx = 1;

    receivedText = new TextArea(3, 20);
    gridBag.setConstraints(receivedText, c);
    add(receivedText);

}
```

continued

```
// As a client, we create a socket bound to the specified port,
// connect to the specified host, and then spawn a thread to
// read data coming coming in over the network via the socket.

private void client() {
    try {
        if (hostname.equals("local"))
            hostname = null;

        InetAddress serverAddr = InetAddress.getByName(hostname);
        sock = new Socket(serverAddr.getHostName(), port, true);
        remoteOut = new DataOutputStream(sock.getOutputStream());

        System.out.println("Connected to server " +
                serverAddr.getHostName() +
                " on port " + sock.getPort());

        new MultiChatReceive(this).start();

    } catch (IOException e) {
        System.out.println(e.getMessage() +
            ": Failed to connect to server.");
    }
}

// Send data out to the socket we're communicating with when
// the user hits enter in the text field.

public boolean action(Event e, Object what) {

    if (e.target == sendText) {

        try {
            // Send it.
            remoteOut.writeUTF(username + ": " + sendText.getText());

            // Clear it.
            sendText.setText("");
```

continued

```
                } catch (IOException x) {
                    System.out.println(x.getMessage() +
                        ": Connection to peer lost.");
                }
            }

            return super.action(e, what);
        }


        protected void finalize() throws Throwable {
            try {
                if (remoteOut != null)
                    remoteOut.close();
                if (sock != null)
                    sock.close();
            } catch (IOException x) {
            }
            super.finalize();
        }

    }


    /*
     * ExitFrame allows us to exit when the user closes the frame.
     */
    class ExitFrame extends Frame {
        ExitFrame(String s) {
            super(s);
        }

        public boolean handleEvent(Event e) {
            if (e.id == Event.WINDOW_DESTROY) {
                hide();
                dispose();
                System.exit(0);
            }
            return super.handleEvent(e);
        }
    }
```

continued

```java
/*
 * MultiChatReceive takes data sent on a socket and displays it in
 * a text area. This receives it from the network.
 */
class MultiChatReceive extends Thread {
    private MultiChat chat;

    MultiChatReceive(MultiChat chat) {
        this.chat = chat;
    }

    public synchronized void run() {
        String s;
        DataInputStream remoteIn = null;
        try {
            remoteIn = new DataInputStream(chat.sock.getInputStream());

            while (true) {
                s = remoteIn.readUTF();
                chat.receivedText.setText(s);
            }

        } catch (IOException e) {
            System.out.println(e.getMessage() +
                ": Connection to peer lost.");

        } finally {
            try {
                if (remoteIn != null)
                    remoteIn.close();
            } catch (IOException x) {
            }
        }
    }
}
```

The only real difference between the client version of MultiChat and the client portion of SingleChat is that one of the command-line parameters is the user's name. This name is placed in front of the user's message to identify the speaker when the message is broadcast.

Cleaning Up

You'll also notice that, once again, we're very careful about closing the streams and sockets after we're through with them.

Exercise 22.1

Write a standalone character-mode client/server chat application using sockets. The server should accept only one connection from the client. Each peer should write what the user types via the keyboard to its communication socket, and read what comes in over this communication socket and display it in the standard output.

Exercise 22.2

Write a standalone character-mode client/server application where the client guesses a number between 0 and 9 chosen by the server. The client should send messages that follow this protocol:

If the client wants to know whether the number chosen by the server is greater than some number, it should send a String in the format:

```
>#
```

For example, to guess if the number is greater than 5, the client can send:

```
>5
```

To ask whether the number is less than a value, the client can send:

```
<#
```

To guess if the number is equal to a particular value, the client can send:

```
=#
```

The server should send true or false, depending on the number it has chosen and on the client's guess. When the client has guessed the number correctly, the server should send a congratulatory message and then end the connection with the client.

What's Not on the Developer Assignment

Uniform Resource Locator

Here's a quick word about URLs (you won't really have to program using URLs on the programming assignment).

Java defines a class called URL. When you use this class, you don't have to concern yourself with what's really going on with TCP/IP. All you have to do is point to the Internet address you are interested in and use the java.io classes to read from (and write to) that location.

The basic format of a URL address is:

```
access-method://server-name[:port]/dir/file
```

As you can see from this, a URL indicates the access method, server name, and file name of an Internet resource. Typically, the access method is something like http or ftp. The server name for a Web address might be www.bluehorse.com. The server name for an ftp address might be ftp.bluehorse.com. The directory and file name refer to the directory structure of the server.

You can create a URL object using a variety of constructors. The easiest way is to create a new URL like this:

```
URL myHome = new URL("www.bluehorse.com");
```

You can then use a method called openConnection() to begin reading from this URL, using the same I/O classes and methods you've already learned about. The openConnect() method returns a URLConnection object. With this, you can obtain an input stream or an output stream by calling getInputStream() or getOutputStream(). As you might suspect, you can then use this stream to access the resource.

Answer to the Exercises

Exercise 22.1

The only important change in this particular solution, compared to the example programs in the text, is that I used two threads: one to continually monitor what the user types and one to read from the socket.

```
import java.io.*;
import java.net.*;
import java.awt.*;

/**
 * CharChat -- A chat program between a server and one client.
 *
 * To run as a client, name the server as the first command line
 * argument:
 *    java SingleChat bluehorse.com
 * or
 *    java SingleChat local         // to run locally
 */

public class CharChat {
    private int                 port = 5001;    // The default port.

    public static void main(String args[]) {

        String s = null;
        if (args.length > 0)
            s = args[0];

        CharChat chat = new CharChat();
        if (s == null)
            chat.server();
        else
            chat.client(s);
    }

    // As a server, we create a server socket bound to the specified
    // port, wait for a connection, and then spawn a thread to
    // read data coming in over the network via the socket.

    private void server() {
        Socket sock = null;
        ServerSocket serverSock = null;

        try {
            serverSock = new ServerSocket(port, 1);

            //We'll only accept one connection for this server.
            sock = serverSock.accept();
```

continued

```
        new CharChatSend(sock).start();
        new CharChatReceive(sock).start();

    } catch (IOException x) {
        System.out.println(x.getMessage() +
            ": Failed to connect to client.");
        System.exit(1);

    } finally {

        // At this point, we don't need the ServerSocket anymore.
        if (serverSock != null) {
            try {
                serverSock.close();
            } catch (IOException x) {
            }
        }
    }

}

// As a client, we create a socket bound to the specified port,
// connect to the specified host, and then spawn a thread to
// read data coming coming in over the network via the socket.

private void client(String serverName) {
    try {
        if (serverName.equals("local"))
            serverName = null;

        InetAddress serverAddr = InetAddress.getByName(serverName);
        Socket sock =
            new Socket(serverAddr.getHostName(), port, true);

        new CharChatSend(sock).start();
        new CharChatReceive(sock).start();

    } catch (IOException e) {
        System.out.println(e.getMessage() +
            ": Failed to connect to server.");
    }
}

}
```

continued

```
/*
 * CharChatReceive takes data sent on a socket and displays it in
 * the standard output.
 */
class CharChatReceive extends Thread {
    private Socket sock;
    private DataInputStream remoteIn;
    private boolean listening = true;

    public CharChatReceive(Socket sock) throws IOException {
        this.sock = sock;
        remoteIn = new DataInputStream(sock.getInputStream());
    }

    public synchronized void run() {
        String s;
        try {

            while (listening) {
                s = remoteIn.readUTF();
                System.out.println(s);
            }

        } catch (IOException e) {
            System.out.println(e.getMessage() +
                ": Connection to peer lost.");

        } finally {
            try {
                if (remoteIn != null) {
                    remoteIn.close();
                    remoteIn = null;
                }

                if (sock != null) {
                    sock.close();
                    sock = null;
                }

            } catch (IOException x) {
            }
        }
    }
```

continued

```java
    protected void finalize() throws Throwable {
        try {
           if (remoteIn != null)
              remoteIn.close();
           if (sock != null)
              sock.close();
        } catch (IOException x) {
        }
        super.finalize();
    }


}

/*
 * CharChatSend takes data entered on the standard input and
 * sends it out over a socket.
 */
class CharChatSend extends Thread {
    private Socket sock;
    private DataOutputStream remoteOut;
    private boolean listening = true;

    public CharChatSend(Socket sock) throws IOException {
        this.sock = sock;
        remoteOut = new DataOutputStream(sock.getOutputStream());
    }

    public synchronized void run() {
        DataInputStream in = null;
        String s;
        try {

            in = new DataInputStream(System.in);
            while (listening) {
                s = in.readLine();
                if (s.equals(""))
                   break;
                remoteOut.writeUTF(s);
            }

        } catch (IOException e) {
            System.out.println(e.getMessage() +
               ": Connection to peer lost.");
```

continued

```
        } finally {
          try {
            if (in != null)
              in.close();

            if (remoteOut != null) {
              remoteOut.close();
              remoteOut = null;
            }

            // Socket closed in receive thread

          } catch (IOException x) {
          }
        }
      }

    protected void finalize() throws Throwable {
      try {
        if (remoteOut != null)
          remoteOut.close();

        // Socket closed in Recive thread

      } catch (IOException x) {
      }
      super.finalize();
    }
  }
```

Exercise 22.2

Here is the client:

```
import java.io.*;
import java.net.*;
import java.awt.*;

/**
 * NumberClient -- The client program for the guessing game.
```

continued

```
 * To run as a client, name the server as the first command line
 * argument:
 *    java NumberClient bluehorse.com
 * or
 *    java NumberClient local           // to run locally
 */

public class NumberClient {
    private int             port = 5001;    // The default port.
    private Socket          sock;
    private DataInputStream  remoteIn;
    private DataOutputStream remoteOut;
    private boolean         listening = true;

    public static void main(String args[]) {

        if (args.length != 1) {
            System.out.println("format is: java NumberClient <host-
name>");
            return;
        }

        new NumberClient().client(args[0]);
    }

    // As a client, we create a socket bound to the specified port,
    // connect to the specified host, and then start communicating
    // over the network via the socket.

    private void client(String serverName) {
        DataInputStream in = new DataInputStream(System.in);

        try {
            if (serverName.equals("local"))
                serverName = null;

            InetAddress serverAddr = InetAddress.getByName(serverName);
            sock = new Socket(serverAddr.getHostName(), port, true);
            remoteIn = new DataInputStream(sock.getInputStream());
            remoteOut = new DataOutputStream(sock.getOutputStream());
```

continued

```
            while (listening) {
                String s = in.readLine();
                if (s.equals(""))
                    listening = false;
                else
                    remoteOut.writeUTF(s);

                String response = remoteIn.readUTF();
                System.out.println(response);
            }

        } catch (IOException e) {
            System.out.println(e.getMessage() +
                ": Connection with server closed.");

        } finally {
            try {
                if (remoteIn != null) {
                    remoteIn.close();
                    remoteIn = null;
                }

                if (remoteOut != null) {
                    remoteOut.close();
                    remoteOut = null;
                }

                if (sock != null) {
                    sock.close();
                    sock = null;
                }

            } catch (IOException x) {
            }
        }
    }

    protected void finalize() throws Throwable {
        try {
            if (remoteIn != null)
                remoteIn.close();
            if (remoteOut != null)
                remoteOut.close();
            if (sock != null)
```

continued

```
            sock.close();
        } catch (IOException x) {
        }
        super.finalize();
    }


}
```

Here is the server:

```
import java.io.*;
import java.net.*;
import java.awt.*;


/**
 * NumberServer -- The server for a number guessing application.
 *
 * To run as a server, name the server as the first command line
 * argument:
 *    java NumberServer bluehorse.com
 * or
 *    java NumberServer local          // to run locally
 */

public class NumberServer {
    private int              port = 5001;    // The default port.
    private boolean          listening = true;

    public static void main(String args[]) {
       new NumberServer().server();
    }

    // As a server, we create a server socket bound to the specified
    // port, wait for a connection, and then spawn a thread to
    // read data coming in over the network via the socket.

    private void server() {
        ServerSocket serverSock = null;
```

continued

```
        try {
            serverSock = new ServerSocket(port, 50);
        } catch (IOException x) {
            System.out.println(x.getMessage() +
                ": Failed to create server socket.");
            System.exit(1);
        }

        while (listening) {
            try {

                Socket sock = serverSock.accept();
                new HandleGuesses(sock).start();

            } catch (IOException x) {
                System.out.println(x.getMessage() +
                    ": Failed to connect to client.");
                System.exit(1);
            }
        }

        // At this point, we don't need the ServerSocket anymore.
        if (serverSock != null) {
            try {
                serverSock.close();
            } catch (IOException x) {
            }
        }
    }

}


/*
 * HandleGuesses communicates with the client.
 */
class HandleGuesses extends Thread {
    private Socket sock;
    private DataInputStream remoteIn;
    private DataOutputStream remoteOut;
    private boolean listening = true;
    private int num = (int)(Math.random() * 10);
```

continued

```
public HandleGuesses(Socket sock) throws IOException {
    this.sock = sock;
    remoteIn = new DataInputStream(sock.getInputStream());
    remoteOut = new DataOutputStream(sock.getOutputStream());
}

public synchronized void run() {
    String s;
    String op;
    String guessString;
    int guessInt;
    try {

        while (listening) {
            s = remoteIn.readUTF();
            op = s.substring(0, 1);
            guessString = s.substring(1, 2);
            guessInt = new Integer(guessString).intValue();

            if (op.equals(">"))
                handleGreaterThan(guessInt);
            else if (op.equals("<"))
                handleLessThan(guessInt);
            else
                handleEquals(guessInt);
        }

    } catch (NumberFormatException x) {
        System.out.println(x.getMessage() +
            ": Protocol problem: expected a number.");

    } catch (IOException x) {
        System.out.println(x.getMessage() +
            ": Connection to peer lost.");

    } finally {
        try {
            if (remoteIn != null) {
                remoteIn.close();
                remoteIn = null;
            }
```

continued

```
                if (remoteOut != null) {
                    remoteOut.close();
                    remoteOut = null;
                }

                if (sock != null) {
                    sock.close();
                    sock = null;
                }

            } catch (IOException x) {
            }
        }
    }

    private void handleGreaterThan(int i) throws IOException {
        if (num > i)
            remoteOut.writeUTF("true");
        else
            remoteOut.writeUTF("false");
    }

    private void handleLessThan(int i) throws IOException{
        if (num < i)
            remoteOut.writeUTF("true");
        else
            remoteOut.writeUTF("false");
    }

    private void handleEquals(int i) throws IOException {
        if (i == num) {
            remoteOut.writeUTF("You guessed it!");
            listening = false;
        }

        else
            remoteOut.writeUTF("false");
    }
```

continued

```
protected void finalize() throws Throwable {
    try {
        if (remoteIn != null)
            remoteIn.close();
        if (remoteOut != null)
            remoteOut.close();
        if (sock != null)
            sock.close();
    } catch (IOException x) {
    }
    super.finalize();
    }
}
```

Review Questions

Question 1:   A socket encodes:

a) a port number
b) an IP address
c) both a port number and an IP address
d) none of these

Question 2:   To wait for a client to request a connection, your server can use the class:

a) Socket
b) ServerSocket
c) Server
d) URL

Question 3: The ServerSocket's accept() method returns an object of type:

a) Socket
b) ServerSocket
c) Server
d) URL

Question 4: When you create a new Socket instance using a constructor that takes a host address:

a) Java attempts to establish a connection over the Internet with the host.
b) Java starts a server running on the host.
c) Nothing special happens until you invoke the Socket's `accept()` method.

Question 5: To acquire an output stream to use to communicate via a socket given a Socket instance named sock, you can write:

a) `sock.accept();`
b) `sock.getDataOutputStream();`
c) `sock.getOutputStream();`
d) `new DataOutputStream(sock);`

Question 6: TCP is used to:

a) Identify a machine on the Internet based on a dotted octet or domain name.
b) Ensure packets arrive in the same order they are sent.
c) Both a and b.
d) Neither of these.

Answers to the Review Questions

Question 1   c.   A socket encodes both a port number and an IP address.

Question 2   b.   Invoke the ServerSocket's `accept()` method to wait for an incoming request.

Question 3   a.   The ServerSocket's `accept()` method returns an instance of class Socket, which the server can use to communicate with the client.

Question 4   a.   Creating a Socket using a constructor that specifies a host causes Java to attempt to establish a connection with that host.

Question 5   c.   Use `getOutputStream()` to acquire a stream. You can then create a DataOutputStream by passing this stream to its constructor.

Question 6   b.   TCP (Transport Control Protocol) guarantees packets arrive in the same order they are sent. IP (Internet Protocol) identifies machines on the Internet.

CHAPTER 23

Comments and Style

None.

As with any programming language, you have a free hand when it comes to coding style. Indentation, white space, variables names, and so on are up to you. There are some standard conventions in Java. We'll explore those here.

What's on the Programming Assignment

The person who will grade your programming assignment gives you points based on your programming style and the comments you supply. This does not mean you should provide a page of comments for each method you write—far from it! It means you must program in the style that your grader expects. This chapter will show you what that is.

Objectives for this Chapter

- Indent your code according to common practice.
- Comment only the non-obvious lines.
- Use consistent coding style.
- Handle errors appropriately.
- Use javadoc-style comments.

Styles and Conventions

Indentation

Indent your code according to common practice.

Every programmer knows how to indent code so that all code in a block is easy to spot. Regardless of how many spaces you indent compared to the next programmer, your main objective, whatever your style, is to *be consistent!*

Beware of some integrated development environments (IDEs) with their own code editors. Some of these automatically indent code for you, and you're probably apt to use the tab key in these editors. That's fine, but take a look at your code using a plain ASCII editor at some point. You might find that what looks good in the editor with your IDE doesn't look so hot with another editor. If this is the case, you might want to think about changing your tabs to spaces and making sure that no matter what editor Sun engineers use to view your program, it's going to look the way you intended.

Identifiers

Use consistent coding style.

Again, you can use any style you would like to, but be consistent. A common practice is to make your class names start with a capital letter and your variable and method names start with a lower-case letter. Usually, identifiers that are really multiple words—like "max value" and "the applet"—start with a small letter but have a capital at the start of each word, such as `maxValue` and `theApplet`.

Another common practice is to make constants—usually defined as `public static final`—all upper-case and connect words with an underscore, as in `MAX_VALUE` and `THE_APPLET`.

Names also are usually self-documenting. Unless it's a temporary variable, you might want to use descriptive names like `maxValue` instead of `m`, for example. However, it's common to name temporary variables (such as loop indexes or nested user interface objects such as panels) with just a letter or two.

If you have a style you're comfortable with now, don't change it just for this programming assignment. If you do, it might cause you to inadvertently mix styles, and that's what you're trying to avoid.

Comments

Comment only the non-obvious lines.

Most programmers hate documentation. If you do too, this next piece of advice might not apply to you. I am one of those who like comments; I feel the more, the better. However, be aware: you'll lose points if you put in excessive comments. In particular, you should not comment lines that essentially document themselves. You should only include comments for those lines that are tricky or not immediately obvious.

Error Handling

Handle errors appropriately.

Sometimes it's easy to fall into a trap where you let your application take a guess at what to do, even when it encounters an unexpected situation. For example, consider these `switch-case` statements:

```
switch (userSelection) {
    case MOVE: moveItem(); break;
    case DELETE: deleteItem(); break;
}
```

What if `userSelection` is not equal to either MOVE or DELETE? Should you do nothing? Or perhaps you should add a `default` case:

```
switch (userSelection) {
    case MOVE: moveItem(); break;
    case DELETE: deleteItem(); break;
    default: editItem();
}
```

In this case, what you should do depends on whether `userSelection` is supposed to *absolutely*, *positively* equal either MOVE or DELETE. If it is but doesn't equal either one, then this is a very serious problem. You may even want to throw an exception:

```
switch (userSelection) {
    case MOVE: moveItem(); break;
    case DELETE: deleteItem(); break;
    default: throw
        new UserSelectionException("Should be move or delete");
}
```

I have assumed there is a class defined for this application called UserSelectionException.

It might be tempting to throw an unchecked exception rather than make your own exception class. For example, you might think you could throw NumberFormatException or ArithmeticException if a number is not in the right format or if you are about to divide by 0. The problem is that you should never throw an unchecked exception from your own code. As we reviewed in Chapter 8, you should only throw checked exceptions—exceptions which must be caught.

Another problem with throwing a generic, unchecked exception is that it does not fully identify the application-specific problem. Perhaps the problem with the number not being in the right format is a protocol error. It might make better sense to create a new class called ProtocolException and throw that when an error arises. By supplying a message for this object before you throw it, your exception handler can display this message to help with debugging.

When you handle the error, also give some thought about what it is you would like to do in your `catch` block. Should you print out a debugging message, end the application, or take a guess as to what to do? You might want to do something differently each time, but similar problems should be handled in similar ways. Remember your credo: be consistent.

Java's Documentation Problem

In C/C++, documentation is often placed into header files. This is because a header file contains the function definitions and variables shared by more than one program in an application. Since this file is shared by any program that needs it, the header file is the right place to put these comments. A great advantage of this approach is that a developer can distribute only the binary files for the actual program which keeps the implementation hidden, but still distribute the header files which provide all the public documentation for these files, as well as means for using them.

This approach does not even begin to work in Java. Why? Because there are no header files! There are no declarations of methods separate from their implementation (unless you've defined an interface or abstract method). All methods are implemented where they are declared.

This might appear to mean that distributing documentation concerning how to use a Java package would run the risk of one of two extremes:

1. Distribute the source code that contains the in-line documentation for the public classes, variables, and methods, or
2. Keep the documentation in separate files, far away from the original source, and potentially fall out of sync with the code.

Happily, the JDK provides relief from both of these port choicesby supplying a special utility called *javadoc*. This utility pulls out the important information concerning your classes, variables, and methods, and automatically generates great-looking documentation. The advantage of this approach is that you can run javadoc whenever you want and generate new documentation that reflects the current state of your code.

javadoc

Use javadoc-style comments.

When you run javadoc and pass it the name of a class or package, javadoc generates documentation in HTML format for all of your `public` classes, and your `public` and `protected` variables and methods.

You're no doubt familiar with the HTML format that javadoc generates, because this is the same format that the API files are published in. Javadoc creates an HTML file for each class. Each HTML file lists the fields, then the constructors, and then the methods for a class. Javadoc also places a class hierarchy at the top of the HTML file and provides an index to the fields, constructors, and methods after that.

All you have to do to generate this documentation is run the command **javadoc** and place the resulting HTML files into the same directory as the API files for the JDK.

Javadoc will generate four types of files:

- `packages.html`: A listing of each package you generated documentation for and the class they contain.
- `AllNames.html`: An alphabetical index of all of your method and variable names.
- `tree.html`: A listing of all of the classes you've generated documentation for and where these fit into the class hierarchy, going all the way back to `java.lang.Object`.
- `classname.html`: Documentation for that class.

Naturally, all of these files contain hypertext links to the classes, methods, and variables they refer to, including Java's own classes.

Helping javadoc

In addition to the two common ways of writing a comment:

```
// everything to the end of the line is a comment
```

and

```
/* everything in here is a comment */
```

Java also defines a special third way:

```
/** everything in here is a javadoc comment */
```

Tip

By default, this special javadoc comment only has meaning before a public class, or before a public or protected variable or method. You can see javadoc-style comments for private variables or methods if you use the -private option when you run javadoc.

With a javadoc comment, you can help javadoc to document your code. For example, here is a simple class definition:

```
public class PrimeNumber {
    private int number;
    public int getNumber() {
        return number;
    }
    public void setNumber(int num) {
        number = num;
    }
    public boolean isPrime() { /* code to test number */ }
}
```

Javadoc will automatically generate the documentation shown in Figures 23-1 and 23-2 (these show the top half and bottom half of a Web browser displaying the file that javadoc generated).

Figure 23-1
The javadoc-Generat-
ed Index

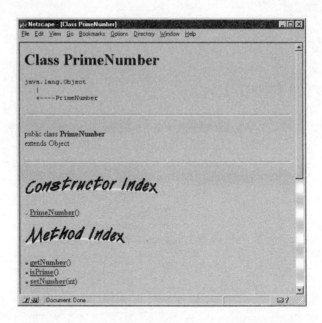

Figure 23-2
The javadoc-Generat-
ed Method Docu-
mentation

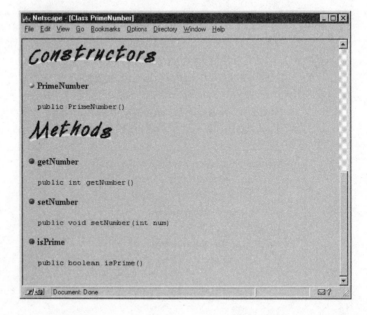

This is fine as far as it goes. What you'd really like to do is add some of your own comments to this documentation. By adding documentation to this class using special javadoc comments, like this:

```
/**
 * Identify a number as prime or not prime.
 */
public class PrimeNumber {
    private int number;

    /** Retrieve the number. */
    public int getNumber() {
        return number;
    }

    /** Set the number. */
    public void setNumber(int num) {
        number = num;
    }

    /** Test whether the number is a prime. */
    public boolean isPrime() { /* code to test number */ }
}
```

you can generate the documentation shown in Figures 23-3 and 23-4:

Figure 23-3
The javadoc Index,
with Comments

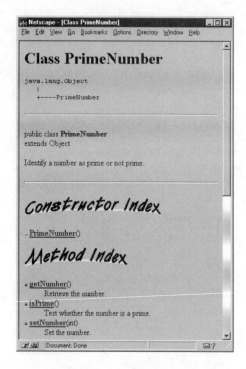

Figure 23-4
The javadoc Methods, with Comments

javadoc Tags

You can also use special tags within your javadoc comments. javadoc seeks out these tags and creates special documentation based on them. First, let's look at the tags. Then I'll show some examples of how to use them and what their resulting documentation looks like.

Variables

When you define a variable, you can use an `@see` tag to reference a different object or method. There are a few different versions of this tag. First, here's the format for `@see` to refer to a class:

@see classname

The `classname` can simply be the class' name if the class is in the same package as the class defining the comment. The `classname` can also be fully qualified if it's in a different package. For example, if Lightning is the name of a class, you can write:

```
@see Lightning
```

or

```
@see phenomenon.natural.Lightning
```

You can also reference a method name using the `@see` tag by writing:

@see classname#methodname

For example, you might write:

```
@see Lightning#flash
```

As before, you can also fully qualify the class name.

Classes

You can use any of these `@see` tags with classes. There are also two other tags you can use with the class that are useful only with special keywords passed to javadoc. These tags are `@version` and `@author`:

@version anytext

You would typically put a version number following this tag, such as 1.0 or 2.1:

```
@version 1.0
```

@author anytext

As you might guess, you would normally place your name after this tag, as in:

```
@author Albert Einstein
```

To see these @version and @author values in the documentation, you must use the options:

```
-author -version
```

when you invoke javadoc, as in:

```
javadoc -author -version MyClass.java
```

Methods

Methods can use any of the @see tags. In addition, there are three other tags that document the method's signature: @return, @param, and @exception.

@return anytext

For example, you might write:

```
@return a true or false value indicating whether the number is a prime
```

@param paramname anytext

For example, you might write:

```
@param    number    a number to test to see if it is a prime or not
```

@exception exceptionname anytext

For example, you might write:

```
@exception ProtocolException Throws this exception when the client
    has not supplied data following the agreed-upon protocol
```

Tip

In all cases, the text following a particular tag can go over multiple lines.

Rules for Using javadoc Comments and Tags

A typical javadoc comment and set of javadoc tags follows this format:

```
/**
 * Summary comment line
 * Any number of additional comment lines
 *    this could even include HTML
 * @tag any number of lines providing text for this tag
 */
```

There's no need to have a row of asterisks along the left hand side of the comments like this, but you'll see this done in most Java programs. However, it's perfectly acceptable to also write:

```
/**
   Summary comment line
   Any number of additional comment lines
      this could even include HTML
   @tag any number of lines providing text for this tag
 */
```

Notice that the first line in a javadoc comment is special. It is a summary line, and javadoc uses this in its indices. For example, the method index at the top of the class's HTML file displays this one sentence description, as does the index file AllNames.html for each method and variable.

Following this summary line, you can include any number of lines you'd like to. javadoc will strip away any leading spaces (even any leading asterisk as in the first comment sample above), and will wrap the text as appropriate.

Any HTML tags it finds it will use as is, so that you can format your documentation with references, links, bold or italic styles, or code snippets.

Following these general comments, you should place any special javadoc tags.

Always place all of your tags at the end of your javadoc comments. Since tags can be spread over multiple lines, the only way for javadoc to identify the end of a tag is when it hits the start of a new one.

Examples of javadoc Comments and Tags

Here is an example of class documentation for a class called Tester:

```
/**
 * Test machine for objects.
 * This class tests objects for performance and accuracy
 *    by executing standard tests.
 * @see CanBeTested
 * @version 1.0
 * @author Barry Boone
 */
public class Tester { . . . }
```

Javadoc will generate the display in Figure 23-5 based on this.

Figure 23-5
Class Documentation

public class **Tester**
extends Object

Test machine for objects. This class tests objects for performance and accuracy by executing standard tests.

Version:
　　1.0
Author:
　　Barry Boone
See Also:
　　CanBeTested

Similarly, based on the following method documentation:

```
/**
 * Performs the standard test.
 * Invokes test() for the object to be tested and informs
 *    this method how much testing should be performed.
 * @return A String that explains the results of the test
 * @param target The debug level
 * @see CanBeTested
 */
public String runTest(int debugLevel) { . . . }
```

Javadoc will generate the html file shown in Figure 23-6.

Figure 23-6
Method Documenta-
tion

```
public String runTest(int debugLevel)
```

Performs the standard test. Invokes test() for the object to
be tested and informs this method how much testing
should be performed.

Parameters:
    target - The debug level
Returns:
    A String that explains the results of the test
See Also:
    CanBeTested

And for this variable documentation:

```
/** Debug output level.
 *   @see CanBeTested
 */
public int debugLevel;
```

Javadoc will generate the html file shown in Figure 23-7.

Figure 23-7
Variable Documenta-
tion

```
public int debugLevel
```

Debug output level.

See Also:
    CanBeTested

Review Questions

Question 1:   Which javadoc tags are useful for documenting a class? (For this question, pick all that apply.)

a)   `@see`
b)   `@param`
c)   `@version`
d)   `@return`
e)   `@author`

Question 2:   If you use the `@author` tag:

a)   You will see the author when you use javadoc, no options required.
b)   You will only see the `author` if you use the -author option when you invoke javadoc.
c)   The `@author` tag never displays the author; it is only used for reference within the source code.

Question 3:   The proper use of the `@exception` tag is:

a)   `@exception exceptionname anytext`
b)   `@exception anytext`
c)   `@exception exceptionname`
d)   There is no `@exception` tag.

Answers to the Review Questions

Question 1   a, c, e.   The `@param` tag and `@return` tag are only useful when documenting a method.

Question 2   b.   You must invoke javadoc using the -author keyword to see the author information.

Question 3   a.   Specify the name of the exception class, followed by your own descriptive text.

Practice Exams
and
What to Expect

CHAPTER 24

The Scoop
on Java Certification

The better prepared you are for the logistics of taking the test, and the more you understand what Sun is looking for, the more comfortable you'll feel in the testing center and the better you're likely to do. I've gathered all the information in this chapter on the test, signing up for the test, and rules at the testing center to help you see where to go and what to do. I've also spoken with the people at Sun who are responsible for creating and administering the exams, and I've summarized their thoughts on the exams here.

After this chapter, you'll find two practice exams for the Programmer test, a practice programming assignment for Developer certification, and a practice Developer exam. This section also contains strategies and tips for taking the exams and a little bit about what to expect when you go through the certification process.

A Quick Overview

First you take the Programmer exam. This is exam number 310-020. If you pass, you can proudly call yourself a Sun Certified Java Programmer. You can then download a programming assignment from a Web site that you must complete as part of Developer certification. Once you complete the assignment and sign up for the Developer exam, you can upload the assignment on the Web site and take the Developer exam. This exam number is 310-020 for Java 1.0.2, and exam 310-022 for Java 1.1. Once you submit a successful programming assignment and pass the Developer exam, you become a Sun Certified Java Developer, which is the highest level of Java certification.

Figure 24-1 shows your path to full certification, starting with taking the Java Programmer exam.

Figure 24-1
The Steps to Full Java
Certification

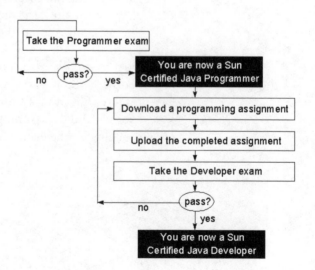

What the Programmer Test is Like

The Programmer exam consists of 70 multiple choice and short-answer questions. You have up to 2 hours and 15 minutes to complete the exam.

There are two kinds of multiple choice questions: those that require only a single answer, and those that allow you to select all of the right answers (usually up to five right answers).

What the Developer Assignment and Test are Like

The programming assignment consists of a complete set of specifications that you must implement. Some code is already completed for you. You can download this assignment from a Web site after you have passed the Programmer exam. You can do this assignment as your schedule allows, and upload it once you have finished.

The Developer exam consists of five essay questions regarding the assignment. These questions ask you to justify your design choices.

How the Test is Administered

The Programmer and Developer tests are administered on PCs by a company called Sylvan Prometric. They have test centers all over the U.S. and the world. When you show up, you sign in, identify yourself by showing two forms of ID (one with a picture, and both with signatures), and then you take the test at your scheduled time.

You can't bring any paper into or out of the testing room. They don't want you taking a crib sheet in with you, or writing out test questions during the test. (Of course, once you leave the testing area, you can try to recall as many questions as possible. However, be aware that the tests are copyrighted, so you can't turn around and publish the questions, make copies of them, and so on.)

You also can't bring in any pagers or cellular phones. After all, in this day and age, it would be a simple matter to have your local Java guru talk you through the test.

Even though you can't take any paper in with you, the people at Sylvan Prometric do give you either some scratch paper or a small marker board and a marker to help you work out answers.

How to Sign Up For and Take the Exams

You must call Sun and buy a voucher (or buy or get a voucher from your company, who has in turn purchased a voucher through Sun). The idea behind the voucher system is that your company may offer vouchers for free or at a discount to the regular price of the test if they are encouraging you to become certified.

The main number for Sun Educational Services in the United States is 1-800-422-8020. Listen to the options from the phone menu and make sure you tell them what test you want to sign up for! Outside the U.S., check out the Web site at http://www.hibbertco.com/sun/suncontacts/contacts.html for additional phone numbers

The good people at Sun will ask for a credit card to pay for the voucher. You've got to then wait for the voucher to arrive before you can sign up for the test. They send the vouchers by FedEx, so you'll get any vouchers you purchase by the next business day. Once you get it, don't misplace it—it's like money. You can't replace them and if you drop it on the street, that's that. Some random person can pick it up and go take a Java test.

The voucher is supposed to be good for up to one year after you purchase it. However, mine came with an expiration date set to seven months after the purchase. Voucher expiration dates cannot be extended! However—here's the loophole—after you sign up for a testing appointment, you can extend the appointment for up to one year.

You may have your voucher, but you're not done yet. You've still got to register for the test. You can do this by calling Sylvan Prometric. Their number is 1-800-795-EXAM. (I know, I hate dialing by letters, too: their number in numbers is 1-800-795-3926.)

You'll have to give them your social security number for identification, and they'll ask you some questions, such as which company you're with, your phone number, and your address. Then they'll schedule you for a test.

When they schedule you, they'll find a time that's convenient for you to visit one of their testing centers. You need to be there on time, because you can't stay past your stop time—the computer will shut you off! What they do is distribute the test electronically to the test center you'll be at.

According to a person I spoke with at Sylvan, ou need to be there when the test is ready to go.

If they can fit you in the next day and that's what you want, they'll do their best to accommodate you. The only possible problem might be that a space is not available at the test center closest to you.

Just so that your friendly neighborhood Java expert doesn't show up in your place as a ringer, you need to bring two forms of ID, one of which must be a photo ID.

If you want to postpone for some reason—if you're panicking or you just plum can't make it—you can do so up until the day before the test.

You'll find out immediately whether or not you've passed the exam, because the software that administers the test prints out your results. You need to get at least 70% of the questions right to pass. You can always restudy and take it again if you do fail, and, since it's a difficult test, lots of people go this route.

How to Acquire the Programming Assignment for the Developer Test

After you've taken and passed the Programmer exam, you can obtain the programming assignment that's part of Developer certification. You obtain the assignment by downloading it off the Web. Go to:

```
http://www.sun.com/sunservice/suned/java certification.html
```

and enter your last name and social security number (which is your Sylvan candidate ID). You should allow at least a week after passing the exam for Sylvan to let Sun know that you passed, and for Sun to update their server. Until then, the server will say "User not found." Don't worry—the records will be updated as soon as they can get to them. If you've allowed a week to go by and it really looks like the server is not being updated, you can call the main numbers at Sun Educational Services, explain the situation, and they'll patch you through to someone who can help you.

Once your record has been updated, then entering your last name and candidate ID will bring you to a screen that displays your current status in the testing cycle. If you have passed the Programmer exam, you'll see a button on the bottom of the screen that says "Download assignment." Go ahead and click that for instructions on how to access the assignment.

Once you've downloaded the .zip or .tar file that contains the assignment, you'll see a new button back on the page you just came from. This button reads "Upload assignment." When you're all done, you'll come back here, click this button, and upload your work to Sun.

You'll get a number of files, including a postscript document, a Word for Windows document, and an RTF (Rich Text Format) document, all containing the same instructions. There are also .gif images that show some design diagrams, as well as a number of source and class files that you'll use as part of your programming assignment.

The first thing you should do, before even reading over the documents, is to make backups of everything! The test is customized for *you*, and you need to be able to get back to what you downloaded if something goes wrong, or if you want to start over again.

Only after you complete this programming assignment and sign up for the Developer exam can you submit your assignment for grading. You submit the assignment by uploading it through the download Web site.

All of the programming assignments are marked very carefully and it takes time to ensure the quality and consistency of this process.

Strategies for Approaching the Developer Assignment

First and foremost, give yourself time—a few days, if not a week or more. The assignment is long and complicated. Think about the issues. Read the design document over two, three, four times. Print it out and mark it up. Make sketches.

After you've thought about the design for a while, create the user interface. Seeing a user interface can make the assignment more tangible. This is especially true if you feel overwhelmed by what to do. You'll begin to realize which pieces have to connect with which other pieces. What's more, it's comforting to have part of it done and working!

Look over the source code that comes with the assignment. That can really help you figure out what is already done for you and what you've got to write yourself.

One of the wonderful things about this assignment is a test harness that's distributed with the assignment. You can run this test harness to see if your program is working well enough to submit. Passing the test harness can go a long way to making you feel comfortable with your work.

Make backups of the database files before you start testing, because, depending on your particular version of the assignment, you might start changing things!

How and When to Sign Up for the Developer Exam

You should sign up for the Developer exam once you know you have uploaded your Developer assignment. You must be sure you pass the automated tests based on the test harness, because you'll fail immediately if you submit code that fails the test harness. There are instructions in the programming assignment that explain how to write your code so that the test harness can interact with it and perform its tests.

Like the Programmer exam, the Developer exam costs $150, and you call the same numbers to sign up.

The Developer exam consists of 5 essay questions. You have 90 minutes to answer them. These questions ask you to discuss what you did on the programming assignment and to justify your design decisions. There are no absolute right or wrong answers. The people grading your assignment and the exam will look for your understanding of the issues involved.

Whom to Contact

The main table of contents concerning Java certification information is available at:

```
http://www.sun.com/sunservice/suned/java_certification.html
```

From here, you'll find information about the exam and whom to call to schedule your test.

Test-Taking Tips for the Programmer Exam

What the Test Program Looks Like for the Programmer Exam

When you first sit down at the computer, you'll be asked to type in your test-taking ID, which is most likely your social security number (Sylvan Prometric will tell you). The test software will then ask whether or not you're familiar with the application. If you'd like, you can take a short tutorial. The test does not begin until you look at the first question, so looking over the tutorial doesn't take away from your testing time. If you're ready, then go ahead and start the exam.

The font is large and easy to read. There are buttons on the bottom to go to the next or a previous question.

The program that administers the test is very friendly. There's a clock in the top right of the screen that counts down from 2 hours and 15 minutes. You can double-click this clock to see what time you started, the maximum time allowed for the exam you're taking, and the current time.

You can go through most of the test just by clicking. For the multiple choice questions, there are two types: exclusive and non-exclusive. The non-exclusive questions allow you to pick as many answers as are valid. The exclusive answer questions have round radio buttons. The multiple answer questions have square check boxes. In addition to the way the check boxes look for the different question types, a small message at the bottom of the question indicates whether you should select just one right answer or all valid answers.

The questions that require you to type in a response have a single-line text field, so this is a good indication to you that all of your typed responses should be short—no full class definitions, no algorithms. All you'll need to do is invoke a method or specify a class name. You should click in the text field to begin typing.

At the end of the test, after you've answered the last question, you'll see a list of all the questions and your responses. You can double-click on a question/answer in this list to jump to it and review it.

There's a little check box in the top left that says "mark." If you click this, then when you go to review your questions at the end, you'll see a little yellow square with the letter "m" beside your question in the question/answer list. This little yellow square can remind you that you had a question about something and wanted to go back to review your answer.

If you have any incomplete answers, you'll see this in the review screen at the end, as well. Incomplete answers have a red square with an "I" to indicate their incomplete status.

There's a help button that provides a good overview of what you're seeing on the screen. And if there's really a problem, there's always a real, live person you can call into the room.

Be Careful!

Sometimes, a question is too long to fit in one screen. This is usually the case when the question contains a code snippet or a full program for you to analyze. If you want to scroll down, you might inadvertently click in the answer area instead of over the scroll bar. If that happens, check your answers! If you click over the same row as an answer, even if it's all the way over to the right, the test application recognizes that click and will mark the answer in that row!

Take Your Time and Answer the Easy Ones First

You have close to 2 minutes per question. Believe me, unless you fall asleep, you won't run out of time; you'll have plenty of time to read over each question and think about it.

Not all questions take the same amount of time. Some questions you'll answer right off the bat. Some are so easy you'll read them over a second time, thinking you missed some trick. Most take about a minute to answer.

You should aim to have completed at least 35 questions in the first hour. If you can do that, you know you're right on schedule and you'll finish with a bit of time to spare.

If you get impatient with a long question involving a big class definition, feel free to skip it and go back to it later. You can answer all the easy ones first, and then return to the more difficult or long questions later. All questions are worth the same number of points, so you might as well. Sometimes, this strategy works particularly well, because a later question might contain in it, inadvertently, the answer to something you were pondering earlier.

You might remember from your days in high school or graduate school that one of the tricks in taking the SATs or GREs is to eliminate the wrong answers first to increase your odds. That's a great technique for this test as well. You'll find some answers that are obviously wrong (trust me, you will). When you do, you'll be that much closer to picking the right one.

It's also better to answer a question than to not answer it at all. You're only marked for right answers—there's no penalty for a wrong answer, so you should always at least guess rather than leaving something blank.

Beware of Tricks

Sometimes the test questions try to trick you. For example, a particular question might present answers where you should pick all the valid ones. For example, you might see a question like this:

```
Which identifiers are valid in Java?

  a) max_num

  b) max-num

  c) 3DogNight

  d) star*power

  e) (train)
```

Since this question allows more than one correct answer, you might think that there must be more than one correct answer. But that's not so. In fact, only one of these is a valid Java identifier:

```
a)   max_num
```

The rest are not valid at all.

Another trick is to present some irrelevant information in a question. For example, check out the following:

```
Given the following preliminary specification for a class that
will be shared by different packages, write the beginning of a
class definition that indicates the new class' access control key-
words (if any) and what the new class inherits from.

"A Satellite is a SpaceCraft. It maintains information for its
orbital information, which is an array of 6 double values."
```

This might lead you to think your answer should look something like this:

```
public class Satellite extends SpaceCraft {
   double[] orbitalInfo = new double[6];
}
```

However, the question asked only to indicate the access control for the class and which class it inherits from. What's more, you can only enter one line anyway for short answer questions. So, the answer it's really looking for is simply:

```
public class Satellite extends SpaceCraft
```

Both types of trick questions really arise because the test is assembled semi-randomly from components in a question database. (The assembly of questions is not completely random, because the program that assembles the questions makes sure that there is not a concentration of questions in any particular area.) Sometimes there will be multiple answers for a question that allows multiple answers, but sometimes there won't be. And sometimes more information will appear in a question than you need to answer that question. Don't be fooled. Think about the question and give the best answer you can, not what you think the question requires for an answer.

Understand Why the Question is on the Test

One great way to feel good about an answer to a question is to understand why it is on the test. For example, imagine the following question:

```
Given the following code:

class ClassA {
   public static void main(String[] args) {
      ClassA a = new ClassA();
      ClassB b = new ClassB();
      ClassA a2 = b;

      System.out.println("test() for a is: " + a.test());
      System.out.println("test() for a2 is: " + a2.test());
   }

   String test() {
      return "ClassA";
   }
}
```

```
class ClassB extends ClassA {
    String test() {
        return "ClassB";
    }
}
```

If you invoke main() for ClassA, what messages appear in the standard output?

a)
test() for a is: ClassA
test() for a2 is: ClassA

b)
test() for a is: ClassA
test() for a2 is: ClassB

c)
test() for a is: ClassB
test() for a2 is: ClassA

d)
test() for a is: ClassB
test() for a2 is: ClassB

You probably have this narrowed down to either a or b. The answer is b. The reason is that the method that is invoked depends on the *actual* object type referenced by the variable, not on the *declared* type of the variable.

Once you realize this, it's obvious why this question would appear on the test: it's making sure you understand this concept.

Know Your Test Center

It's helpful to show up early to get the feel for what the test center is like. And it can eliminate problems—I showed up about 20 minutes early and was told that my name wasn't on the list of test takers for that day! The people at the test center had to call Sylvan Prometric's "Hot Line" and ask them to download the test right then, which took some time. By the time this was accomplished, it was time to take the test.

Not all test centers are created equal. Some have 14-inch monitors and some have 17-inch monitors; some have 486 processors and some have Pentiums. If you're lucky enough to have a choice of test centers, call ahead and ask what their screen size is and what kind of computers they use. I'd say your first priority is a big screen, followed by a fast processor as a close second. Some questions (in fact, most questions) take up more screen real estate than a 14-inch monitor can supply. Long code snippets are particularly annoying to look at when you have to keep on scrolling up and down. It's not tragic if you have a 14-inch screen; I had one and it wasn't debilitating. However, that said, the bigger the screen, the better.

And the faster the computer, the better. Remember, your test is being administered by a computer. The last thing you want to do is wait around for the question to pop up on your screen.

What Happens When You're Done?

When you tell the computer you're done, it will grade your exam right there, on the spot. It then displays the percentage of questions you got right and whether you passed or not. You need 70% to pass. With 70 questions, this means you need to get 49 right (of course, this also means you can get up to 21 wrong).

If you pass, the computer will print a certificate, which the people at your Sylvan test center will then emboss, stamp, and hand to you for your safe-keeping.

At that point, it's official. You're a Sun Certified Java Programmer!

Passing the Developer Assignment and Exam

Feedback on passing the Developer programming assignment and exam is not as immediate, because there are no absolute right or wrong answers. The programming is graded based on a set of criteria that includes good object-oriented design, documentation, efficiency, and style. You should follow the directions that come with the programming assignment as exactly as possible.

After you've uploaded your assignment, you can register the exam. There are five essay questions that ask you to justify your design decisions. When you walk out of the test center this time, you won't know whether you've passed or not (though you might have a good feel for how things went).

The programming assignment and exam are graded by professionals outside of Sun, consultants in the business of providing high-level Java services. Sun Educational Services doesn't want to be accused of having a vested interest in who passes and fails, so they farm this job out. However, if there's a borderline case, the exam might go back into Java-Soft. JavaSoft engineers will then grade the assignment and test and act as a moderator.

Sun will contact you to let you know the results.

Sun's Take on Certification

In talking with a number of people at Sun Educational Services, including those responsible for creating the certification program, I have come to a good understanding of how they view the certification process. Here's a summary of their thoughts, many of which I've already touched on throughout this book.

Java certification is a way for individuals to differentiate and promote their skills and for employers and clients to know that a programmer is credible.

Sun needed to implement a certification program because Java is so new. It's simply not possible for a programmer to claim he has several years of experience with Java. So it's a challenge to employees to demonstrate they know what they say they know. Becoming certified in Java is a recognized way of validating your skills.

If you'd like to get up to speed as quickly as possible, Sun Educational Services offers courses that cover many of the topics that are part of Java certification. Other courses (both live and on the Web) cover these topics as well, as do books, seminars, and lectures. There is also no substitute for real-world experience. Regardless of how you learned Java in the first place, *remember to study for the test*. You can't know too much going into the exams!

As you prepare, you should also give some thought as to what your goals are for becoming certified. Are you studying just to pass the exams, or are you truly trying to become an expert?

You are certified according to a particular Java release. Therefore, you are Java certified in 1.0.2 or 1.1, depending on when you took the certification exam. If you would like to be certified in a new version of the language, you must take the certification exams again (which means paying the testing fees once more).

When you become certified, Sun sends you some material in the mail. This includes a logo that you can place on your business cards to tell the world you're Sun certified, a certificate, and a lapel pin (so others can see you're certified without even glancing at your business cards).

How Sun Manages the Certification Process

Sun Educational Services sends the questions to Sylvan Prometric with all the right answers. The Programmer test takes into account that there can be more than one right answer for a question. For example, the difference between a comma and a semicolon could be that one's right and one's wrong. But the question, "What if I put spaces around my parameters in a parameter list?" has a different answer. They're both right, and the test will mark both answers as correct.

Sun is constantly monitoring the feedback they receive from test takers to make sure they did not miss anything.

Sun does not publish numbers of how many people take the test and how many people pass. Sun did not want this to be the kind of test where you can just walk in, sign your name, and pass. This is not simply certification on paper. Passing really means you know your stuff.

Where Certification is Heading

Sun certification is becoming the standard in the industry. As the inventors of the Java language, other companies are looking to Sun to verify their skills. For example, IBM's own certification program will include Sun's Java certification exams.

Java certification is part of the 100% pure Java initiative. JavaSoft administers the applications and systems side of this initiative; Java certification represents the people side. Java certification answers the question "Do you have the capability to develop 100% pure Java programs?"

Java certification is also becoming important in corporate education. For example, when an employee is trained in Java, how does a company know if the training hit the mark? Java certification is a standardized way to make sure that employees learn what they need to know.

Sun Certified Programmer Exam

Practice Exam Number 1

Here are the rules:

Allow 2 hours and 15 minutes to complete this exam. You should turn off the telephone, go someplace where you won't be disturbed, check the time on your watch, and begin. Don't bring any books with you, because you won't have them during the test. You can take breaks, but don't look anything up. You can have a piece of scratch paper and a pen or pencil, but you can't have any crib sheets!

If you get 49 questions right, you've hit the 70% mark, and you've passed. Good luck!

Questions

Question 1: Which of the following class definitions defines a legal abstract class?

Select all right answers.

☐   a)
```
class Animal {
    abstract void growl();
}
```

☐   b)
```
abstract Animal {
    abstract void growl();
}
```

☐   c)
```
class abstract Animal {
    abstract void growl();
}
```

☐   d)
```
abstract class Animal {
    abstract void growl();
}
```

☐   e)
```
abstract class Animal {
    abstract void growl() {
        System.out.println("growl");
    }
}
```

Question 2: For an object to be a target for a Thread, that object must be of type:

Fill in the blank.

Question 3: What is the proper way of defining a class named Key so that it cannot be subclassed?

Select the one right answer.

○ a)
```
class Key { }
```

○ b)
```
abstract final class Key { }
```

○ c)
```
native class Key { }
```

○ d)
```
class Key {
    final;
}
```

○ e)
```
final class Key { }
```

Question 4: What modes are legal for creating a new RandomAccessFile object?

Select all valid answers.

☐ a) "w"

☐ b) "r"

☐ c) "x"

☐ d) "rw"

☐ e) "xrw"

Question 5:   Given the following code:

```
class Tester {
    public static void main(String[] args) {
        CellPhone cell = new CellPhone();
        cell.emergency();
    }
}

class Phone {
    final void dial911() {
        // code to dial 911 here . . .
    }
}

class CellPhone extends Phone {
    void emergency() {
        dial911();
    }
}
```

What will happen when you try to compile and run the Tester class?
Select the one right answer.

○   a)   The code will not compile because Phone is not also declared as `final`.

○   b)   The code will not compile because you cannot invoke a `final` method from a subclass.

○   c)   The code will compile and run fine.

○   d)   The code will compile but will throw a NoSuchMethodException when Tester is run.

○   e)   Phone and CellPhone are fine, but Tester will not compile because it cannot create an instance of a class that derives from a class defining a `final` method.

Question 6: Which assignments are legal?

Select all valid answers.

❐ a) long test = 012;

❐ b) float f = -412;

❐ c) int other = (int)true;

❐ d) double d = 0x12345678;

❐ e) short s = 10;

Question 7: Given this class definition:

```
abstract class Transaction implements Runnable { }
class Deposit extends Transaction {
   protected void process() {
       addAmount();
   }
   void undo(int i) {
       System.out.println("Undo");
   }
}
```

What will happen if we attempted to compile the code?
   Select the one right answer.

○ a) This code will not compile because the parameter i is not used
       in undo().

○ b) This code will not compile because there is no main() method.

○ c) This code will not compile because Deposit must be an
       abstract class.

○ d) This code will not compile because Deposit is not declared
       public.

○ e) Everything will compile fine.

Question 8: Which exception might wait() throw?

Fill in the blank.

Question 9: Which of the following are not Java keywords:

abstract	double	int	static
boolean	else	interface	super
break	extends	long	√ superclass
byte	final	native	switch
case	finally	new	synchronized
catch	float	null	this
char	for	√ open	throw
class	goto	package	throws
√ close	if	private	transient
const	implements	protected	try
continue	import	public	void
default	instanceof	return	volatile
do	integer	short	while

Select all valid answers.

- ❏ a) superclass
- ❏ b) goto
- ❏ c) open
- ❏ d) close
- ❏ e) integer
- ❏ f) import
- ❏ g) try
- ❏ h) they are all valid keywords

Question 10: Which of the following represents an octal number?

Select all that apply.

- ☐ a)   0x12
- ☐ b)   32O
- ☐ c)   032
- ☐ d)   (octal)2
- ☐ e)   12

Question 11: What will appear in the standard output when you run the Tester class?

```
class Tester {
    int var;
    Tester(double var) {
        this.var = (int)var;
    }
    Tester(int var) {
        this("hello");
    }
    Tester(String s) {
        this();
        System.out.println(s);
    }
    Tester() {
        System.out.println("good-bye");
    }
    public static void main(String[] args) {
        Tester t = new Tester(5);
    }
}
```

Select the one right answer.

- ○ a)   nothing
- ○ b)   "hello"
- ○ c)   5
- ○ d)   "hello" followed by "good-bye"
- ○ e)   "good-bye" followed by "hello"

Question 12: Write a line of code to use the String's `substring()` method to obtain the substring "lip" from a String instance named s that is set to "tulip".

Fill in the blank.

```

```

Question 13: There are a number of labels in the source code below. These are labeled a through j. Which label identifies the earliest point where, after that line has executed, the object referred to by the variable `first` may be garbage collected?

```
class Riddle {
    public static void main(String[] args) {
        String first, second;
        String riddle;

        if (args.length < 2)
            return;
a:      first = new String(args[0]);
b:      second = new String(args[1]);
c:      riddle = "When is a " + first;
d:      first = null;
e:      riddle += " like a " + second + "?";
f:      second = null;

g:      System.out.println(riddle);

h:      args[0] = null;
i:      args[1] = null;

j:

    }
}
```

Select the one right answer.

○   a)   d:
○   b)   e:
○   c)   h:
○   d)   i:
○   e)   j:

Question 14: What are the range of values for a variable of type `byte`?

Select the one right answer.

○   a) -2^7 to $2^7 - 1$
○   b)   0 to 2^8
○   c) -2^8 to 2^8
○   d) -2^7 to $2^7 - 1$
○   e) $-2^8 - 1$ to 2^8

Question 15: What will happen when you try to compile and run the following program?

```
class Car {
   int mpg;
   int index;
   Car(int mpg) {
      this.mpg = mpg;
      index = 0;
   }
   Car() {
   }
   public static void main(String[] args) {
      int index;
      Car c = new Car(25);
      if (args.length > 0)
         if (args[index].equals("Hiway"))
            c.mpg *= 2;
      System.out.println("mpg: " + mpg);
   }
}
```

Select the one right answer.

○ a) The code compiles and displays "mpg: 50" if the command-line argument is "Hiway." If the command-line argument is not "Hiway," the code displays "mpg: 25."

○ b) The code compiles and displays "mpg: 50" if the command-line argument is "Hiway." If the command-line argument is not "Hiway," the code throws an ArrayIndexOutOfBoundsException.

○ c) The code does not compile because the automatic variable named `index` has not been initialized.

○ d) The code does not compile because `milesPerGallon` has not been initialized.

○ e) The code does not compile because the no-args constructor is not written correctly.

Question 16: What will happen when you compile and run this program:

```
class Array {
   public static void main(String[] args) {
      int length = 100;
      int[] d = new int[length];
      for (int index = 0; index < length; index++)
         System.out.println(d[index]);
   }
}
```

Select the one right answer.

○ a) The code will not compile because the `int[]` array is not declared correctly.

○ b) The code will compile but will throw an IndexArrayOutOfBoundsException when it runs and nothing will appear in the standard output.

○ c) The code will display the numbers 0 through 99 in the standard output, and then throw an IndexOutOfBoundsException.

○ d) The code will compile but the `println()` method will throw a NoSuchMethodException.

○ e) This code will work fine and display 100 zeroes in the standard output.

Question 17: What is the result of attempting to compile and run the following class?

```
class Ar {
    public static void main(String[] args) {
        int[] seeds = new int[3];
        for (int i = 0; i < seeds.length; i++)
            System.out.println(i);
    }
}
```

Select all valid answers.

- ☐ a)   0
- ☐ b)   1
- ☐ c)   2
- ☐ d)   3
- ☐ e)   the program does not compile because the seeds array is not initialized

Question 18:   What method name can you use from the applet to read a String passed to an applet via the `<param>` tag? (Supply the method name only, without parameters.)

Fill in the blank.

Question 19: Given these class definitions:

```
class Superclass { }
class Subclass1 extends Superclass { }
```

and these objects:

```
Superclass a = new Superclass();
Subclass1 b = new Subclass1();
```

which of the following explains the result of the statement:

```
a = b;
```

Select the one right answer.

- ○ a) Illegal at compile time
- ○ b) Legal at compile time but possibly illegal at runtime
- ○ c) Definitely legal at runtime

Question 20: Given these class definitions:

```
class Superclass { }
class Subclass1 extends Superclass { }
class Subclass2 extends Superclass { }
```

and these objects:

```
Superclass a = new Superclass();
Subclass1 b = new Subclass1();
Subclass2 c = new Subclass2();
```

which of the following explains the result of the statement:

```
b = (Subclass1)c;
```

Select the one right answer.

- ○ a) Illegal at compile time
- ○ b) Legal at compile time but possibly illegal at runtime
- ○ c) Definitely legal at runtime

Question 21: How can you use the escape notation \u to set the variable c, declared as a char, to the Unicode character whose value is hex 0x30A0?

Fill in the blank.

Question 22: Which operators are overloaded for String objects?

Select all valid answers.

☐ a) –

☐ b) +=

☐ c) >>

☐ d) &

☐ e) none of these

Question 23: How can you change the **break** statement below so that it breaks out of both the inner and middle loops and continues with the next iteration of the outer loop?

```
outer: for (int x = 0; x < 3; x++) {
   middle: for (int y = 0; y < 3; y++) {
      inner: for (int z = 0; z < 3; z++) {
         if (arr(x, y, z) == targetValue)
            break;
      }
   }
}
```

Select the one right answer.

○ a) break inner;

○ b) break middle;

○ c) break outer;

○ d) continue;

○ e) continue middle;

Question 24: Given this code snippet:

```
try {
   tryThis();
   return;
} catch (IOException x1) {
   System.out.println("exception 1");
   return;
} catch (Exception x2) {
   System.out.println("exception 2");
   return;
} finally {
   System.out.println("finally");
}
```

What will appear in the standard output if tryThis() throws a Number-FormatException?

Select the one right answer.

O   a)   Nothing

O   b)   "exception 1" followed by "finally"

O   c)   "exception 2" followed by "finally"

O   d)   "exception 1"

O   e)   "exception 2"

Question 25: Given these class definitions:

```
class Superclass { }
class Subclass1 extends Superclass { }
```

and these objects:

```
Superclass a = new Superclass();
Subclass1 b = new Subclass1();
```

which of the following explains the result of the statement:

```
b = a;
```

Select the one right answer.

- ○ a)   Illegal at compile time
- ○ b)   Legal at compile time but possibly illegal at runtime
- ○ c)   Definitely legal at runtime

Question 26: Given these class definitions:

```
class Superclass { }
class Subclass1 extends Superclass { }
```

and these objects:
   which of the following explains the result of the statement:

```
Superclass a = new Superclass();
Subclass1 b = new Subclass1();
b = (Subclass1)a;
```

Select the one right answer.

- ○ a)   Illegal at compile time
- ○ b)   Legal at compile time but possibly illegal at runtime
- ○ c)   Definitely legal at runtime

Question 27: To invoke **read()** from an InputStream subclass, you must handle what type of exception?

Fill in the blank.

Question 28: Imagine there are two exception classes called Exception1 and Exception2 that descend from the Exception class. Given these two class definitions:

```
class First {
    void test() throws Exception1, Exception2 { . . . }
}
class Second extends First {
    void test() { . . . }
}
```

Create a class called Third that extends Second and defines a `test()` method. What exceptions can Third's `test()` method throw?

Select all valid answers.

❑　a)　Exception1

❑　b)　Exception2

❑　c)　no checked exceptions

❑　d)　any exceptions declared in the `throws` clause of the Third's `test()` method.

Question 29: What is the result of executing the following code:

```
class Test {
    public static void main(String[] args) {
        Test t = new Test();
        t.test(1.0, 2L, 3);
    }
    void test(double a, double b, short c) {
        System.out.println("1");
    }
    void test(float a, byte b, byte c) {
        System.out.println("2");
    }
    void test(double a, double b, double c) {
        System.out.println("3");
    }
    void test(int a, long b, int c) {
        System.out.println("4");
    }
    void test(long a, long b, long c) {
        System.out.println("5");
    }
}
```

Select the one right answer.

○ a) 1

○ b) 2

○ c) 3

○ d) 4

○ e) 5

Question 30: Given this code snippet:

```
double a = 90.7;
double b = method(a);
System.out.println(b);
```

If this snippet displays 90 in the standard output, what Math method did
method() invoke?

Select all valid answers.

☐ a)   abs()

☐ b)   min()

☐ c)   floor()

☐ d)   round()

☐ e)   ceil()

Question 31: In Java 1.0.2, to make a Button object non-responsive to mouse clicks, you can invoke which method? (Only supply the method name, without a parameter list.)

Fill in the blank.

Question 32: Given this code snippet:

```
double a = 14.9;
double b = method(a);
System.out.println(b);
```

If this snippet displays 15 in the standard output, what Math method(s) could method() have invoke?

Select the one right answer.

○   a)   ceil() and round()

○   b)   floor() and round()

○   c)   ceil() only

○   d)   floor() only

○   e)   round() only

Question 33: What methods does Java define in the Math class specifically for trigonometric calculations?

Select all valid answers.

❐   a)   cos()

❐   b)   asin()

❐   c)   tan()

❐   d)   sin()

❐   e)   angle()

Question 34: What String instance method would return true when invoked like this:

```
a.method(b);
```

where a = "GROUNDhog" and b = "groundHOG"?
Select the one right answer.

○ a) equals()

○ b) toLowerCase()

○ c) toUpperCase()

○ d) equalsIgnoreCase()

○ e) none of the above

Question 35: At the end of these two lines of code:

```
String s = "hypertext";
String t = s.substring(2, 5);
```

What does the object reference t contain?
Select the one right answer.

○ a) "yper"

○ b) "ype"

○ c) "pert"

○ d) "per"

○ e) "perte"

Question 36: What access control keyword should you use to allow other classes to access a method freely within its package, but to restrict classes outside of the package from accessing that method?

Select all valid answers.

❏ a) public

❏ b) protected

❏ c) private

❏ d) do not supply an access control keyword

Question 37: After these two lines of code:

```
String s = "Dolly ";
String t = s.concat("Hello, ");
```

What characters will the object reference t contain?
Select the one right answer.

○   a)   "Hello, Dolly "

○   b)   "Dolly Hello, "

○   c)   "Hello, "

○   d)   "Dolly "

○   e)   none of the above

Question 38: What does the following code do?

```
File f = new File("hello.test");
FileOutputStream out = new FileOutputStream(f);
```

Select the one right answer.

○   a)   Create a new file named "hello.test" if it does not yet exist. It also opens the file so you can write to it and read from it.

○   b)   Create a new file named "hello.test" if it does not yet exist. The file is not opened.

○   c)   Open a file named "hello.test" so that you can write to it and read from it, but does not create the file if it does not yet exist.

○   d)   Open a file named "hello.test" so that you can write to it but cannot read from it.

○   e)   Create an object that you can now use to create and open the file named "hello.test," and write to and read from the file.

Question 39: Which expressions are *illegal?*

Select all valid answers.

☐   a)   (true & true)

☐   b)   (4 & 5)

☐   c)   (int myInt = 0 > 3)

☐   d)   float myFloat = 40.0;

☐   e)   boolean b = (boolean)99;

Question 40: Which label name(s) are illegal?

Select all valid answers.

☐   a)   here:

☐   b)   _there:

☐   c)   this:

☐   d)   that:

☐   e)   2to1odds:

Question 41: Given this code:

```
import java.io.*;

class Write {
   public static void main(String[] args) throws Exception {
      File file = new File("temp.test");
      FileOutputStream stream = new FileOutputStream(file);

      // write integers here. . .

   }
}
```

How can you replace the comment at the end of main() with code that will write the integers 0 through 9?
   Select the one right answer.

○   a)

```
        DataOutputStream filter = new
DataOutputStream(stream);

        for (int i = 0; i < 10; i++)
            filter.writeInt(i);
```

○   b)

```
        for (int i = 0; i < 10; i++)
            file.writeInt(i);
```

○   c)

```
        for (int i = 0; i < 10; i++)
            stream.writeInt(i);
```

○   d)

```
        DataOutputStream filter = new
DataOutputStream(stream);

        for (int i = 0; i < 10; i++)
            filter.write(i);
```

○   e)

```
        for (int i = 0; i < 10; i++)
            stream.write(i);
```

Question 42: What keyword, when used in front of a method, must also appear in front of the class?

Fill in the blank.

Question 43: What letters get written to the standard output with the following code?

```
class Unchecked {
    public static void main(String[] args) {
        try {
            method();
        } catch (Exception e) {
        }
    }

    static void method() {
        try {
            wrench();

            System.out.println("a");
        } catch (ArithmeticException e) {
            System.out.println("b");
        } finally {
            System.out.println("c");
        }
        System.out.println("d");
    }

    static void wrench() {
        throw new NullPointerException();
    }
}
```

Select all valid answers.

☐   a)   "a"

☐   b)   "b"

☐   c)   "c"

☐   d)   "d"

☐   e)   none of these

Question 44: What happens if the file "Ran.test" does not yet exist and you attempt to compile and run the following code?

```java
import java.io.*;

class Ran {
   public static void main(String[] args) throws IOException {
      RandomAccessFile out = new RandomAccessFile("Ran.test", "rw");
      out.writeBytes("Ninotchka");
   }
}
```

Select the one right answer.

- ○ a) The code does not compile because RandomAccessFile is not created correctly.

- ○ b) The code does not compile because RandomAccessFile does not implement the writeBytes() method.

- ○ c) The code compiles and runs but throws an IOException because "Ran.test" does not yet exist.

- ○ d) The code compiles and runs but nothing appears in the file "Ran.test" that it creates.

- ○ e) The code compiles and runs and "Ninotchka" appears in the file "Ran.test" that it creates.

Question 45: If you run the following code on a on a PC from the directory c:\source:

```java
import java.io.*;

class Path {
   public static void main(String[] args) throws Exception {
      File file = new File("Ran.test");
      System.out.println(file.getAbsolutePath());
   }
}
```

What do you expect the output to be?
Select the one right answer.

○   a)   `Ran.test`

○   b)   `source\Ran.test`

○   c)   `c:\source\Ran.test`

○   d)   `c:\source`

○   e)   `null`

Question 46: If you supply a target object when you create a new Thread, as in:

```
Thread t = new Thread(targetObject);
```

What test of `instanceof` does `targetObject` have to pass for this to be legal?
Select the one right answer.

○   a)   `targetObject instanceof Thread`

○   b)   `targetObject instanceof Object`

○   c)   `targetObject instanceof Applet`

○   d)   `targetObject instanceof Runnable`

○   e)   `targetObject instanceof String`

Question 47: What appears in the standard output when you run the Dots class?

```
class Dots {
   DotThread t;
   public static void main(String[] args) {
      Dots d = new Dots();
      d.t = new DotThread();
   }
   public void init() {
      t.start();
      new DashThread().start();
   }
}
```

Question 47 continued

```
class DotThread extends Thread {
   public void run() {
       for (int index = 0; index < 100; index++)
          System.out.print(".");
   }
}
class DashThread extends Thread {
   public void run() {
       for (int index = 0; index < 100; index++)
          System.out.print("-");
   }
}
```

Select the one right answer.

○ a)   nothing

○ b)   100 dots (.)

○ c)   200 dots (.)

○ d)   100 dashes (-)

○ e)   100 dots (.) and 100 dashes(-)

Question 48: When you invoke `repaint()` for a Component, the AWT package calls which Component method?

Select the one right answer.

○ a)   repaint()

○ b)   update()

○ c)   paint()

○ d)   draw()

○ e)   show()

Question 49: How you can you test whether an object referenced by `ref` implements an interface named MyInterface? Replace *your test here*-with this test:

```
if (your test here) {
    System.out.println("ref implements MyInterface");
```

Fill in the blank.

Question 50: What does the following line of code do?

```
TextField tf = new TextField(30);
```

Select the one right answer.

- ○ a) This code is illegal; there is no such constructor for TextField.
- ○ b) Creates a TextField object that can hold 30 rows, but since it is not initialized to anything, it will always be empty.
- ○ c) Creates a TextField object that can hold 30 columns, but since it is not initialized to anything, it will always be empty.
- ○ d) Creates a TextField object that can hold 30 rows of text.
- ○ e) Creates a new TextField object that is 30 columns of text.

Question 51: Given these code snippets:

```
Boolean b1 = new Boolean(true);
Boolean b2 = new Boolean(true);
```

Which expressions are legal Java expressions that return true?
Select all valid answers.

☐ a) `b1 == b2`

☐ b) `b1.equals(b2)`

☐ c) `b1 & b2`

☐ d) `b1 | b2`

☐ e) `b1 && b2`

☐ f) `b1 || b2`

Question 52: Which LayoutManager arranges components left to right, then top to bottom, centering each row as it moves to the next?

Select the one right answer.

○ a) BorderLayout

○ b) FlowLayout

○ c) GridLayout

○ d) CardLayout

○ e) GridBagLayout

Question 53: A component will automatically be resized horizontally, but not vertically, when it is placed in which region of a BorderLayout?

Select the one right answer.

○ a) North or South

○ b) East or West

○ c) Center

○ d) North, South, or Center

○ e) any region

Question 54: How can you place three Components along the bottom of a Container?

Select the one right answer.

○ a) Set the Container's LayoutManager to be a BorderLayout and add each Component to the "South" of the Container.

○ b) Set the Container's LayoutManager to be a FlowLayout and add each Component to the Container.

○ c) Set the Container's LayoutManager to be a BorderLayout; add each Component to a different Container that uses a FlowLayout, and then add that Container to the "South" of the first Container.

○ d) Use a GridLayout for the Container and add each Component to the Container.

○ e) Do not use a LayoutManager at all and add each Component to the Container.

Question 55: What will happen when you attempt to compile and run the following program by passing the Test class to the Java interpreter?

```
class Test {
  public static void main() {
     System.out.println("hello");
  }
}
```

Select the one right answer.

○ a) The program does not compile because main() is not defined correctly.

○ b) The program compiles but when you try to run the interpreter complains that it cannot find the main() method it needs to run.

○ c) The program compiles but you cannot run it because the class is not declared as public.

○ d) The program compiles and runs without an error but does not display anything in the standard output.

○ e) The program compiles and displays "hello" in the standard output when you run it.

Question 56: Which of the following is a valid way to embed an applet class named Q56 into a Web page?

Select all right answers.

☐ a)
```
<applet class=Q56.class width=100 height=100>
</applet>
```

☐ b)
```
<applet code=Q56 width=100 height=100>
</applet>
```

☐ c)
```
<applet code=Q56.class width=100 height=100>
</applet>
```

☐ d)
```
<applet param=Q56.class width=100 height=100>
</applet>
```

☐ e)
```
<applet param=Q56 width=100 height=100>
</applet>
```

Question 57: How would you make the background color red for a Panel referenced by the variable p?

Fill in the blank.

```

```

Question 58: How can you retrieve a circle's radius value that's passed to an applet as a parameter named `radius`?

Select the one right answer.

a)
```
public void init() {
    String s = getParameter("radius");
    doSomethingWithRadius(s);
}
```

b)
```
public static void main(String[] args) {
    String s = args[0];
    DoSomethingWithRadius(s);
}
```

c)
```
public static void main(String[] args) {
    String s = getParameter("radius");
    DoSomethingWithRadius(s);
}
```

d)
```
public void init() {
    int radius = getParameter("radius");
    doSomethingWithRadius(radius);
}
```

e)
```
public void init() {
    int radius = getParameter();
    doSomethingWithRadius(radius);
}
```

Question 59: What is the result of invoking `main()` for the classes D and E?

```
class D {
    public static void main(String[] args) {
        String s1 = new String("hello");
        String s2 = new String("hello");
        if (s1.equals(s2))
            System.out.println("equal");
        else
            System.out.println("not equal");
    }
}

class E {
    public static void main(String[] args) {
        StringBuffer sb1 = new StringBuffer("hello");
        StringBuffer sb2 = new StringBuffer("hello");
        if (sb1.equals(sb2))
            System.out.println("equal");
        else
            System.out.println("not equal");
    }
}
```

Select the one right answer.

○ a) D: equal; E: equal

○ b) D: not equal; E: not equal

○ c) D: equal; E: not equal

○ d) D: not equal; E: not equal

○ e) nothing appears in the standard output for either class

Question 60: What does the following code do?

```
drawArc(50, 40, 20, 20, 90, 180);
```

Select the one right answer.

- ○ a) Draw an arc that is centered at x = 50, y = 40, is 20 pixels wide, as a semicircle from the top of the circle to the bottom along the left-hand side.

- ○ b) Draw an arc that is centered at x = 50, y = 40, is 20 pixels wide, as a semicircle from the 3:00 position to the 9:00 position along the bottom of the circle.

- ○ c) Draw an arc that is centered at x = 50, y = 40, is 20 pixels wide, as a semicircle from the top of the circle to the bottom along the right-hand side.

- ○ d) Draw an arc in a circle whose left side is at 50, whose top is at 40, is 20 pixels wide, as a semicircle from the top of the circle to the bottom along the left-hand side.

- ○ e) Draw an arc in a circle whose left side is at 50, whose top is at 40, is 20 pixels wide, as a semicircle from the top of the circle to the bottom along the right-hand side.

Question 61: What does the following code do (if anything)?

```
drawLine(0, 10, 20, 30);
```

Select the one right answer.

- ○ a) draw a line from x = 0, y = 20 to x = 10, y = 30

- ○ b) draw a line from x = 0, y = 10 to the coordinates x = 20, y = 30

- ○ c) draw the outline of a box whose left, top corner is at 0, 10 and that is 20 pixels wide and 30 pixels high

- ○ d) nothing—this code does not compile because it does not provide the correct number of arguments

- ○ e) nothing—this code does not compile because the arguments make no sense

Question 62: What Graphics methods can draw the outline of a square?

Select all right answers.

☐ a) drawRect()

☐ b) fillRect()

☐ c) drawPolygon()

☐ d) fillPolygon()

Question 63: What method from Java 1.0.2 can you use to remove a Component from a user interface display?

Select all right answers.

☐ a) disable()

☐ b) hide()

☐ c) remove()

☐ d) delete()

☐ e) unhook()

Question 64: Returning a value of `false` in Java 1.0.2 from an event handler:

Select the one right answer.

○ a) passes that event up the container hierarchy

○ b) stops that event from being passed up the container hierarchy

○ c) has no effect on whether the event is passed up the container heirarchy

Question 65: Which statements about garbage collection are true?

Select all valid answers.

☐ a)   You can directly free the memory allocated by an object.

☐ b)   You can directly run the garbage collector whenever you want to.

☐ c)   The garbage collector informs your object when it is about to be garbage collected.

☐ d)   The garbage collector reclaims an object's memory as soon as it becomes a candidate for garbage collection.

☐ e)   The garbage collector runs in low-memory situations.

Question 66: If you'd like to change the size of a Component, you can use the Java 1.1-specific method:

Select the one right answer.

○ a)   `size()`

○ b)   `resize()`

○ c)   `area()`

○ d)   `setSize()`

○ e)   `dimension()`

Question 67: The `setForeground()` and `setBackground()` methods are defined in class:

Select the one right answer.

○ a)   Graphics

○ b)   Container

○ c)   Component

○ d)   Object

○ e)   Applet

Question 68: How many bits are used to maintain a `char` data type?

Fill in the blank.

(blank box)

Question 69: The `&&` operator works with which data types?

Select all valid answers.

- ❑ a)   int
- ❑ b)   long
- ❑ c)   double
- ❑ d)   boolean
- ❑ e)   float

Question 70: To place a 1 in the high-bit of an `int` named `ref` that's set to `0x00000001`, you can write:

Select the one right answer.

- ○ a)   ref >> 31;
- ○ b)   ref >>= 31;
- ○ c)   ref << 31;
- ○ d)   ref <<= 31;

Answers and Explanations

Question 1   d.   An abstract class is defined using the keyword abstract in front of the class keyword and almost always defines at least one abstract method. An abstract class does not have to define an abstract method. If there are no abstract methods in an abstract class, then any subclasses of the abstract class can be instantiated (as long as they are not, in turn, defined using the abstract keyword). (See Chapter 1.)

Question 2   "Runnable."   Only classes that implement the Runnable interface (and so are of type Runnable) can be targets of threads.

Question 3   e.   Use the final keyword in front of the class to make the class unable to be subclassed. (See Chapter 1.)

Question 4   b, d.   Only "r" and "rw" are legal modes for a RandomAccessFile.

Question 5   c.   This code is perfectly fine. (See Chapter 1.)

Question 6   a, b, d, e.   The other tries to cast a boolean to an int, which is illegal.

Quesiton 7   c.   Since the superclass is abstract and implements Runnable, but does not supply a run() method, the subclass must supply run() or also be declared abstract. (See Chapter 1.)

Question 8   "InterruptedException" or "IllegalMonitorException"

Question 9   a, c, d, e.   superclass, open, close, and integer are not Java keywords. goto is a keyword, though it isn't used as of Java 1.1. (See Chapter 2.)

Question 10   c.

An octal number in Java is preceded by a 0.

Question 11   e.

There are three constructors that come into play. First, the constructor that takes an int is invoked. This invokes the constructor that takes a String. This invokes the no-args constructor, which displays "good-bye." Then, the constructor that takes a String displays "hello." (See Chapter 3.)

Question 12   "s.substring(2, 5)" or "s.substring(2)" *or*

s.substring (2, s.length()) ;

Question 13   a.

A new String is created based on args[0], but args[0] does not have to be nulled out before first can be garbage collected. As soon as the line with the label d is executed, the object that first has referred to is ready to be garbage collected, because there is no way to recover a reference to this object again. (See Chapter 4.)

Question 14   d.

The range of integer types goes from minus $2^{(number\ of\ bits\ -\ 1)}$ to $2^{(number\ of\ bits\ -\ 1)}$ minus 1. (See Chapter 5.)

Question 15   c.

Even though there is an instance variable named index defined in the Car class, the *local* or *automatic* variable named index takes precedence. Since automatic variables do not have a default value, this code will not compile because it is uninitialized when we attempt to access the element in the args array. (See Chapter 5.)

Question 16   e.

There's nothing wrong with this code. 100 0's will appear in the standard output. (See Chapter 5.)

Question 17	a, b, c.	The elements in arrays are initialized to their default values: 0, 0.0, null, false, or \u0000, depending on the data type.
Question 18	"getParameter"	
Question 19	c.	Assigning a subclass type to a superclass type is perfectly legal and will run fine at runtime.
Question 20	a.	You cannot assign an object to a sibling object reference, even with casting.
Question 21	"c = '\u30A0';"	You can set a `char` to a Unicode sequence by matching the template `\udddd`, where `dddd` are four hexadecimal digits representing the Unicode character you want. (See Chapter 5.)
Question 22	b.	Only + and += are overloaded for String objects.
Question 23	b.	Changing the `break` statement to `break middle` will break out of the loop named using the label `middle` and continue with the next iteration of the outer loop. The statement `continue outer` would also have this effect. (See Chapter 7.)
Question 24	c.	NumberFormatException will be handled in the `catch` clause for Exception. Then, regardless of the `return` statements, the `finally` clause will be executed before control returns to the calling method. (See Chapter 8.)
Question 25	a.	An explicit cast is needed to assign a superclass type to a subclass type.
Question 26	b.	If the object contained in a is not actually a Subclass1 object, the assignment will cause Java to throw a CastClassException. That would be the case in the code in this example.

Question 27   "IOException" or "java.io.IOException"

Question 28   c.   A method in a subclass cannot add new exception types that it might throw. Since its superclass, Second, does not define any exceptions in its `test()` method, Third can't either. (See Chapter 8.)

Question 29   c.   The method with all double parameters is actually the only version of `test()` that the Java Virtual Machine can legally coerce the numbers to. The reason the other versions of `test()` are not invoked is that at least one of the parameters would have to be automatically coerced from a type with greater accuracy to a type with less accuracy, which is illegal. (See Chapter 9.)

Question 30   c.   The Math method `floor()` finds the integer closest to but less than the parameter to `floor()`. The methods `round()` and `ceil()` would both result in 91, and `min()` and `max()` both require two parameters. (See Chapter 10.)

Question 31   "disable"

Question 32   a.   Both `ceil()` and `round()` will produce 15 from 14.9. The `floor()` method yields 14. (See Chapter 10.)

Question 33   a, b, c, d.   The methods Java defines for trig operations include `sin()`, `asin()`, `cos()`, and `tan()`. (See Chapter 10.)

Question 34   d.   The method `equalsIgnoreCase()` would return true for the two Strings a and b in the question. (See Chapter 10.)

Question 35   d.   The method `substring()` starts at the first index, inclusive, with 0 being the first character), and ends at the end index - 1 (that is, exclusive of the end index). (See Chapter 10.)

Question 36 d.

This is the default access control for methods and member variables.

Question 37 b.

The concat() method appends the characters passed to it to the characters in the String responding to the method call. The concat() method creates a new String, since Strings cannot be changed once they are created. (See Chapter 10.)

Question 38 ~~a.~~ d

The file as shown in the code is available for writing but not reading.

The first line creates a File object that represents the file. By creating a FileOutputStream, you create the file if it does not yet exist, and open that file for reading and writing. (See Chapter 11.)

Question 39 c, d, e.

You cannot assign an integer to a boolean—not even with casting. Also, the default type for a floating-point literal is double, and you cannot assign a double to a float without casting.

Question 40 c, e.

this is a reserved word, so it cannot be used as an identifier (such as a label). 2to1odds starts with a number, so it is also invalid as an identifier.

Question 41 a.

In order to write a primitive data type such as an int, you need to use a Filter~~Input~~Output Stream subclass such as Data~~Input~~Output Stream. This class defines writeInt(), which is perfect for our needs. (See Chapter 11.)

Question 42 "abstract"

Question 43 c.

Only the "c" from finally gets written out. The exception thrown doesn't match the exception caught, so the catch block is not executed. Control returns to the caller after finally to see if there is a catch block there to handle this unchecked exception. If there is not (as is the case here), execution comes to an end.

Question 44   e.   This code compiles and runs fine. RandomAccessFile implements the DataOutput interface, so it does implement `write-Bytes()`, among others. RandomAccessFile creates the file if it does not yet exist. (See Chapter 11.)

Question 45   c.   The absolute path includes the drive name and the top-level directories, as well as the file name itself. (See Chapter 11.)

Question 46   d.   The target object for a Thread must implement Runnable, which means it will pass the test:

`targetObject instanceof Runnable`

(See Chapter 12.)

Question 47   a.   The thread with `start()` method is never invoked. (This is not an applet, so `init()` is not automatically invoked.) (See Chapter 12.)

Question 48   b.   The AWT invokes `update()` for the Component, which invokes `paint()` in its default behavior. (See Chapter 13.)

Question 49   "ref instanceof MyInterface"

Question 50   e.   TextField defines a constructor that takes the number of columns, as shown in the example. TextField objects can have their text updated at any time, including long after they're created. (See Chapter 13.)

Question 51   b.   The first yields `false`, and the others are not legal Java expressions (this is a wrapper type we're using here).

Question 52   b.   A FlowLayout arranges components in this way. (See Chapter 13.)

Question 53   a.   North and South only can resize a component horizontally, to the width of the Container. (See Chapter 13.)

Question 54   c.   Complicated as it might seem, this is the best way to accomplish this goal. First, you set the Container's LayoutManager to be a BorderLayout. Then, you create an intermediate Container and add each Component to this new Container that uses a FlowLayout. Finally, you add that Container to the "South" of the original Container. (See Chapter 13.)

Question 55   b.   The program will compile fine. However, the Java interpreter specifically looks for a `main()` method declared as `public` and `static`, that returns no value, and that takes an array of String objects as its parameter.

Question 56   c.   The `<applet>` tag requires three keywords: `code`, `width`, and `height`.

Question 57   "p.setBackground(Color.red);"

Question 58   a.   Use the `getParameter()` method, passing it the name of the value you want to retrieve. This method retrieves a String representing that value. (You can convert the String to a primitive data type using a wrapper class if you need to.)

Question 59   c.   The StringBuffer class does not override `equals()`. Hence, this class returns `false` when passed two different objects. (See Chapter 6.)

Question 60   d.   The four parameters are the left, top, width, height, start angle (0 is the 3:00 position), and the arc angle (the arc ends at start angle plus the arc angle), drawn counter-clockwise.

Question 61   b.   The `drawLine()` method takes four parameters: the starting point and the ending point of the line to draw.

Question 62   a, c.

You can use `drawRect()` to draw a rectangle outline given its upper left point and width and height, and `drawPolygon()` to draw each of the four points of the square, plus an end point that is the same as the first point.

Question 63   b.

The `hide()` method is more or less the opposite of `show()` and removes a Component from the display.

Question 64   a.

Returning `false` indicates that method did not handle the event, which means AWT passes the event up the container hierarchy looking for someone who does want to handle it.

Question 65   b, c, e.

You cannot directly free the memory allocated by an object, though you can set an object reference to null. Also, the garbage collector only runs in low-memory situations, and so does not always reclaim an object's memory as soon as it becomes a candidate for garbage collection.

Question 66   d.

`setSize()` is specific to Java 1.1.

Question 67   c.

These are Component methods. (The `set-Color()` method is defined in the Graphics class.)

Question 68   "16"

Question 69   d.

The `&&` operator combines two `boolean` expressions.

Question 70   d.

The `<<` operator shifts the bits the given number of places to the left.

CHAPTER 26

Sun Certified Programmer Exam

Practice Exam Number 2

As before, here are the rules:

Allow 2 hours and 15 minutes to complete this exam. You should turn off the telephone, go someplace where you won't be disturbed, check the time on your watch, and begin. Don't bring any books with you, because you won't have them during the test. You can take breaks, but don't look anything up. You can have a piece of scratch paper and a pen or pencil, but you can't have any crib sheets!

If you get 49 questions right, you've hit the 70% mark, and you've passed. Good luck!

Questions

Question 1: Given that a Processor class has an `int` to maintain a clock speed, a Computer class has a Processor, and a PC class is a type of Computer, specify a class definition for a PC class based on the information available so that it can be accessed by many different packages.

Fill in the blank.

```
                                                          
                                                          
```

Question 2: What will happen if you try to compile the following code and execute the Tester class?

```java
class Tester {
    public static void main(String[] args) {
        Groucho g = new Groucho();
        g.speak("You said the magic word");
    }
}

abstract class Person {
    abstract void speak();
}

class Groucho extends Person {
    void speak(String s) {
        System.out.println(s);
    }
}
```

Select the one right answer.

○   a)   The program will compile and when run display "You said the magic word" in the standard output.

○   b)   The program will compile and when run will not display anything.

   ○   c)   The code will compile but when run will throw an Unimple-
mentedMethodException.

   ○   d)   The code will not compile because speak() is abstract and
there is no method matching this method's signature in the
Groucho subclass.

   ○   e)   The code will not compile because Tester does not inherit from
Groucho.

Question 3:   Given these class definitions:

In a file named `Transaction.java`:

```
package Transaction;

public class Transaction {
   public String account;
   private double amount;
   public Transaction(double amt, String acct) {
      amount = amt;
      account = acct;
   }
   synchronized double getAmount() {
      return amount;
   }
   protected synchronized void addAmount(double amt) {
      amount += amt;
   }
   protected synchronized void subAmount(double amt) {
      amount -= amt;
   }
}
```

In a file named `Main.java`:

```
import Transaction.*;

class Deposit extends Transaction {
   protected void process(double amt) {
      addAmount(amt);
   }
}
```

Transaction

Which fields and methods defined in ~~Withdrawal~~ can the Deposit class access?
Select all valid answers.

- [ ] a) account
- [ ] b) amount
- [ ] c) getAmount()
- [ ] d) addAmount()
- [ ] e) subAmount()
- [ ] f) the constructor

Question 4: Which set of relationships between classes named Amount, Account, Transaction, and Deposit makes the most sense? Here are the elements each class should have access to.

- An Amount maintains a `double` representing the amount.
- An Account has a balance, which can be an Amount.
- A Transaction has an Account and the Amount of the transaction.

Select the one right answer.

- ○ a)
  ```
  class Account extends Amount
  class Transaction extends Account
  ```

- ○ b)
  ```
  class Account has a reference to Amount
  class Transaction extends Account and has a reference to Amount
  ```

- ○ c)
  ```
  class Account has a reference to Amount
  class Transaction has a reference to Account and Amount
  ```

- ○ d)
  ```
  class Account extends Transaction and has a reference to Amount
  ```

- ○ e)
  ```
  class Account has a  reference to Amount
  class Amount extends Transaction
  ```

Question 5: How can you return the return value of your superclass from the method `handleEvent()`, if you have declared your own `handleEvent()` method like this:

```
public boolean handleEvent(Event e) { . . . }
```

Fill in the blank.

Question 6: What will happen if you attempt to compile the three classes below and run the Tester class?

```
class President {
   int born;
   President(int born) {
      this.born = born;
   }
}
class Washington extends President {
}
class Tester {
   public static void main(String[] args) {
      Washington w = new Washington();
      System.out.println(w.born);
   }
}
```

Select all valid answers.

- ☐ a) The code will compile.

- ☐ b) The code will not compile.

- ☐ c) The `println()` method will display 0 to the standard output.

- ☐ d) When you run Tester, the Java Virtual Machine will halt the program by throwing a ClassNotFoundException.

- ☐ e) The compiler will complain that Washington does not have a default constructor.

- ☐ f) The compiler will complain that President does not have a default constructor.

Question 7: What will appear in the standard output when you attempt to compile both classes and run the Washington class below?

```
abstract class President {
    int born;
    President(int born) {
        this.born = born;
        System.out.println("born: " + born);
    }
}


class Washington extends President {
    Washington(int born) {
        super(born);
    }
    public static void main(String[] args) {
        Washington w = new Washington(1732);
    }
}
```

Select the one right answer.

○ a) The code will compile and "born: 1732" will appear in the standard output.

○ b) The code will compile but nothing will appear in the standard output.

○ c) The code will not compile because President is abstract.

○ d) The code will not compile because there is no default, no-args constructor for Washington.

○ e) The code will not compile because there is no default, no-args constructor for Washington.

Question 8: What keyword would you use to indicate that a method's behavior is supplied by platform-specific code?

Fill in the blank.

Question 9: Given the following code, which letters get written to the standard output?

```
class Unchecked {
   public static void main(String[] args) {
      try {
         method();
      } catch (Exception e) {
      }
   }

   static void method() {
      try {
         wrench();
         System.out.println("a");
      } catch (ArithmeticException e) {
         System.out.println("b");
      } finally {
         System.out.println("c");
      }
      System.out.println("d");
   }

   static void wrench() {
      throw new NullPointerException();
   }
}
```

Select all valid answers.

☐   a)   a

☐   b)   b

☐   c)   c

☐   d)   d

Question 10: Which answers provide a valid definition for a `main()` method that you can use to invoke a class?

Select all valid answers.

- ☐ a) `void main(String[] args) { }`
- ☐ b) `static public void main(String args[]) { }`
- ☐ c) `public static void main(String[] args) { }`
- ☐ d) `public static int main(String[] args) { }`
- ☐ e) `public static void main(String args[]);`

Question 11: The valid arguments for a switch statement are:

Select all valid answers.

- ☐ a) `int`
- ☐ b) `float`
- ☐ c) `char`
- ☐ d) `boolean`
- ☐ e) `Object`

Question 12: What type of a layout manager arranges components according to the directions "North" and "South"?

Fill in the blank.

Question 13: Select all valid Java keywords from those presented below.

Select all valid answers.

☐ a)   zero

☐ b)   instanceof

☐ c)   implements

☐ d)   NULL

☐ e)   sizeof

☐ f)   goto

Question 14: Given the following code:

```
public class exam1 {
   public static void main(String args[]) {
      StringBuffer sb1 = new StringBuffer("top");
      StringBuffer sb2 = new StringBuffer("top");
      convert(sb1, sb2);
      System.out.println("sb1 is " + sb1 + "\nsb2 is " + sb2);
   }

   public static void convert(StringBuffer sb1, StringBuffer sb2) {
      sb1.insert(0, 's');
      sb2 = sb1;
   }
}
```

Which one of the following correctly describe the behavior when this program is compiled and run?

Select the one right answer.

○ a)   compilation is successful and the output is:

```
sb1 is top
sb2 is top
```

○   b)   compilation is successful and the output is:

```
sb1 is stop
sb2 is top
```

○   c)   compilation is successful and the output is:

```
sb1 is stop
sb2 is stop
```

○   d)   the assignment 'sb2 = sb1' is rejected by the compiler because the StringBuffer class cannot overload the operator '='.

○   e)   the expression (sb1 is " + sb1 + "\nsb2 is " + sb2) is rejected by the compiler because the StringBuffer class cannot overload the operator '+'.

Question 15: What will happen when you try to compile and run the following class?

```
class DataTypes {
    int intType = 4;
    double doubleType;
    boolean booleanType;
    String s;
    DataTypes() {
        System.out.println(intType);
        System.out.println(doubleType);
        System.out.println(booleanType);
        System.out.println(s);
    }
    public static void main(String[] args) {
        DataTypes dt = new DataTypes();
    }
}
```

Select the one right answer.

○ a) It will compile and display the following:

```
4
0.0
false
null
```

○ b) It will compile and display the following:

```
0
0.0
false
```

Then, the `println()` method will throw a NullPointerException.

○ c) It will not compile because three variables are undefined.

○ d) It will not compile because `intType` cannot be initialized when it is defined.

○ e) It will not compile because you cannot access instance variables from a `static` method.

Question 16: What will happen when you compile and run this program:

```
class Array {
    public static void main(String[] args) {
        int length = 100;
        int[] d = new int[length];
        for (int index = 0; index <= length; length++)
            d[index] = index;
        for (int index = 0; index <= length; length++)
            System.out.println(d[index]);
    }
}
```

Select the one right answer.

○ a) The code will not compile because the `int[]` array is not declared correctly.

○ b) The code will compile but will throw an IndexArrayOutOf-BoundsException when it runs.

○ c) The code will compile but the `println()` method will throw a NoSuchMethodException.

○ d) The code will compile and the numbers 1 through 100 will appear in the standard output.

○ e) The code will compile and the numbers 0 through 99 will appear in the standard output.

Question 17: What does this code write to the standard output?

```
class Array {
    public static void main(String[] args) {
        int[] d = {1, 2, 3, 4, 5};
        System.out.println(d[3]);
    }
}
```

Select the one right answer.

○ a) 0

○ b) 1

○ c) 2

○ d) 3

○ e) 4

Question 18: What class implements `notify()`?

Fill in the blank.

Question 19: What is the outcome of this program?

```
class Bit {
    public static void main(String[] args) {
        int i = 0x00000021;
        int ans;

        System.out.println("before: " + i);
        ans = i >> 2;
        System.out.println("after: " + ans);
    }
}
```

Select the one right answer.

○ a)
```
before: 31
after: 16
```

○ b)
```
before: 33
after: 8
```

○ c)
```
before: 33
after: 9
```

○ d)
```
before: 33
after: 1
```

○ e)
```
before: 33
after: 0
```

Question 20: What test using `instanceof`, in this pattern:

```
objRef instanceof _____
```

where objRef is an object reference pointing to a legal object, will always return true?

Select all valid answers.

☐ a) null

☐ b) void

☐ c) Object

☐ d) objRef

☐ e) Class

Question 21: What string will s and t contain after this code snippet executes:

```
String s = "Here's to you ";
String t = s + "Mrs. ";
String t += "Robinson.";
```

Select the one right answer.

○ a) s = "Here's to you ", t = "Here's to you Mrs. Robinson."

○ b) s = "Here's to you Mrs. ", t = "Here's to you Mrs. Robinson."

○ c) s = "Here's to you Mrs. ", t = "Mrs. Robinson."

○ d) s = null, t = "Here's to you Mrs. Robinson."

○ e) s = null, t = "Robinson."

Question 22: What is the result of attempting to compile and executing a program containing this code snippet?

```
Object b1 = new Boolean(false);
Object b2 = new Boolean(false);
System.out.println(b1.equals(b2));
```

Select the one right answer.

○ a) This code will not compile because you cannot assign a Boolean to an Object.

    ○   b)   This code will not compile because you cannot test for equality of two Boolean values using `equals()`.

    ○   c)   This code compiles and when it runs, it displays the word "true."

    ○   d)   This code compiles and when it runs, it displays the word "false."

    ○   e)   This code runs but throws NoSuchMethodException.

Question 23: What is the result of this expression:

(4 & 3) + (2 | 1)

in base ten.
Select the one right answer.

    ○   a)   0

    ○   b)   1

    ○   c)   2

    ○   d)   3

    ○   e)   8

Question 24: You write a method named `tryThis()` declared like this:

```
void tryThis() { . . . }
```

This method invokes the method `test()`, declared like this:

```
void test() throws TestException { . . . }
```

TestException is declared like this:

```
class TestException extends Exception { }
```

You do not want to handle TestException in your `tryThis()` method. How can you declare `tryThis()` so that not handling TestException when you call `test()` is legal?

Select all valid answers.

☐ a)   `void tryThis()`

☐ b)   `void tryThis() throw new TestException()`

☐ c)   `void tryThis() throw TestException`

☐ d)   `void tryThis() throws TestException`

☐ e)   `TestException void tryThis()`

Question 25: Given this method definition:

```
double avg(double a, double b) {
    return (a + b) / 2.0;
}
```

How would this method definition look if it was modified throw an exception called AvgException, an Exception subclass, if either number was less than 0?

Select the one right answer.

○ a)
```
double avg(double a, double b) throws AvgException {
    return (a + b) / 2.0;
}
```

○ b)
```
double avg(double a, double b) {
    if (a < 0 || b < 0)
        throw AvgException();
    return (a + b) / 2.0;
}
```

○ c)
```
double avg(double a, double b) {
    if (a < 0 || b < 0)
        throw new AvgException();
    return (a + b) / 2.0;
}
```

○　d)

```
double avg(double a, double b) throw AvgException {
    if (a < 0 || b < 0)
        throw new AvgException();
    return (a + b) / 2.0;
}
```

○　e)

```
double avg(double a, double b) throws AvgException {
    if (a < 0 || b < 0)
        throw new AvgException();
    return (a + b) / 2.0;
}
```

Question 26: What keyword do you use to obtain an object's monitor?

Fill in the blank.

Question 27: What will happen when you attempt to compile and run the following code?

```
class First {
    String test() {
        return "First";
    }
    public static void main(String[] args) {
        First f = new Second();
        System.out.println(f.test());
    }
}

class Second extends First {
    String test() {
        return "Second";
    }
}
```

Select the one right answer.

○ a) The First class will not compile because the object reference f in test() is used illegally.

○ b) The Second class will not compile because test() is not over-ridden legally.

○ c) The code will compile and run and "Second" will appear in the standard outout.

○ d) The code will compile and run and "First" will appear in the standard output.

○ e) The code will compile and run but nothing will appear in the standard output.

Question 28: Given this code snippet:

```
double a = -4.3;
double b = method(a);
System.out.println(b);
```

If this snippet displays -4 in the standard output, what Math method did method() invoke?

Select all right answers.

☐ a) abs()

☐ b) cos()

☐ c) floor()

☐ d) round()

☐ e) ceil()

Question 29: What would be possible output from the following program:

```
class Ran {
   public static void main(String[] args) {
       System.out.println(Math.random());
       System.out.println(Math.random());
       System.out.println(Math.random());
   }
}
```

Select the one right answer.

○   a)

```
104.676471
3020.0196787
12113.132725
```

○   b)

```
0.676471
0.0196787
0.132725
```

○   c)

```
0.676471
0.0196787
-0.132725
```

○   d)

```
1029204
9729543
6004347
```

○   e)

```
5032.3032E18
3203.32E-2
932.40329E8
```

Question 30: In the following code snippet:

```
String s = "Maybe ";
s += " not";
```

Which of the following statements is true:
  Select all right answers.

❏   a)   s contains "Maybe not" at the end.

❏   b)   This code produces a String object that becomes a candidate for garbage collection.

❏   c)   Only one String object is created.

❏   d)   This code produces an exception because a String object cannot be modified once it is created.

Question 31: The String method `indexOf()` is overloaded to accept which combinations of parameters?

Select all right answers.

☐ a) `indexOf(int c)`

☐ b) `indexOf(int c, int fromIndex)`

☐ c) `indexOf(int c, char fromChar)`

☐ d) `indexOf(String s);`

☐ e) `indexOf(String s, int fromIndex)`

Question 32: Write code that tests whether the String s is set to the text "Hello".

Fill in the blank.

```
┌─────────────────────────────────────────────────────────────┐
│                                                               │
│                                                               │
└─────────────────────────────────────────────────────────────┘
```

Question 33: The `trim()` method defined in class String:

Select all valid answers.

☐ a) Can remove all leading white space.

☐ b) Can remove all trailing white space.

☐ c) Can trim the String to a substring specified as a parameter.

☐ d) Can trim the String to start and end indexes specified as parameters.

Question 34: DataInput and DataOutput are:

Select all valid answers.

☐ a) the top-level, `abstract` classes defined in `java.io` that all other stream classes inherit from.

☐ b) classes you can instantiate to read and write primitive data types.

☐   c)   interfaces that define methods that can be used to read and
              write primitive data types.

☐   d)   descendants of FilterInputStream and FilterOutputStream that
              can be used to chain together streams.

☐   e)   interfaces that define methods to open and close files.

Question 35: A valid way to create a FilterInputStream instance is to write:

Select all valid answers.

☐   a)   `new FilterInputStream();`

☐   b)   `new FilterInputStream(System.in);`

☐   c)   `new FilterInputStream(System.out);`

☐   d)   `new FilterInputStream(new File("hello.test"));`

☐   e)   `new FilterInputStream(new File());`

Question 36: What can you do with a File object by invoking File methods?

Select all valid answers.

☐   a)   create files

☐   b)   rename files

☐   c)   delete files

☐   d)   write to files

☐   e)   open files

Question 37: Position the file pointer for a RandomAccessFile object named out to the end of the file.

Fill in the blank.

Question 38: How can you tell if a node in the file system already exists by using the File class?

Select the one right answer.

- ○ a) Create a File object and invoke an instance method called exists().

- ○ b) Use a static method called exists().

- ○ c) If creating a new File object throws an IOException, then the node does not yet exist.

- ○ d) Create a file object and check a variable called exists.

- ○ e) You cannot tell if a node already exists by using the File class.

Question 39: To read an entire line of input at once from the standard input, and ignoring exceptions, you can write the following code:

Select the one right answer.

- ○ a)
  ```
  String s = System.in.readLine();
  ```

- ○ b)
  ```
  String s = System.in.read();
  ```

- ○ c)
  ```
  DataOutputStream in = new DataOutputStream(System.in);
  String s = in.readLine();
  ```

- ○ d)
  ```
  DataInputStream in = new DataInputStream(System.in);
  String s = in.read();
  ```

- ○ e)
  ```
  DataInputStream in = new DataInputStream(System.in);
  String s = in.readLine();
  ```

Question 40: Which exception do you have to catch if you invoke `wait()`?

Fill in the blank.

Question 41: Which method do you have to define if you implement the Runnable interface?

Select the one right answer.

- ○ a)   `start()`
- ○ b)   `runnable()`
- ○ c)   `run()`
- ○ d)   `init()`
- ○ e)   `main()`

Question 42: What class can you use to create a new directory in the file system?

Fill in the blank.

Question 43: Given this outline for a class definition:

```
class Test {
    boolean method(int arg) { }
}
```

Which of the following methods can be added to Test so that Test is still a valid class?

Select all valid answers.

☐ a) `void method(int arg2) { }`

☐ b) `void method() { }`

☐ c) `boolean method(long arg) { }`

☐ d) `boolean method(int arg1, int arg2) { }`

☐ e) `public static void main(String[] args) { }`

Question 44: Which identifiers are legal?

Select all valid answers.

☐ a) `taxman20`

☐ b) `strawberry-fields`

☐ c) `_status`

☐ d) `100bottles`

☐ e) `xMachina`

Question 45: What operator shifts the bits to the right and fills the sign bit with 0?

Fill in the blank.

Question 46: Why is this class unable to compile?

```
class Bounce implements Runnable {
   public static void main(String[] args) {
      new Thread(this).start();
   }
   public void run(int milliseconds) {
      while (true) {
         System.out.print("boing. . . ");
         try {
            sleep(1000);
         } catch (InterruptedException ie) {
         }
      }
   }
}
```

Select the one right answer.

○ a) `sleep()` is not invoked correctly.

○ b) The Runnable interface is not implemented correctly.

○ c) `sleep()` does not throw InterruptedException.

○ d) Objects cannot implement the Runnable interface.

○ e) The compiler will complain that the `run()` method loops forever.

Question 47: What numbers does the following code write to the standard output?

```
class Loop {
   public static void main(String[] args) {
      int x = 1;

      while (x++ < 3)
         System.out.println(x);
   }
}
```

Select all valid answers.

☐ a)   1

☐ b)   2

☐ c)   3

☐ d)   4

Question 48: Which of the following correctly overrides the `paint()` method defined in the Component class?

Select the one right answer.

○ a)
```
private void paint(Graphics g) {
    // . . .
}
```

○ b)
```
public boolean paint(Graphics g) {
    // . . .
}
```

○ c)
```
public void paint(Graphics g) {
    // . . .
}
```

○ d)
```
public void paint() {
    // . . .
}
```

○ e)
```
public void paint(Graphics g) throws Throwable {
    // . . .
}
```

Question 49: How can you create a TextArea object that displays 10 lines of text and is wide enough to display approximately 20 characters?

Select the one right answer.

○ a)   `TextArea text = new TextArea(10, 20);`

○ b)   `TextArea text = new TextArea(20, 10);`

○ c)   `TextArea text = new TextArea(10);`

○ d)   `TextArea text = new TextArea(20);`

○ e)   none of the above

Question 50: Define a new List object and assign it to a predefined List variable named `myList`. This List object should display a maximum of 5 rows and should allow multiple selections.

Fill in the blank.

```

```

Question 51: Given a valid File object referenced by `f`, how can you create a new file?

Select all valid answers.

❑ a)   `FileOutputStream out = new FileOutputStream(f);`

❑ b)   `FileInputStream out = new FileInputStream(f);`

❑ c)   `f.create();`

❑ d)   `RandomAccessFile out = new RandomAccessFile(f, "rw");`

Question 52: Just before an object is garbage collected, the Java Virtual Machine runs that object's method called (write the method name only):

Fill in the blank.

```
                                                                    
```

Question 53: Which of the following represent valid lines of code?

Select all valid answers.

- ❑ a) `String[] args = { "1" };`
- ❑ b) `int values[] = 1;`
- ❑ c) `int values[3] = {1, 2, 3};`
- ❑ d) `boolean switches = new boolean[3];`
- ❑ e) `String myArgs[] = new myArgs[101];`

Question 54: A method indicates which exceptions it can throw by using the keyword:

Fill in the blank.

```
                                                                    
```

Question 55: What are valid regions in a BorderLayout?

Select all valid answers.

- ❑ a) Top
- ❑ b) Bottom
- ❑ c) East
- ❑ d) Middle
- ❑ e) Center

Question 56: What is the effect of the following method?

```
public boolean handleEvent(Event e) {
    return true;
}
```

Select the one right answer.

○   a)   This method ensures that the event is passed to its Container.

○   b)   This method ensures that the event is not passed to its Container.

○   c)   This method has no effect on the event.

○   d)   This method will not compile, because the arguments to `han-dleEvent()` are not correct.

○   e)   This method will not compile, because the return type of `han-dleEvent()` is not correct.

Question 57: When you invoke a program by passing a class to the Java interpreter, the Java interpreter:

Select the one right answer.

○   a)   Invokes your class `init()` method.

○   b)   Invokes your class `start()` method.

○   c)   Invokes your class `main()` method.

○   d)   Invokes the method that you tell it to start at.

○   e)   Does not invoke any method but waits for interaction with the user.

Question 58: If you invoke a class using the Java interpreter like this:

java Q58 Albany Boston Chicago Detroit

which version of `main()` will display "Chicago" in the standard output?
Select the one right answer.

○   a)
```
class Q58 {
    System.out.println(args[2]);
}
```

○   b)
```
class Q58 {
   public void main(String[] args) {
      System.out.println(args[2]);
   }
}
```

○   c)
```
class Q58 {
   public static void main(String[] args) {
      System.out.println(args[3]);
   }
}
```

○   d)
```
class Q58 {
   public static void main(String args) {
      System.out.println(args[2]);
   }
}
```

○   e)
```
class Q58 {
   public static void main(String[] args) {
      System.out.println(args[2]);
   }
}
```

Question 59: How can you pass the value of a circle's radius, in this case 12, to an applet? What line of HTML code can be placed between the `<applet>` and `</applet>` tags?

Select all valid *answers*.

☐   a)   <param=radius value=12>

☐   b)   <param keyword=radius value=12>

☐   c)   <param radius=12>

☐   d)   <param name=radius value=12>

☐   e)   <radius=12>

Question 60: What is the result of invoking `main()` for classes A, B, and C?

```
class A {
   public static void main(String[] args) {
      Integer myInt = new Integer(5);
      Integer otherInt;
      otherInt = myInt;
      if (otherInt.equals(myInt))
         System.out.println("equal");
      else
         System.out.println("not equal");
   }
}

class B {
   public static void main(String[] args) {
      Integer myInt = new Integer(5);
      Integer anotherInt = new Integer(5);
      if (anotherInt.equals(myInt))
         System.out.println("equal");
      else
         System.out.println("not equal");
   }
}

class C {
   public static void main(String[] args) {
      MyClass mc1 = new MyClass(5);
      MyClass mc2 = new MyClass(5);
      if (mc1.equals(mc2))
         System.out.println("equal");
      else
         System.out.println("not equal");
   }
}

class MyClass extends Object {
   int value;
   MyClass(int value) {
      this.value = value;
   }
}
```

Select the one right answer.

○ a) A: equal; B: equal; C: equal

○ b) A: equal; B: equal; C: not equal

○ c) A: equal; B: not equal; C: not equal

○ d) A: not equal; B: equal; C: equal

○ e) none of the above

Question 61: Which of the following are valid class definitions?

Select all valid answers.

❒ a) `protected class MyClass { }`

❒ b) `public class MyClass { }`

❒ c) `private class MyClass { }`

❒ d) `final class MyClass { }`

❒ e) `abstract class MyClass { }`

Question 62: Which method call draws a solid rectangle whose corners are at (0, 10), (20, 10), (20, 30), and (0, 30)?

Select the one right answer.

○ a) `drawRect(0, 10, 20, 20);`

○ b) `drawRect(0, 10, 30, 30);`

○ c) `drawLine(0, 10, 20, 30);`

○ d) `fillRect(0, 10, 20, 20);`

○ e) `fillRect(0, 10, 30, 30);`

Question 63: How can you draw a String within an applet that reads "Maltese Falcon" that is 30 pixels from the left edge and whose baseline is at 20 pixels from the top?

Select all right answers.

☐ a) `paint("Maltese Falcon", 30, 20);`

☐ b) `System.output.println("Maltese Falcon", 30, 20);`

☐ c) `g.drawString("Maltese Falcon", 30, 20);` (where g is a Graphics object)

☐ d) `g.drawString(30, 20, "Maltese Falcon");` (where g is a Graphics object)

☐ e) `g.drawString("Maltese Falcon", 30, 20);` (where g is a Graphics object)

Question 64: The following code draws something in the applet. What does this "something" most closely resemble?

```
import java.awt.*;
import java.applet.*;

public class Pol extends Applet {
    public void paint(Graphics g) {
        int[] a = {20, 20, 60, 60};
        int[] b = {60, 20, 60, 20};
        g.drawPolygon(a, b, 4);
    }
}
```

Select the one right answer.

○ a) a box

○ b) a bow-tie

○ c) the letter "n"

○ d) the letter "m"

○ e) the letter "z"

Question 65: What method could you invoke, given the right parameters, to draw a rectangle filled with the current color?

Select all valid answers.

☐ a)   `drawRect()`

☐ b)   `fillRect()`

☐ c)   `fillPolygon()`

☐ d)   `drawPolygon()`

☐ e)   `drawLine()`

Question 66: What keyword do you use to place all of the classes in a particular file in the same class library?

Fill in the blank.

```
┌─────────────────────────────────────────────────────┐
│                                                       │
│                                                       │
└─────────────────────────────────────────────────────┘
```

Question 67: What will happen when you attempt to run this code?

```java
import java.awt.*;

class Q67 {
   public static void main(String[] args) {
      Frame f = new Frame();
      f.resize(100, 100);
      f.add("Center", new Button("click me"));
   }
}
```

Select the one right answer.

○ a)   The code does not compile because the arguments to `add()` are not correct.

○ b)   The code does not compile because you cannot create a Frame with a no-args constructor.

○ c)   The code compiles but nothing appears when you run this program.

○ d)   The compile compiles and a window appears but the button does not appear inside it.

○ e)   The compiles and a button appears in a frame, filling the frame.

Question 68: What happens when you try to compile and run the following program?

```java
import java.awt.*;
import java.applet.*;

public class Q102 extends Applet {
    Button stop, go;
    public void init() {
        stop = new Button("stop");
        go = new Button("go");
        add(stop);
        add(go);
    }
    public boolean action(Event e, Object what) {
        if (e.target == stop) {
            stop.disable();
            go.enable();
        } else {
            stop.enable();
            go.disable();
        }
        return super.action(e, what);
    }
}
```

Select the one right answer.

○ a)   Buttons named "stop" and "go" appear. When you click one, that one becomes disabled and the other becomes enabled.

○ b)   Buttons named "stop" and "go" appear. When you click one, they both become disabled, so you cannot click either one again.

○ c)   Buttons named "stop" and "go" appear. When you click them, nothing happens.

○ d)   This program compiles fine but nothing appears when you run it.

○ e)   This program does not compile.

Question 69: The `size()` method for a Component in Java 1.0.2 returns:

Select the one right answer.

○ a) nothing

○ b) an array of two `int` values representing the width and height of the Component.

○ c) aSize object representing the size of the Component.

○ d) a Dimension object representing the size of the Component.

○ e) a Point object whose two `int` values represent the size of the Component.

Question 70: To set a thread to the highest possible priority, what `static` variable defined by Thread can you pass to the thread's `setPriority()` method?

Fill in the blank.

┌───┐
│   │
└───┘

Answers and Explanations

Question 1 — "public class PC extends Computer { }" — Since a PC is a type of Computer, PC should extend Computer. The class should be public since it will be accessed by many different packages. (See Chapter 1.)

Question 2 — d. — Even though there is a `speak()` method defined in the Groucho subclass, this method does not match the signature of the `abstract` method defined in the Person class. Hence, Groucho must either be defined as abstract itself, or it needs to change its `speak()` method, or Person can change its speak method to take a String parameter. (See Chapter 1.)

Question 3   a, d, e, f.   Since Deposit is defined in a different ~~class~~ package than Transaction, it can only access public members (and protected members if it is a subclass—which it is). (See Chapter 1.)

Question 4   c.   An Account has an Amount, and a Transaction has both an Account and an Amount.

An Account is *not* an Amount, but an Account does have an Amount. A Transaction is *not* an Account, though it does have one. (See Chapter 1.)

Question 5   "return super.handleEvent(e);" (See Chapter 13.)

Question 6   b, f.   Java provides a default, no-args constructor only if you have not provided one yourself. This is the case in the Washington class, but not in the President class. The default constructor invokes the default constructor in the superclass. Since President does not have a default constructor, the compiler complains. (See Chapter 3.)

Question 7   a.   There's no problem here. Everything will compile and run fine. The constructor for Washington will invoke the proper constructor for President, which will display the year this particular president was born. (See Chapter 3.)

Question 8   "native" (See Chapter 2.)

Question 9   c.   The letter "c" is the only letter to get written to the standard output. ArithmeticException and NullPointerException are unchecked, so they don't have to be caught.

When `wrench()` throws NullPointerException, control skips over "a". Since there is no `catch` for NullPointerException, control goes to the `finally` clause, so "c" gets written out. After this, control returns to the caller and NullPointerException gets passed up the call stack. The exception is handled in `main()`. (See Chapter 11.)

Question 10   b, c, e.

Both of these are valid. The order of the keywords is unimportant, but they must all be there.

Question 11   a, c.

Only `int` and `char` are legal.

Question 12   "BorderLayout".

This type of layout manager arranges components by "North," "South," "East," "West," and "Center."

Question 13   b, c, and f.

The others either are keywords in other languages or I made them up because they sounded good.

Question 14   b.

Java passes all parameters to a method *by value*.

The `convert()` variables `sb1` and `sb2` are different variables altogether than the variables `sb1` and `sb2` in `main()`. However, the objects they refer to are the same.

When we invoke `insert()` given `sb1` from within `convert()`, we change the object itself. However, if the variable containing the object reference is changed (such as by assigning `sb1` to `sb2`) inside `convert()`, that means nothing back in `main()`, because, again, the parameters were passed *by value*. We are dealing with different variables entirely—different physical locations in memory—even though their contents are the same. (See Chapter 4.)

Question 15 a.   If a variable is not initialized when it is defined, it takes on its default values of 0, 0.0, false, or null, depending on its type. (See Chapter 5.)

Question 16 b.   This code will compile, but it will throw an ArrayIndexOutOfBoundsException when it tries to access element number 100 from the array, which contains elements at positions 0 through 99, but not 100. (See Chapter 5.)

Question 17 e.   The elements in the array are accessed using the indexes 0 through 4. At index 3, the value is 4. (See Chapter 5.)

Question 18 "Object".   The Object class implements wait(), notify(), and notifyAll().

Question 19 b.   At first, the value is 0x00000021, which is 33:

0000 0000 0000 0000 0000 0000 0010 0001

or 32 + 1 = 33. Shifting this two bits to the right makes the 1 fall off the sequence, and makes value in the bit in the 32 position move to the 8 position:

0000 0000 0000 0000 0000 0000 0000 1000

So the result after the operator has been applied is 8. (See Chapter 6.)

Question 20 c.   All objects inherit from class Object, so testing to see whether objRef is an instance of a class Object will always yield true for allocated, legal objects. (See Chapter 6.)

Question 21 a.   Note that t is a different object after line 3 than it is after line 2. However, it still contains the full line of the old Simon and Garfunkel tune. (See Chapter 6.)

Question 22   c.

This code compiles and runs fine. It displays the word "true," because the two Boolean objects represent the same Boolean value. (See Chapter 6.)

Question 23   d.

The expression:

```
(4 & 3) + (2 | 1)
```

is, in binary:

```
(100 & 011) + (10 | 01)
```

The binary combination is:

```
(000) + (11)
```

or, in base ten: 3. (See Chapter 7.)

Question 24   d.

You can use the `throws` keyword to indicate your method might throw an exception. (See Chapter 8.)

Question 25   e.

You must declare the thrown exception using the `throws` clause in the method definition, and then you must actually `throw` that exception somewhere in the method. (See chapter 8.)

Question 26   "synchronized".

Question 27   c.

The method that is invoked depends on the actual type of the object, not on the declared type of the object reference. The actual object is of type Second, so Second's `test()` method is invoked. (See Chapter 9.)

Question 28   d, e.

`round()` will bring this from -4.3 to -4, and `ceil()` will find the next highest integer, which is -4. `ceil()` will yield -5. (See Chapter 10.)

Question 29   b.

`Math.random()` produces a random number between 0.0 and 1.0. (See Chapter 10.)

Question 30 a, b.   A String object cannot be changed once it is created, but you can reassign an object reference to a different object. That's what this code does by creating a String, and then using the += operator to create a new String. So, the first String object becomes a candidate for garbage collection; the final string contains "Maybe not." (See Chapter 10.)

Question 31 a, b, d, e.   There are four versions of the indexOf() method. The versions that take a character use an int as the character value. (See Chapter 10.)

Question 32 s.equals("Hello"); The equals() method for String returns true if the String's text is equal to the String passed to it.

Question 33 a, b.   The trim() method removes leading and trailing white space. White space is defined as any code less than or equal to '\u0020'. (See Chapter 10.)

Question 34 c.   DataInput and DataOutput are interfaces that are implemented by classes such as DataInputStream, DataOutputStream, and RandomAccessFile. (See Chapter 11.)

Question 35 b.   A FilterInputStream object must be constructed by passing an InputStream object to its constructor. An example of an InputStream object is System.in. (See chapter 11.)

Question 36 b, c.   You can delete and rename files with a File object. To create a stream in the first place you need to create a OutputStream or RandomAccessFile object. (See Chapter 11.)

Question 37 out.seek(out.length()); The RandomAccessMethod length() finds the length of the file. Using seek() to set the file pointer to this position sets the file pointer to the end of the file; new data written to the file will then be appended to it. (See Chapter 11.)

Question 38   a.   The instance method exists() will return true if that node in the File system already exists. (See Chapter 11.)

Question 39   e.   Use DataInputStream and the method readLine() to read an entire line from the standard input. DataInputStream takes the standard input as its constructor parameter. (See Chapter 11.)

Question 40   "InterruptedException".

Question 41   c.   The Runnable interface declares the run() method.

Question 42   "File".   You can use the mkdir() method given a File instance.

Question 43   b, c, d, e. All of these methods can be added to the class definition, except for the first one, because, except for the return value which doesn't count, the signature is identical to the method already defined in the class.

Question 44   a, c, e.   An identifier must start with a letter or underscore.

Question 45   ">>>"

Question 46   b.   The Runnable interface defines a method named run() that does not take any parameters. The run() method defined in the Bounce class takes an int parameter. So, the Bounce class does not implement the run() method defined in the Runnable interface. (See Chapter 12.)

Question 47   b, c.   The variable x is incremented after the while expression is evaluated. So, first it displays 1++, or 2, and then 2++, or 3. Then the while loop ends.

Question 48   c.   The paint() method defined in Component is declared public, does not return a value, and takes a Graphics object as its argument. (See Chapter 13.)

Question 49   a.   There are four different constructors for TextArea. One of them takes the number of rows, followed by the number of columns. (See Chapter 13.)

Question 50   "myList = new List(5, true);"

Question 51   a, d.   Only FileOutputStream and RandomAccessFile create new files.

Question 52   "finalize"

Question 53   a.

Question 54   "throws"

Question 55   c, e.   You can arrange components in any of these five regions: North, South, East, West, and Center. (See Chapter 13.)

Question 56   b.   When an event method returns true, that event is not passed to that Component's Container. (See Chapter 13.)

Question 57   c.   The Java interpreter runs your class by invoking its main() method.

Question 58   e.   The other versions may or may not compile, but this is the only version that will work as intended.

Question 59   d.   You can use the <param> tag to pass a value to an applet. The <param> tag takes two keywords: name and value.

Question 60   b.   The new class MyClass does not override equals(). The default behavior in Object is to return the result of the == operator. Hence, class C displays "false" in the standard output. (See Chapter 6.)

Question 61   b, d, e.   A class cannot be defined with the protected or private keywords. A class can be abstract, even if it does not contain abstract methods.

Question 62   d.   The `fillRect()` method draws a solid rectangle given four `int` values: the left, top, width, and height of the rectangle.

Question 63   c.   The Graphics class defines the `drawString()` method which takes the String to draw plus the x and y of the baseline to draw it at.

Question 64   ~~c.~~ b   The `drawPolygon()` method connects the dots passed to it in two arrays. The first array contains the x positions points, and the second array contains the y positions for the points. The third parameter indicates how many points to draw.

Question 65   b, c.   Both `fillPolygon()` and `fillRect()` would work, given the proper parameters.

Question 66   "package"

Question 67   c.   The reason that nothing appears is that this code does not show the frame. Adding

```
f.show();
```

as the last line of the `main()` method will make the frame appear with a button filling the frame.

Question 68   a.   This code is fine and runs exactly as described in this answer.

Question 69   d.   The Dimension class defines two `int` values: width and height.

Question 70   "MAX_PRIORITY"

CHAPTER 27

Practice Programming Assignment

Developer certification takes place in stages. First, you complete a programming assignment that you download from the Web. Then, you take a test that asks you to justify decisions you made in completing the programming assignment.

The assignment consists of implementing a client/server application, where the client and server talk to each other using TCP/IP. While the actual assignment is of course different from this one, the two are similar in scope and the topics they cover.

Read over the scenario and instructions for this assignment, and then go to it.

The Scenario

"Aunt Edna's Airlines" started as a one-woman operation. Edna rented a small two-seater and flew passengers to the San Juan Islands from Seattle, a short hop of less than an hour. No one thought her business would make it, but her flying was flawless and her service professional. She now owns two planes, capable of carrying five passengers each. She hired her niece as the other pilot. She set up regular flight schedules.

Edna has been taking reservations over the phone, but with business booming, that has became too cumbersome. She has allowed travel agents to mail in reservations, but this is not a very efficient system. What's more, they keep on booking passengers in the same seats (numbered 1 through 5) because there is no coordination between them. (Remember the discussion of this scenario back in Chapter 12 when we talked about threads?)

Edna talked things over with her niece, and they came up with a plan. They have this idea that travel agents would tap directly into their reservation computer over the Internet. They could maintain a simple database that travel agents could use to make reservations and assign passengers to seats.

Her niece worked on a piece of this program for a few days when it was rainy and no one wanted to visit the San Juans. Being a Mac person, she bought "Learn Java on the Macintosh." She got as far defining what the prototype database would look like and providing a few simple methods to access the database. However, business soon picked up, and she headed back into the skies (where she preferred to be, anyway).

Edna has looked around for a qualified Java programmer, and since you are Sun Certified as a Java Programmer, she thought you would be ideal for the task. She would like you to write a prototype system so that she can begin to get a sense of what this might look like. The prototype is only proof of a concept that she hopes will do the following things:

- Offer a simple user interface that displays the date, flight number, and passenger list.
- Allow the user to make a new reservation, type in the passenger's name, and assign the passenger a seat from a list of those available.
- Let the user delete a reservation.
- Provide access to the database over the Internet, possibly by multiple travel agents at a time.

She wants this done in a very particular way, because she wants to make sure that, if you decide to move on to other projects after implementing the prototype, her niece can understand how the program works and maintain it. This means that you should favor code that is easy to understand over code that might be slightly more efficient. And you should provide all of the javadoc-style comments necessary so that the code is well-documented, without being filled with unnecessary, trivial comments.

The Prototype Specifications

The rest of this document describes:

- The design completed so far.
- The protocol you will use to communicate between the client and server.
- The code completed so far.
- What you will add to the code.
- What the user interface will look like.

The Design Completed So Far

The current design identifies the class names for the prototype. However, the only classes that have been completed are those for the record layout for the database (the classes PassengerRecord and FileHeader) and some support methods to manipulate the database file (in the class DB). The database file is simply an ASCII file that we'll read from and write to using the `java.io` classes—especially RandomAccessFile. There is also an interface called CanUpdate and two new Exception classes that are complete, but their definitions are very simple. You will implement all of the other classes yourself as you think best, but you should try to follow the designs presented here.

Figure 27-1 shows the user interface classes for the prototype. The only one of these currently written is an interface called CanUpdate. This interface defines a single method that other classes can call to force the user interface to update to reflect the current state of the database.

Figure 27-1
The Current Design

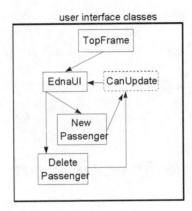

Figure 27-1 shows the intended flow of control between these classes. A user can launch the client by invoking the Java interpreter and passing it a top-level frame. The `main()` method of this new Frame subclass creates an instance of a Panel subclass called EdnaUI. EdnaUI implements the CanUpdate interface.

When the user wants to add a new passenger to the passenger list, the user interface will bring up a new window—a Frame subclass called New-Passenger. (I'll discuss the exact look and feel of the user interface later in this chapter.) When the user wants to delete a passenger from the passenger list, the user interface will bring up a new window—a Frame subclass called DeletePassenger.

Once the user has added or deleted a passenger, these Frame subclasses invoke `updateUI()` for the EdnaUI object. The method `updateUI()` is the method defined by the CanUpdate interface and implemented by EdnaUI, so that the user interface reflects the new state of the database.

If this were not to be a client/server application, NewPassenger and DeletePassenger could access the database directly, as shown in Figure 27-2.

Figure 27-2
Directly Accessing the
Database

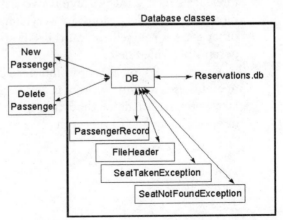

The DB class reads from and writes to a file called Reservations.db. It uses the FileHeader and PassengerRecord classes to keep track of the data in each record. There are also two exceptions that the DB class can use if it encounters any trouble assigning seats.

All of the classes are currently part of the same default package.

The New Design

To complete this assignment, you should place the classes into one of two packages: client or server. Any new classes you create should go into one of these packages. You can import classes from one package to another as you require. However, you may only need to import a class called server.Server (which I'll discuss shortly) in the a class called client.Client. You can probably find ways around this, if you would like to.

Figure 27-3 shows the new design on the client side. This is the final design that you should achieve in your solution.

Figure 27-3
The Design on the Client Side

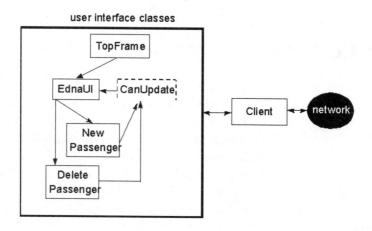

NewPassenger and DeletePassenger do not communicate directly with the database. Instead, they create a new instance of a class called Client. Client defines methods that establish a TCP/IP connection with a server and communicate with the server to perform database operations.

On the server side, there are two new classes. These are shown in Figure 27-4.

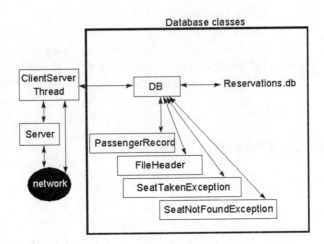

The first server class is called Server. This class simply loops forever, waiting for a client to connect to it. When it establishes a connection, Server creates a new instance of a Thread subclass called ClientServerThread and starts this thread. This thread reads data from the network, interacts with the database, and passes the appropriate data back out over the network.

The Code Completed So Far

You must use the following code as part of your solution. This code defines the database entries and specifies how you will access the database. Optimizations such as compressing the database by squeezing out deleted records will be a future consideration, implemented at some point after the prototype is completed, so don't concern yourself with this now.

Here are two classes that define the record layout. Each record consists of a header and passenger information.

The class FileHeader can be placed in the file DB.java (which I'll discuss in just a second):

```
class FileHeader {
    int totalRecords;
    int numPassengers;
}
```

The class PassengerRecord must be placed in its own file, PassengerRecord.java:

```
public class PassengerRecord {
   private long ptr;
   private String name;
   private int seat;

   public String getName() {
      return name;
   }

   public void setName(String n) {
      name = n;
   }

   public int getSeat() {
      return seat;
   }

   public void setSeat(int s) {
      seat = s;
   }

   public long getPtr() {
      return ptr;
   }

   public void setPtr(long p) {
      ptr = p;
   }
}
```

As far as the code to manipulate a database, here is the start of the class called DB that does this (there are three methods still to implement). This class is defined in DB.java:

```
import java.io.*;

/**
 * Record format is:
 * <num records>
 * <name> <seat #>
 * repeat as necessary
 */
public class DB {
   public static final String FILE_NAME = "Reservations.db";
   public static final int MAX_SEATS = 5;
```

continued

```java
private static final int ACTIVE_REC = 0;
private static final int DELETED_REC = 1;

private boolean open;
private RandomAccessFile file;

public DB() throws IOException {
   try {
      File test = new File(FILE_NAME);
      boolean alreadyExisted = test.exists();
      file = new RandomAccessFile(FILE_NAME, "rw");
      open = true;

      if (!alreadyExisted) {
         FileHeader header = new FileHeader();
         writeHeader(header);
      }

   } catch (IOException x) {
      close();
      throw x;
   }
}

public synchronized String[] getPassengerList() throws IOException {
   String[] reservations = null;

   // PLACE YOUR CODE HERE.

   return reservations;
}

public synchronized int getSeat(String passenger)
   throws IOException, SeatNotFoundException
{
   int seat = 0;

   // PLACE YOUR CODE HERE.

   return seat;
}
```

continued

```
public synchronized void reservePassenger(String passenger, int seat)
   throws IOException, SeatTakenException
{

   // PLACE YOUR CODE HERE.

}

public synchronized int[] getOpenSeats() throws IOException {
   PassengerRecord record;

   FileHeader header = readHeader();
   // Do the case where there are no seats:
   if (header.numPassengers == MAX_SEATS)
      return new int[0];

   // Do the case where all seats are still available.
   if (header.numPassengers == 0) {
      int[] open = {1, 2, 3, 4, 5};
      return open;
   }

   // Determine the open seats from the reserved seats.
   boolean[] reserved = new boolean[MAX_SEATS];
   String passenger;
   for (int i = 0; i < header.numPassengers; i++) {
      record = readNextRecord();
      reserved[record.getSeat() - 1] = true;
   }

   // Make the int array only as large as it needs to be.
   int[] open = new int[MAX_SEATS - header.numPassengers];
   int next = 0;
   for (int i = 0; i < MAX_SEATS; i++) {
      if (reserved[i] == false)
         open[next++] = i + 1;
   }

   return open;
}
```

continued

```
public synchronized void deletePassenger(String name)
    throws IOException
{
    FileHeader header = readHeader();

    boolean found = false;
    PassengerRecord record = null; // make the compiler happy
    for (int i = 0; i < header.numPassengers && !found; i++) {
        record = readNextRecord();
        if (name.equals(record.getName()))
            found = true;
    }

    // Delete at the position before we read the record to be deleted.
    if (found) {
        file.seek(record.getPtr());
        file.write(DELETED_REC);

        header.numPassengers--;
        writeHeader(header);
    }
}

public synchronized void close() {
    if (open) {
        try {
            file.close();
        } catch (IOException x) {
            System.out.println(x.getMessage());
        } finally {
            open = false;
        }
    }
}

public void finalize() throws Throwable {
    close();
    super.finalize();
}
```

continued

```
private synchronized PassengerRecord readNextRecord()
   throws IOException
{
   boolean looking = true;
   PassengerRecord record = new PassengerRecord();

   try {
      while (looking) {
         record.setPtr(file.getFilePointer());
         int type = file.readInt();
         record.setName(file.readUTF());
         record.setSeat(file.readInt());
         if (type == ACTIVE_REC)
            looking = false;
      }
   } catch (EOFException x) {
      System.out.println("read past the end of the file");
   }

   return record;
}

private synchronized void writeRecord(PassengerRecord record)
   throws IOException
{
   FileHeader header = readHeader();
   header.totalRecords++;
   header.numPassengers++;
   writeHeader(header);

   file.seek(file.length());
   file.writeInt(ACTIVE_REC);
   file.writeUTF(record.getName());
   file.writeInt(record.getSeat());
}

private synchronized FileHeader readHeader() throws IOException {
   FileHeader header = new FileHeader();
   file.seek(0);
   header.totalRecords = file.readInt();
   header.numPassengers = file.readInt();
   return header;
}
```

continued

```
    private synchronized void writeHeader(FileHeader header)
        throws IOException
    {
        file.seek(0);
        file.writeInt(header.totalRecords);
        file.writeInt(header.numPassengers);
    }


}

class FileHeader {
    int totalRecords;
    int numPassengers;
}
```

The three methods you need to implement are getPassengerList(), get-Seat(), and reservePassenger(). You will invoke these methods from ClientServerThread when appropriate. The two other methods that you will invoke from ClientServerThread are deletePassenger() and getOpenSeats(), which are already implemented for you.

There is a new exception called SeatNotFoundException defined in SeatNotFoundException.java like this:

```
public class SeatNotFoundException extends Exception { }
```

There is also a new exception called SeatTakenException defined in SeatTakenException.java like this:

```
public class SeatTakenException extends Exception { }
```

On the client side, the interface CanUpdate looks like this:

```
public interface CanUpdate {
    void updateUI();
}
```

(You will find all of this code on the CD-ROM included with this book.)

What You will Add to the Code

You need to complete the DB class, create the user interface for accessing the database, and turn this into a client/server application by defining client and server classes.

The Database

The basic structure of the database has already been implemented for you. However, here's what's going on, if it helps you to write your software.

The database consists of a header followed by any number of records. Only five records will be active at a time; if there are more, it is only because the others have been deleted.

The database's header consists of two numbers: the total number of records in the database, and the total number of passengers. (Nothing is currently done with the integer for the total number of records.)

Each record in the database consists of an integer indicating whether it is active or deleted, a String indicating the passenger's name, and an integer specifying the passenger's seat assignment.

The DB class already implements methods to append a new record to the database, delete a record, and retrieve the open seats.

The Server

The server should be able to handle multiple clients. Each transaction with a client should be one complete connect-process-close cycle. For example, if the client wants to add a new passenger to the database, it should connect with the server and pass the server the new passenger name and seat assignment. The server should add this passenger to the database if it can, and tell the client whether or not it was successful. Then, the connection ends.

The server and the client can both run on the local machine by default for the purposes of this exercise. However, all of the proper TCP/IP should be in place so that they could reside on different machines if necessary. (You can pick a port you think is appropriate for the client and server to use to communicate. The port number 5001 is one candidate.)

The server consists of the Server class and the ClientServerThread class. The server handles connections arriving over the network and interacts with the DB class to work with the database.

The Client

The client consists of the user interface and a class called Client that knows how to establish a connection with the server, communicate with the server, and close the connection. The Client class can define different methods to perform different transactions—add a new passenger to the list, delete a passenger, and so on.

The User Interface

The user interface is discussed below, after the discussion of protocol. Your user interface should match the figures in this chapter as closely as possible. The user interface can create a new Client instance when it needs to talk to the server, and invoke the proper method in the Client instance to make the client communicate with the server.

The Protocol

In order for the client and the server to talk to each other, they have to speak the same language. In other words, they need to agree on a protocol. Each transaction represents a new connection between the client and the server.

Making a New Reservation

The client sends: an integer opcode that means "make a new reservation," followed by a String representing the passenger name, followed by an integer for the seat number.

The server returns: a 0 if the reservation was made successfully, or a 1 if it was not.

Delete a Passenger's Reservation

The client sends: an integer opcode that means "delete this reservation," followed by a String representing the passenger name.

The server returns: a 0 if the reservation was deleted successfully, or a 1 if it was not.

Finding a Passenger's Seat

The client sends: an integer opcode that means "get this passenger's seat," followed by a String representing the passenger name.

The server returns: an integer representing the passenger's seat number.

Finding All Open Seats

The client sends: an integer opcode that means "find all open seats."

The server returns: an integer that indicates how many open seats there are, followed by integers that specify the open seat numbers. If there are no open seats, the first integer is 0, followed, of course, by no other numbers.

Retrieving the List of Passengers

The client sends: an integer opcode that means "return the passenger list."

The server returns: an integer that indicates how many passengers there are, followed by Strings that contain the passenger names. If there are no passengers, the first integer is 0, followed by no other Strings.

What the User Interface Should Look Like when You're Done

Figure 27-5 shows what will first appear on the screen when the user launches the client.

Figure 27-5
The Initial Client
Interface

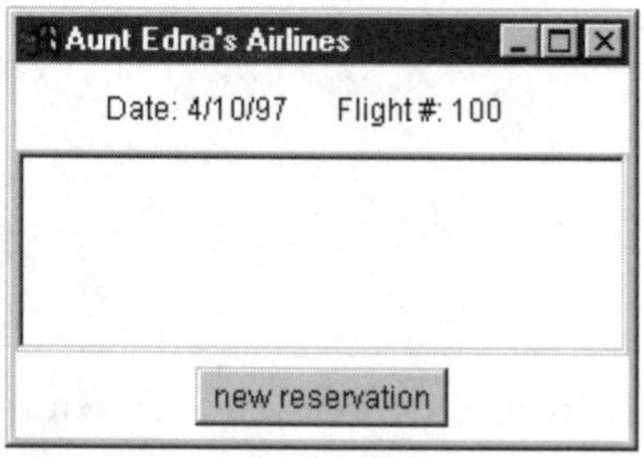

(The client is a standalone graphical program. It does not run within a Web browser.)

There are three regions to this user interface:

1. At the top are the date and flight number. These can be labels purely for aesthetic purposes that don't have to reflect any real data.
2. In the center is the list of passengers. This list will reflect the current state of the database.
3. At the bottom is a button that allows the user to make new reservations.

When the user first launches the client, it should connect with the server. Once it establishes a connection, it should update the passenger list if there is already data in the database, so that the user interface displays any passenger data when it first appears.

As the user enters data into the database, the center portion of the user interface will show this data. Figure 27-6 shows the list of passengers after the user has made two new reservations:

Figure 27-6

The List of Passengers

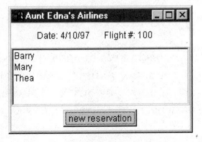

The database method getPassengerList() returns an array of Strings that you can use to display in this list, one String per list item.

To make this clearer, Figure 27-7 shows the generic arrangement of the user interface components you need to implement:

Figure 27-7

The User Interface Components

There are two other features of this user interface that you should implement:

1. The **new reservation** button becomes disabled when the flight is full (that is, when there are five passengers).
2. The client program ends when the user clicks the **close** button in the frame enclosing this interface.

In addition to these, clicking the **new reservation** button and double-clicking a list entry both cause the user interface to bring up other windows. The **new reservation** button brings up a window that allows you to add passengers to the database. Double-clicking a list entry brings up a window that allows you to delete that passenger.

Updating the Passenger List

When the user clicks the **new reservation** button, a new window appears that floats separately from the main user interface. This window should look like Figure 27-8:

Figure 27-8
The New Passenger
Window

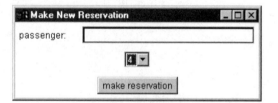

The only entries in the choice box should be those for the open seats. (The seats are numbered 1 through 5.) You can use the database method getOpenSeats() to determine which entries to place into the choice box. The user will type the passenger name into the text field and click the **reserve seat** button to make the reservation. To make this work, you'll have to implement the database method reservePassenger(). If the seat the user is trying to reserve is already taken (because another thread has beaten the user to it), then no reservation should be made. (If the text field is all spaces or blank, the **reserve seat** button should not change the database.)

Then, the window should vanish. If the user clicks the **close** button for this enclosing frame, the floating window should go away without the user having made a reservation.

When the window vanishes, the main user interface's list of passengers should be updated to reflect the new passenger in the database. To do this, the window can invoke EdnaUI's implementation of updateUI().

When the user double-clicks an entry in the list, a new window appears that floats separately from the main user interface. This window should look like Figure 27-9:

Figure 27-9
The Delete Passenger
Window

This window shows the passenger's name and seat assignment. To show the seat assignment, you'll have to implement the database method get-Seat(). Two buttons on the bottom of this floating window allow the user to either keep or delete this reservation. If the user clicks **delete**, the passenger should be removed from the database. (To do this, you should implement the database's deletePassenger() method.) Then, the window should vanish. If the user clicks **keep** or clicks the **Close** button in the enclosing frame, the floating window should simply go away.

Again, when the window vanishes, the main user interface's list of passengers should be updated to reflect the change to the database.

Final Words of Advice

Implement this as you think best. Keep in mind the chapters we've covered in the previous section, especially regarding TCP/IP and building user interfaces by placing layout managers inside other layout managers.

I have provided few lines of working code on purpose. The more you work through the issues yourself, the easier you'll find the actual developer programming assignment. Don't worry if it takes some time.

You can always look at the answer at the end of this chapter if you get stuck. But try to get as far as you can to really think about what's happening.

One Possible Answer for the Client Side

Client.java

```java
package client;

import java.io.*;
import java.net.*;
import server.Server;

/**
 * Communicates with the database server.
 * @see server.Server
 * @version 1.0
 * @author Barry Boone
 */
public class Client {

    /* Data stream to read from server. */
    DataInputStream remoteIn;

    /* Data stream to write to server. */
    DataOutputStream remoteOut;

    private int port = 5001;
    private Socket sock;
    private String server = null;
        // name of the remote server (null if on same machine)

    /**
     * Establish a connection with the database server.
     * @exception IOException  Thrown if there's trouble
     *    connecting to the server
     */
    void establishConnection() throws IOException {
        try {
            InetAddress serverAddr = InetAddress.getByName(server);
            sock = new Socket(serverAddr.getHostName(), port, true);
```

continued

```
            remoteIn = new DataInputStream(sock.getInputStream());
            remoteOut = new DataOutputStream(sock.getOutputStream());

        } catch (IOException e) {
            System.out.println(e.getMessage() +
                ": Failed to connect to server.");
            throw e;
        }


    }


    /*
     * Close the connection with the database server.
     */
    void closeConnection() {
        try {
            if (remoteOut != null) {
                remoteOut.close();
                remoteOut = null;
            }

            if (remoteIn != null) {
                remoteIn.close();
                remoteIn = null;
            }

        } catch (IOException x) {
            System.out.println(x.getMessage());
        } finally {
            try {
                if (sock != null) {
                    sock.close();
                    sock = null;
                }
            } catch (IOException x) {
                System.out.println(x.getMessage());
            }
        }
    }
```

continued

```
int[] getOpenSeats() throws IOException {
   establishConnection();
   remoteOut.writeInt(Server.OP_GET_OPEN_SEATS);
   int numSeats = remoteIn.readInt();
   int[] seats = new int[numSeats];
   for (int i = 0; i < numSeats; i++)
      seats[i] = remoteIn.readInt();

   closeConnection();
   return seats;
}

String[] getPassengerList() throws IOException {
   establishConnection();
   remoteOut.writeInt(Server.OP_GET_PASSENGER_LIST);
   int numPassengers = remoteIn.readInt();
   String[] passengers = new String[numPassengers];
   for (int i = 0; i < numPassengers; i++)
      passengers[i] = remoteIn.readUTF();

   closeConnection();
   return passengers;
}

int reservePassenger(String name, int seat) throws IOException{
   establishConnection();
   remoteOut.writeInt(Server.OP_MAKE_RESERVATION);
   remoteOut.writeUTF(name);
   remoteOut.writeInt(seat);
   int rv = remoteIn.readInt();
   closeConnection();
   return rv;
}

int deletePassenger(String name) throws IOException {
   establishConnection();
   remoteOut.writeInt(Server.OP_DELETE);
   remoteOut.writeUTF(name);
   int rv = remoteIn.readInt();
   closeConnection();
   return rv;
}
```

continued

```
    int getSeat(String name) throws IOException {
        establishConnection();
        remoteOut.writeInt(Server.OP_GET_SEAT);
        remoteOut.writeUTF(name);
        int seat = remoteIn.readInt();
        closeConnection();
        return seat;
    }

    protected void finalize() throws Throwable {
        super.finalize();
        closeConnection();
    }

}
```

TopFrame.java

```
package client;

import java.awt.*;

public class TopFrame extends Frame {
    public TopFrame(String s) {
        super(s);
    }

    public boolean handleEvent(Event e) {
        if (e.id == Event.WINDOW_DESTROY) {
            hide();
            System.exit(0);
        }
        return super.handleEvent(e);
    }

    public static void main(String[] args) {
        TopFrame frame = new TopFrame("Aunt Edna's Airlines");
        EdnaUI ui = new EdnaUI();
        frame.add("Center", ui);
        frame.pack();
        frame.show();

        ui.updateUI();
    }
}
```

EdnaUI.java

```java
package client;

import java.awt.*;
import java.util.Date;
import java.util.StringTokenizer;
import java.io.IOException;

public class EdnaUI extends Panel implements CanUpdate {
    private static final int MAX_SEATS = 5;

    private List      passengerList;
    private Button    reserve;

    public EdnaUI() {
        setLayout(new BorderLayout());

        Panel p;
        p = new Panel();

        p.add(new Label("Date: 4/10/97"));
        p.add(new Label("Flight #: 100"));

        add("North", p);

        passengerList = new List(5, false);
        add("Center", passengerList);
        p = new Panel();
        reserve = new Button("new reservation");
        p.add(reserve);

        add("South", p);

    }


    /**
     * Show frame to make a new reservation when the user clicks
     * the "new reservation" button.
     * Show frame to delete a reservation when the user double-clicks
     * the list.
     */
    public boolean action(Event e, Object what) {
        try {
```

continued

```
            if (e.target == reserve)
                showNewWindow();
            else if (e.target == passengerList)
                showDeleteWindow();
        } catch (IOException x) {
            System.out.println("could not edit passenger list");
        }


        return super.action(e, what);
    }

    private void showDeleteWindow() throws IOException {
        Frame pass;

        // Get the selected entry in the list, if there is one.
        String name = passengerList.getSelectedItem();
        if (name != null) {
            pass = new DeletePassenger(name, this);
            pass.pack();
            pass.show();
        }
    }

    private void showNewWindow() throws IOException {
        Frame pass;

        pass = new NewPassenger(this);
        pass.pack();
        pass.show();
    }


    public void updateUI() {
        String[] reservations;
        try {
            reservations = new Client().getPassengerList();
        } catch (IOException x) {
            System.out.println("Unable to show list");
            System.out.println(x.getMessage());
            return;
        }
        passengerList.clear();
```

continued

```
      int total = reservations.length;
      for (int i = 0; i < total; i++)
         passengerList.addItem(reservations[i]);

      // Update the "make reservation" button as appropriate.
      if (reservations.length == MAX_SEATS)
         reserve.enable(false);
      else
         reserve.enable(true);

      validate();
   }

}
```

NewPassenger.java

```
package client;

import java.awt.*;
import java.io.IOException;

public class NewPassenger extends Frame {
   String    thePassenger;
   TextField passengerField;
   Choice    seatNumber;
   Button    makeRes;
   CanUpdate ui;
   int[]     openSeats;

   public NewPassenger(CanUpdate edna) throws IOException {
      super("Make New Reservation");

      ui = edna;

      setLayout(new GridLayout(3, 1));
      Panel p;

      p = new Panel();
      p.add(new Label("passenger: "));
```

continued

```
    passengerField = new TextField(30);
    p.add(passengerField);
    add(p);

    p = new Panel();
    openSeats = new Client().getOpenSeats();

    seatNumber = new Choice();
    for (int i = 0; i < openSeats.length; i++) {
        String s = new Integer(openSeats[i]).toString();
        seatNumber.addItem(s);
    }
    p.add(seatNumber);

    add(p);

    p = new Panel();
    makeRes = new Button("make reservation");
    p.add(makeRes);
    add(p);
}

public boolean handleEvent(Event e) {
    if (e.id == Event.WINDOW_DESTROY) {
        hide();
        return true;
    }
    return super.handleEvent(e);
}

public boolean action(Event e, Object what) {
    if (e.target == makeRes) {

        String passenger = passengerField.getText();
        passenger = passenger.trim();
        if (passenger.length() > 0) {
            int seatIndex = seatNumber.getSelectedIndex();
            int seatNum = openSeats[seatIndex];
            try {
                new Client().reservePassenger(passenger, seatNum);
            } catch (IOException x) {
                System.out.println("Unable to reserve " + passenger +
                    "for seat number " + seatNum);
            }
        }
```

continued

```
        hide();
        ui.updateUI();
        return true;
    }
    return super.action(e, what);
}
}
```

DeletePassenger.java

```java
package client;

import java.awt.*;
import java.io.IOException;

public class DeletePassenger extends Frame {
    String    thePassenger;
    Button    keepRes;
    Button    deleteRes;
    CanUpdate ui;

    public DeletePassenger(String s, CanUpdate edna) throws IOException {
        super("Delete Reservation");

        thePassenger = s;
        ui = edna;

        setLayout(new GridLayout(2, 1));
        Panel p;

        p = new Panel();
        p.add(new Label("passenger: " + thePassenger));

        int seat = new Client().getSeat(thePassenger);

        p.add(new Label("seat #: " + seat));

        add(p);
```

continued

```
        p = new Panel();
        keepRes = new Button("keep");
        p.add(keepRes);
        deleteRes = new Button("delete");
        p.add(deleteRes);

        add(p);
    }

    public boolean handleEvent(Event e) {
        if (e.id == Event.WINDOW_DESTROY) {
            hide();
            return true;
        }
        return super.handleEvent(e);
    }

    public boolean action(Event e, Object what) {
        if (e.target == keepRes) {
            hide();
            return true;
        }

        if (e.target == deleteRes) {
            try {
                new Client().deletePassenger(thePassenger);
            } catch (IOException x) {
                System.out.println(x.getMessage());
            }
            hide();
            ui.updateUI();
            return true;
        }

        return super.action(e, what);
    }
}
```

One Possible Answer for the Server Side

Server.java (Including ClientServerThread)

```java
package server;

import java.io.*;
import java.net.*;

/**
 * The DataServer processes requests from clients to access the
 * database.
 * The DataServer runs until you hit control-c. It is a multithreaded
 *    server and spins off threads to process each connection from
 *    a client.
 * @see server.DB
 * @version 1.0
 * @author Barry Boone
 */
public class Server {

    /** opcode for making a reservation. */
    public static final int OP_MAKE_RESERVATION = 1;

    /** opcode for deleting a reservation. */
    public static final int OP_DELETE = 2;

    /** opcode for getting a passenger's seat. */
    public static final int OP_GET_SEAT = 3;

    /** opcode for getting all open seats. */
    public static final int OP_GET_OPEN_SEATS = 4;

    /** opcode for getting all passengers. */
    public static final int OP_GET_PASSENGER_LIST = 5;

    private int port = 5001;
    private boolean listening = true;
    private DB db;
    private ServerSocket serverSock;
```

continued

```java
/** Start the database server spinning. */
public static void main(String args[]) {
   int portnum = 5001;

   System.out.println("The Server runs until you hit control-c");

   try {
      Server server = new Server();
      server.start();
   } catch (IOException x) {
      System.out.println("Could not create server socket: " +
         x.getMessage());
      System.exit(1);
   }
}


/**
 * Put the Server object into action.
 * @exception IOException thrown if we cannot create a ServerSocket
 *      bound to the specified port
 */
public void start() throws IOException {

   serverSock = null;
   Socket sock;

   db = new DB();

   try {
      serverSock = new ServerSocket(port, 50);

      while (listening) {

         // Wait for a client to connect with the server socket.
         // Then spin off a thread to handle the connection
         // with the client, repeat.
         try {
            // Wait here until contacted by a client.
            sock = serverSock.accept();

            new ClientServerThread(sock, db).start();
         } catch (IOException e) {
            System.out.println("Connection dropped?: " +
               e.getMessage());
         }
      }
```

continued

```
       } finally {
          serverSock.close();
          serverSock = null;
       }
   }

   protected void finalize() throws Throwable {
      super.finalize();
      if (serverSock != null) {
         serverSock.close();
         serverSock = null;
      }
   }
}

// Handles one transaction with a client.
class ClientServerThread extends Thread {

   private static final int SUCCESS = 0;
   private static final int FAILURE = 1;

   private static final int PAUSE_FOR = 50;

   private DB db;
   private Socket sock;
   private DataInputStream remoteIn;
   private DataOutputStream remoteOut;

   ClientServerThread(Socket sock, DB db) {
      this.sock = sock;
      this.db = db;
   }


   // Ths run() method processes just one request from a client and
   // then ends.
   public void run() {
      try {
         remoteIn = new DataInputStream(sock.getInputStream());
         remoteOut = new DataOutputStream(sock.getOutputStream());

         // Get the opcode so we know how to handle this transaction.
         int opcode = remoteIn.readInt();
```

continued

```
        switch (opcode) {
            case (Server.OP_MAKE_RESERVATION):
                makeReservation();
                break;
            case (Server.OP_DELETE):
                delete();
                break;
            case (Server.OP_GET_SEAT):
                getSeat();
                break;
            case (Server.OP_GET_OPEN_SEATS):
                getOpenSeats();
                break;
            case (Server.OP_GET_PASSENGER_LIST):
                getPassengerList();
                break;
            default:
                done();
                return;
        }

    } catch (IOException e) {
        error(e);
    }
}


// Make a reservation.
// in:  <opcode> <passenger name> <seat number>
// out: <0 OR 1 (success or failure)>

private void makeReservation() {
    try {
        String name = remoteIn.readUTF();
        int seat = remoteIn.readInt();
        db.reservePassenger(name, seat);
        sendToClient(SUCCESS);
    } catch (SeatTakenException x) {
        sendToClient(FAILURE);
    } catch (IOException x) {
        System.out.println(x.getMessage());
        sendToClient(FAILURE);
    } finally {
        done();
    }
}
```

continued

```
// Delete a reservation.
// in:   <opcode> <passenger name>
// out: <0 OR 1 (success or failure)>
private void delete() {
   try {
      String name = remoteIn.readUTF();
      db.deletePassenger(name);
      sendToClient(SUCCESS);
   } catch (IOException e) {
      error(e);
      sendToClient(FAILURE);
   } finally {
      done();
   }
}

// Get a seat given a passenger.
// in:   <opcode> <passenger name>
// out: <seat number> (-1 if no seat found)
private void getSeat()
{
   try {
      String name = remoteIn.readUTF();
      int seat = db.getSeat(name);
      sendToClient(seat);
   } catch (Exception x) {
      sendToClient(FAILURE);
   } finally {
      done();
   }
}

// Get all open seats.
// in:   <opcode>
// out: <number of open seats> { <seat number> }
private void getOpenSeats()
{
   try {
      int[] seats = db.getOpenSeats();
      sendToClient(seats.length);
      for (int i = 0; i < seats.length; i++)
         sendToClient(seats[i]);
   } catch (Exception x) {
   } finally {
      done();
   }
}
```

continued

```java
// Get passenger list.
// in:  <opcode>
// out: <number of passengers> { <passenger name> }
private void getPassengerList()
{
    try {
        String[] passengers = db.getPassengerList();
        sendToClient(passengers.length);
        for (int i = 0; i < passengers.length; i++)
            sendToClient(passengers[i]);
    } catch (Exception x) {
    } finally {
        done();
    }
}


// Close the connection with the client.
private void done() {
    try {
        if (remoteOut != null) {
            remoteOut.close();
            remoteOut = null;
        }

        if (remoteIn != null) {
            remoteIn.close();
            remoteIn = null;
        }
    } catch (IOException x) {
        error(x);

    } finally {
        try {
            if (sock != null) {
                sock.close();
                sock = null;
            }
        } catch (IOException x) {
            error(x);
        }
    }
}
```

continued

```
    private void sendToClient(int i) {
        try {
            remoteOut.writeInt(i);
        } catch (IOException x) {
            error(x);
        }

        pause();
    }

    private void sendToClient(String s) {
        try {
            remoteOut.writeUTF(s);
        } catch (IOException x) {
            error(x);
        }

        pause();
    }

    // On Windows95, at least, when the client and server are running on
    // the same machine, we have to pause for the client to read
    // the data when the server writes it to the socket.
    // Otherwise, the client hangs.
    private void pause() {
        try {
            sleep(PAUSE_FOR);
        } catch (InterruptedException x) {
            error(x);
        }
    }

    private void error(Exception x) {
        System.out.println("Connection dropped?: " + x.getMessage());
    }

    protected void finalize() throws Throwable {
        super.finalize();
        done();
    }

}
```

The Three Missing Methods from DB.java

```java
public synchronized String[] getPassengerList() throws IOException {
    String[] reservations = null;
    PassengerRecord record;

    FileHeader header = readHeader();

    reservations = new String[header.numPassengers];

    for (int i = 0; i < header.numPassengers; i++) {
        reservations[i] = readNextRecord().getName();
    }
    return reservations;
}

public synchronized int getSeat(String passenger)
    throws IOException, SeatNotFoundException
{
    boolean found = false;
    PassengerRecord record;

    int seat = 0; // satisfy the compiler
    FileHeader header = readHeader();

    for (int i = 0; i < header.numPassengers && !found; i++) {
        record = readNextRecord();
        if (passenger.equals(record.getName())) {
            found = true;
            seat = record.getSeat();
        }
    }

    if (!found)
        throw new SeatNotFoundException();

    return seat;
}
```

continued

```
public synchronized void reservePassenger(String passenger, int seat)
    throws IOException, SeatTakenException
{
    // Make sure the seat is still available
    boolean taken = true; // prove it false
    int[] open = getOpenSeats();
    for (int i = 0; i < open.length && taken; i++) {
        if (seat == open[i])
            taken = false;
    }

    if (taken)
        throw new SeatTakenException();

    PassengerRecord record = new PassengerRecord();
    record.setName(passenger);
    record.setSeat(seat);
    writeRecord(record);
}
```

CHAPTER 28

Practice Developer Exam

For the developer exam, there are no absolute right or wrong answers. Instead, there are five essay questions. Each of these questions asks you to justify your design decisions, comment on your approach to designing applications in Java, and, to some extent, explain how an aspect of Java works in the first place.

You have 90 minutes to answer these questions. On the test, you read over the question (which often has multiple parts), and then, by clicking a button that says **comment**, you bring up a window to type in your response. You can bring up the comment window as many times as you would like to so that you can keep on adding to or tweaking your answer. At the end, you can easily go back over your answers and change them yet again before submitting them.

Once you do submit them, you'll have to wait until Sun Microsystems has a chance to look over your answers, which can take up to four weeks. So relax until then; you have no choice, anyway. You'll generally know if you did okay. Remember, *there are no right or wrong answers*. If you justified your design decisions in a way that makes sense, you'll do fine.

So that you don't have to worry about whether you've written too much or not enough, the question instructions state very clearly the maximum number of sentences, words, or some other appropriate measure you should stay within as you're typing away.

These practice questions relate to the sample programming assignment from Chapter 27. Of course, the questions on the real exam relate to the programming assignment you're asked to complete after you pass the Programmer Certification exam.

Questions

Question 1:   Many of the methods of the DB class are `synchronized`.

a) In a paragraph, explain why you think this is. What might happen if they were not `synchronized`?

b) The `reservePassenger()` method in DB is one of the three methods in that class that you were asked to implement. Did you throw a SeatTakenException (the method declares this method might throw such an exception)? Why or why not? In no more than two paragraphs, describe how it might be possible for this situation to arise (that is, for a seat to be already taken when you call this method) even though most of the DB methods are `synchronized`.

Question 2:   The following questions relate to how you might extend the client's design.

a) When your client communicates with the server, does your client wait for the server to respond before it continues? If so, provide an overview in no more than 100 words on how you might redesign your client so that the user has the ability to cancel the client's wait for a response, so that the client does not hang indefinitely if the server is no longer running. If your client already does this, describe your design.

b) Does your client provide some kind of feedback when it is attempting to communicate with the server? Describe at least two ways to provide feedback and name one advantage for each of them.

Question 3: What types of layout managers did you use in EdnaUI?

a) What did you use for the overall layout manager for EdnaUI? In no more than two sentences, describe what led to your choice.
b) How did you make the **new reservation** button centered in the bottom of EdnaUI without stretching from side to side? If your button *did* stretch from side to side, how might you use a combination of layout managers so that this does not occur?

Question 4: Describe how TCP/IP works in relation to this program by answering the following questions.

a) In not more than three paragraphs, describe how the client and server establish a dedicated connection with each other.
b) In an additional one or two paragraphs, explain how it is possible for there to be two clients and one server all with dedicated connections on the same machine. (In your answer, mention how sockets are used in Java.)

Question 5: In order for the client and server to talk to each other, they need to agree on a protocol involving opcodes.

a) *Where* did you define the opcodes? Did you define these in one place, or in more than one? If you only defined the opcodes in one place, how did you use the opcode numbers in other classes? (If you did not need to use opcodes in more than one class, explain why.)
b) *How* did you define the opcodes? For example, what did the opcode for making a reservation look like (its value is equal to 1)? Did you create a constant, or did you use these numbers inline, written directly in the code? In either case, describe your design decisions that led to your choice.

Answers

Question 1

a) The methods in DB that are synchronized are those that access and change the database. If they were not synchronized, then multiple threads could act on different parts of the database at once. This could easily result in the database becoming corrupted. For example, imagine one thread that deleted records as another added records. This could throw off the record count, or cause records to be overwritten.

b) Even though the methods in DB are synchronized, that does not mean you don't have to guard against data becoming corrupted by some other mechanism. Synchronized methods cannot be executed at the same time by multiple threads. However, in a client/server application such as this one, a client can acquire data, then disconnect, then connect again to act on that data.

That's exactly what happens when a client gets the open seats, then allows a user to pick an open seat. If more than one client is active at a time, both clients will obtain the open seats (one at a time), and then (again, one at a time), they will try to reserve a seat. This means that there's nothing stopping one client from booking a passenger in the same seat as another client—that's why you must check for the seat still being available and inform the client if it is not.

Question 2

a) The client could spawn a separate thread to perform the communication with the server. In addition, the client could display a window that contained a **stop** button. If the user clicked **stop**, this button would halt the communication thread. Otherwise, this window would go away by itself when the server responded. (Note that with Java 1.1, we could make this even better, and make the cursor a busy cursor over all parts of the application except for the **stop** button.)

b) Two ways to provide feedback to the user are to change the cursor and provide a window containing an informative message. With a cursor, the user knows that any click he makes will be ineffective until the cursor changes back to a normal cursor. With a message, the user can read exactly what the application is doing because the message can explain it to him in detail. (A combination of these two approaches might also work well.)

Question 3

a)   The EdnaUI object uses a BorderLayout overall. The specifications indicate it should arrange objects within it in three sections, which happen to fall naturally into a "North," "Center," and "South" arrangement.

b)   Since EdnaUI uses a BorderLayout, if the **new reservation** button were added directly in the "South" region, it would stretch from the left edge of EdnaUI to the right. To stop this from happening, we can place the button into a panel. This keeps the button centered and at its natural size. We can then place the panel "South" in EdnaUI's BorderLayout.

Question 4

a)   An instance of class ServerSocket waits for a connection by invoking `accept()`. At this point, the ServerSocket is listening on a particular port for a client to try to connect with it. A client tries to establish a connection by creating a Socket instance, specifying the server and the port the server is listening to.

   The ServerSocket passes back a new port number to the client that the client should use for all further communication with the server. This port number gets encoded into the Socket object the client creates; it also is encoded into the Socket object returned by `accept()`.

b)   Once the client has a port to use for the dedicated connection, the server continues to listen for more connections on the original port. Each new client, even if it's on the same machine, uses a different port to communicate with the server (even though each client originally connects to the server on the server's one known port).

   Java uses Socket objects to communicate via TCP/IP. A Java socket object encodes an IP address and a port to use for communication. ServerSocket ensures each port is different, so each socket is different, and multiple clients can communicate with the same server—each is using a different port.

Question 5

a) The opcodes were defined in the Server class. This is the only place they were defined. So, when the Client class in the client package needed them, it had to import the Server class, like this:

```
import server.Server;
```

b) The Server class created constants to define each of the opcodes. The opcode for making a reservation, looked like the following:

```
public static final int OP_MAKE_RESERVATION = 1;
```

APPENDIX A

The Web-Based Course

My goal for this book is to help you become certified in Java. To achieve this goal, I have tried to create a book flexible enough to be used in a variety of ways. You can read this book straight through, or you can skip around. You can work through every exercise, or you can jump right to the answers. The choice is up to you.

While you can use this book however you think best, I did have some specific uses in mind. In particular, this book can be used as a textbook.

DigitalThink, which you can find on the Web at http://www.digital-think.com, delivers courses right to your Web browser. DigitalThink has many great courses, from computer science to wine. They also have courses on preparing for the Java Certification exams, and this book is the text for those courses.

DigitalThink's home page looks like Figure A-1 and I've included a link to their site on the CD.

Figure A-1
DigitalThink's
Home Page

While this book goes into more depth than the online courses, the courses from DigitalThink provide some things that are not possible to obtain from this book (or from any book), such as tutors, a community of other students, graded assignments and exercises, discussion groups, chat sessions, audio, and a classroom instructor.

The Web-based courses for Java Certification at DigitalThink consist of eight modules for the Programmer's Certification review, and four for the Developer's Certification review. Each module contains up to ten lessons with clear objectives, side bars, running applets, sample code, and links to other activities such as discussions, quizzes, and exercises. Figures A-2 and A-3 show some sample pages from this course.

Figure A-2
Part of a Lesson from
the Java Course

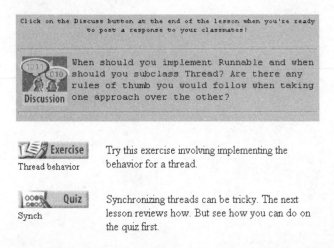

Figure A-3
Part of a Quiz from
the Java Course

Access control

1. **To use a class defined in another package, you must first:**

   ⊙ A.   make your class a subclass of that class.

   ⊙ B.   import that class.

2. **To allow access of a member to a subclass, but restrict access to
   other classes, use the keyword:**

   ⊙ A.   private.

   ⊙ B.   package.

The material in the Web-based course is similar to but, for the most part, different from what you'll find in this book. All the material in the course has been written expressly for the Web. The Programmer's course takes about 15 hours to work through, the Developer's course about 12 hours.

DigitalThink runs a promotion from time to time offering a money-back guarantee as long as you've only worked your way through the first module. So if you want the interaction of a course from the convenience of your Web browser, try it. If you find the course useful, if you like being part of a group of other students, and if you get helpful answers from the tutors, you can decide to continue with the class with confidence. If you find the course is not for you, no problem; the experience won't have set you back a dime.

The CD-ROM

The CD that comes with this book contains resources to help you use this book more effectively. I've included all the source code in the chapter and exercises, Web links to key sites, as well as Sun's latest JDK and the javadoc-style API files for the Java packages in HTML format.

How the CD is Organized

For the source files and Web links, the CD is organized like a Web site. At the top level of the CD, you'll find a directory named "Web Links and Code." Within this there's a file called index.html. You can view this HTML file with any standard Web browser.

I have included links to these categories:

- Code Listings for the Chapter Text
- Code Listings for the Exercises
- Answers to the Exercises
- Code Listings for the Review Questions
- Code for the Programming Assignment
- Where to Find More About Java and Java Certification
- McGraw-Hill Computing Books (on the Web)
- DigitalThink, where you can join other students in a prep class for certification (on the Web)
- Barry Boone (on the Web)

Source Code

The code listings are organized by chapter. Just follow the links until you're looking at Java code.

Sun's JDK

The reason this book includes the JDK is that the exam assumes you are using the JDK to develop your code. You can always grab newer versions of the JDK off of the JavaSoft Web site, but for convenience it's included on the CD, as well. To find installation notes and troubleshooting ideas for the JDK, you can visit: http://www.javasoft.com/products/jdk//.//.

Web Links

For all the latest and greatest information concerning this book and Java certification, I've included links to places on the Web. You'll find this on the CD in the HTML files by following the link titled "Where to Find More About Java and Java Certification."

The JDK

The Programmer test assumes you are using Sun's Java Development Kit. The JDK often insists on things being a certain way, and it has its own commands and characteristics not shared by all development environments. Let's take a quick look at how to use the JDK. I'll also touch some aspects of the JDK that might appear on the test.

The Pieces of the JDK

First, in case you're using a different development environment, you might find it useful to get an overall picture of the JDK. This environment is not graphical; instead, you issue commands from the command-line. For example, to compile a program, you type `javac`, list any options, and then type the name of the file or files you wish to compile.

The JDK comes with:

- a compiler
- a Java Virtual Machine runtime environment for stand-alone programs
- an applet viewer to run applets without the need for starting a full-blown Web browser
- a debugger
- documentation

The debugger is not mentioned on the exam, and we've already covered javadoc-style comments in Chapter 24, which is the format that the JDK's documentation comes in. That leaves the compiler, the runtime environment for stand-alone programs, and the applet viewer.

The Compiler

Execute the compiler using the command `javac`. Invoking `javac` can be as simple as naming the Java source file you want to compile:

```
javac Bagel.java
```

Here are three compiler options you might find useful:

- You can specify the `-classpath path` option to tell the compiler where your class files exist. Without this option, the compiler relies on the `CLASSPATH` environment variable to find where your class files are that you want to include.
- The `-d directory` option tells the compiler to place the classes it generates into a particularly directory. You can use this option when creating classes that belong in packages. For example, if you have defined a source file named `CertClass.java` that contains code like this:

```
package cert.util;
class CertClass { }
```

You can compile this class and generate the directory structure Java expects to be in place with packages by issuing the command:

```
javac -d . CertClass.java
```

javac will create a new directory at the same node as your source file, called cert. Below that, it will create a directory called util. And it will place CertClass.class within util.

- There's also a compiler option -O that allows the compiler to generate inline code for static, final, and private methods. This option stands for "optimize."

The JDK enforces the rule that public classes must be placed in a file named after the class. So, if CertClass above were declared as public, it would have to be placed in a file named CertClass.java. While you can place as many classes in the same source file as you would like, you can only have one public class per file.

The Runtime Environment for Stand-Alone Programs

You can invoke the Java interpreter using the command java. You pass the interpreter the name of the class you want to run (not the file name). For example, you can run the Bagel class by typing:

```
java Bagel
```

The interpreter will seek out this class's public, static main() method. This method must not return a value, and it must take an array of String objects. If the main() method is declared in any other way, the interpreter will complain that it could not find the main() method it was looking for, and it will not run your class.

You might be interested in the -classpath, -noasyncgc, and -verbosegc options.

- As with the compiler, you can specify the -classpath *path* option to tell the compiler where your class files are. Without this option, the compiler relies on the CLASSPATH environment variable to find where your class files are that you want to include.
- The -noasyncgc option turns off garbage collection.
- The -verbosegc option asks the interpreter to tell you when it has performed garbage collection.

The Applet Viewer

You can use the `appletviewer` command to test an applet without ever starting a full-fledged Web browser. You pass the `appletviewer` command the name of an HTML file that references your applet class. For example, if you have an HTML file named `Bagel.html` that includes an `<applet>` tag referencing an Applet subclass, you can type:

```
appletviewer Bagel.html
```

You don't have to only provide the name of a local HTML file. You can supply any URL as the parameter to `appletviewer`.

A useful feature is the `-debug` option, which writes debugging messages to the standard error.

INDEX

Exhibit A
Java™ Development Kit
Version 1.1
Binary Code License

This binary code license ("License") contains rights and restrictions associated with use of the accompanying software and documentation ("Software"). Read the License carefully before installing the Software. By installing the Software you agree to the terms and conditions of this License.

1. **Limited License Grant.** Sun grants to you ("Licensee") a non-exclusive, non-transferable limited license to use the Software without fee for evaluation of the Software and for development of Java‰ compatible applets and applications. Licensee may make one archival copy of the Software. Licensee may not re-distribute the Software in whole or in part, either separately or included with a product. Refer to the Java Runtime Environment Version 1.1 binary code license (http://www.javasoft.com/products/JDK/1.1/index.html) for the availability of runtime code which may be distributed with Java compatible applets and applications.

2. **Java Platform Interface.** Licensee may not modify the Java Platform Interface ("JPI", identified as classes contained within the "java" package or any subpackages of the "java" package), by creating additional classes within the JPI or otherwise causing the addition to or modification of the classes in the JPI. In the event that Licensee creates any Java-related API and distributes such API to others for applet or application development, Licensee must promptly publish an accurate specification for such API for free use by all developers of Java-based software.

3. **Restrictions.** Software is confidential copyrighted information of Sun and title to all copies is retained by Sun and/or its licensors. Licensee shall not modify, decompile, disassemble, decrypt, extract, or otherwise reverse engineer Software. Software may not be leased, assigned, or sublicensed, in whole or in part. **Software is not designed or intended for use in on-line control of aircraft, air traffic, aircraft navigation or aircraft communications; or in the design, construction, operation or maintenance of any nuclear facility. Licensee warrants that it will not use or redistribute the Software for such purposes.**

4. **Trademarks and Logos.** This License does not authorize Licensee to use any Sun name, trademark or logo. Licensee acknowledges that Sun owns the Java trademark and all Java-related trademarks, logos and icons including the Coffee Cup and Duke ("Java Marks") and agrees to: (i) to comply with the Java Trademark Guidelines at http://java.com/trademarks.html; (ii) not do anything harmful to or inconsistent with Sun's rights in the Java Marks; and (iii) assist Sun in protecting those rights, including assigning to Sun any rights acquired by Licensee in any Java Mark.

5. **Disclaimer of Warranty.** Software is provided "AS IS," without a warranty of any kind. ALL EXPRESS OR IMPLIED REPRESENTATIONS AND WARRANTIES, INCLUDING ANY IMPLIED WARRANTY OF MERCHANTABILITY, FITNESS FOR A PARTICULAR PURPOSE OR NON-INFRINGEMENT, ARE HEREBY EXCLUDED.

6. **Limitation of Liability.** SUN AND ITS LICENSORS SHALL NOT BE LIABLE FOR ANY DAMAGES SUFFERED BY LICENSEE OR ANY THIRD PARTY AS A RESULT OF USING OR DISTRIBUTING SOFTWARE. IN NO EVENT WILL SUN OR ITS LICENSORS BE LIABLE FOR ANY LOST REVENUE, PROFIT OR DATA, OR FOR DIRECT, INDIRECT, SPECIAL, CONSEQUENTIAL, INCIDENTAL OR PUNITIVE DAMAGES, HOWEVER CAUSED AND REGARDLESS OF THE THEORY OF LIABILITY, ARISING OUT OF THE USE OF OR INABILITY TO USE SOFTWARE, EVEN IF SUN HAS BEEN ADVISED OF THE POSSIBILITY OF SUCH DAMAGES.

7. **Termination.** Licensee may terminate this License at any time by destroying all copies of Software. This License will terminate immediately without notice from Sun if Licensee fails to comply with any provision of this License. Upon such termination, Licensee must destroy all copies of Software.

8. **Export Regulation.** Software, including technical data, is subject to U.S. export control laws, including the U.S. Export Administration Act and its associated regulations, and may be subject to export or import regulations in other countries. Licensee agrees to comply strictly with all such regulations and acknowledges that it has the responsibility to obtain licenses to export, re-export, or import Software. Software may not be downloaded, or otherwise exported or re-exported (i) into, or to a national or resident of, Cuba, Iraq, Iran, North Korea, Libya, Sudan, Syria or any country to which the U.S. has embargoed goods; or (ii) to anyone on the U.S. Treasury Department's list of Specially Designated Nations or the U.S. Commerce Department's Table of Denial Orders.

9. **Restricted Rights.** Use, duplication or disclosure by the United States government is subject to the restrictions as set forth in the Rights in Technical Data and Computer Software Clauses in DFARS 252.227-7013(c)(1)(ii) and FAR 52.227-19(c)(2) as applicable.

10. **Governing Law.** Any action related to this License will be governed by California law and controlling U.S. federal law. No choice of law rules of any jurisdiction will apply.

11. **Severability.** If any of the above provisions are held to be in violation of applicable law, void, or unenforceable in any jurisdiction, then such provisions are herewith waived to the extent necessary for the License to be otherwise enforceable in such jurisdiction. However, if in Sun's opinion deletion of any provisions of the License by operation of this paragraph unreasonably compromises the rights or increase the liabilities of Sun or its licensors, Sun reserves the right to terminate the License and refund the fee paid by Licensee, if any, as Licensee's sole and exclusive remedy.

SOFTWARE AND INFORMATION LICENSE